Benjamin Wisner Bacon

The Genesis of Genesis

Benjamin Wisner Bacon

The Genesis of Genesis

ISBN/EAN: 9783337140526

Hergestellt in Europa, USA, Kanada, Australien, Japan

Cover: Foto ©Lupo / pixelio.de

Weitere Bücher finden Sie auf **www.hansebooks.com**

THE
GENESIS OF GENESIS

A STUDY OF THE DOCUMENTARY SOURCES OF THE
FIRST BOOK OF MOSES IN ACCORDANCE WITH
THE RESULTS OF CRITICAL SCIENCE
ILLUSTRATING THE PRESENCE OF

BIBLES WITHIN THE BIBLE

BY

BENJAMIN WISNER BACON

WITH AN INTRODUCTION BY GEORGE F. MOORE
Professor in Andover Theological Seminary

" The books of the Old Testament in their present form, in many instances are not, and do not profess to be, the original documents on which the history was based. There was (to use a happy expression employed of late) " A BIBLE WITHIN A BIBLE," an " Old Testament before an Old Testament was written." To discover any traces of the lost works in the actual text, or any allusions to them even when their substance is entirely perished, is a task of immense interest."

STANLEY

HARTFORD
THE STUDENT PUBLISHING COMPANY
1892

BIBLES WITHIN THE BIBLE.

TO

EDWARD E. SALISBURY, LL. D.

LATE PROFESSOR IN

YALE UNIVERSITY,

THIS BOOK

IS DEDICATED IN TOKEN OF GRATITUDE

AND AFFECTION.

PREFACE.

The attention of the reading public of America has been called frequently of late to the claims of the science of Higher Criticism, a study all-important to a correct understanding of the Scriptures ; and in particular to that theory of the science which maintains the origin of the Pentateuch from a compilation of older documents. They have been assured of the practically unanimous acceptance of this theory abroad, and have been themselves witnesses of the divided opinions of scholars at home. Considering the importance of the subject, the enormous mass of accumulated evidence pro and con, the conflicting claims of scholars as to the resulting benefit or injury to accrue to Christian faith from the acceptance of the theory, it should be apparent to all, as a primary axiom, that the reading public are entitled to judge for themselves.

As to the method of presenting the facts to the public, two propositions are easily established.

I. The public require, not controversial argument, but explanation.

The method of the controversialist, which ever side be championed, rarely gains more than a partisan applause guaranteed in advance, and the converts to be made among those "convinced against their will." It assumes that the public has already made up its mind, or else to judge for the public. The assumption is either false or impertinent. A public accustomed to exercise the right of private judgment demands, in the case of so important and widely supported a theory, a plain statement of the case, an explanation of the general principles involved, of the nature, rather than the details, of the argument, and as simple a presentation of methods and results as possible. It wants "the documents in the case."

II.   It is not necessary that the presentation of the case should be made from a standpoint of hostility to the new theory, nor even from one of indifference.

The public wishes to do justice to the new theory.   Until it has had opportunity to obtain a general conspectus thereof it occupies the standpoint of traditional opinion.   It has not time to give to the minutiæ of controversial discussion, but desires to be informed in general outline of the method pursued by the critics and the results propounded.   Such an explanation can only be given by one familiar with the critical argument and at least in some degree in sympathy with the theory.   The position of such an expositor differs however from that of the advocate and special pleader, in that he undertakes to explain and not to argue.   He does not pretend to have no opinion, but refrains from obtruding his opinion upon the reader, preferring to state the most general facts and grounds of critical procedure in an unbiassed way, and leave the reader to draw his own conclusions.

In accordance with the general proposition first laid down, the present work is addressed not merely to scholars and technical investigators, but to the general public.   The author believes that critics and biblical scholars will find contributions of value to the science of documentary analysis within its pages ; but argument in support of these original investigations has been relegated to technical reviews, and even notes which require the use of Hebrew text have been inserted in a special appendix, reference being made by means of the numerals (1), (2), (3), etc.   Chapter III. is a reprint of the author's articles in *Hebraica* iv. 4 and v. 1 (1888) intended to exhibit the present state of the documentary analysis.   The articles have been deprived of the footnotes, in which all divergences from the analysis of Dillmann —given in the text—by six of the foremost critics were presented, and for the purpose of a minute comparison of the analyses of Wellhausen, Kuenen, Budde, Jülicher, Delitzsch and Kittel, the reader will be obliged to consult the articles in their original form.   One of the principal results of the articles has been, however, to establish beyond the possibility of dispute the existence of a real and extraordinarily minute agreement of all schools of documentary analysis. The citation of the authority of Dillmann alone will therefore serve the purposes of the general reader, as it is, in the main and essentially, identical with that of all critics. The present work will be found accordingly to be in general a graphic presentation of the consensus of modern criticism. But the author has not restricted himself to a following of authorities. The analysis has been carried through independently, with results in a number of cases diverging from those of all former critics. For the process and evidence in these cases of original analysis the reader is referred to *Hebraica*, October, 1890, and following numbers, where it is given in detail. Technical argument has thus been avoided in the present volume, but the general reader will have opportunity by consulting chapter III. to assure himself that the recognized authorities in this field are fairly represented, while at the same time the more exact student has placed at his disposal, through the notes and references, the means of verifying all statements and examining the grounds of independent analysis. A careful study of the opening paragraphs of chapter III. is especially recommended. If the few lines of Hebrew in this chapter and in Appendix II. appear somewhat formidable, the main ideas will be found available and even indispensable to the thoughtful reader.

In recent years, thanks largely to the efforts of Profs. W. R. Harper of Chicago and C. A. Briggs of Union Seminary, the claims of Semitic literature to a position in the curriculum of study for every person of liberal education are coming to be felt. The literary and scientific study of the development of the Hebrew and Hellenistic religious consciousness as exhibited in their literature—the Bible—is beginning to be recognized as something not to be left merely to the pulpit orator and the Sunday-school teacher, but to be eagerly welcomed into the domain of school, college and university training. With the recognition has come a perception of the transcendent interest of these studies and a growing demand from beyond the academic walls for admission to at least a gleaner's share in these new fields of scientific investigation.

The author desires to meet this demand, and to present to all classes of Bible students, in churches, Sunday-schools, academies and other institutions of learning, as well as to the general public, that which might be expected to be gained from a course of lectures on the Documentary Theory of the Pentateuch, if delivered on one of the recently endowed university foundations for instruction in Biblical Literature.

The method of the book explains itself. Part I. is introductory. The science of Documentary Analysis and that inseparable from it of Historical Criticism are briefly explained and illustrated. A more complete idea of each, and of their mutual relations, can be gained by reading the articles "Israel" and "Pentateuch" in Enc. Brit., 9th ed. ; W. Robertson Smith's "Old Testament in the Jewish Church," and "Prophets of Israel," D. Appleton and Co., 1882 and 1883 ; Prof. Geo. T. Ladd's "What is the Bible?" Scribner's, 1888 ; and Prof. C. A. Brigg's "Biblical Study" (3d ed., 1890) ; and "Messianic Prophecy," Scribner's, 1886. Fr. Lenormant's "Beginnings of History" (translated), Scribner's, 1883, and Geo. Smith's "Chaldean Account of Genesis ;" new ed. ; Sampson Low, Marston and Co., London, 1880, are books of kindred aim adapted to the requirements of the general reader. Of a more technical character are Prof. Ladd's "Doctrine of Sacred Scripture," Scribner's, 1883 ; and, as standard works respectively of historical and analytical criticism, J. Wellhausen's "History of Israel" (translated), A. and C. Black, Edinburgh, 1885 ; and Kuenen's "Hexateuch" (translated), Macmillan and Co., London, 1886. To readers of German, Dutch and French, an inexhaustible field is opened. A bibliography will be found in almost any one of the larger works just enumerated.

Part II. affords to the eye a general view of the processes and results of Pentateuch analysis during the 138 years of its labor. The typographical means employed display the text of Genesis according to the revised version, the portions assigned to sources, compilers, editors and interpolators characteristically exhibited, and the loss or displacement of material indicated, so that at a glance the reader may comprehend the whole process of untwisting of each supposed strand in the composite thread, and judge whether or not it be reasonable. The references at the foot of the page are for the most part intelligible to the reader unfamiliar with Hebrew, and are mainly concerned with resemblances and contrasts in style and subject matter among the supposed documents. In a few cases they are intended to elucidate the thought, and go beyond the limits of the Hexateuch.

Part III. affords a connected view of the supposed documents **J**, **E** and **P**, as they are restored by the analysis. Lost material has sometimes been conjecturally supplied, but all such supplemental material is marked with [. . . . . .] These gaps can sometimes be filled with certainty from subsequent references in the same document (e. g. **J**'s version of the first interview of Joseph with his brethren in Egypt corresponding to **E** in Gen. xlii., from **J** in xliii. 3–7, 18–21 ; xliv. 19–29) ; sometimes all attempts at restoration of lost material must be mere guesswork. But gaps are fortunately the exception, not the rule. A few conjectural readings and amendments to the text of good authority, spoken of in the notes to Part II., are introduced in Part III. ; also preferred marginal renderings, and, in a small number of cases, new translations suggested by the analysis, and an arrangement of the text in verses, intended to exhibit the traces of metrical form displayed by the original.

The first Appendix presents a group of passages connected with the Creation and Flood story, exhibiting remarkable affinity with the well-known Assyrian Flood and Creation tablets. Critics now regard these passages in Genesis as having been grafted upon the stock of Hebrew tradition, the majority considering them as an interpolation into the document **J**, others as incorporated by **J** together with the national epos. These passages are taken out as a group and placed, in Appendix I., in juxtaposition with the cuneiform narratives for purposes of comparison.

In joining the number of those who are endeavoring to awaken a new interest in biblical study by means of the remarkable results of analytical criticism, the author wishes to express his most grateful acknowledgments to Prof. A. Kuenen of Leyden and President W. R. Harper of Chicago for the kindness experienced at their hands. Also to Prof. George F. Moore of Andover for his scholarly revision and criticism of the new readings of Part III., beside innumerable other services of value, and to the eminent scholars to whom he is indebted for their courteous commendation of the book to the English-speaking public at home and abroad. To the reader who may approach these pages in the endeavor to find a deeper, clearer meaning in the ancient book than hitherto, he would express the sincere and sanguine hope that new light upon the unknown history of this long revered and cherished literature may prove it ever more and more clearly a "word of God," fragments providentially preserved of religious thought from that people whose history is the history of the development of the religious consciousness. If "given unto the fathers in the prophets by divers portions and in divers manners," it was no less "given of God," because the gift extended over many centuries, "line upon line and precept upon precept." It is no less divine if the fruit of generations of consecrated human hearts and consciences, rather than the utterance of a single individual.

What is true of the individual investigator is in a still higher degree true of any science, the science of criticism included. "We can do nothing against the truth, but for the truth." If reassurance is needed in regard to the effect of presenting to the public these claims of the higher criticism, I prefer to give it in the words of others rather than my own. Says Prof. Briggs of Union Seminary : "The higher criticism has rent the crust with which rabbinical tradition and Christian scholasticism have encased the Old Testament, overlaying the poetic and prophetic elements with the legal and the ritual. Younger biblical scholars have caught glimpses of the beauty and glory of biblical literature. The Old Testament is studied as never before in the Christian Church. It is beginning to exert its charming influence upon ministers and people. Christian theology and Christian life will be ere long enriched by it. God's blessing is in it to those who have the Christian wisdom to recognize, and the grace to receive and employ it."*

In the firm confidence that a general acquaintance with the discoveries claimed to have been made by the higher criticism in the Pentateuch can only conduce to the lasting benefit of His cause, who said, "Thy word is Truth," this volume is respectfully submitted to the Christian public.

BENJAMIN WISNER BACON.

Parsonage, Oswego, N. Y., October, 1891.

* *Biblical Study*. By Chas. A. Briggs. New York: Scribner and Sons, 1886. Page 247.

ANALYTICAL TABLE OF CONTENTS.

PREFACE, ... vii.–xiii.

INTRODUCTION, ... xxiii.–xxx.

PART FIRST: INTRODUCTORY.

CHAPTER I.

HIGHER CRITICISM AND THE SCIENCE OF DOCUMENTARY ANALYSIS.

1. Criticism is appreciation.—Biblical criticism, both textual and "higher," is necessary to do justice to the Bible, and is the indispensable foundation of a valid doctrine of Revelation and Inspiration ; hence also of a scientific Revealed Theology........Pp. 1, 2

2. The Documentary Analysis: Its field and function.—Treatises on its history and method.—Illustrations of its success from patristic literature...Pp. 2–6

3. General nature and history of Oriental MSS.—Agglomerative in their origin, and accretive in their transmission.—Explanation, and testimony to the fact................................Pp. 6–10

4. Origin of prose histories.—The minstrels the first historians.—Literature at first mnemonic in purpose.—Illustrations from extra-Pentateuchal literature..........................Pp. 10–22

5. Relation of poetic sources to incorporating narrative.—Illustrations from Joshua x. and Judges xv.—Higher criticism goes behind the author to his sources.—The Book of Jashar............Pp. 12–17

6. Sources cited as such by the Pentateuch.—The Book of the Wars of Yahweh.—Prose sources named.—Deuteronomy and the Book of

the Covenant.—Other writings attributed to Moses.—Relation of the sources quoted as such to the Pentateuch narrative.—Theory of the analysis...Pp. 17-21

7. The analysis has the right to search the Scriptures.—*A priori* exclusion refuted.—An unreasonable demand complied with.—Unity can only be certified by the results of attempted analysis..Pp. 21-24

8. The demand for " credentials " complied with...........Pp. 24-25

CHAPTER II.

THE SCIENCE OF HISTORICAL CRITICISM.

1. Documentary analysis is only preliminary to Historical Criticism.—Indispensableness of the latter to appreciation of both history and literature.—Results...P. 27

2. Illustration from secular literature needless.—Historical criticism is a cross-examination of the witnesses................Pp. 27, 28

3. Biblical historical criticism illustrated from the Psalms and Deutero-Isaiah.—Two methods of accounting for the phenomena.—Practical results of the critical method.................Pp. 28-30

4. Biblical archæology and the history of historical criticism to be studied in other treatises.—The purely literary branch of the science, in the single department of the Hexateuch, alone treated here.—A scriptural discrimination......................Pp. 30, 31

5. External and Internal evidence.—The former includes Tradition.—All New Testament references belong under this head.—The doctrinal argument irrelevant.—Internal evidence.—For determination of dates the two kinds of evidence are complementary...Pp. 31-34

6. Date and authorship of the Pentateuch in the light of external and internal evidence.—The tradition.—Other external evidence assures its existence circ. 300 B. C.—Anonymity..........Pp. 34–36

7. Evidence opposed to Mosaic authorship.—External *e silentio*, (a) from the history, (b) from the prophetic literature.—Relation of Chronicles to the older historical books.—Pre-exilic history ignores the ritual law.—The contrast might be due to disappearance of the Pentateuch...Pp. 36–39

8. The prophetic literature ignores the ritual law and positively disclaims a knowledge of its existence.. ....Pp. 39–42

9. Internal evidence.—How its force may be nullified.—*Post-Mosaica.*—Destructive criticism of Colenso.—Illustrations.—Its object:...Pp. 42–46

10. The date 620 B. C. for Deuteronomy the key to historical criticism of the Pentateuch.—Why critics identify Hilkiah's law-book, II. Kings xxii.f, with Deuteronomy.—External evidence for this date...Pp. 46–49

11. Internal evidence in Deuteronomy.—*Post-Mosaica.*—Character and style of the Code.—The religious revolution demanded.—Its necessity and radical nature.—Deuteronomy providentially if not miraculously fitted to the necessities of reform in the seventh century, B. C.............................. ....Pp. 49–54

12. Position of the priestly code in regard to the great reform.—Characterization of P. — Relation to the history and literature...Pp. 54–57

13. Relation of Deuteronomy to P an unbroken silence.—Deuteronomy "analyzes" Exodus and Numbers.—Internal evidence for post-exilic origin of P.—Illustration from Ezekiel of legal development.... ....Pp. 57–59

14. Characterization of JE.—External and internal evidence of date.—
Its function in the prophetic movement..................Pp. 59–62

15. J and E.—Relation and contrast of J and E.,............Pp. 62, 63

16. Results of the Critical Theory.—An inductive doctrine of revelation and inspiration......................................Pp. 63, 64

CHAPTER III.

The Documentary Theory of To-day.

1. Purpose of the articles.—Method pursued.—The Grafian theory.—
History of the amalgamation of JE.—Origin and incorporation
of Deuteronomy.—The "prophetic" element of the Hexateuch.—
Growth of the priestly legislation.—Rewriting of the history as a
framework to the priestly legislation.—Supplementation.—Amalgamation of the priestly with the prophetic elements.—Final
redaction...Pp. 65, 66

2. The theory of Dillmann.—Mainly a peculiar theory of the origin of
P.—The earliest priestly codes.—The great priestly writer.—
Simultaneous combination of **E**, **P²**, **J** and parts of **P¹** by **R.**
—Deuteronomy and the Deuteronomist................Pp. 66, 67

3. Evangelical critics.—List of authorities...................P. 67, 68

4. Table of Dillmann's analysis of **P**, **E** and **J** throughout the Hexateuch...Pp. 68–94

PART II.

The text of Genesis according to the Revised Version in varieties of
type to exhibit the constituent sources and method of their compilation
according to the general consensus of critical analysis, with notes
explanatory of the phenomena of redaction..................Pp. 97–223

PART III.

The separate documents J, E and P conjecturally restored, with revised translation according to emended text and conjectural readings of good authority.......................................Pp. 225-334

APPENDICES.

Appendix I.   The great Flood Interpolation and connected passages, placed in juxtaposition with a translation of their cuneiform parallels.......................................Pp. 335-350

Appendix II.   Hebrew Notes...........................Pp. 351, 352

INTRODUCTION.

"If you penetrate the secret of the twelve [last verses of Deuteronomy, containing the account of Moses' death], also 'And Moses wrote' (Ex. xxiv. 4; Num. xxxiii. 2; Deut. xxxi. 9, 22), 'And the Canaanites were then in the land' (Gen. xii. 6; cf. xiii. 7), 'In the mountain of the Lord he appears' (Gen. xxii. 14), 'And his bedstead was an iron bedstead' (Deut. iii. 11), you will discover the truth." In these enigmatical words Aben Ezra [† 1168], the acutest of the mediæval Jewish commentators, calls attention to a number of indications in the Pentateuch of a later hand than that of Moses. He leaves the inference to his readers with a caution; "He who understands will hold his tongue" (Comm. on Gen. xii. 6). It is not certain what inference he himself drew. The mystery he makes about it might easily lead us, as perhaps it did Spinoza, to exaggerate the extent of Aben Ezra's departures from the received opinion. He deprecates in an outburst of orthodox horror the temerity of a certain Isaac, who ascribed the list of kings in Edom "before there was any king in Israel" (Gen. xxxvi. 31), to the time of Jehoshaphat. On the other hand, it is not clear that Aben Ezra meant no more than to point out the existence of some later glosses in the Mosaic text of the Pentateuch. However that may be, with these observations criticism had made a beginning. It was a long time before anything more came of it. The new impulse to Bible study in the Reformation century did not take a critical direction. The erratic reformer Carlstadt [† 1541] declared the authorship of the Pentateuch unknown and unknowable; the Catholic Andreas Maes [† 1573], one of the men of learning whom scholars will always delight to honor, held that long after Moses the

Pentateuch had passed through the hands of an editor (perhaps Ezra), who had at least introduced words and clauses here and there to make the meaning clearer, and substituted for obsolete names of places those .by which they were known in his time. The Church responded by putting Maes's Joshua on the Index.* Biblical scholarship had, indeed, much to do before addressing itself to the problems of the higher criticism. The ancient versions of the Old Testament were to be edited and the entire apparatus brought together in the great Polyglot Bibles ; the interpretation of the Old Testament on the basis of the original text—wholly neglected among Christians since Jerome—was to be taken up, and the tools of the interpreter created ; the history, geography, chronology, archæology of the Bible to be worked up ; the versions to be compared with the Hebrew text, and the beginnings of systematic text criticism made. This work was done in the seventeenth century with a comprehensive learning and an indefatigable diligence which command not only our admiration but our lasting gratitude. There were giants in the earth in those days. Toward the end of the century the Mosaic authorship of the Pentateuch, as we have it, was again challenged. Hobbes in his "Leviathan," 1651 and La Peyrère in his fantastic "Preadamites," 1655, did little more than enlarge and comment on Aben Ezra's list of difficulties ; though the latter argues also from the obscurity, confusion, and disorder of many parts of the narrative that we have a jumble of excerpts and transcripts rather than an original work. He does not doubt, however, that Moses wrote the greater part of the Pentateuch. Spinoza, *Tractatus Theologico-politicus*, 1670, making Aben Ezra's obscure hints his point of departure, went much farther and anticipated many of the observations and inferences of subsequent criticism. He shows that there are much more serious difficulties in the way of the long-established opinion that Moses is the author of the Pentateuch than the superficial anachronisms

* This did not deter other Catholic scholars from following in his footsteps. The Spaniard Pereira and the Flemish Jesuit Bonfrère are particularly to be named.

which would at most warrant the conclusion that it had been glossed here and there by copyists or revised by an editor. The whole history of Joseph and Jacob, for example, shows by its internal inconsistencies that it is extracted and compiled from different histories. No author could have put Genesis xxxviii. (the story of Judah and Tamar), with its introduction, "And it came to pass at that time," where it now stands, interrupting the history of Joseph and involving the most patent chronological absurdities; it must be taken from another book, and introduced here by the compiler without sufficient examination. The hypotheses by which the commentators seek to relieve such difficulties, if true, would prove that the ancient Hebrews were entirely ignorant both of their own language and of the way to tell a story; in which case there would be no principle or norm in the interpretation of Scripture, but every man might invent any explanation he pleased. This clear statement of the inevitable outcome of the attempt to remove critical difficulties by exegetical inventions contains the judgment not only of the rabbinical commentators whom Spinoza had immediately in view, but of much modern exegesis as well. Such a method is not to interpret the Scripture but to correct it; or as he says in a note, to corrupt it, and give it, like a piece of wax, as many shapes as you please. His own theory was that the Pentateuch and older Historical Books (Josh., Jud., Sam., Kings) were the work of a single historian, who proposed to write the antiquities of the Jews from the beginning to the first destruction of Jerusalem, and who largely compiled his work from older writings. Who this historian was, cannot be certainly established; but there are considerations of some weight which support the conjecture that it was Ezra.

The criticism of the seventeenth century is best known by the names of Richard Simon, *Histoire critique du Vieux Testament*, 1678 (edition suppressed; authorized reprint, Rotterdam, 1685), and Jean Le Clerc, *Sentimens de quelques théologiens de Hollande sur l' Histoire Critique*, etc., 1685, etc.; to whom may be added Anton van Dale, 1696. These scholars agree only in their negative conclusion : the Pentateuch as we have it can not be the work of Moses. Each has his own hypothesis of its origin. According to Simon it grew out of the public archives under the direction of prophets and scribes ; Le Clerc imagined it the work of the Samaritan priest, 1 Kings xvii. 28 ; Van Dale makes Ezra the author.

Without some new instrument, criticism could not get beyond negative results. Its researches could make it increasingly clear that the Pentateuch in its present form is not Mosaic ; that it is a compilation rather than an original work ; but that true history of the book which, as Spinoza justly says, is the basis of its interpretation, it could not divine. The course of criticism in the seventeenth century, and again in Germany in the end of the eighteenth, shows that the logical drift of opinion was to bring the compilation of the Pentateuch down to the age of Ezra ; in which case, as no criteria other than the intrinsic probability of the relation existed, by which to determine the age or work of the sources employed by the author, the historical value of the work was effectually destroyed.

The necessary instrument, the critical analysis, was put in the hands of criticism by the French physician, Jean Astruc. Astruc's father, a Reformed pastor, who abjured before the revocation of the Edict of Nantes, had given him a thorough education.* He rose to eminence in his profession, not only as a practitioner, but as the author of treatises which are still named with honor. It was the man of science, not the theologian, who discovered the secret of Genesis. The repetitions, or parallel narratives (e. g. the two accounts of the creation of the world and especially of man ; the threefold repetition of some of the particulars of the flood) ; the peculiar use of the names Elohim and Jehovah in Genesis, in contrast with Exodus iii.ff ; the antichronisms, or disturbances of the chronological order, led him to conjecture that the author (Moses) had employed at least two older nar-

* It is often said (e. g. by Renan in his preface to the French translation of Kuenen's Introduction) that Astruc was not a Hebrew scholar. This is contradicted, however, by his own language, *Conjectures*, p. 18 ; cf. Note p. 31, 32, etc.

ratives, one of which used the name Elohim, the other, Jehovah. This hypothesis he tested by carrying through the analysis. His success in this attempt was itself a verification; but the verification became demonstrative when it appeared that upon the separation of the Elohim and the Jehovah Memoirs the repetitions, contradictions, and antichronisms which had so much exercised commentators and critics, disappeared of themselves. With the confidence of the man of science in scientific method, he wrote at the end of his prefatory exposition of these results: "So we must either renounce all pretence of ever proving any thing in any critical question, or agree that the proof which the combination of these facts affords amounts to a complete demonstration of the theory of the composition of Genesis which I have propounded." Unfortunately, few theologians had sufficient scientific or historical training to recognize the absolute cogency of the demonstration.

Astruc's motive and his application of the results were conservative. He congratulated himself that his surgeon's knife had effected a radical cure of what he calls the "malady of the last century," the doubt of the Mosaic authorship of Genesis; and especially that he had "annihilated the vain triumph of Spinoza," in the matter of Genesis xxxviii. The father of analytic criticism was an apologist. His own analysis was tentative and imperfect; his criteria were too simple; his application of them too mechanical. His hypothesis of the way in which the "Memoirs" were combined was artificial and improbable. But when all that is said, his discovery remains one of the most brilliant and fruitful in the history of criticism.

His *Conjectures* had no better fortune than the works of laymen usually experience at the hands of scholars of the schools. J. D. Michaelis, in a review of the book the year after its appearance, gave the author the credit of being a well-meaning man; but added that he seemed not to be acquainted with the literature of Old Testament studies since Clericus, and that his original contributions were worthless!

The theory of the composition of Genesis from two principal narratives was taken up in Germany by Michaelis's younger colleague, Eichhorn (from 1779), and improved on by Ilgen (1798), who recognized a second Elohist (E), and in other ways displayed remarkable insight.

In the early years of the present century the hypothesis of Astruc-Eichhorn-Ilgen, that our Genesis is the harmonistic combination of two or three continuous narratives, gave place for a time to the theory of Geddes (1792) and Vater (1805), who regarded the Pentateuch as a planless and disorderly congeries of loose scraps, of various age and worth, brought together by a late compiler. This was the direction in which German criticism had been feeling its way before Eichhorn, and to which it now returned. This "Fragment Hypothesis" succumbed to the demonstration, which was ere long forthcoming, that the Pentateuch is not such a hodge-podge; but has, in spite of a certain appearance of disorder, a manifest unity and strongly marked plan.

This plan appears most conspicuously in the main Elohistic narrative, the "Groundwork" of the Pentateuch, as it now began to be called. And this led to the hypothesis, which enjoyed for a while the adhesion of the leading critics, that the Groundwork has received extensive additions by a later writer. These pieces of new cloth do not always match the old garment; they are often misplaced, and have sometimes made rents: the disorder on the surface of a well-ordered composition is thus accounted for. In this theory ("Supplement Hypothesis") the Fragment Hypothesis is only half overcome. A juster and more discriminating analysis soon showed that the Jehovistic parts of Genesis have a plan and order of their own, and when separated form a tolerably complete whole. This was demonstrated by Hupfeld, whose work on the Sources of Genesis appeared, by a noteworthy coincidence, in 1853, the centennary of the publication of Astruc's *Conjectures.* Hupfeld rediscovered Ilgen's second Elohist, and demonstrated that Genesis is a cord, not of two, but of three strands. Criticism had now nothing to do but to return to the original hypothesis, that Genesis is a combination of older histories (so-called "Document Hypothesis"); and did so with more assured confidence, since all conceivable alternatives had been tried and excluded.

Since this return to the right path much progress has been made in the details of the analysis by the studies of Nöldeke, Wellhausen, Kuenen, Dillmann, Budde, and others. In Genesis, at least, we are approaching, if we have not already reached, the limit to which it can be carried. There will always be a remainder which defies our analysis. And, as in all other historical investigations, the evidence varies from the highest degree of probability to the most delicate balancing of seemingly contradictory indicia. But there is no reason to think that the general results in which critics now agree will be overturned.

In this volume the actual status of the analysis is graphically exhibited by the use of different fonts of type for the different narratives which have been combined to make our Genesis. The composite character of the whole having been thus made apparent, the unity and substantial integrity of the three main sources is shown by bringing together the *disjecta membra* of each of them. Synthesis must be the test of analysis.* Of the author's qualification for the task he has undertaken, the work itself is the best witness. It is the fruit of long and thorough study of the text, and of intimate acquaintance with the extensive and widely scattered literature of recent criticism. Mr. Bacon has proved his ability to do original work of value in this field by various articles in *Hebraica* and the *Journal of Biblical Literature* which have

---

*Earlier attempts to present the results of the analysis to the eye are—not to mention Astruc's parallel columns—E. Boehmer, *Liber Genesis Pentateuchicus,* 1860 (the Hebrew text in different fonts of type); followed by his *Das erste Buch der Thora. Uebersetzung seiner drei Quellenschriften u. s. w.,* 1862. Lenormant, *La Genèse. Traduction d' après l'Hebreu avec distinction des élémens constitutifs du texte, suivie d' un essai de restitution des livres primitifs,* 1883; English translation under the title : *The Book of Genesis,* etc., 1886. (On this translation see *Andover Review* X., 654.) Kautzsch and Socin, *Die Genesis mit äusserer Unterscheidung der Quellenschriften, u. s. w.,* 1889; second edition, 1891. It is proper to say that the present work was far advanced before the appearance of the first edition of Kautzsch and Socin's excellent little volume.

received merited commendation from scholars. A more competent guide through the labyrinth of the analysis would be hard to find.

It would not be strange if the very clearness with which the results of criticism are here exhibited should give rise to some apprehension of the consequences if they should be generally accepted. But surely apprehension is groundless. That a better understanding of the way in which God has revealed Himself in the history of the true religion, whose early chapters are written in the Old Testament, will diminish men's faith in religion or the Scripture, or their reverence for them, is no less unreasonable than to suppose that better knowledge of Astronomy or Geology must impair faith in the God of Heaven and Earth.

PART. I.

CHAPTER I.

Higher Criticism and the Science of Documentary Analysis.

CHAPTER II.

The Science of Historical Criticism.

CHAPTER III.

Pentateuchal Analysis.

PART I. INTRODUCTORY.

CHAPTER I.

Higher Criticism and the Science of Documentary Analysis.

1. Criticism is appreciation. To criticise means, both by etymology and correct usage, to do justice; but as all things partaking in any degree of a human character are imperfect, and justice implies the exposing of imperfection, the word is naturally apt to acquire a sinister sense to which it is not justly entitled. Biblical criticism is therefore in reality not merely an innocent pursuit for specialists, but in the highest degree a science to be cultivated by all who honor and revere the Scriptures. To fail to criticise the Bible is to fail to do it justice.

In former times when it was customary to deny even the existence of a human element in the Bible, textual criticism was denounced as an attack upon revealed religion. But textual criticism is now universally admitted to have corrected vast numbers of errors on the part of scribes and copyists, and may justly claim to have brought us by means of its marvellous apparatus for minute comparison of texts, to a position by many centuries nearer to the original writers of the Scriptures.

The Higher Criticism* accepts the text which textual criticism furnishes as the closest possible approximation to the original, and identical for all practical purposes with the autograph of the latest editor or compiler as the case may be; but beyond this point it undertakes to carry us still further back. It inquires how the text thus established came to assume that form. Was the writer an editor or compiler

---

* "By the Higher Criticism is meant that study which tries to reproduce the influences and circumstances out of which the biblical books arose, and thus exhibit them as true children of their own time." Ladd. *What is the Bible?* p. 126.

I

merely, as the writers of Kings and Chronicles declare themselves to be? Then what were his sources, and what was their authority? Was he an author, as in the case of the fourth gospel? Then who was he? When and where did he live? Under what circumstances and for what purpose did he write? What were his materials, and, if his personal opinions enter into the writing, what is the ground and degree of the respect to which his opinions are entitled? All these questions are essential to a just appreciation of the Scriptures, and at the same time they are such as are legitimately comprised in the field of a special science. Until they are answered on scientific principles there can be no scientific doctrine of revelation and inspiration, no valid interpretation, and consequently no scientific science of Revealed theology.

It is not assumed that there is no divine element in the Bible. It is not of course assumed that there is no human element in it, beside the mistakes of copyists. Nothing is assumed. One thing however is regarded as certain: that whether the Bible as it left the hands of the final editors was all divine, or all human; or whether it was neither the one nor the other, but partook, as it is now admitted to partake, of the nature of both, there is no other way to do it justice than by criticism. By no other means can the human element, if there be one, be made to disclose its imperfections, and the divine element, if there be one, be made to disclose its perfections, but by Biblical Criticism, both the textual and the higher.

2. But it is with only a single department of the higher criticism that we have mainly to do in the present volume, the subordinate branch of Documentary Analysis, whose principal function is the extrication of sources. Even here we do not go beyond the first six books of the Old Testament, which critics regard as a literary unit and call the Hexateuch.

It has been the unique privilege of the present century to succeed in unearthing veritable libraries of ancient literature.

Monuments of stone, tablets of clay, scrolls of parchment and papyrus have yielded up many secrets of the past to the patient search and scrutiny of the archæologist. But a field of discovery by no means the least fruitful has been the page of authors and historians long known to our libraries, as well as of others recently brought to light. When we hear the ancient authors Sanchoniathon, Berosus, Manetho, and others quoted, the impression is apt to be made that copies of their works are in existence. This is not the case; the works of a great proportion of these ancient writers are known to us only as they are quoted by Eusebius, Josephus, or some ancient historian whose works survive. But it necessarily happened that in many instances, especially in the earlier times, sources were not quoted by title and name, but simply incorporated; for ideas of copyright and plagiarism, author's privileges and citation of authorities, are of modern invention. It is obvious, however, that no historian can write without sources, either oral or written, and if we possess more than one book wherein the same material appears, it becomes at once a problem within the ability of science to solve, at least in some degree, what the source was. A familiar instance is the book of Chronicles, which reproduces *verbatim* page after page of the earlier books of Samuel and Kings. Another kind of problem, almost equally familiar, is that of the Synoptic Gospels, Matthew, Mark and Luke, where again we have the same material employed three times over in long passages verbally identical, but where the phenomena are such as to make the theory of direct transfer of limited application.

That which is not so well known to the general public is the fact that a science exists, and has existed for more than a century, with definite method and rules for going beneath the surface of ancient writings, and, so to speak, examining the material of their foundations and tracing thereon the masons' marks, and that many important results of this science have already secured universal acceptation among those competent to judge.

At present the trustworthiness of the science in its

general methods and results can be best exhibited by an illustration drawn from patristic literature, since thus we shall not raise the mooted question of the documentary theory of the Pentateuch.*

Up to the time of the publication in 1883 of the extremely ancient Christian document entitled, *The Teaching of the Twelve Apostles*, the eminent German critics, Bickell and Gebhardt had concluded from their studies of the so-called *Apostolic Constitutions* and *Apostolic Epitome* that some more ancient document underlay these writings. In 1882 appeared the work of Krawutzky, "in which he undertook to recover and reconstruct the imbedded earlier and simpler document." When, in 1883, this Teaching of the Twelve Apostles was brought forth from its hiding-place of centuries in a neglected convent library of Constantinople and given to the Christian world, the close correspondence of it with the document conjecturally reproduced by the processes of "documentary analysis" demonstrated the latter to be "a success of the most pronounced and brilliant character."†

Like work to this so successfully accomplished in patristic literature, can be done, and has been done in the biblical writings, and its results have been scrutinized, checked and corroborated by the mutual criticism of many schools of higher criticism, comprising the most illustrious names in Biblical scholarship for a century past. Corroboration by the discovery of the actual documents supposed to have been imbedded in the Hexateuch is scarcely to be expected; for the discovery of the Assyro-Chaldean Flood and Creation tablets,‡ though furnishing unmistakeable evidence of a rela-

---

* Instead of a minute description of the history and methods of this science of Documentary Analysis, the reader is referred to the article *Pentateuch* in the Enc. Brit. IX. ed., or, if accessible, to a very excellent French history of Pentateuch analysis by A. Westphal, *Les Sources du Pentateuque* (Paris, Librairie Fischbacher, 1888.) The methods can best be studied by the English reader in Kuenen's *Hexateuch* already referred to: by readers of German in Kuenen, and in Wellhausen's *Composition des Hexateuchs*, Berlin, 1890.

† Professors Hitchcock and Brown of Union Theological Seminary. Introduction to their edition of the *Didachè*.

‡ See Appendix I.

tionship between the two versions, affords no material verbally incorporated into the narratives supposed to have been
interpolated in Genesis. The archæologist has however
brought to light quite recently a document whose bearing
upon the documentary theory of the Pentateuch is too direct
and important to permit an ignoring of it in any work assuming to present the claims of the analysis. Professor Geo. F.
Moore of Andover, in an article published in the *Journal
of Biblical Literature* 1890, Part II, and entitled, "Tatian's
Diatessaron and the Pentateuch," shows how every process
attributed by the critics to **R.** the Redactor, or assumed compiler and editor of the Pentateuch, is paralleled, and more
than paralleled, by those applied by the long-lost author Tatian
to the material taken by him from our own canonical four
gospels. That which in the analysis of the Hexateuch has
been ignorantly denounced as "a crazy patchwork" is seen
to be more sober, more credible by far, than the process
actually applied by Tatian to Matthew, Mark, Luke and John
to make his *Diatessaron*, or "Harmony of the four gospels."

This work is itself an illustration of the constructive power
of the documentary analysis, for it was reconstructed by
Zahn in 1881 "with conspicuous success" by means of a
Latin Harmony of the sixth century and the Armenian commentary on it of Ephraem Syrus. In 1888 Ciasca edited the
Diatessaron itself from two codices, the Vatican Cod. Arab.
xiv., and a MS. recently acquired by the Museum Borgianum.

For details of the comparison between the mode of construction of this composite gospel—for such it is, rather than
a harmony—and the composite Pentateuch assumed by the
overwhelming majority of modern scholars, the reader is
referred to the above mentioned article. It is however the
history of Tatian's Diatessaron which has a more immediate
bearing than even its text upon the Pentateuchal theory.
Prof. Moore will allow me to quote his language.

"This harmony of the Gospels was made after the middle of the
second century. . . . It was for several generations the Gospel of a
large part of the Syrian church, and is quoted simply as such. . . . .
After the beginning of the fifth century, however, there came a change.

Rabbula, Bishop of Edessa (411–435), ordered that the churches of his diocese should be supplied with copies of the Separate Gospels, and that they should be read. A few years later, Theodoret, Bishop of Cyrrhus (423–457), found the Diatessaron in use in two hundred churches in his diocese—one in four of the whole number. He sequestered them, and replaced them by copies of the Gospels of the Four Evangelists. These names are not without significance. They are the opposite of 'Composite Gospel,' the common name for the Diatessaron. The title of Matthew in the Curetonian fragments, which puzzled Cureton, and of which Bernstein proposed a wholly untenable explanation, expresses this contrast ; it is ' The Separate Gospel Matthew.' "

Had it not been for the forcible intervention of the bishops, the Syrian church would doubtless have repeated to the letter the history of the supposed documentary sources of the Pentateuch **J. E. D.** and **P;*** for in an uncritical age motives of convenience and the tendency to assimilation far outweigh the claims of literary comparison for the sake of historical accuracy. What the Separate Gospels did for the Syrian church the analysis aims to do for us by a Separated Hexateuch. The greater the number of witnesses and the wider the divergence in their standpoint, the longer will be the base-line of critical measurement and the stronger and more accurate the history determined by it.

3. Complete as is the parallel between the history of Tatian's Diatessaron and the supposed history of the Pentateuch, no one pretends to say that such a supposition would be probable in the case of a modern Occidental work. Two facts coöperate to make the supposition credible in the case of ancient Oriental books which in the case of modern books would be quite improbable: first, their long and checkered history in the MS. form, subject to all kinds of manipulation and interpolation such as textual criticism bears witness to†; second, ancient, and especially Oriental methods of book-making.

So nearly universal is the rule that very ancient documents are conglomerate, having incorporated in their history larger or smaller quantities of older or foreign material, that scarcely

* I. e., Jahvist, Elohist, Deuteronomist and Priestly writer. See p. 21.

† E. g., Mark xvi. 9–20 and John vii. 53—viii. 11. Rev. Ver.

one exists to which the process of analysis has not been applied with more or less striking success.

The Egyptian Book of the Dead, perhaps the oldest writing in existence, and the Homeric poems, are generally regarded as conglomerate, though so far back as traceable in history they have been protected from divergent forms by canonization and hence afford but slight crevices for the wedge of analytical criticism. Other sacred books of antiquity, however, the Vedas, the Bundehesch and the Edda, are mines of primitive documentary treasure; while the clay tablets of Sardanapalus avow themselves copies of works dating from 2000 B. C., and earlier. In fact it is the general expectation of the antiquarian that investigation of an early document will disclose still earlier fragments. Hence discoveries of ancient writings are no sooner made than appeal is taken both to historical and analytical criticism, to discover whatever may be underlying the present text. An example is The Teaching of the Twelve Apostles, wherein already the discovery of a still earlier portion by critical analysis has been announced and is generally accepted. .

These facts necessarily presuppose a somewhat different character and structure in ancient documents from that to which we are accustomed in modern literature. No one would think, for example, of trying to analyze one of Dickens's novels or a story of the war of the Rebellion or Bancroft's History of the United States, into component parts. We might indeed be sure, in cases like the last, that certain sources must underlie the work of the author; but we should know it a hopeless task to attempt anything like a reconstruction of more than minute parts of such authorities employed, because of their great number and the thorough process of mental review and assimilation which they had undergone before composition began. But with respect to the writings here dealt with the case is wholly different.

In the first place, works of fiction spun out of the author's individual mind are notoriously (with exceptions too few to be considered) not to be found in primeval literatures.

Secondly, a certain class of writings, manifestly the autographs of individuals, such as monumental inscriptions, are of course excepted in any case from the sphere of analysis. Such autographs are however, in the nature of the case, comparatively rare and brief. When transmitted to us by literary transcription and incorporation into larger works, they are liable to those modifying processess—revision, emendation, expansion—which always accompany such transmission, and of which we shall have more to say in the course of the argument. Writings of this class are therefore more apt to be the finished product of documentary analysis than its raw material.

Thirdly, in the case of historic, poetic and religious writings (the usual form in which the literary legacy of the early past is transmitted to us), we must expect a very different character and structure from that of modern books. A modern writer has a vast number of works on kindred topics, which are also accessible to his readers. He cannot quote at length from all, he dare not plagiarize at length from one or two. With the ancient writer the case is entirely different. He has but very few sources—three or four at the utmost. He has neither the capacity nor the desire to compare critically, to digest and reproduce in his own language. On the other hand there is no objection to unlimited transfer of material. He may simply copy a whole book. He may copy the whole or parts of two books or three, and add as much or as little as he chooses of his own. In either case his work will be equally serviceable and equally approved. A book was a book, individually and by itself, before the days of systematic publication; it was judged by its contents as true or untrue, interesting or uninteresting, without regard to authorship, sources, or possible relation to other books, previous or contemporary, like or unlike. The man who owned it owned so much parchment or paper, on which he copied what he chose and wrote what he chose. His successor owned it in like manner and could treat it in like manner. It is no wonder that ancient documents, of even a few pages only, contain elements extremely heterogeneous in character. It is no wonder either that we should find (as we do) that documents usually tend to swell in bulk as they pass on from generation to generation. Even supposing the owner of a book to abstain from inserting on the margin or between the lines observations of his own—an abstinence more apt to flow from mental indolence than from any idea of literary impropriety—he cannot be expected to abstain from inserting into his volume any floating scrap of history or poetry which strikes him as valuable, especially if he has a notion that it emanates from the same author as the volume in his possession. Omission, on the other hand, would be comparatively rare, occurring only in very obvious cases of duplication or contradiction.

These *a priori* conclusions were strikingly confirmed, as we have seen, by the discovery of Tatian's Diatessaron; further illustration and authority for these statements will be afforded by the following extract from a review of vol. III. of Renan's *History of Israel* in the *Christian Union* for April 9, 1891 :—

"Oriental history is compilation, in which the several parts retain their individuality. There is less desire for smoothness and unbroken connection than for the inclusion of all matters bearing on the subject in hand. That 'the pieces exist in their entirety, not digested (p. 58), is to a large extent true. Renan cites as examples of the habit the Chronicle of Malalas of Antioch, among the Greek compilations ; Moses of Chorene, Firdusi. The materials thus used are preserved in their new combination, but lost as separate works. 'It is, in fact, the law of Oriental history-writing that a book kills its predecessor. The sources of a compilation rarely survive the compilation itself. A book in the Orient is hardly ever copied just as it is. It is brought up to date by the addition of whatever is known, or believed to be known, besides. The individuality of a historical book does not exist in the Orient. The substance is held to, not the form ; there is no scruple at mixing authors and styles. The desire is to be complete, that is all.'" (Pp. 61, 62.)

Says Prof. W. Robertson Smith of Cambridge :—

"When critics maintain that some Old Testament writings traditionally ascribed to a single hand, are really of a composite origin, and that many of the Hebrew books have gone through successive redactions,—or, in other words, have been edited and re-edited, in different ages, receiving some addition or modification at the hand of each editor,—it is often supposed that these are mere theories devised to account for facts which may be susceptible of a very different explanation. . . . . . Here it is that the Septuagint comes in to justify the critics, and provide external evidence of the sort of thing which to the conservative school seems so incredible. The variations of the Greek and Hebrew text, reveal to us a time when the functions of copyist and editor shaded into one another by imperceptible degrees. They not only prove that Old Testament books were subjected to such processes of successive editing as critics maintain, but that the work of redaction went on to so late a date that editorial changes are found in the present Hebrew text which did not exist in the MSS. of the Greek translators. . . . .   No one who has been personally occupied with old Eastern MSS., and has observed the way in which copyists, on account of the scarcity and costliness of writing material, were accustomed to fill up blank pages at the end of a book by writing in some other work or passage which they wished to preserve, and that without any note or title whatever, will for a moment venture to affirm that the title at the beginning of the book must necessarily apply to the whole contents of the volume." *

The testimony of competent witnesses is unanimous that early, and especially Oriental MSS. are far from being universally homogeneous in original structure, while their transmission has been exposed to almost unlimited interpolation and manipulation. The earliest Semitic authorship seems to have been frequently a process of agglomeration, of which the Diatessaron is only one of the latest and most elaborate examples. The transmission of these early works has again been not merely copying, but during a considerable part of the history a process of accretion. There are however two considerations which relieve the sense of dissatisfaction occasioned by this disclosure. First: elimination is much rarer than addition. Second : the very fact of great antiquity, although in one respect complicating the problem of analysis, makes the probability the stronger that the writing, if composite, is the resultant of few elements rather than many.

4. There will be no disposition in any quarter to dispute the general proposition that the earliest prose histories are found to rest upon a foundation of folk-lore and minstrelsy. The history of literature presents to us in the earliest period the age of war-songs and ballads sung at feasts or round the camp fire by bards whose music is but a step from the ringing shield or twang of bow-string; of legends, too, that cluster around sacred groves or venerated shrines. The Homeric poems, the Runic sagas, survived thus in oral form for an in-

* *Old Test. in the Jewish Church*, pp. 105 and 109.

definite period. While the treasury of tribal tradition was still small, for a period indeed which to the modern seems almost incredible, the memory alone was sufficient to preserve the most memorable of these traditions entire; but gradually the increasing burden compelled reluctant resort to the laborious and costly method of writing. In most cases if not all, literature begins in the attempt to preserve the overflowing treasures of oral tradition ; the different forms of poetic expression, cadence, rhythm, rhyme and alliteration, being mnemonic expedients previously resorted to. We need not be surprised therefore to find underlying a primitive historical writing, as one of its principal sources, individual songs, sometimes of even epic proportions ; and not infrequently whole collections of early poems, usually of a warlike, often of a religious character. The prose Edda reduces to the form of a continuous story the earlier lyric mythology. Herodotus and his predecessors draw upon the earlier legends of poetic form. Livy looks back to Ennius "the Homer of Rome." But most nearly allied to Hebrew writings is the Arabic epic *Kitab-el-Aghâni*, whose resemblance in its mingled prose and verse to some of the Old Testament writings is a favorite illustration of Renan.

"Rhythmic structure," he says, "especially when conformed to the rules of the Semitic parallelism, is like the *quipou*, the knotted string which holds fast what would otherwise drop out of memory. Thus it is that every Arab tribe, making no use of writing, preserved, in old times, the whole Divan of its poems ; thus it is that the memory of the pre-islamic Arabs, from which it would have been in vain to expect a single accurate statement of historic fact, preserved, down to the time of the scribes of Baghdad, one hundred and fifty years after Mohammed, the immense poetic treasure of the *Kitab-el-Aghâni*, the *Moallakât*, and other poems of the same sort. The Tuareg tribes in our own day exhibit phenomena of the same kind."*

It is well known to what extent the historical writings of the Old Testament, especially the Pentateuch, Joshua and the book of Judges, are strewn with poems and poetic fragments antique in structure and often of great beauty. It will hardly be supposed that the author of the prose work himself composed the poems for the embellishment of the history. But

* E. Renan. *Histoire du peuple d' Israël.* I. p. 304.

if not, here is already a "source" easily separable, whose relation to the work which now incorporates it we should do well to discover. What if the Song of Lamech, the Blessing of Noah, the Oracle of Rebekah, the Blessings of Isaac and of Jacob form parts of such a fund of folk-lore and minstrelsy! In that case not only will the separate study of these fragments carry us back to an earlier period of the history, but a comparison of their standpoint with that of the writer who incorporates them, will shed an invaluable light upon the question how the latter shall be understood, and to what extent our view of his narrative is to be affected by the sources to which he thus invites our study.

Illustrations are abundant. The 4th and 5th chapters of Judges give respectively a prose and a poetic account of the victory of Deborah and Barak. There can be no question as to the relative antiquity of the two, since the song bears every mark of a pæan of victory dating from the immediate remembrance of the triumph. The prose narrative in this instance makes a highly favorable impression by its correspondence with and at the same time its seeming independence of the poem, as if its author had at command some further details of the battle, written or traditional, though he manifestly looks back to "that time" as one more or less remote.

5. But let us turn to another instance even more noted. Joshua x. 12, 13, contains a quotation expressly assigned to its source. The author, perhaps because what he relates might seem to require more authority than his mere statement, after quoting four lines of poetry says, "Is not this written in the book of Jashar?" The quotation is a poetic apostrophe to the sun and moon, placed no doubt in the mouth of Joshua, and reminds us of the impassioned assertion of Deborah's Song, "The stars in their courses fought against Sisera." It read as follows:

> Sun, stand thou still upon Gibeon,
> And thou, moon, in the valley of Aijalon.
> And the sun stood still, and the moon stayed
> Until the nation had avenged themselves of their enemies.

We recognize at once the force and beauty of a poetical figure. But there is no evidence that the author of the prose narrative did so. To him it was simply a miracle, but one the stupendous character of which in its cosmical relations he of course could not appreciate. In a tone of wonder he declares: "And the sun stayed in the midst of heaven, and hasted not to go down about a whole day. And there was no day like that before it or after it, that Yahweh hearkened unto the voice of a man; for Yahweh fought for Israel."

Here we see an author distinctly citing his authority by title, and apparently misconceiving it. This is quite a different matter from that in Judges iv., and if we succeed in establishing unity of authorship between this prose account and other parts of the historical writings, we learn to treat such other parts with the caution suggested by the discovery that the writer is dependent on a poetical source, the book of Jashar, which in at least one case he failed to interpret correctly.

That which is so undeniably true in the case of this passage in Joshua must be admitted to be at least possible in other cases. We find ourselves thus prompted by the very letter of the Scriptures themselves to this inquiry: Is it permissible to go behind the letter of the text in these other cases also?— It is by this process of "searching the Scriptures," that we are led toward an answer. Where the narrative is not actually set face to face with the cited authority we cannot proceed with the same confidence; but we can proceed with a degree of probability which makes the whole study one of the profoundest interest to the lover of sacred history.

No fault has been found with the revisers for eliminating from the book of Judges one of its most remarkable prodigies by a simple modification of the translation of xv. 19, from "God clave a hollow place that was in the jaw" to "God clave the hollow place that is in Lehi," although such attempts to lighten the task of faith are wont to be resented. *Lehi* of course means "jawbone" and the spring called *En-hakkore* ("spring of him that called"), which is at Lehi, is said by the writer to have derived its origin and name from Samson's prayer.   The name of the place Lehi or Ramath-Lehi ("hill of the jawbone") corresponds to the Greek name for a certain promontory which Strabo gives as *Onugnathos*, "ass's jawbone," and is supposed by critics to be derived from the appearance of the cliff,* as in Hebrew a rock is called a "tooth," *shen*,† and a cliff a "jaw."   Will it be resented if after the revisers, by simply regarding Lehi as a proper name in v. 19, have eliminated one of the most incredible prodigies of the Old Testament, the higher criticism proceeds to remove the equally stupendous one which immediately precedes it, by doing exactly the same thing in v. 16, viz., translating Lehi as a proper name?   If this is permissible, verse 16 will read literally, "And Samson said,

> At Lehi an ass [or a heap] a heap, two heaps,
> At Lehi an ass [or a heap] I have slain a thousand men."

The merest tyro in criticism will see at a glance that the word translated "an ass" in the text, which is identically the same word (*hamor*) as that twice repeated at the end of the first line, is simply what is called a dittograph, the commonest of scribal errors, by which a word is accidentally duplicated in writing.   Either because the word Lehi ("jawbone of") suggested the translation "an ass" for the first *hamor* or because the reduplication of the word ("a heap, two heaps") to signify great numbers made confusion, the simple fragment of a war song,

> *At* (Heb. *be*) Lehi, a heap, two heaps,
> At Lehi I have slain a thousand men,

was transformed into

" *With* (a secondary sense of *be*) the jawbone of an ass heaps upon heaps,
With the jawbone of an ass I have slain a thousand men." ‡

---

* Cf. note to Gen. xvi. 14, the well of *Lehi-roi*.

† Cf. French *dent*, *Dent du Midi*, *Dent du Dru*.

‡ Cf. Heb. Notes. (1)

But since the elimination of the prodigy is effected in this case by the removal of a single dittographic word from the text, many will be inclined to consider this textual criticism. It is not. The author of the chapter himself read and wrote "jawbone of an ass," and builds all his story on the fact. We must go behind the author to his source, which in this instance is unquestionably an ancient song, probably the same twice quoted in the preceding chapter. When it becomes manifest from verses 15 and 17 that the author himself understood his material in the sense, "With the jawbone of an ass," no matter how absurd the rendering, textual criticism has no more to say. It becomes the duty of the higher criticism to put the inquiry, How far does the author correctly interpret his source? To most minds the conclusion will be inevitable that we have here instead of a stupendous prodigy the simple misinterpretation of an ancient song.

Outside the Pentateuch it is therefore entirely possible to trace in some of the historical books, certain fragments of the sources employed, and even to place the source itself in comparison with the narrative deduced from it. Not only is this true, but we know the title of one of the most important of the earlier works quoted, and can make a beginning already toward reconstructing it. For the *Sepher haj-Jashar*, or "Book of the Upright," quoted by the author of Joshua x. 10, ff. is referred to elsewhere in the Old Testament and considerable extracts made from it. The noble elegy upon the death of Saul and Jonathan, II Samuel i. 17–27, there called (or perhaps directed to be sung to the melody of) "The Song of the Bow," and attributed to David, is the most important excerpt, and easily constitutes the most authentic and earliest witness to David's skill as a minstrel, besides corroborating the touching story of the friendship of David and Jonathan.

> "I am distressed for thee, my brother Jonathan,
> Very pleasant hast thou been unto me :
> Thy love to me was wonderful,
> Passing the love of woman.
> Behold it is written in the book of Jashar."

But while this corroboration of I Samuel and of the tradition which in Amos's time (Amos vi. 5) gave to David the reputation of a bard, is most welcome, it must be admitted that the period to which we should assign the collection quoted here and in Joshua x., is brought down to a later date than we have been accustomed to assign to the composition of Joshua itself.   Even if we assume with Renan in his brilliant but inexcusably superficial and dogmatic *Histoire du Peuple d'Israël*, that the Song of the Bow marks the closing of the collection of *haj-Jashar*, we cannot place this date earlier than the reign of David.   But M. Renan, who avowedly depends more upon the instinctive intuition of a French Semitic scholar than on the patient industry and cautious method of German critics, has in this instance been led astray by his intuition that the *Sepher haj-Jashar must* have been completed in, or soon after, the period of David.

" It is therefore our opinion that the battle of Gilboa and the elegy on the death of Jonathan occupied the last pages of the book. *Certainly there was no allusion to the last period of David nor to the reign of Solomon.*" *

A glance at the LXX. version, however, at I Kings viii. 12, would have proved that the building and dedication of the temple were also treated in the book of Jashar.   The poetic fragment which, according to the Hebrew, begins—

Then spake Solomon :

" Yahweh hath said that he would dwell in the thick darkness ;
But I have built thee an house to dwell in,
A place for thine habitation forever ;"

was more complete and correct in the text possessed by the LXX., and read in a way which restores both the parallelism and poetic thought of the opening line.

" Yahweh created the sun in the heavens,
But he hath determined to dwell in darkness,
I have built an house of habitation for thee,
A place to dwell in eternally.
Behold is it not written in the book of Jashar."

* " Nous pensons donc que la bataille de Gelboé et l'élégie sur la mort de Jonathas occupaient les dernières pages du livre. Assurément, il n' y était question ni des derniers temps de David ni du regne de Salomon." *Hist. d' Isr.* II. 226.

How much beyond the dedication of the temple it would be necessary to bring down the date of compilation of the Book of Jashar it is of course impossible to say, but Renan is doubtless right in comparing the work to the Arab anthology *Kitab-el-Aghâni* with its ancient ballads loosely connected by brief prose narratives. To what extent it may underlie the older historical books is as yet a question which admits only of conjecture.

6. In deference to the traditional belief in the Mosaic authorship of the Pentateuch, reference to the poetic sources incorporated by it has been avoided hitherto.* We may however, without pre-judging the question, at least refer to the sources which the Pentateuch itself expressly presents as such. Thus Deut. xxxii. 1–43 is introduced in the preceding and following verses as a song which Moses and Hoshea spake in the ears of the people. Deut. xxxiii. is another long poem introduced by the simple phrase, "This is the Blessing, wherewith Moses the man of God blessed the children of Israel before his death." We pass over the great mass of Songs and Blessings, from the so-called "Sword-song" of Lamech, Gen. iv. 23 f. down, which, by advocates of the Mosaic authorship, may be considered in the light either of incorporated material,† or as the composition of Moses,‡ and come at once to a case precisely similar to that of Joshua x. 10.

---

* Josh. x. 10, while belonging on the critical theory to E, one of the Pentateuch sources, is of course not regarded as " Mosaic " by the supporters of the traditional view.

† So Rev. E. Cowley in his *Writers of Genesis* just issued (1891) by Thos. Whittaker, 2 Bible House, New York: "My belief is, and I shall endeavor to show, that Noah, Abraham, Isaac, Jacob, Judah and Joseph were the original writers of those portions of Genesis in which they appear as the active subjects. . . . . . My treatment will assign to Moses the first editing of the records of Judah which ended with the death of Joseph. In Egypt and Midian he collected all the Hebrew records and traditions. They had kindled his enthusiasm and incited him to undue haste when he slew the offending Egyptian."

‡ It is, I believe, customary on the traditional theory to assume that records of the utterances of Lamech, Noah and the patriarchs were transmitted in oral or written form to Moses. (See note preceding.) I am not aware, however, in what way the long poem in Numbers xxiii. f. is considered to have reached Moses in time for incorporation in his work, unless Balaam himself is supposed to have personally communicated the substance of his prophecy.

2

In Numbers xxi. 14 ff. we have a poetic citation concerning Israel's coming into "the field of Moab," introduced by the words, "Wherefore it is said in the *Sepher Milchamoth Yahweh*," or "Book of the Wars of Yahweh." A longer poetic fragment in the same chapter is attributed by the historian to "them that speak in proverbs," or, as we might better translate, "folk-lore."

In the case of these and the other lyric fragments scattered through the non-legal parts of the Hexateuch the fact that the same type is employed in the analysis contained in Part II. of this volume is not to be understood as indicating an opinion that the authors **J** and **E** themselves composed the poems. On the contrary criticism frequently traces the origin of the prose narrative to the existence and sometimes to the misinterpretation of the earlier poem.*

No other poetic citation of the Pentateuch beside Numbers xxi. 14 ff. is referred by actual title to its source, but several of the codes of law incorporated, including all which by critics are regarded as the oldest, are explicitly referred by the Pentateuchal writer to certain "books," or "writings," which in his judgment were Mosaic. Whether by this he meant that he supposed himself possessed of an autograph of the great legislator, and transcribed *verbatim ;* or whether the "Mosaic" character of these writings was indirect, admitting of free transcription, interpretation and expansion from tradi-

---

* By referring to Dillmann's analysis of Ex. xiv. (see chap. III.) the reader will see that in J, generally regarded as the oldest document, the crossing of the Red Sea cannot be called a miraculous occurrence though manifestly providential. The strong wind drives back the shallow water till Israel is able to ford the narrow gulf. On the further shore the battle takes place between them and their pursuers, who are embarrassed by the returning tide and finally turn to "flee against it" leaving their dead upon the seashore. The transition from this providential but purely natural relation to the prodigy of the later story, in which the cleft mass of waters stand as a wall on either side of the host and collapse at the signal from Moses' rod as the Egyptian host enters behind, is traced by some critics in the poetic license of the ode of victory, ch. xv., which in verse 8 passes from the poetic description of the wind as "the blast of Yahweh's nostrils," "piling up the waters," to the purely figurative

    " The floods stood upright as an heap,
    The deeps were congealed in the heart of the sea."

Still this idea is open to grave objections, based however not upon the earliness, but the lateness of the psalm. Cf. verse.17.

tional understanding, both on his part and on the part of his predecessors; or whether, finally, he had no positive judgment to express, but simply adopted the current tradition which attributed all legislation to Moses, as in the Graeco-Roman world to Lycurgus, Draco, Solon, Minos, the Twelve Tables, we do not now inquire. Argument can of course be made to great extent on all three suppositions. The fact remains that these codes are referred, in the narrative which frames them in, to Moses, and are spoken of as "written" documents. No argument is here intended against the Mosaic authorship, for we do not impugn the possibility that the narrative, even where it goes on, at the end of Deuteronomy, to tell the story of Moses' death on Mount Nebo, may be of Moses' own writing* as well as the incorporated codes. But the codes are incorporated as sources and we have no choice but to accept the fact when it is so distinctly written. Thus the author of Deut. xxxi. 9, expressly distinguishes the "book of the law" which "Moses wrote and delivered it unto the priests, the sons of Levi, which bare the ark of the covenant of Yahweh, and unto all the elders of Israel" from the book he is engaged in writing. Of *that* book he says, xxxi. 24 ff., that when Moses had written it "till it was finished," he commanded the Levites to "take it and put it by the side of the ark of the covenant of Yahweh your God that it may be there for a witness." The present book of Deuteronomy purports to be a transcript or reproduction (verse 9, "this law") of the book of the law which Moses wrote, and *that* book, if we can discover it, was the *source* of the Deuteronomic Code.

In the opinion of critics we actually possess the book attributed by the writer of Deuteronomy to Moses, incor-

---

* Jewish tradition is represented in the *Gemara*: "It is taught [Dt. xxxiv. 5]: 'And Moses the servant of the Lord died there.' How is it possible that Moses died and wrote: 'and Moses died there'? It is only unto this passage Moses wrote, afterwards Joshua wrote the rest. These are the words of Rabbi Jehuda, others say of Rabbi Nehemiah, but Rabbi Simeon said to him: Is it possible that the book of the law [Pentateuch] could lack one letter, since it is written [Dt. xxxi. 26]: 'Take this book of the law?' It is only unto this the Holy One, blessed be He! spoke, and Moses [both] spoke and wrote. From this place and onwards the Holy One, blessed be He! spoke, and Moses wrote with weeping." Briggs, *Bibl. Study*, p. 177.

porated in Exodus xx.–xxiii., and in the narrative attached to
it, xxiv. 3–8, called "the Book of the Covenant" and again
stated to have been "written by Moses" (xxiv. 4).*

Whether or not this opinion of the critics is adopted, the
remarks just made concerning the narrative framework of
the Deuteronomic Code apply in exactly the same way, and
with the same force, to the narrative incorporating "The
Book of the Covenant." The author of Ex. xxiv. 4–8, and
consequently of the narrative of Yahweh's speaking, again
distinguishes "the Book of the Covenant," which included
"all the Words of Yahweh and all the Judgments" (cf. xx. 1
and xxi. 1.), from his own narrative, and incorporates it as a
source which he considers to be Mosaic. We need not necessarily assume that Moses did not write both code and narrative, but they are two separate documents written at different
times, and the one serves as material to the other. The only
other passages in the Pentateuch where Moses is said to write
anything are Ex. xvii. 14, where it is natural, but not necessary, to suppose that the author had before him a narrative
of the battle with Amalek; Ex. xxxiv. 27 f, where some will
perhaps assume that the writing referred to was accessible;
and Num. xxxiii. 1–49, to which the remarks upon Deuteronomy and the Book of the Covenant apply with equal force.

It is certain therefore that the Pentateuch has *sources* both
prose and verse, distinguishable from the text, and tolerably
numerous. Of these sometimes only fragments are taken up,
but in at least two cases the entire document.

It is a well-known fact that besides these sources which are
explicitly named, and sometimes described, by the Pentateuch
itself, modern critics believe it to incorporate two principal
narratives extending from Gen. i. 1. to Joshua xxiv. 33, called
respectively from their supposed characteristics the Priestly
Law-book and the Prophetic Narrative. The latter, now
generally regarded as the older, is supposed to be itself com-

*Those who wish to know the grounds on which Ex. xx.–xxiv. 8 is regarded as
the "source" referred to by Deuteronomy, will find in *The Old Testament in the
Jewish Church*, by W. Robertson Smith, Note 2 to Lecture xi., p. 431, a detailed
table of the laws in Ex. xx.–xxiii. and their equivalents in Deuteronomy.

posite, a braiding together of a strand **J** derived from Judah*
and a strand **E** derived from Ephraim.   The interweaving in
these two cases is regarded as similar in character to that illustrated in the Diatessaron and exemplified within the canon
by the confessed practise of the authors of Kings and Chronicles.   (Cf.I Kings xi. 41, xiv. 29, xv. 7, 23, 31, xvi. 5, etc.)   The
reader himself will have opportunity to judge of the value of
the theory, and the author purposely refrains from argument.
On one point however he is unfortunately obliged to assume
temporarily the controversial attitude.

7.   Strange as it may seem to the student who approaches
the Bible without prepossessions, to learn simply what it has
to teach concerning itself, and gather, but not monopolize, its
hid treasure, a certain class of writers demand that all
attempts to learn by critical analysis what its component
parts are shall be forbidden *a priori*.   Unless the critical
prospector can demonstrate beforehand that there is treasure
beneath the surface, not a sod shall be turned by pick or
spade ; he is peremptorily warned off the premises.   Would-be
monopolists, and self-constituted "defenders" of the Scriptures of this kind, the expounder of criticism is obliged to
meet with a straightforward and positive denial of their
assumption.   A typical instance is furnished in a recently
published argument for "The Mosaic Origin of the Pentateuchal Codes." †
It is remarkable in many places for missing the point at
issue, misconceiving the true principles and methods of the
inquiry, and failing to appreciate the force of evidence.   One

---

* The letters J and E are abbreviations of Jahvist and Elohist, names applied
from the characteristic use of *Elohim* in one document and *Yahweh* (Jahvé) in the
other, to designate the Deity ; but as all critics agree that E must be of northern
(i. e., Ephraimite) origin and nearly all (Kuenen excepted), consider J to have originated in Judah, the letters serve a double mnemonic purpose.   JE stands for Jehovistic narrative, the combination of J and E forming the so-called Prophetic Narrative.   Sometimes it stands for their compiler personally.

† *The Mosaic Origin of the Pentateuchal Codes,* by Geerhardus Vos, fellow of
Princeton Theological Seminary.   With an introduction by Prof. Wm. Henry
Green.   New York : A. C. Armstrong and Son, 714 Broadway, 1886.

passage in the book so forcibly exhibits what the Pentateuch and the Pentateuchal question are *not* that it may well be transcribed in full.

The author lays down as his general thesis No. 1 :—

" There must be, in the first instance, some reasonable ground why the critical analysis should be applied to the Pentateuchal code, to justify any use being made of it whatever. If there be no presumptive evidence that it consists of various documents, it will be justly condemned as a most arbitrary and unscientific procedure to divide it into several pieces, more or less strongly marked by linguistic or stylistic peculiarities. The question is not whether the process admits of being made plausible by apparently striking results, but whether it be necessary, or at least natural, on *a priori* considerations. We might take a chapter or poem of any one author, sunder out a page, note the striking expressions, then examine the other parts of the work, combine all the passages where the same terms appear, give them the name of a document, and finally declare that all the rest constitutes a second document, and that the two were interwoven by the hand of a redactor so as to form now an apparent unity. Our first demand therefore, is that the critical analysis shall rest on a solid foundation, and show its credentials beforehand." *

If we take every sentence and thought of this passage and reverse it, we shall come very near to a proper and reasonable first principle of biblical study. The assumption with which the writer starts out is that there is no presumptive evidence of various documents in the Pentateuch, or at least in the Pentateuchal Code.

We will not take so cruel an advantage as to refer the author to his own title, but surely it is presumptive evidence that the Pentateuch itself refers to its sources. For the required "reasonable ground" it is only necessary to refer to the many Christian scholars who before the days of the analysis, were hopelessly puzzled and confused by the apparently duplicate accounts of the same event, incongruities in the material placed in juxtaposition, and other phenomena which the analysis explains. †

* Vos. *Mosaic Origin*, &c. p. 25.

† Cf. Briggs, *Bibl. Study*, 196–202 for examples of higher criticism before the days of the analysis. Thus Spinoza 1670 regarded the Pentateuch as conglomerate. Richard Simon 1678 distinguished a Mosaic Code and a "prophetic" narrative, and called attention to: (1) The double account of the deluge. (2) The lack of order in the arrangement of the narratives and laws. (3) The diversity of the style. Clericus, Van Dale, Semler, Vitringa and others shared these views. See also Ladd. *Doctrine of Sacred Scripture*, Vol. I. pp. 501 ff.

Peyrerius declared it "*non vero simile regem Gerarae voluisse Saram vetulam cui desierant fieri muliebria ;*" and even the rabbis found stumbling blocks in the way of their own theory.*

But supposing it to be admitted that there is no "presumptive evidence" for the analysis; how shall we decide whether or not it is "a most arbitrary and unscientific procedure?" Here is a substance traditionally and popularly believed to be homogeneous, elementary. The chemist proceeds to test or prove this belief. How ?—There is only one way. By applying the process of analysis. If the substance is not composite it cannot be decomposed, and in spite of the strange declaration in a passage we are about to take up, it is as true in literature as in chemistry that the supreme, perfect and only valid proof of non-composite structure is resistance to all attempts at analysis or decomposition. Division into all possible elements is just the process by which,—and by which alone—literary unity can be demonstrated. If the work is a real unit the process fails; that is all.

But the class of defenders of the faith with whom we have now to deal would rest their proofs on other grounds. "The question," we are told, "is not whether the process admits of being made plausible by apparently striking results, but whether it be necessary, or at least natural, on *a priori* considerations."†

With every apology for so square a contradiction, we are constrained to say that in our view the question is precisely what the above statement says it is not; otherwise analysis is not analysis. *A priori* considerations doubtless persuade the

---

* So Aben Ezra found difficulty with Gen. xii. 6, xxxvi. 31. Num. xii. 6f. and Dt. xxxiv. 10. Observe also the singular legend alluded to in 1. Cor. x. 4, that the rock struck by Moses *followed* the marching host throughout the wilderness, a movable reservoir, which would seem a difficult conception to account for. May it not be that the fact that the story of its being struck and giving out water is *twice* related, once at the outset of the 40 years wandering, Ex. xvii. 1-7, and once at its conclusion, Num. xx. 1-13, the very name of the cliff (Meribah) being the same in both instances, was the ground for the belief? Such a deduction would be far from unexampled in the Talmudic writings. Cf. also the legend of Lilith, Adam's first wife, based upon Gen. i. 27f. compared with ii. 18-25.

† Vos. *Mosaic Origin*, &c. p. 26.

average man that water is an elementary substance; it is simply the *results* of analysis that remove the cherished error. As to the rash offer to "sunder out a page of any one author," let the writer simply try the experiment upon any admittedly non-composite writing and see what the "results" will be.

For by "results" is the decision made at the tribunal of science; and upon the results, and nothing else, will the verdict be given in this question before the court of ultimate appeal, which is the forum of the Christian public. We deem it therefore a work not only permissible, but deserving of commendation and good-will from all quarters rather than hostility and suspicion, to bring these *results* before the public.

8.   There is but one thing to detain us before proceeding to the presentation of the results required, and that is the "demand" formulated in the passage above quoted, which seems to be made in the name of the whole traditionary school. "Our first demand therefore, is that the critical analysis shall rest on a solid foundation, and show its credentials beforehand." I assume that the writer does not mean that the analysis shall show its results before beginning its work, or rest on a solid foundation before being allowed to enter the field of operations or to even begin to build. By "credentials" therefore must be meant "testimonials" from scholars whom the Christian world is wont to respect. We will content ourselves with quoting one which sums up and includes the testimony of all. Our "credentials" shall be the statement of Prof. C. A. Briggs of Union Theological Seminary N. Y., (Presbyterian), as it is quoted and endorsed by Prof. Geo. T. Ladd of Yale University (Congregational).

"In several places in this book the claim has been made that Christian scholars are almost unanimous in their opinion that the Hexateuch is a composite composition, an historical development, and therefore cannot have been the work of Moses. This claim of scholarly unanimity is sometimes disputed in the presence of the Christian multitude. I wish therefore to enforce it by quoting the words of Prof. C. A. Briggs (in the *Presbyterian Review* for April, 1887, p. 340). 'The critical analysis of the Hexateuch,' says this Christian scholar, 'is the result of more than a century of profound study of the documents by the greatest critics of the age. There has been a steady advance until the present position of agreement has been reached in which Jew and Christian, Roman Catholic and Protestant, Rationalistic and Evangelical scholars, Reformed and Lutheran, Presbyterian and Episcopal, Unitarian, Methodist and Baptist, all concur. The analysis of the Hexateuch into several distinct original documents is a purely literary question in which no article of faith is involved. Whoever in these times, in the discussion of the literary phenomena of the Hexateuch, appeals to the ignorance and prejudices of the multitude as if there were any peril to the faith in these processes of the Higher Criticism, risks his reputation for scholarship by so doing. There are no Hebrew professors on the continent of Europe, so far as I know, who would deny the literary analysis of the Pentateuch into the four great documents [J. E. P. and D.] The professors of Hebrew in the Universities of Oxford, Cambridge and Edinburgh, and tutors in a large number of theological colleges, hold the same opinion. A very considerable number of the Hebrew professors of America are in accord with them. There are, indeed, a few professional scholars who hold to the traditional opinion, but these are in a hopeless minority. I doubt whether there is any question of scholarship whatever in which there is greater agreement among scholars than in this question of the literary analysis of the Hexateuch.'"*

The opinion of scholars is not to take the place of a judgment made, each man for himself, by the Christian public "from the results." But since the right of the analysis to appear at all has been challenged, and its credentials demanded, it becomes necessary to quote the above statement as one of the facts to be considered *a priori.*

* *What is the Bible?* p. 486.

CHAPTER II.

The Science of Historical Criticism.

1. A mere separation of Scripture into documents is of course very far from securing that appreciation of the literature which we have seen to be the purpose and significance of Biblical criticism. If documents are traceable here we need to know their character, age, authorship, and mutual relation ; but above all, their relation to the course of events in which their place is to be determined. To do them justice we must know the history out of which they sprang and the history which grew from them. To make us acquainted with this history is an essential part of the purpose of the documents themselves. If then we can better appreciate both the history itself and the narrative of it by applying to them the methods which Niebuhr and Wolf applied to the historians of ancient Greece and Rome, and which have since been recognized as indispensable to the understanding of all historical writings, this will be the truest way to honor the Bible and to give it the systematic study of which it is worthy. If the results are revolutionary in theology, the revolution will be simply the substitution of an *inductive* method for the *a priori* method of dogmatics, and thus identical in nature with that which since the days of Francis Bacon has taken place in all other branches of science.

2. We do not need to illustrate the methods and success of historical criticism, which undertakes the tasks above defined, in secular literature. Every intelligent reader is aware that historical critics are universally regarded as competent to fix, from style, language and thought, from subject-matter and relation to external events and to other literature, the date and probable authorship of ancient anonymous or pseudonymous documents. But more, we have already seen that it is

(27)

possible to go behind an author and compare his own statements with his sources.   A large part of historical criticism is simply cross-examination of a witness, a cross-examination not hostile, but friendly, to ascertain how accurate his knowledge is, and in what sense and degree of literalness he wishes his statements to be taken.   Testimony can be cross-examined in the absence of the witness by comparison with itself, even where no parallel account exists; but it is characteristic of the Bible that it presents almost every narrative in two-fold, three-fold, even five-fold form.   This system of cross-examination is now so universally recognized as indispensable to do justice to all secular history that we may simply sum up the facts in the saying of the late historian Von Ranke, "There is no *history* but critical history."

3.   Within the Bible an illustration drawn from the sphere in which historical criticism is least effective would be the book of Psalms.   Prayers, hymns and lyrics adapted for the general uses of public worship must of necessity be of a character having but little that is distinctive of any one epoch.   Yet how easy it is to see when once we raise the question of date and authorship that Ps. xlii.–xliii. belongs to the period of exile in Babylon, and comes from one whose "soul is cast down" as he remembers Jerusalem and how he "was wont to go up to the house of God with the multitude that kept holy day!"   How meaningless is it if read without raising these questions!   If the Psalm-book as a whole be considered, as historical criticism suggests, a product of the post-exilic period, the single outlet for the old religious feeling of the people not yet quenched by priestly ritual in the temple, and scribal and pharisaic pettifogging in the synagogue, what a light does this throw on that dark epoch when prophecy seemed extinct and only its germs were slowly maturing beneath the soil, to bloom forth at length in the unparalleled glory of the teaching of John the Baptist and of Jesus!

If we turn now to some of the more generally accepted

results of historical criticism, we may take as a second illustration the great anonymous prophecy appended after the prose chapters, Is. xxxvi.–xxxix., which terminate the collection of prophecies attributed to Isaiah the son of Amoz. A traditional theory, now nearly obsolete, considers Is. xl.–lxvi. to have been written by the author of Is. i.–xxxix. circ. 720 B. C., but separately, "as a deep and rich bequest to the church of the Exile . . . . left to be understood in the future." In point of fact this bequest would have been incomprehensible for nearly two centuries; for Isaiah lived in the Assyrian period, when the long struggle against the foreign invader had just culminated in the overthrow of Sennacherib, and Jerusalem was left safe and triumphant. Babylon has yet to come into prominence; the Exile is more than a century in the future. But every thought and expression of Isaiah xl.–lxvi. is inseparably linked with the end of the Babylonian Captivity. The author stands behind the "bars of iron and gates of brass" (the one-hundred brazen gates of Babylon) soon to be broken in sunder by the Redeemer of Israel, and hears a voice from the desert that stretches between him and Jerusalem, bidding him speak comfort to the exiles and that they prepare to get them up from Babylon and return to their own land, for Yahweh will lead them back as he led their fathers thither.

"He saith of Jerusalem, She shall be inhabited; and of the cities of Judah, They shall be built, and I will raise up the waste places thereof: He saith to the deep, Be dry, and I will dry up thy rivers: He saith of Cyrus, He is my shepherd, and shall perform all my pleasure; even saying of Jerusalem, She shall be built, and to the temple, Thy foundation shall be laid. Thus saith Yahweh to his Messiah, to Cyrus, whose right hand I have holden, to subdue nations before him, and I will loose the loins of kings; to open the doors before him, and the gates shall not be shut; I will go before thee, and make the rugged places plain; I will break in pieces the doors of brass and cut in sunder the bars of iron."*

There are two ways of accounting for this outburst of welcome from a captive in Babylon to Cyrus as Yahweh's messenger to redeem Israel. By assuming a prodigious miracle, we may suppose that Isaiah the son of Amoz wrote it more

---

* Is. xl. 1 ff. and xliv. 26 ff.

than a century before Cyrus was born or the Jews had gone into captivity, being miraculously enabled to put himself into the situation of the exiled people. This method has the merit of justifying the entire accuracy of the scribe who put this prophecy upon the same roll of parchment as that containing the prophecies of Isaiah the son of Amoz.

Another way regards the mention of Cyrus, the allusions to Jerusalem as "burnt with fire," and to the people as in captivity in Babylon, from whence they are now to be delivered, as indications of the period in which the prophecy was actually written. This latter, which is the method of historical criticism, is not so wonderful as the other, and admits the possibility that the inclusion of these chapters without separate title after Is. xxxix. was due to mistake, but it claims to treat the Scriptures with at least equal respect, and has the advantage of throwing a glory of meaning into this last and noblest fruit of the prophetic spirit which it could not otherwise possess. At the same time it displays to us the inner workings of divine providence at the critical period when the question was, Shall Jerusalem be rebuilt, or shall Judah also pass into oblivion as Ephraim did, and the treasures of Hebrew religious life and literature remain forever buried in the mounds of Mesopotamia. Thus understood we recognize in Is. xl.–lxvi. not merely the swan-song of the ancient prophetic spirit, but the clarion-call which summons into being the "faithful seed" from which is to come forth a new Israel, a new Jerusalem, and at last a Kingdom of God.

4. Aside from these mere excerpts we cannot better describe what historical criticism has done for biblical literature and history than by a brief review of its treatment of that mass of material which has come down to us as the Pentateuch Narrative. This material, when coördinated and systematized, will give us (a) a rational conception of the continuous working of God in the providential events of Israel's career; (b) a view in perspective of the gradually enlarging apprehension of this working of God in their history which

filled the minds of Israel's teachers and writers. We shall scarcely be able to find God in the Bible until we find him there in these two ways, in the events which he decreed, and in the minds which he enlightened. Biblical archæology is of value for the former, but historical criticism is indispensable for the latter.*

Historical criticism we understand then to be a loyal response to the distinct summons of the Scriptures themselves to go behind the letter and beneath the surface, distinguishing between the testimony and the facts testified to, between the mere literature and the sources and causes, material and spiritual, human and divine, which gave rise to it; even as Paul himself warns us not to be blind supporters of this name or that, but to count both him and Apollos "ministers through whom ye believed." Above all is this discrimination inculcated by our Lord in his rebuke to the scribes and pharisees for their servile clinging to the letter of the Scriptures. "Ye search the Scriptures because ye think that in them ye have eternal life ; and they are they which *testify* of me; but ye would not come unto me that ye might have life."† Be it our task then to draw as near as may be to the mind of the writers, and ask what it is that has affected them. And first we must obtain, so far as may be through brief explanation and illustration, a general outline of the method and theory of historical criticism within the domain of the Hexateuch. We turn then to the two great classes of evidence which criticism relies on for its fundamental inquiry as to date and authorship.

5. External evidence may be conclusive of the date of a writing so far as regards the *terminus a quo* or fixed point of departure in the backward tracing of a document. Thus the

* An excellent synopsis of the progress of the science in recent times will be found in Prof. O. Pfleiderer's *Development of Theology*, New York, Macmillan and Co., 1890. Book III., ch. II. The *Histories of Israel* by Wellhausen and Renan, already quoted, the articles *Israel* and *Pentateuch* in Encyc. Brit. ed. ix. and *The Religion of Israel* by A. Kuenen, London, Williams and Norgate, 1874, are all accessible to the English reader, beside " Introductions " and minor works innumerable.

† John v. 39 f. (R. V.)

quotations from Matthew in the "Teaching of the Twelve Apostles" positively establish the existence of Matthew in the early part of the 2d century ; and the LXX. version proves the existence of the Pentateuch in nearly its present shape in the third century B. C. But as to the *terminus ad quem* external evidence is not conclusive. We can by no means argue that Matthew did not exist in the year 90 A. D. because Clement of Rome does not use it. The mere silence of authors from Ezra down would not prove that Matthew was not written in 500 B. C. Neither can we establish the non-existence of the Pentateuch from the mere fact, if fact it be, that none of the prophets allude to it. Such arguments *e silentio* are only of force when a strong independent probability can be established that the writers would have used it, or would at least have expressed themselves otherwise than they did, if they had known of it.

Under external evidence must be included traditional views of date and authorship. Tradition which can be traced back to a period wherein men might be supposed to know the date and authorship would be very valuable, especially if there were no other way of accounting for the origin of the tradition than to regard its statements as fact. The tradition, for example, attributing the origin of the second gospel to John-Mark gains very much in weight from the difficulty of accounting for an untrue tradition fixing upon so obscure a character rather than the prominent one which popular rumor usually prefers. If, on the other hand, the tradition cannot be traced to a period competent to know, but is of a piece with numerous other traditions known to be worthless, and is easily accounted for, it will have scarcely any weight at all.

It is true that certain supporters of the Mosaic authorship of the Pentateuch have attempted to introduce a *tertium quid* of the nature neither of external nor internal evidence, by excepting the utterances of our Lord from the general class of tradition and exalting them into a kind of dogmatic or doctrinal argument. If our Lord had ever expressed an opinion for or against the critical theory we should indeed be obliged to take sides either with those who should deny his competency to judge, and insist upon drawing their own conclusions in literary criticism, or else with those who should hold that the *ipse dixit* of Jesus forbade all critical investigation as impious. The modern attempt to occupy both positions at once is irrational. Fortunately there is no such desperate alternative presented. The dogmatic argument has no relevancy whatever, for Jesus expressed no opinion in the case. The fact that Jesus in quoting from the Pentateuch referred the citation to "Moses" proves simply that the books were called then, as they are now, "the Books of Moses." It shows that the tradition of Mosaic authorship was then unquestioned, which we knew before, and that Jesus would not precipitate discussion of such a question, which we might have known before. We must decline to stake the authority of Jesus Christ on a question of literary criticism.

The second line of critical evidence is internal. If external evidence is conclusive of the *terminus a quo* in the question of date, internal evidence is in exactly the same degree conclusive as to the *terminus ad quem*. If the quotations from Matthew in the *Didachē* are external evidence positively proving that Matthew existed before the *Didachē*, they are internal evidence for the *Didachē* proving with equal positiveness that the *Didachē*, at least in these parts, did *not* exist until after Matthew. By means of internal evidence it is almost always easy to detect a forgery, as none but the most finished scholar could possibly construct even the briefest document which would not by some anachronism in style, language, subject-matter, or mode of treatment, betray an acquaintance with matters occurring subsequently to its supposed origin.

Internal evidence however is capable of furnishing far more, as we have already seen, than merely data from which to determine date and authorship. The writer of a document is the best teacher from whom to learn its purpose and character, and, although rarely in ancient times announcing

3

his own authorship, can yet be made a willing witness upon questions of interpretation (whether as legend, myth, allegory or simple fact) and the degree of literalness with which the statements of the document are meant to be received.

6. As we enter now upon the consideration of the general argument and theory of the historical criticism of the Pentateuch, the reader who does not wish to know even in outline what the character of the evidence is which leads critics to a practically unanimous decision against Mosaic authorship, is invited to skip the pages which follow. For the sake of those who wish to know the outline and basis of that theory, we will attempt briefly to illustrate and explain the character of the evidence, beginning with tradition.

The Talmud, from which we have already quoted an important passage on this question (p. 19), is explicit in attributing the Pentateuch to Moses; but not the Pentateuch only. *Job* also is assigned to Moses.*   Josephus† likewise ascribes the Pentateuch to Moses including the last eight verses describing his own death.   So also Philo.‡

These witnesses from the first century confirm the evidence from the New-Testament of the existence of the tradition. They also shed light upon the character of it.   But if desired we can trace the tradition a step farther back, and obtain still more light upon its character.

The Apocalypse of Ezra is an apocryphal book frequently printed in the English Bible under the title of II Esdras, and dating from the first century A. D.   Readers who find it accessible are referred to II Esdras xiv. 19–46 for the tradition of Mosaic (?) authorship in full, in the form in which it was adopted by the Christian fathers Clement of Alexandria, Tertullian, Chrysostom, in pseud-Augustine, and the Clementine Homilies.   This tradition represents that the law (Pentateuch) and all the holy books were burnt at the destruction

---

*For a description of these mediæval opinions the reader is referred to Prof. Briggs, *Biblical Study*, pp. 173-180.

† *Antiquities*, IV. 8, 48.

‡ *Life of Moses*, III. 39.

of Jerusalem by Nebuchadnezzar.   Ezra miraculously restored them all, composing also others.   In the words of Clement of Alexandria :

"Since the Scriptures perished in the Captivity of Nebuchadnezzar, Esdras the Levite, the priest, in the time of Artaxerxes, king of the Persians, having become inspired in the exercise of prophecy, restored again the whole of the ancient Scriptures." *

Another form of the same tradition adopted by Irenæus, Theodoret, Basil, Jerome, and later Christian writers, represents the "restoration" of Ezra to have been a "recasting of all the words of the former prophets" and a "reëstablishment" of the Mosaic legislation.   Carrying back the tradition thus to the earliest form in which it is directly stated it becomes a difficult matter indeed to say whether tradition is more favorable to the so-called "traditional" view, or to the critical theory which attributes to Ezra and the later scribes the incorporation of the priestly element **P** into the Hexateuch and the recasting of the whole.   A scientific judgment of the character of the tradition however, must simply classify it with a mass of similar traditions which attribute Samuel, Judges and Ruth to Samuel, Kings to Jeremiah, and the Psalms to "David with the aid of the ten ancients, Adam the first, Melchizedek, Abraham, Moses, Heman, Jeduthun, Asaph, and the three sons of Korah."   In other words there is nothing to recommend it as anything more than an *a priori* assumption of the crudest kind on the part of the scribes.

But external evidence for the existence of the tradition and of the Pentateuch as a whole may be traced still earlier. Allusions in the books of Chronicles, Nehemiah and Ezra to the Book of the Law of Moses, are admitted to refer to our present Pentateuch and furnish evidence perhaps a little earlier than the LXX.   Further back it is not possible to go ; for the work now divided into First and Second Chronicles, Ezra and Nehemiah mentions Darius Codomannus (336 B. C.), and brings down its genealogies to a still later date. Earlier allusions to the law of Moses cannot be shown to refer

---

* Stromata i. 22.

to more than some one of the codes now incorporated in the Pentateuch, and there attributed to him. There is therefore no disposition in any quarter to deny the fact that the Pentateuch, approximately in its present shape, existed circ. 300 B. C., and was then attributed, by a more or less rational tradition, in a more or less direct sense, to Moses. More than this can scarcely be drawn in favor of the traditional date and authorship from external evidence.

If there is internal evidence for Mosaic authorship beside the passages attributing, as has been shown, certain *sources* to Moses, it is of too general and desultory a character to be taken into serious consideration; for the book itself, like all the ancient historical books, is simply anonymous.*

7. We turn with some dismay to the mass of evidence both external and internal accumulated by historical criticism against the traditional view. External evidence as we have already seen partakes necessarily of the weakness of an *argumentum e silentio* when we depart from the *terminus a quo* or date before which it *must* have existed (viz., 300 B. C.) and seek a *terminus ad quem* before which it *cannot* have existed. Here we find ourselves at once confronted with masses of evidence derived from both the history and the literature of Israel from the time of Moses, 1320 B. C., to the time of Ezra 450 B. C. to prove, *e silentio*, that before Ezra the Pentateuch as we have it was not in existence, or at least not known to any one of all those whom we should expect to be most familiar with it.

The force of this evidence will depend upon the degree of probability with which it can be established that these persons would have acted differently, or written differently, from the way in which they did act, and write, if they had known our Pentateuch. This external evidence divides itself therefore into evidence from the history, and evidence from

---

* The degree of familiarity with Egyptian customs evidenced in Gen. 1. 1 ff. and other passages is so easily attributable to any fairly well-informed writer of the period of the monarchy, that none but a special pleader would think of advancing it as evidence.

the literature.   We can do no more than briefly summarize both.

The history admittedly presents no agreement with the requirements of the Pentateuch, even in the case of the most earnest zealots for Yahweh and the greatest reformers, from the period of Moses down to that of Ezra.   The contrast between the history as it was, and the history as it would have been if the actors had been guided by the "law of Moses" according to the Pentateuch, is brought out very vividly by the post-exilic book of Chronicles, which re-writes the history of the pre-exilic books of Samuel and Kings, omitting and amending so as to bring the history into conformity with the ritual law.   A comparison in detail exhibiting the system by which the chronicler proceeds can be found in Wellhausen's *History of Israel*, chap. vi.   For the present we can only ask the reader to compare the story of the rebellion against Athaliah as it appears in II. Kings xi. 4–12, heedless of all the elaborate provisions of the Levitical law against the entrance of any save a consecrated foot into the house of Yahweh, and the same story in II. Chron. xxiii. amended by the substitution of *the Levites* for the king's body-guard of mercenaries.   The example is characteristic of the way in which Chronicles fills out the unbroken silence of the older historical books in regard to the whole vast Levitical system and Aaronic hierarchy, with its elaborate ritual and centralized worship, and brings into conformity with the Levitical system the actions of David, Samuel, Elijah and other devout characters, who in Samuel and Kings act as if they never had heard of the Pentateuch or the ritual law.   As a further illustration of the contrast between the early and the late religious *praxis* the reader may compare the worship and ritual at the primitive temple at Shiloh, where Eli and his sons are the priests and the little *Ephraimite* (not Levite) boy Samuel, clad with *the ephod*, performs the service of the sanctuary "before Yahweh," lies down to sleep "*in the temple of Yahweh where the ark of God was*" before "*the lamp of God was gone out*" (cf. Lev. xxiv. 1–4), and "opens the doors of the house of Yahweh in the morning," I. Sam. i.–iv., with the elaborate provisions of the Levitical code, consigning the care and even the sight of the most holy things exclusively to the house of Aaron and of the holy things to the Levites, with the injunction, Num. i. 51, "the stranger that cometh nigh shall be put to death." To take the post-exilic testimony of Chronicles in preference to that of its acknowledged sources, from 400 to 600 years earlier in date, reverses every principle of common sense. We have no alternative but to assume that the Pentateuch as we know it, was not in existence, or that it was unknown to men like Samuel, David, Elijah, and Isaiah, who could not voluntarily have so completely ignored and transgressed its most emphatic requirements, as in the earlier historical books they are uniformly related to have done. Upholders of tradition have, of course, preferred the latter, assuming a disappearance of the Pentateuch for ages, and subsequent re-discovery. In connection with the explanation of the critical treatment of Deuteronomy we shall meet again this assumption, and hence at present will confine ourselves to the above setting-forth of the indisputable fact that the history, from Joshua to the Exile, completely ignores the Levitical law. It should be observed, however, that the immense presumption against the accidental reappearance of a book lost for more than six centuries makes it incumbent upon the propounders of the theory to show reason for its acceptance. The Levitical law is a system of elaborately developed ritual worship, centralized about the inner shrine of the temple of Jerusalem, which itself is regarded as simply a copy of a portable temple or "tabernacle" of the previous epoch, unknown, however, to the pre-exilic writers. Concentric circles of sanctity, which it is death for the unprivileged to cross, surround the Holy of holies, holy-place, and successive temple courts, and elaborate ritual prescriptions make the temple, its service and its hierarchy, the all-absorbing, all-controlling interest of the nation. The older history knows nothing whatever of this; worship is free and untrammeled. Prophets, kings, and common people build altars at any place to offer sacrifice with entire acceptance. There is simply no thought or mention whatever of the Levitical requirements, the breach of which in the least degree in the Pentateuch is visited with instant death. Every man approaches God freely and spontaneously where he chooses or where he happens to be. The sanctuaries are numerous, but very simple and unpretentious, and open to all the people. The people worship Yahweh "upon every high hill and under every green tree ;" but the surprising thing is not this, which is admitted to be true, and might be accounted for on the theory of rebellion and degeneracy, but that this worship is regarded as entirely acceptable to God by the older historians and equally so by all the greatest reformers down to the time of Josiah.*

8. We turn to the external evidence from the literature of the period in which the Levitical law now incorporated in the Pentateuch and forming by far the largest part of "the law of Moses" as there presented, is supposed to have existed. The authors of the older historical literature, as we have seen, simply ignore this ritual system. These, however, are less important than the writings of the prophets, which by way of exception in Semitic literature have both the author's name and date prefixed,† and which bring into broad daylight the religious life of the people both in Ephraim and Judah throughout nearly three centuries preceding the Exile.

---

*Observe I. Kings iii. 4–15 in contrast with II. Chron. i. 1–13 ; also, Elijah's *complaint* to God at Horeb. "They have thrown down thine altars," I. Kings xix. 10, 14. All these altars, according to the Pentateuch and the later literature, were an abomination, to destroy which was piety.

† "This remark [the law of anonymity] applies with full force only to works like the Historical Books, which were products of the study, and did not derive their value from their connection with the author's public life. It is not equally applicable to lyric poetry, where, as in the case of David's elegy on Saul and Jonathan, the interest of the poem frequently depends on the authorship. Least of all could the law of anonymity apply to the written collections of the sermons of the prophets, which were summaries of a course of public activity in which the personality of the prophet could not be separated from his words. Thus, while the historical books are habitually anonymous, and poetical pieces only sometimes bear an author's name, it is the rule that each group of prophecies, and often each individual oracle, has the name of the author attached." W. Robertson Smith, *Old Testament in Jewish Church,* 108.

The first trace of an allusion to anything contained in the priestly legislation of the Pentateuch, or to the existence of any ordinance of Moses concerning ritual, will be searched for in vain throughout the writings of the pre-exilic prophets.

This *argumentum e silentio* is met by the explanation that the specific work of the prophets led them to exalt the ethical feature of the law at the expense of the ritual, and indeed we should by no means ignore the contrast in function between the prophet and priest. Both were teachers of the people, the priest however being the interpreter and mouthpiece of the ritual law (Ez. xliv. 23f.), and the prophet usually taking a more generally ethical ground. Both "sat in Moses' seat" as trustees of the national inheritance of law and custom, but their relations were far from antagonistic, as the friendship of Isaiah with Uriah the chief priest sufficiently shows. Several of the later prophets, including both Jeremiah and Ezekiel, were at the same time priests as well as prophets, and Ezekiel devotes all the latter part of his book to the construction of an elaborate ritual system. Nevertheless in weighing the evidential force of the silence of the prophets on this subject full consideration must be given to the peculiarly ethical work of prophetism in general.

It is not, however, upon this mere silence that historical criticism depends for its external evidence. It is claimed that the repeated expressions of these writers are such as to make it absolutely insupposable that they knew the Pentateuch, or had ever heard of the enactment of an elaborate ritual law by Moses. More explicit language, for example, than that of Jeremiah vii. 21ff. could scarcely be expected.

"Thus saith Yahweh of hosts, the God of Israel: Add your burnt offerings unto your sacrifices, and eat ye flesh. For I spake not unto your fathers, nor commanded them in the day that I brought them out of the land of Egypt, concerning burnt offerings or sacrifices: but this thing I commanded them, saying, Hearken unto my voice, and I will be your God, and ye shall be my people: and walk ye in all the way that I command you, that it may be well with you."

An appeal to the public to say whether any such law was ever given will perhaps be even stronger testimony, especially if it be made in the name of Yahweh himself. Such an appeal the critics find in Amos v. 21ff., where the period of the wilderness-wandering is spoken of as a time of special manifestation of Yahweh's favor (so, frequently, in the Pss. and prophets, cf. Hos. xi. 1ff., xiii. 4f., etc.), and the question asked whether *then* there was any of this sacrificing and ritual observance. The reader of the Pentateuch of to-day would be inclined to call that the period of sacrifice and ritual *par excellence.*

"I hate, I despise your feasts, and I will take no delight in your solemn assemblies. Yea, though ye offer me your burnt offerings and meat offerings, I will not accept them : neither will I regard the peace offerings of your fat beasts. Take thou away from me the noise of thy songs ; for I will not hear the melody of thy viols. But let judgment roll down as waters, and righteousness as a mighty stream. Did ye bring unto me sacrifices and offerings in the wilderness forty years, O house of Israel ?

Equally plain is the noble appeal in Micah vi. 6–8 :—

"Wherewith shall I come before Yahweh, and bow myself before the high God? shall I come before him with burnt offerings, with calves of a year old? Will the Lord be pleased with thousands of rams, or with ten thousands of rivers of oil? shall I give my firstborn for my transgression, the fruit of my body for the sin of my soul? He hath shewed thee, O man, what is good : and what doth Yahweh require of thee, but to do justly, and to love mercy, and to walk humbly with thy God?"

Isaiah i. 11f. demands to know on what authority ritual observances are practised :—

"To what purpose is the multitude of your sacrifices unto me, saith Yahweh : I am full of the burnt offerings of rams, and the fat of fed beasts ; and I delight not in the blood of bullocks, or of lambs, or of he-goats. When ye come to appear before me, who hath required this at your hand, to trample my courts?"

One might indeed reconcile with a knowledge of the Pentateuch utterances of the prophets deprecating the *too great* regard paid to ritual, and urging as of equal or greater importance the "weightier matters of the law ;" but how can it be supposed that the authors of these appeals to know when and where Yahweh had ever authorized anything of the kind, were aware of the existence of a Mosaic law, nine-tenths of which were devoted to inculcating this very thing in the most explicit terms as of immediate divine authority, and with the imposition of most fearful penalties for its neglect. Can we suppose that Jeremiah and Isaiah knew of this body of law? And if Jeremiah and Isaiah and those they appealed to knew nothing of it, who did? Such are the questions an examination of the external evidence brings. Whether or no such facts are compatible with the traditionary view, or are susceptible of explanation, the reader himself must judge.

We need add but one more piece of external evidence to do justice to the case of historical criticism in this department, although of course the presentation here made is a mere abstract. Some of the most important evidence for the date of *codification* of the ritual law is found in the book of Ezekiel. Here we have a prophet of the Exile planning for the reconstruction of the nation after its return. Ezekiel was both prophet and priest. The last part of his book is an elaborate ritual system devised on a purely ideal foundation, but of course far less elaborate than the Pentateuchal provisions. Was he aware of the existence of a Mosaic code covering in greater detail than his the whole ground of his code, or did he think of superseding it by his own? If Ezekiel knew nothing of it, who knew of it?

It is the attempt to answer these questions which has driven nearly all Old Testament scholars to abandon the idea of the Pentateuch ritual code as a revelation to Moses fixed for all subsequent time in all its detail, and substituted that of a growth whose roots go back in the consuctudinary law and traditional practise of the sanctuary for an indefinite period previous to the Exile, but whose *codification* began at the same time and for the same reasons as Ezekiel's code.

9. We have seen why from the nature of the case external evidence can furnish only an argument from silence, when we seek a date before which a writing *cannot* have existed. This argument from silence admits of being strengthened almost indefinitely by the establishing of a probability that if a book had been in existence it would have been known to

the authors consulted, and they in consequence would have used it, referred to it, or at least have written or acted in some way differently from what they did. Still it is necessarily internal evidence, exactly complementary to external, which can alone definitely fix a date before which a writing cannot have existed. Even here however we may escape the conclusion if we are willing to assume a miracle in support of Rabbinic tradition.*

In reply to this nothing can be said except to grant to all to whom this method of meeting difficulties is satisfactory that internal evidence is powerless before it. Supposing, however, that there are some to whom this short and easy method with the critics will not be satisfactory, we will briefly refer to some of the best-known phenomena of the Pentateuch which may be termed the *post-Mosaica ;* clauses which cannot be severed from the text except by resorting, as in the case of Deut. xxxiv. 5–12, to the very process of analysis denounced by the traditionary school, passages for which, nevertheless, it is necessary to assume a miracle to attribute them to Moses. As our purpose is merely illustrative, the following must be regarded not as a complete list, but as examples of a class :—

Gen. xxxvi. 31, " Before there reigned any king over the children of Israel," on critical principles would imply authorship subsequent to the establishment of the monarchy ; Gen. xl. 15, " the land of the Hebrews ;" Gen. xii. 6b, xiii. 7b and a series of passages implying that the Canaanites in the author's day had long disappeared, brings down the date to the period subsequent to Solomon (I. Kings ix. 16, 20f.) Deut. ii. 12 refers explicitly to Israel's having driven out the Canaanites and taken full possession of the land. " The Horites dwelt there beforetime, but the children of Esau succeeded them ; and they destroyed them from before them, and dwelt in their stead, *as Israel did unto the land of his possession which Yahweh gave unto them.*" Deut. xix. 14 forbids the removal of " thy neighbor's landmark which *they of old time* have set." Passages like Gen. xxxv. 20, " The same is the pillar of

* Cf. Briggs' *Bibl. Study,* p. 188, a quotation from the commentary of Wm. Gouge, an honored puritan divine, who meets the objections to the Davidic authorship of *all* the psalms, and in particular, " *Objection 5—*The cxxxviith Psalm doth set down the disposition and carriage of the Israelites in the Babylonish Captivity, which was six hundred forty years after David's time, and the cxxvith Psalm sets out their return from that Captivity. *Ans.*—To grant these to be so, yet might David pen those psalms ; for, by a prophetical spirit, he might foresee what would fall out, and answerably pen Psalms fit thereunto.''

Rachel's grave unto this day ;" Deut. iii. 11, " Behold his bedstead was a bedstead of iron ; is it not in Rabbah of the children of Ammon?" with Gen. xxxii. 22 and Deut. x. 8 (" unto this day "), point to mementos and institutions of antiquity to which the reader is referred. Num. xxiv. 7 alludes to Agag, cf. I. Sam. xv. 33. The psalm, Ex. xv. 1–17, refers in vv. 13 and 17 to the temple—" Thou hast guided them in thy strength to thy holy habitation ;" and, " Thou shalt bring them in and plant them in the mountain of thine inheritance,

> The place, O Yahweh, which thou hast made for thee to dwell in,
> The sanctuary, O Yahweh, which thy hands have established."

See also Num. xii. 3 and Deut. xxxiv. 10.

A second class of *post-Mosaica* are the references to position. The Pentateuch writer or writers use invariably the stereotyped expressions for north, south, east and west, which, nevertheless, have no significance except for a dweller in Palestine. Thus south is literally, " *Negeb*-ward," i. e. toward the desert of Beersheba ; west is "sea-ward," i. e. toward the Mediterranean. The expression " beyond Jordan " is frequently accompanied by " toward the sunrising," and is always shown by the context to mean eastward, whereas to Moses " beyond Jordan " would be west.

Passing over the argument from the indications of progressive development in the Pentateuchal codes, which, although considered by many the strongest evidence for the critical theory, is of too technical a nature for a popular treatise, we reluctantly turn to a department of the evidence which cannot be ignored, but which from its very nature is obnoxious to all for whom the religious value of the book is inseparable from historical accuracy in describing the events of the remote past. No small part of the proof deduced from the Pentateuch of its origin from traditionary sources centuries after the events it narrates is the alleged impossibility, and hence historical inaccuracy of its representations. This most thankless task of all criticism, a purely negative work, but one which, like the clearing away of unsound material, must necessarily precede the building of a trustworthy structure upon the actual phenomena of the documents, was taken up by Colenso, Bishop of Natal, in Part I. of his " *Pentateuch and Book of Joshua critically examined*,"* and carried through

*New York, D. Appleton and Co., 1863.

as unflinchingly as the surgeon wields the knife against disease. We can only refer to an instance or two from the period of Moses himself.

The enormous numbers of the Israelites who came out of Egypt (600,000 armed men, beside non-combatants), are *not* due to textual errors, because they are again and again re-iterated, verified by repeated footings and that in two complete censuses, besides agreeing with many of the representations of the story itself. Colenso proceeded to show that they are not only incompatible with the account of the 70 persons who *four generations* before had come into Egypt, but make the account of the Exodus incredible. To mobilize an army of "600,000 armed men" in a single night, Ex. xii. 37ff., is an incredible feat, even if we leave entirely out of account the women and children, the aged and infirm, the "mixed multitude" and the "flocks and herds." But supposing all this done, and the whole company, numbering necessarily between two and three million, provided with the "tents," we find them immediately after (Ex. xvi. 16) occupying, and all other necessary paraphernalia, including the riches required for the tabernacle, why should 600,000 armed men who "went up in battle array out of Egypt" (Ex. xiii.-18), run away from Pharaoh, or cry out for fear of the detachment of troops sent in pursuit? Why need an "armed force" ten times as numerous as the entire allied army at Waterloo submit to intolerable oppression? And how could the petty desert tribe of Amalekites hold them in check and for a considerable time "prevail" against them, Ex. xvii. 8ff.?

Again; the human millions are supported by manna in the "waste howling wilderness," but what supported the great numbers of cattle and flocks and herds of which we hear repeatedly? If they had these "flocks and herds" why did they complain of having no flesh to eat, and twice require a miracle to provide it, Ex. xvi. 1–14, Num xi. 4–35? If they did *not* have them, whence came the innumerable beasts for sacrifice carefully specified, and the passover lambs for 40 successive years required, Ex. xii. 5, to be males of the first year?

Again, the male Levites at the first census, Num. iii. 39, were 22,009; thirty-eight years afterward, Num. xxvi. 62, 23,000. But in Moses' own generation (Ex. vi. 16ff.) there were only *sixteen* all told. These 23,000 Levites were substituted for 22,273 first-born males of all Israel (Num. iii. 43). If we make the total male population only 900,000 (600,000 bore arms) every mother in Israel must then have had at least 42 *male* children.

Other objections of Colenso are of a more general character. Any intelligent person may gain a fair conception of them by simply reading the passages referred to (e. g. Num. xxxi.) and asking himself from time to time, "What does this narrative imply?"

This is indeed purely negative criticism; but its object is not destruction of the records as is often supposed. Negative criticism must be considered part of the evidence tending to show whether the history is that of eyewitnesses or more or less distorted by tradition. We turn, nevertheless, with satisfaction from the negative to the constructive side of historical criticism.

10. The central position of the science as regards the Hexateuch is the date 620 B. C. for the code of Deuteronomy. The argument for this is a volume in itself. In the treatise of DeWette, entitled *Dissertatio Critica*, 1805, Deuteronomy was identified with the "Book of the Law" or "Teaching" (*torah*) found by Hilkiah in the temple under Josiah, who made it the basis for a revolution in the religious history of Israel. It is this religious revolution which, more completely even than the Exile itself, divides the history into two distinct epochs. The story of this discovery and great reform is related at length in II. Kings xxii., xxiii., and the origin of Deuteronomy as an attempt to formulate the *torah* of Moses, as then understood, at a period not long previous to 620 has, since DeWette, acquired the force of an axiom among critics. The briefest possible *resumé* of external and internal evidence is all that we can allow ourselves.

The book brought forward by Hilkiah is positively identified as the Deuteronomic Code (Deuteronomy without the historical introduction and appendix which frame it in to the Hexateuch story), and *not* the whole Pentateuch. The testimony of Jeremiah and Ezekiel already adduced precludes from the point of view of criticism the supposition that this book contained the ritual law, for ignorance cannot be pleaded in their case. The conduct of Josiah is equally conclusive. But further, the book was so short that Shaphan could read it aloud "before the king," II. Kings xxii. 10, and the king "*the whole of it*" before the people, xxiii. 2. (Cf. the reading of the Pentateuch for a whole week, Neh. viii. 2–18). It was in the form of a "covenant" (xxiii. 2 and 21, "this book of the covenant," cf. Dt. xxix. 1), and was distinguished by fearful curses (xxii. 11–20 ; cf. Dt. xxvii. 11—xxviii. 68). Finally its contents may fairly be inferred from II. Kings xxiii. 1–24, which relates in detail the innovations Josiah undertook after pledging himself to carry out the reforms demanded by the book discovered. The whole chapter relates simply how Josiah proceeds step by step to carry out the requirements of the Deuteronomic Code. Thus

II. Kings xxiii.	7 carries out	Dt. xxiii., 7f.
" " "	9 " "	" xviii. 8.
" " "	10 " "	" xviii. 10.
" " "	11 " "	" xvii. 3.
" " "	14 " "	" xvi. 21f.
" " "	21 " "	" xvi. 5.
" " "	24 " "	" xviii. 11.

Further evidence for the identity of the book appears in the fact that it demanded some great and radical reform to justify the language of II. Kings xxii. 13, "Great is the wrath of Yahweh that is kindled against us, because our fathers have not hearkened unto the words of this book to do according unto all that which is written concerning us," and that of xxiii. 22, which extends the period during which no such requirements had been observed, back to the time of Joshua. What this radical reform was we shall soon see. For the present the external evidence of the case is clear to the critic. It was the Deuteronomic Code and nothing else, so far as external evidence can show it, which was brought forward by Hilkiah in the year 620 B. C. The statements of II. Kings are explicit and unanswerable that previous to that time neither the book nor all of its requirements had been known for an indefinite period. The question at once arises, How old was it? In what sense, and on what grounds, was it called " the Book of the Law ?"* On this point also we may learn something from the narrative in II. Kings.

Any one acquainted with ancient MSS. will be inclined to say at once, in answer to the query as to age, " Not very old." If for no other reason, then because only a trained expert can read MSS. of a few centuries back, on account of changes in chirography and language; but further, because Oriental MSS. are written with ink which fades and becomes illegible with dampness, and no MS. can be supposed to have survived, without care, the repeated pillaging of the temple, and the extraordinary vicissitudes of the ark in the ruined temple of Shiloh (Jer. vii. 12, 14, xxvi. 6, 9), in battle, among the Philistine cities, in the house of Obed-Edom, and among the peasants of Beth-shemesh. To suppose that the Book of the Torah which Shaphan claimed to have found in the temple was the actual autograph of Moses referred to in Dt. xxxi. 24ff., is perhaps what the author of Dt. xxxi. 24ff. thought and intended ; but in order to accept his opinion as true and competent, it will be necessary to assume a prodigious miracle. Let us see what means the finders resorted to, to ascertain the origin and authority of the book. The story is short. They did not trouble themselves at all about its origin, but a delegation took it to " Huldah the prophetess, the wife of Shallum, the son of Tikvah, the son of Harhas, keeper of the wardrobe," who returned the very practical answer that what the book required ought to be done. It was " good law ;" beyond this point none seemed to think it necessary to go. So far as the external evidence goes, in the story of the discovery, and aside from the practical difficulties in the way of

* Observe that it is nowhere in the story attributed to Moses.

supposing an extremely ancient MS., Shaphan's "Book of the Torah" might equally well have been an autograph of Moses, or a mere recent embodiment of the traditional "teaching" as understood by the prophets and priests of the period, the prophets being, according to the book itself, Deut. xviii. 15–22, the authorized custodians and interpreters of this "Torah." Or again, it might be neither of these extremes, but, as critics suggest, an expansion and modification (fully within the legitimate province of the prophet) of a Torah of Moses codified from the traditional form at least a century before. Such a Torah unquestionably existed, was attributed to Moses, and is now incorporated as "The Book of the Covenant" in Ex. xx.—xxiv.*

The external evidence of Scripture narrative, therefore, simply determines the year 620 for the *terminus a quo* of Deuteronomy, and throws open, for determination upon internal evidence, the question how much further back this "Book of the Torah" can be carried in its present form (the form described in II. Kings).

11. We need not long delay upon the *post-Mosaica.* In addition to the brief phrases adduced on page 43, we may cite Dt. iv. 38, "To give thee the land . . . . . *as it is this day*," and the use of "Dan" for Laish, xxxiv. 1 (cf. Jud. xviii. 29.) More particular attention, however, is called to the general character of the legislation. It is adapted to the wants, and assumes the existence, of an agricultural people long accustomed to city and village life. (Cf. the precautions of xxii. 1–10 in regard to house-building and agriculture ; also xix. 14.) The same of course holds true of the Book of the Covenant, from which these laws are taken. Chap. xx., especially vv. 5–9, is ill adapted to the period of the conquest. Chap. xvii. 14–20 gives directions for the conduct of kings. Samuel, and the author of I. Sam. viii., as well as the people of that day, seem never to have heard of it, but the directions and prohibitions themselves are scarcely comprehensible except when

* See page 19f.

4

read side by side with the story of Solomon's abuses of the office, II. Kings x. 14—xi. 8.   Chaps. xxix. and xxx. (**D'**, cf. especially xxix. 28), which assume that the alternative of blessing or curse of the preceding chapters is no longer open but that the curse has already fallen, we do not here consider, as they cannot in any case be earlier than the Code, and are regarded by critics as a later appendix.   As negative evidence of a post-Mosaic origin the above should suffice.   Have we any means of determining constructively the date of Deuteronomy ?

For the purely literary critic the resemblance of the style, language, religious conceptions and general standpoint to Jeremiah is so marked as perhaps to outweigh even the historical evidence.   Some critics have indeed claimed Jeremiah as the author, on the ground of identity of expressions and cast of thought ; but the evidence is inconclusive and too technical for our consideration.   We must proceed at once to the examination of that radical religious reform carried through by Josiah according to the requirement of " this Book of the Torah," which in the account itself is stated to have been an innovation upon the practise of all the people from time immemorial.   Both the Code itself, Deut. xii. ff., and the story of the reform, II. Kings xxiii., make it absolutely unmistakable what the nature of the revolution was.   It was the abolition of the *bamoth* (" high places "), or local sanctuaries and altars, and the concentration of the worship of the entire people at Jerusalem, designated as " the place which Yahweh shall choose."   It was demanded on the ground that these local shrines with their altars, " pillars " (*maçceboth*), and sacred trees, or *asherim* (wooden posts used as religious symbols), were of Canaanitish origin, and tended to corrupt the worship of Yahweh into resemblance to the impure worship of the Canaanite *baalim* (Dt. xii. 1–18).   All this was most unquestionably true, and we may even say that had not this radical discrimination of Yahweh-worship from ordinary Semitic Baal-worship (cf. Hos. ii. 16f.) taken place as it did scarcely a generation before the people were scattered in exile, Judah, and with it Yahweh-worship, with all its price-less treasures of revelation and religious thought, would have disappeared as completely as Ephraim did in captivity, by simple assimilation and absorption among kindred peoples. Whatever consequences it may have had in the development of ritualism and the extinction of prophecy in post-exilic times, it was a revolution which was necessary, and one to which we owe the preservation not only of the pre-exilic literature, but actually of the Jewish race itself as a "peculiar people," and the subsequent development of their religious consciousness.

However, it was an innovation, and of the most radical character. The Book of the Covenant, Ex. xx.–xxiv., had dis-tinctly sanctioned the popular worship, "in every place where Yahweh caused his name to be remembered;" the simple "altars of earth and unhewn stone" had dotted the land. Prophets like Amos, Hosea, Micah and Isaiah had deplored the tendency to Canaanitish practises there, but never dreamed of declaring them illegal. Elijah had built up the ruined altar of Carmel and mourned for those which an impious hand had broken down. Samuel (I. Sam. ixf.) honored the simple village sacrifice at the *bamah* ("high-place ") by his presence, and blessed the sacrifice ; from year to year he went in circuit from one to another of the most revered (vii. 16). Not a prophet or reformer or king of the ancient time but had exercised freely the right of private sacrifice and building of altars. If, as the Deuteronomist truly says, they were of Canaanitish origin, hitherto the whole effort of reformers had been to connect them with the history of Yahweh's relations with the patriarchs. The narratives of Genesis * are almost exclusively devoted to connecting this (sacred) tree, that altar, this (sacred) well, with the history of the patriarchs ; and the origin of sanctuary after sanctuary, tree after tree, "pillar" after "pillar" is justified in the relation of how "Yahweh had caused his name to be remem-bered there."

---

* The JE element only. P maintains the strictest silence on the whole subject of sacrifices, altars and sacred places.

Isaiah had begun the movement of reform, but even Isaiah, although the destruction of Ephraim in 722 B. C. removed the most insurmountable obstacle in the way of concentration of the worship at Jerusalem, did not accomplish, if he even attempted, the abolition of the local sanctuaries ; and " a *maççebah* to Yahweh" in the border of Egypt, and an altar in the midst of Egypt (Is. xix. 19), was to him an end to be devoutly prayed for. Compare with this the distinct prohibition of Deut. xvi. 21f., " Thou shalt not plant thee an *asherah* of any kind of tree beside the altar of Yahweh thy God which thou shalt make thee, neither shalt thou set thee up a *maççebah ;* which Yahweh thy God hateth," and that of Lev. xxvi. 1, " Ye shall make you no idols, neither shall ye rear you up a graven image, or a *maççebah*, neither shall ye place any figured stone in your land to bow down to it."

This warfare against material objects of worship as such appears to have been preceded, as we might expect, by a period of warfare against the heathen sacred tree, stone or *maççebah* as distinct from that reared in honor of Yahweh.   The *maççeboth of the Canaanites* are to be broken in pieces, Ex. xxiii. 24 ; xxxiv. 13f. ; Num. xxxiii. 52.   It is this stage of prophetic " zeal for Yahweh " which is presented in the pre-Isaianic prophets and in the narratives of Genesis re-baptizing the sacred trees, wells, stones, cairns, cromlechs, altars and *maççeboth* of the land into memorials of Yahweh's relations with the patriarchs.   So at least the critics understand the records.   (Cf. Gen. xxi. 33 ; xxviii. 18, 22 ; xxxv. 14, 20, and *passim ;* Josh. xxiv. 26 ; Hos. iii. 4.)

We cannot enter further into the story of .this contest of the prophets (and doubtless the priests also), in the seventh century, for the purification of Yahweh-worship from Canaanitish survivals.   Much more can be obtained by reading Part I. of the "History" of Wellhausen.   Whether due to the prophetic insight of Moses discovering in advance the exact wants of the century in which Deuteronomy would come to light ; or whether the book be considered an adaptation to that time of the Mosaic *torah* as it was understood in the circle of prophetic and priestly reformers of the period of Josiah, its legitimate guardians and exponents ; certain it is that the Deuteronomic Code plunges into the very thick of the contest, at the opportune moment when the long reactionary policy of Manasseh and Amon has been displaced by that of a docile youth under a priestly regency. It summons reformers to the vital issue of that very day in its opening words : " Ye shall not do after all the things that we do here this day, every man whatsoever is right in his own eyes." (Dt. xii. 8. Cf. also Dt. xvii. 3 with II. Kings xxi. 3.)

Even the consequences of its radical innovation in the worship are foreseen and provided for in Deuteronomy. For the ancient Israelite sacrifice and slaughter were the same thing. The Hebrew has but one word for both. Meat was rarely eaten, and whenever an animal was killed it was brought "*unto God,*" Ex. xxi. 6—of course not to the distant temple at Jerusalem, but to the village sanctuary and altar. Slaughter without this consecrating of the blood at the altar was impious, I. Sam. xiv. 32–35 ; but when animals were taken in the chase, it was provided as a substitute for the altar service, that the blood should be poured out upon the ground, Lev. xvii. 1–14. Among other consequences of the revolution effected by Deuteronomy would be the impossibility of bringing animals to Jerusalem to be slaughtered. This difficulty of distance is foreseen and provided for in Dt. xiv. 24f., and express provision is made for this case in the second part of the opening chapter of the Code, Dt. xii. 15–27, which extends the provisions previously applying to "the gazelle and hart" to all kinds of flesh.

A more serious difficulty was the providing of support for the priests who would be made destitute by the abolition of the *bamoth.* These rural priests (*Chemarim*) are recognized in Deuteronomy as on a footing of equality with the Jerusalem priesthood of the house of Zadok. They were Levites, and in Deuteronomy, just as in Jeremiah, the phrases, "the priests the Levites" and "the Levites the priests" are interchangeable. The distinction so strongly marked in the

Priestly Code between a priest and a Levite has here no existence whatever.* The author accordingly not only commends repeatedly the Levite, in connection with the widow and fatherless, to the compassion of the people, but devotes the section xviii. 1–8 to a special enactment providing that:—

"If a Levite come from any of thy gates out of all Israel, where he sojourneth, and come with all the desire of his soul unto the place which Yahweh shall choose ; then he shall minister in the name of Yahweh his God, as all his brethren the Levites do, which stand there before Yahweh. They shall have like portions to eat, beside that which cometh of the sale of his patrimony."

The Levites who thus became dependent upon the charity of the people and of their Jerusalem (Zadokite) brethren could not of course expect to remain on a footing of equality with these latter, and, as we shall see, it is from the history of the ever-widening discrimination between the mere Levites, and the Zadokite priesthood, that one of the strongest arguments is derived for the date of the Priestly Code.

With this exhibition of the internal evidence for Deuteronomy as the product of the great struggle for reform in the seventh century B. C., an adaptation of the *torah* of Moses, both oral and written, to the necessities of the struggle for pure worship, we must leave the reader to decide for himself how much weight may be given to the argument of historical critics for this their cardinal position, and proceed briefly to describe the subordinate propositions of current historical criticism.

12. We have already seen (p. 38) that the concentration of worship around the single altar at Jerusalem, which is the great innovation of Deuteronomy, is in the Priestly Code of the Pentateuch already a fundamental axiom. The central altar protected by concentric rings of sanctity is the core and kernel of all the Levitical ritual law. Totally unknown to the earlier history, to prophets, legislators and reformers, and

* Cf. Deut. xviii. 1, "the priests, the Levites *even all the tribe of Levi*," with the repeated denunciation of the death penalty in the Priestly Code for a usurpation of the least function of the priest by a Levite, in particular the destruction of Korah and his company, Num. xvi.

indeed totally impracticable under the conditions previous to the captivity of Ephraim, it comes first to light when Ezra "the priest, the scribe of the law of the God of heaven" returns empowered by Artaxerxes to reconstruct the unfortunate little colony at Jerusalem "according to the law of his God which was in his hand," Ezra vii. 1–26. From this time Judaism begins. In the words of Dean Stanley, "it was not a nation but a church which returned." The prophet is displaced by the scribe ; the local sanctuary by the synagogue ; king, nobles and people, by high-priests and priests, Levites and laity. There can be no question when the Priestly Law was *introduced*, the only question must be, When did it *originate* in a written form? and what was the function of "Ezra the priest, the scribe, even the scribe of the words of the commandments of Yahweh, and of his statutes to Israel?" (Ezra vii. 11.)

It cannot again be necessary to enter into all the minutiæ of external and internal evidence. Suffice it to say that the Documentary Analysis distinguishes in the Hexateuch a priestly element, **P**, easily separable, all the way from Gen. i. to Josh. xxiv., from the so-called "prophetic narrative," **J E**, and comprising the whole Levitical or ritual law. The nucleus of the work is supposed to be a priestly code (**P'**) incorporated in Lev. xvii–xxvi. to which the great majority of critics assign a date nearly contemporaneous with Ezekiel. The rest of **P** (**P²**,) is mainly a code of ritual law presented in the form of a history of the conquest of Canaan. A certain amount of material incorporated at a still later date is classified as **P³**. The great mass of the book is naturally located at Sinai (Ex. xxv–xl. Lev. i–xxvii. Num. i–x.) but special laws or "covenants" are brought in at important epochs : the Sabbath, at creation ; Noachic law of bloodshed, Gen. ix. ; circumcision, Gen. xvii. ; passover, Ex. xii. Another important object for the writer seems to be the deduction of exact genealogies from Adam down, in the case of all characters of the history ; and still another the distribution of the land of Canaan by lot according to the heads of the fathers' houses of each tribe. Thus the patriarchal period is divided into ten *Toledoth* or genealogies, of which Gen. v. is an example, only interrupted here and there by something of legal or ritual importance. The story is a mere skeleton or framework, derived, according to the dominant school of criticism, from J E. In Joshua it is almost purely occupied with assigning boundaries, to the tribal "lots;" in the middle books of course with ritual prescriptions.

The style is inexpressibly verbose, artificial and repetitious, and is comparable to nothing but the genealogies and inventories of Chronicles, Ezra and Nehemiah. (Cf. Num. vii., the same passage of six verses *repeated verbatim twelve times over*, with Ezra ii.) The decimal system is introduced everywhere and a minute chronology extends up to the very day of creation, including the birth-day and death-day of every descendant of Adam down to the Flood, and of all the patriarchs since. The minutest detail of numbers, statistics and measurements (the same which drew the unsparing criticism of Colenso) pervades all the history, and gives to the whole document the tone of a mathematical calculation. In the judgment of Nöldeke, the great critic of the Priestly Code, a more artificial, unnatural and purely mechanical treatment of the story can scarcely be conceived. It is needless to add that **P** is absolutely barren of poetic material.

No anachronism is traceable in the document, for the writer never permits himself for one moment to anticipate the course of revelation as he has mapped it out. The name Yahweh, for example, is not used until Ex. vi. 2, where it is related to have been revealed to Moses. Thereafter it is used uniformly. The frequent sacrificing, altar-building, and other religious observances which in J E so largely occupy the time of the patriarchs, in **P** are wholly wanting until the instituting of the ritual at Sinai sets the system in regular motion.

Mechanical and artificial as is the Priestly Code in both style and conception, the religious ideas which it embodies are the loftiest of the Pentateuch. The justly admired monotheistic representations of Gen. i. are characteristic of **P**. The naif, poetic and striking but crude anthropomorphisms of **J**, which only partially disappear in **E**, are wholly removed from **P**. The life has gone out of the narrative of **J E** in the form **P** gives it, but at least we must recognize here the work of one who desires to embalm for perpetual preservation the records of a past replete with divine significance. The treatment of the history is a process of smoothing out all the wrinkles and reducing of every thing to an absolute and stereotyped uniformity of perfection, and this naturally excites the antipathy of the historical critic ; but the very changes which obliterate for example from the story of the patriarchs all traces of dissension and wrong conduct, leaving nothing but an ideal and uniform existence of unbroken serenity, or which in Joshua transform the checkered history of the Conquest into a simple division of Canaan among the tribes by lot, after we have been told in two words how Joshua converted the whole territory into a *tabula rasa*, are due to nothing else than the very vividness with which a mind extravagantly devoted to minute and mechanical systematizing, and utterly unprotected from its own vagaries by the first scintillation of historical imagination or critical sense, has grasped the fundamental idea of a divine purpose and a divine revelation in the history. Crude and artificial as it is, from the point of view of the historian, this extraordinary document had a providential task to fulfill in the year 444 B. C. and whether then new or old it was providentially adapted to fulfill it. We can take but a single illustration from each department of the evidence adduced by historical criticism for assigning the work to about this date.*

13. Deuteronomy is regarded by the traditionary school as

---

* See chapter III., p 67, for Dillmann's dissenting view. His opposition to the opinion of the dominant school is however more apparent than real, since he also although claiming an existence of P before the Exile—some portions excepted— would consider it to have been quite unknown, its existence being merely latent. He also considers P entirely dependent upon E and some of the *sources* of J for his historical material. As the Dillmann theory is certainly losing ground it will not be necessary to pay it further attention in what follows.

later than the priestly legislation.   It professes to set forth
the law of Moses given at Horeb.   It rehearses the history of
all the period from Sinai to the Jordan, in which the great mass
of the priestly document falls.   It is singular, in this view, that
the minutest search of critic after critic in both the narrative
and the legislative parts of Deuteronomy has failed, as even
Dillmann, who maintains the origin of **P** *before* Deuteronomy,
confesses, to reveal one trace of acquaintance with any part
of this great mass of mingled law and narrative.   But not even
is this all.   The analysis of Num. xvi., for example, reveals a **JE**
element narrating the revolt of Dathan and Abiram, Reuben-
ites, against Moses, and their punishment by being swallowed
up alive.   Intimately inwoven and blended with this is the
narrative of **P** of an attempt of Korah with 250 Levites to
usurp the functions of the priesthood.   Fire came out from
Yahweh and devoured them.   Dt. xi. 6 quotes this chapter,
but only the J E element.   Korah and all pertaining to him are
simply ignored.   As external evidence that **P** was unknown
to the Deuteronomist facts like these must be admitted to
have weight.

The internal evidence for the late origin of **P** is mainly
derived from evidences of development in the legislation
beyond the point of Deuteronomy and Ezekiel.   We select
as a single example the regulations discriminating between
priest and Levite.   In the chapter just quoted, Num. xvi., **P**
exhibits his conception of the inferiority of the Levites.   It
is in **P** a matter of birth, the priests being exclusively descendants of Aaron of the house of Zadok.   The distinction
is thus for him primeval.   But in considering Deuteronomy
we found an equality between priests and Levites only just
beginning to separate into a distinction of rank between the
Zadokites and the ordinary Levite.   How came this little
rift to widen to such a chasm?   The transition point is found
in Ezekiel's legislation.   Here in Ez. xliv. 7–16 "the Levites
that went far from me, when Israel went astray" are assigned a menial position in the sanctuary (displacing the for-

eign *hierodouloi*, apparently Philistines,* who had performed such services),

> " Because they ministered unto them before their idols, and became a stumbling-block of iniquity unto the house of Israel : therefore have I lifted up my hand against them saith the Lord Yahweh, and they shall bear their iniquity.   And they shall not come near unto me, to execute the office of priest unto me nor to come near unto any of my holy things. . . . . Yet will I make them keepers of the charge of the house for all the service thereof and for all that shall be done therein. *But the priests the Levites, the sons of Zadok, that kept the charge of my sanctuary when the children of Israel went astray from me,* they shall come near unto me to minister unto me ; and they shall stand before me to offer unto me the fat and the blood, saith the Lord Yahweh, they shall enter into my sanctuary, and they shall come near to my table to minister unto me, and they shall keep my charge."

That which in the Priestly Law is regarded as primeval, is here instituted as a punishment for ministering in illegitimate worship. The passage looks both forward and backward ; backward to a time when, as in Deuteronomy, "the priests, the Levites" were "all the tribe of Levi ;" forward to the time when, as in the Priestly Code, the Zadokites shall be the only legitimate priests and the other Levites mere servants. In this development Deuteronomy stands earliest, Ezekiel midway, **P** latest.

A striking detail of the phenomenon is the fact of the retention in Num. xvii. 1, 23 (**P**) of the very phrase "they shall bear their iniquity" twice employed by Ezekiel. In the Priestly Code however all odium is removed from it. The sense attached is simply "act as mediators for the people."

14. Referring the reader to the technical works already cited for evidence as to the origin of **P**, and to the document itself for further characterization, we turn to the other element of the Hexateuch, the Prophetic Narrative **J E**. Although recognized by critics as duplicate, the two strands of **J E** are so closely similar in style, content, purpose and general characteristics, and withal are so closely intertwined,

---

* So considered from the fact that they were "uncircumcised," Ez. xliv. 7-9, "leaped over the threshold," Zeph. i. 9—cf. 1 Sam. v. 4 f., and were perhaps no other than the king's body-guard of Cretans and Philistines, 2 Sam. viii. 18 ; xv. 18 ; xx. 7, 23 ; 1 Kings i. 38, 44.

that it is better to treat **J E** first as a unit.   Such indeed relatively to **D** and **P** it really is.   Afterward I shall refer more briefly to some of the characteristics which distinguish **E** from **J**.

The external evidence for **J E** in Deuteronomy is as complete as it was absolutely wanting for **P**.   The narrative parts of Deuteronomy reproduce **J E** throughout the period covered in Exodus and Numbers, precisely as extricated by the analysis, and in frequent cases *verbatim*.   The legal enactments again reproduce the whole of the Book of the Covenant, Ex. xx–xxiv. 8 (**E**), with scarcely an exception.   For the separate parts of **JE** references can be found of a still higher antiquity.   Thus **E** in Ex. iv.–xv. can be traced in Is. x. 24, 26, and later ; and Hosea, at a still earlier period, repeatedly refers to the narratives of **J**.   In view of this it is not necessary to refer again to the pre-deuteronomic attitude assumed in **JE** toward the local sanctuaries, trees, altars, wells and *maṣṣeboth*, which are universally put in a favorable light and connected with theophanies to, or experiences of, the patriarchs.   The style, language and religious standpoint is in general that of Isaiah and his period, though betraying of course in the older portions a much more archaic type.   If, however, the judgment of historical critics is worth anything, the religious standpoint of both elements of **JE** is such as cannot possibly be supposed to antedate the great religious revival of Elijah.   The whole work is in fact permeated through and through with the " prophetic " spirit of Elijah and his successors, of "jealousy for Yahweh " (I. Kings xix. 10, 14).   It is to paint in most vivid colors the action of Yahweh for his people from the beginning, his favor for their obedience, and wrath for their frowardness, that this incomparable collection of the folk-lore of Israel was made.   With a distinctly religious purpose it was shaped into a national epos of Yahweh's dealing with his people from the time when he called Abram and promised him the land, till that promise was fulfilled to the children of Abram. There is no period which it so appropriately fits as that golden age of prophetic activity, where literature and the religious consciousness seem to have sprung at once and together almost to their perfect bloom. Whenever it may have found its origin, it found its significance in the age of the great prophets Amos, Hosea, Micah, Isaiah ; the age which begins with the brilliant and prosperous reigns of Jeroboam II. and Uzziah, and ends with the tragic fate of Josiah. Here, as part of the great prophetic movement, if guided by historical criticism, we must place the origin of the Bible ; for this, and nothing less, was the function of the Prophetic Narrative, especially after its combination with Deuteronomy, to be *the Bible* of pre-exilic Israel.

With this date agrees every indication of the text, the references to the monarchy, to the extinction of the Canaanites, to the temple, to the Book of Jashar (Josh. x. 12f=**E**), and others already noted. From the standpoint of literary and historical criticism **JE** is of the very bone and flesh of the Assyrian period, 850–722 B. C. If it was already in existence before the conquest of Canaan it was a miraculous removal during deep sleep.

Of the character and purpose of **JE** we can speak but briefly in addition to what has been already spoken and implied. Contrast in style could not be stronger than between **JE** and **P**. Graphic narrative, brilliant coloring, dramatic power, idyllic simplicity and freshness take the place of "endless genealogies" and ponderous artificiality. Poetry and imaginative genius illuminate every page. We visit each local shrine and sanctuary and learn the story of its origin. We live the life of the patriarchs, and find it that of the peasant of pre-exilic Israel. Love-stories, tales of feats of cunning over-reaching cunning, of gigantic strength, of heaven-sent wisdom and kind-heartedness, puns and jokes even (Gen. xl. 13 and 19), awaken the interest, sympathy or mirth of the reader. Rarely (least rarely in **J**) do we meet with coarse innuendoes (Gen. xix. 30ff) and popular superstitions (Gen. xxx. 14–16). The fountains of minstrelsy and ballad-lore yet flow copiously through its pages. But through

it all runs the thread of a unifying purpose, a religious *motif*
which betrays the inspiration of the men who made Israel "a
light to lighten the Gentiles." This underlying *motif*, more
clear in **E** than in **J**, in **JE** than in either, is a purpose to
show forth "God in history." The "history" is such only as
the age could provide, but the God apprehended there is the
Everlasting God of Truth and Righteousness.

15. In the ensuing analysis, **J** is presented as antedating **E**
by some fifty years, and as derived from Judah. There are
difficulties in the way of assuming both together. Both style
and material of **J** seem more archaic than **E**. **J** is more secular, **E** more careful to preserve the religious tone.* These
phenomena naturally lead to the conclusion that **J** is older,
especially if, as seems probable, one is dependent upon the
other more or less indirectly. Also the external evidence, it
will be remembered, can be traced further back for **J** than
for **E**. On the other hand, an origin in less prosperous Judah
might account for a less developed literary product, and it is
hard to accept the very considerable evidence for the
southern origin of **J** and at the same time account otherwise
than by dependence upon **E** for the fact of his including the
same list of sanctuaries (all Ephraimite but one), as **E**, whose
Ephraimite proclivities are so marked as to be universally
conceded among critics. Hence Kuenen, convinced of the
earlier origin of **J**, considers the document Ephraimite and **E**
as merely emphasizing its national *tendenz*. The solution is
perhaps to be found in the fact that both **J** and **E** may draw
from an elohistic, Ephraimite (poetic?) source, **E** being the
later, and the common material of the two be thus only
indirectly related. To this source **J** may well have added
his southern material and modified its Ephraimite character,
though he did not remove it. The contrasts between **J** and
E in style, phraseology and religious conceptions are striking

* Cf. Jacob's overreaching of Laban in J xxx. 41-43 with God's providential favor-
ing of Jacob in E xxxi. 7-9 ; similarly xxx. 14-16 (J) with 17f. (E) ; xii. 13 (J), with xx.
12 (E) ; xvi. 6f. (J), with xxi. 11-13 (E) ; and see xlv. 5-8, l. 19f., and other E passages.

and interesting ; as, for example, the revelation by dream or by a voice "from heaven" in **E** (cf. Num. xii. 6–8), in contrast to the personal interviews with Yahweh related by **J**. Certain modes of expression, as e. g. **E**'s formula of address, Gen. xxii. 1, 7, 11, etc., and contrasted historical conceptions, are interesting, but belong rather to the details of analysis than to our present general characterization.

16. We bring to a close our theory and method, and our presentation of the outline of the argument of historical criticism of the Pentateuch, by calling the attention of the reader to the revolution which must follow from it, if adopted, in current modes of conceiving the history of Israel. Instead of starting at the summit and rehearsing nothing but a long series of lapses and reinstatements, the history thus conceived discloses a connected development, a wavering but nevertheless constant line of advance in the development of the religious consciousness of Israel ; first the prophet, the creative genius, emphasizing the moral law ; then the priest and scribe, the conservative power, developing ritual form. From the simple idyllic transcripts of the folk-lore and national tradition which served as the earliest channel by which the devotion of the prophets to Yahweh the God of Israel, the God of Righteousness, was transfused into the veins of the common people, down to the epoch-making Deuteronomic Code, and to the Priestly Legislation, protecting, even while it restricted and seemed almost to stifle beneath its panoply, the germs of religious life in the beginnings of Judaism, we have a progressive revelation of God, a continuous development of the Hebrew religious consciousness. In this development the creative element is the inspired genius of prophetism, apprehending God in history, and in the conscience ; the corrective element is the providential course of events, persistently pruning and training the conception ; and the conservative element, the ritual law. Hebrew history and Hebrew literature, placed side by side and studied by the inductive methods of criticism, lead up to this as a scientific statement of the

doctrine of Divine Revelation, and to the Bible as the ripest and most perfect fruit of this spiritual evolution.

Many doubtless will continue to cling to the tradition of the Mosaic authorship of the Pentateuch, as men long clung to the Davidic authorship of the Psalms. But those who have witnessed the quiet superseding of this now obsolete idea by that of historical criticism, presenting the Psalm-book as a conglomerate which unites in one collection fruits of the religious thought and feeling of Israel during many centuries, have no excuse for regarding the exactly analogous treatment of the heterogeneous elements of the Hexateuch as necessarily subversive of religious faith. Rather let us, with the genuine faith in divine revelation of the late Dean Stanley, see in the results of criticism a dis-covery of "Bibles within the Bible,"—a discovery which testifies to the continuous operation and guidance of the Spirit of Truth in the history of spiritual life in Israel, exactly as the geologist's strata, layer upon layer, bear witness with their embedded fossil survivals of a pre-historic age to the continuous work of the Creator in the sphere of physical life. For here also are "tables of stone written with the finger of God ;" here also are "prophets which have been since the world began."

CHAPTER III.

Pentateuchal Analysis.*†

A few words touching the field of controversy are needed in order to a correct idea of the theories and the stand-point of the authorities cited.

The prevailing theory is the Grafian. Graf's followers, pre-eminent among whom are Kuenen and Wellhausen, consider the "prophetic," so-called (JE), to be the older of the two main sources of the Hexateuch. JE itself is composite, a close amalgamation of two kindred narratives of Hebrew history. J (circ. 800) and E (circ. 750) circulated for a time independently, and were more or less modified. After the destruction of Ephraim and the discovery of Deuteronomy (621) whose origin also must be placed at about this period (650–621), J and E were united into a closely welded whole, and soon after, Deuteronomy, which had, meantime, received an introduction and an appendix, was incorporated.‡

These two processes necessitated further interpolation and modification, and for a considerable period $\dfrac{(J+E)+D}{R_{je}\quad R^d} = JED$ circulated as a well-rounded "prophetic" compilation. But with the interruption of the cultus by the exile began the process of codification of the Levitical,

---

* The subjoined articles were printed in Hebraica, IV. 4 and V. 1 (July and October, 1888), and were intended as a basis for the discussion of the Pentateuchal Question in the columns of that journal; but also, as appears from the note following, as a preliminary to the present volume then in preparation. Lack of space has unfortunately compelled the omission of the foot-notes which contained the divergent analyses of the authorities cited on page 68, and of course also of the analyses of later critics by which the articles had been brought down to date by the author. The omission is the less serious from the fact that the articles themselves are accessible, and moreover from the fact that it was their most striking result to prove an almost exact coincidence in the analyses of independent critics, instead of the "conflicting results" which have been erroneously ascribed to them. With the exception noted the articles are reproduced substantially in their original form.

† A Tabular Presentation according to Representatives of the Principal Schools of Higher Criticism, including Fragments and Portions assigned to Editors, Interpolators, Compilers and Glossators.

The writer has in preparation a volume embodying the subjoined analysis and presenting J, E, and P conjecturally restored.

‡ Wellhausen holds that the amalgamation of J and E preceded the origin of D.

ritual law.   Heretofore it had been consuetudinary, tradition and the living praxis having sufficed for its transmission.   Ezekiel (**40–48**)* inaugurated the new system of a written *Torah*, which progressed during the exile with the formation of the code known as the *Heiligkeitsgesetz*, P¹ (**Lev. 17–26**), an antique body of laws midway in tone between Deuteronomy and the priestly legislation.   It culminated in the priestly code, P².   This great work drew from JE a sketch of the history, made from its own stand-point.   It was subsequently enlarged by the incorporation of P¹ and by expansions and additions designated P³.   Ezra introduced it as the constitution of the post-exilic hierarchical state.   A final redactor, R, combined P with JED at some time between Ezra's promulgation thereof (444 B. C.) and the appearance of the LXX. version (circ. 280 B. C.).   We might express the process by the formula: $\text{Hexateuch} = \dfrac{(J+E)}{Rje} \dfrac{+D}{Rd} \dfrac{+(P^1+P^2+P^3)}{R}$.†

Against the Grafians a minority of critics under the able leadership of Dillmann still maintain the older theory, in a modified form.   This school nearly coincides with the Grafian in the date and origin assigned to the prophetic narrative JE, and to Deuteronomy; but insists upon an earlier origin for P.   Dillmann describes the development of the priestly element (P) somewhat as follows:

The most ancient portions of P are more properly to be considered a cluster of fragments, most densely aggregated together in Lev. 17–26, but scattered also throughout the middle portion of the Hexateuch from Ex. 31 to Num. 15.   In a certain sense they may be considered as having a common "source," since attempts at codification were made probably as early as the period of Jehoshaphat, the material itself being consuetudinary law transmitted in certain cases from a period as remote as the first centuries after the conquest.   But this source P¹ (Dill. S) shows no such unity of design as to enable us to treat it as a specific document.   On the contrary certain portions were incorporated by P² and worked over by him, certain others were taken up by R after complete recasting at his hand, still others adopted in an unassimilated form.‡

---

* Throughout the article, chapters are distinguished from verses by means of bold-faced type.

† The denominators in the formulae are thus placed to indicate the fact that their relation to the factors beneath which they stand is that of compilers and editors.

‡ The Hypothesis broached in Dill. ii. of a version of S (P¹) worked over and incorporated by C (P¹J) is withdrawn in Dill. iii., p. 633; hence the only remaining versions of P¹ recognized by him are P¹p² and P¹r. From these are to be distinguished perhaps unadulterated fragments P¹ (iii., pp. 633–670).

But the differences still remaining between these various fragments of P¹, after allowance has been made for the double redaction of P² and R in the one case and of R alone in the other, is too great to admit of their having existed together in a single code. Two codes of P¹ at least were current, beside individual *toroth*, and the process of redaction of P¹ extended demonstrably into the Exile. A considerable group of fragments from one of these (including its hortatory conclusion, Lev. 26:3–45), still exhibiting its characteristic point of view of "holiness," is preserved to us in Leviticus 17–26, worked over, however, by P².

P², for whom the date 800 B. C. is approximately determined by Dillmann, is held to be dependent for his historical material largely upon E (900–850 B. C.), also upon the *sources* of J, which are frequently very ancient. Here and there he has ancient historical material of his own, but his richest sources are of course the priestly *toroth*. In the first half of the eighth century appeared J, dependent largely upon E, but also using P², though writing from a totally different stand-point. As a popular writer he has access to popular sources. R's work consisted simply in the *simultaneous* combination of E, P², J, and parts of P¹. Very rarely does he use the pen; but in the transposition, clipping, and piecing of his material he shows the utmost freedom. Deuteronomy, the latest document of the Hexateuch, was added by a later redactor, R^d, who used the pen more freely. Thus Dillmann, followed in general by Ed. Riehm ("Handwörterbuch der bibl. Alterthum," Halle).

The most recent period of Hexateuch criticism shows the development of a third school of more conservative character. W. Robertson Smith ("Old Test. in the Jewish Church," Appleton & Co., 1881; and "Prophets of Israel," 1882) made an attempt to show the compatibility of the Grafian theory with evangelical theology; but for a time the only safe course for orthodox scholars who recognized the scientific character of critical methods, was supposed to be to follow Dillmann. Two professors of the Leipzig faculty, however, F. E. König ("Offenbarungs begriff des Alt. Test.," 2 vols.; Leipzig, 1882), and the veteran commentator of world-wide fame, Franz Delitzsch ("Ztschr. f. k. W. und k. Leben," 1880; and "Genesis," Leipzig, 1887) have boldly adopted the Grafian theory in its main outlines as not only in their opinion preferable in itself, but as affording a better basis for the defence of orthodoxy than Dillmann's. W. Graf von Baudissin also ("Heutige Stand der a. t. Wissenschaft," Giessen, 1885) seeks a middle ground between Dillmann and Wellhausen.   But in the special department of Hexateuch analysis a still more recent writer has the best claim to be considered the representative of that modern school which seeks both to avail itself of all the resources of criticism from an evangelical stand-point and to take an independent position while doing full justice to Dillmann on the one hand and to Kuenen and Wellhausen on the other.   This most recent authority is R. Kittel (" Geschichte der Hebräer," Gotha, 1888).

The following is a list of authorities from which our data are derived :

Dillmann, August.
> Kurzgefasstes Exegetisches Hand-buch zum Alten Testament.
> VOL.
> I. Die Genesis. 5. Auflage. Leipzig: 1886.
> II. Die Bücher Exodus und Leviticus. 2. Auflage. Leipzig : 1880.
> III. Die Bücher Numeri Deuteronomium und Josua. 2. Auflage.
> Leipzig : 1886.

Delitzsch, Franz.
> I. Neuer Commentar über die Genesis. Leipzig : 1887.
> II. Zeitschrift für kirchliche Wissenschaft und kirchliches Leben.
> 1. Hefte I–XII. 1880.

Kittel, R.
> Geschichte der Hebräer.
> I. 1. Halbband : Quellenkunde und Geschichte bis zum Tode Josuas.
> 1888.
> II. Theologische Studien aus Württemberg VII. 1886.

Kuenen, A.
> I. Historico-critical Inquiry into the Origin and Composition of the
> Hexateuch. (Trans. by Wicksteed of Historisch-critisch Onderzoek. 2. Uitgave. Leiden : 1885.) London : 1886.
> II. Theologisch Tijdschrift XI., XII., XIII., XV., XVIII. 1877–1884.

Wellhausen, Julius.
> I., II., III. Die Composition des Hexateuches. Three articles in
> Jahrbücher für Deutsche Theologie, XXI., XXII. 1876, 1877. The same reprinted in Skizzen und Vorarbeiten. Part II. Berlin :
> 1885, and translated by Colenso in Wellhausen on the Composition.

Budde, K.
> I. Die Biblische Urgeschichte (Gen. I.–XII. 5) untersucht. Giessen :
> 1883.
> II. Gen. XLVIII. 7 und die benachbarten Abschnitte : Zeitschrift
> für die alttestamentliche Wissenschaft, III. 1883.

III. Richter und Josua. Zeitschrift für die alttestamentliche Wissenschaft, VIII. 1888.

Jülicher, A.

   I. Die Quellen von Exod. I.–VII. 7. Dissertation. Halle : 1880.

   II. Die Quellen von Exod. VII. 8–XXIV. 11. Jahrbuch für Protestantische Theologie, VIII. 1882.

The above cited works furnish the data for the summary of Hexateuch analysis, and are selected for completeness and for their representative character. The divergence between the analysis of Dillmann and Wellhausen measures, probably, the extent of difference on this score among the recognized critical authorities of to-day.

These authorities are referred to under the following abbreviations : Dill. I., II., III.; Del. I. and II. 1, 2, 3, etc.; Kitt. I., II.; Kuen. I. and XI., XII., etc. ; Well. I., II., III.; Bud. I., II., III. ; Jül. I., II., III. For a bibliography of critical works, the reader is referred to Dill. I., II., III. and Kuen. I.*

A. THE PRIESTLY LAW BOOK P².

I. Genesis.

In the following pages the analysis of Dillmann is given as the basis, and that of the other critics in the foot-notes,† an arrangement adopted for convenience and not intended to indicate a preference. Portions included in [ ] are attributed by other critics to a different source. The * indicates a corruption of the text. P³, in our nomenclature, stands for all additions not of a merely editorial nature, appended by second, third or fourth hand to the great law-book whose framework is the priestly history. Similarly J², E², D², include all elements not of an editorial character which have been appended to the original "prophetic" documents. Notes intended according to the critics for harmonizing JE and E, or for the union of JE to D, and glosses and interpolations in general of a minor character, supposed to have preceded the union of JED to P, are included under R⁴. R occupies toward JEDP the same relation that R⁴ does toward JED. Dillmann's theory, of course, makes the activity of R precede that of R⁴ whose work consisted in uniting D to JEP.

1. *The* TOLEDOTH *of the Heavens and the Earth :* an account of creation and of the institution of the Sabbath.

---

* Since the above was written there have appeared in this class of works *Die Genesis :* E. Kautzsch and A. Socin. Freiburg, I. B. 1888 (2d ed. 1891), and *Composition des Hexateuchs :* J. Wellhausen. Berlin, 1890, a reprint of Well. II. with appendices bringing the discussion down to date.

† See note on page 65.

1:2–2:4a (2:4a, the original title, was removed from before 1:2 by R, who supplied instead v. 1).

2. *The Book of the* TOLEDOTH *of Adam:* a genealogy of ten generations, the tenth link branching into three, showing the descent of Noah from Adam in the line of the eldest son.

5:1–32 (exc. v. 29 [= J]).

3. *The* TOLEDOTH *of Noah:* an account of the flood, lasting for two periods of five months and one of two months (365 days), and of the institution of God's covenant with Noah; the Noachic legislation.

6:9-22; 7:6,11,13–16a,18–21,23b,24; 8:1,2a,3b–5,13a,14–19; 9:1–17,28f (7:7–9 = R).

4. *The* TOLEDOTH *of the sons of Noah:* an ethnological table deriving the peoples of the world by descent from the three sons of Noah, beginning with the youngest.

10:1–7,20,22f,31f.

5. *The* TOLEDOTH *of Shem:* a second genealogy in ten generations branching into Abram, Nahor and Haran.

11:10–26.

6. *The* TOLEDOTH *of Terah:* (*a*) a history of the migration of Terah, and of the journey and settlement in Canaan of Abram and Lot his descendants.

11:27,31*,32 (מאור כשרים in v. 31 = R); 12:4b,5; 13:6,11b (from ויפרדו) 12a (to הככר).

(*b*) Further items in the history of the Terachites: Lot delivered from the overthrow of Sodom; Abram begets Ishmael; theophany to Abram and institution of the law of circumcision; promise of Isaac; Isaac's birth; Sarah dies; Abraham buys the field of Ephron and buries Sarah in the cave of Machpelah; death and burial of Abraham.

19:29; 16:1,3,15f; ch. 17 (in v. 1 read אלהים, changed by R to יהוה); 21:1b*,2b–5 (in v. 1b read אלהים); ch. 23; 25:7–11a.

7. *The* TOLEDOTH *of Ishmael:* a table of the twelve tribes of the Ishmaelites and notice of the age and death of Ishmael.

25:12–17.

8. *The* TOLEDOTH *of Isaac:* his marriage and the birth of his sons; Esau's marriage displeasing to his parents; Jacob blessed and sent to Paddan-aram for a wife; his family there; he returns [and is involved in war with the Shechemites]; God meets him at Bethel and there renews the covenant with him; arrived at Hebron his father dies and is buried by Esau and Jacob; Esau removes to Mt. Seir.

25:19,20....26b; 26:34f; 27:46; 28:1-9; (29:24,29; 30:4a,9b?); 31: 18;* 33:18;* 34:1a,2a,4,6,8-10,15-17,20-24....(vs. 13f,18,25,27-29 and טמא in v. 5 = R); 35:6a,9-15 (exc. עוֹד in v. 9 [= R]), 16 in part, 10 in part; 22b (from ויהיו)-29; 36:2a,5b,6-8; 37:1; (36:1,2b-5a = R with a basis of J(?) and P²).

9. *The* TOLEDOTH *of Esau:* an ethnologico-genealogical table deriving the twelve tribes of the Edomites from Esau; the sons of Esau; [the seven *aluphim* of the Horites; the royal succession of Edom]; the *aluphim* of the Edomites.

36:9a*,10*,11,13*,16-18*,19a,29f,31-35a,36-43; (vs. 9b,12 and 14, עמלק in v. 16, and הוא אדם in vs. 19 and 35b = R. The names of Esau's wives also in vs. 10,13f,16-18 were altered by R to bring them into correspondence with his source in vs. 1-5).

10. *The* TOLEDOTH *of Jacob:* Joseph's greatness in Egypt; the sons of Jacob migrate thither [a table of Jacob's descendants]; Pharaoh gives them audience and offers them the land of Ramses; Jacob brings his life to a close in Egypt; adopts the sons of Joseph; gives final directions to his sons; dies, and is buried in the cave of Machpelah.

37:2a (to בצאן or to יעקב); 41:46,(47(?),36(?),50(?)); 46:6f,8-27, (vs. 8,12b,15,20,26f worked over by R); 47:5b, supplying before it from LXX. ויבאו מצרימה אל יוסף יעקב ובניו וישמע פרעה מ' מ'. ויאמר פרעה ליוסף.

Then 5b,6a,7-11,27 in part, 28; 48:3-6; 49:1a,28b-32 (exc. either 30b or v. 32 = R); 48:7 (exc. הוא בית לחם = R); 49:33 in part (המטה ....ויאסף = J); 50:12f.

<h3 style="text-align:center">II. Exodus-Deuteronomy.</h3>

1. "The sons of Israel which came into Egypt;" the cry of their bondage comes up before God.

1:1-5,7 (exc. v. ab), 13f (exc. בשדה....בחמר [= J or E] and את כל עבד [= R]); 2:23 (from ויאנחו on) —25.

2. Theophany to Moses; revelation of the name Yahweh as a pledge of deliverance; Moses commissioned to deliver Israel; [a genealogy of Reuben, Simeon and Levi showing the descent of Moses and Aaron; Aaron appointed Moses' spokesman.

6:2-5,6*,7,10f,13,14-27 (vs. 8f,12,28f,30a = R. Much misplacing is also due to R); 6:30b-7:7.

3. The *five* wonders in Egypt. Aaron's contest with the magicians.

(*a*) The first wonder : Aaron's rod changed to a serpent ; the magicians do likewise.

7:8–13.

(*b*) The second wonder : Aaron's rod turns all the water of Egypt to blood ; the magicians do likewise.

7:19–22 (exc. 20, from יְהוָֹה on, and 21a).

(*c*) The third wonder : Aaron's rod brings frogs ; the magicians do likewise.

8:1–3,11 (from וְלֹא on. Supply וַיֶּחֱזַק לֵב פַּרְעֹה).

(*d*) The fourth wonder : Aaron's rod brings lice ; the magicians fail and acknowledge " the finger of God."

8:12–15.

(*e*) The fifth wonder : Moses and Aaron sprinkle ashes before Pharaoh ; it becomes a boil on man and beast ; the magicians being stricken flee. Pharaoh still obdurate.

9:8–12.

(*f*) [Conclusion of the section. Pharaoh's obduracy provokes the direct intervention of Yahweh.]

11:9,10 (9b perhaps = R).

4. Passover : the deliverance from Egypt.

(*a*) Moses and Aaron receive directions from Yahweh for Israel ; regulations concerning the calendar and the killing and eating of the passover lamb.

12:1–13,28.

(*b*) Egypt smitten ; Israel delivered ; the law of *Mazzoth*. In 12:37 the word מַרְעְמְסֵם ; then vs. 43–49,14–20,50,40,41a (41b = 51), 51.

(*c*) The first-born shall be Yahweh's.

13:1,2.

5. Passage of the Red Sea.

13:20 ; 14:1–4,8,9 in part (exc. וַיִּרְדְּפוּ.…אַחֲרֵיהֶם [= JE] and רֶכֶב וּפָרָשִׁים [= R]), 15–18 (exc. מַה תִּצְעַק אֵלַי in v. 15, and חֶרֶם in v. 16 [= E]), 21ac,22,23 26 ; the first 6 words of 27,28a, 29 (בְּ)רִכְבּוֹ וּבְפָרָשָׁיו in 17,18,23,26,28 and בָּל סוּס רֶכֶב וְגוֹ' in v. 9 = R).

6. The march to Sinai : [Elim] ; Manna given ; Rephidim ; Sinai ; Moses goes up into the mount.

(15:27 ?) ; 16:1–3*,6*,8–14,15b,16–18,22–24,31–34,35* ; 17:1a ; 19:2a,1 ; 24:15–18a (to הֶעָנָן) (15:27 perhaps E(?). Ch. 16 entirely worked over by R and removed from its proper position [to this all the critics agree]. The P[2] elements are given as above in Dill., III., p. 634, but in II., p. 165, somewhat differently, e. g. v. 6f is attributed to P² and v. 8 to R. Vs. 3 in part, 4f,15a, 19f in part, 21,25–30,35a = J, the rest = R).

7. The law and the testimony: the pattern shown in the mount; the institution and regulation of the Levitical ritual.

From Ex. 25 to Num. 10 the entire mass is admitted by all the critics to belong to P in its various stratifications P¹, P², P³. Only Ex. 32–34:28, and a trace of E in 31:18 belongs to the " prophetic " element, and in these three chapters Dillmann alone finds a single trace of P² (in 32:15a). The extrication of P¹, P², P³ in Ex. 25–Num. 10 and the legal chapters of Numbers, with the analysis of the great code of the " prophetic " Hexateuch, Deuteronomy, are reserved for another article. The historical thread of P² is traced by all the critics in Ex. 25ff., (the construction of the tabernacle), Lev. 9,10 in part; (the inauguration of the ritual, and death of Nadab and Abihu), Num. 10:11–28; (the departure from Sinai). We proceed from the point where P² is again combined with J E, viz., in the story of

8. The sending of the spies, murmuring of the people at their report and the punishment.

Num. 13:1–17a,21,25,26a,32 (to הוא); 14:1 in part, 2 in part, 5–7,10, 26.27–29,34–38.

9. The revolt of Korah and the Levites; punishment of the people's murmuring; the plague arrested by Aaron's atonement.

16:1a,2f in part, 4 in part, 5–7 for the most part, 18–24a,35; 17:6–15, 16–28 (16:3 in part, 8–11,16f,24b,27a,32b = R; 17:1–5 = P³).

10. Water from the rock at Meribah; the sin of Moses and Aaron; Aaron's death; fragments of the itinerary.

20:1a (to הראשן), 2,3b,6f,8a*,10a,12*,13*,22–29; 21:10f; 22:1 (many traces of R).

11. Israel misled by the Midianites after the counsel of Baalam; Phinehas' prompt action stays the plague.

25:6–9,14–16,19 (10–13 = P³. 17f = R. Ch. 31 is connected with this account, but in its present form = P³).

12. The census of the nation, preparatory to the occupation of Canaan; regulation of inheritances where the heirs are females; the daughters of Zelophehad.

Ch. 26 (exc. vs. 8–11 and 58–61 [= P³]); 27:1–11.

13. Moses receives directions to prepare for his death; Joshua commissioned; Reuben and Gad receive an inheritance east of Jordan.

Deut. 32:48–52 (exc. glosses in vs. 49 and 52). The passage is a repetition of Num. 27:12–14 [P³ or R], this latter according to Dill. being the copy; Num. 27:15–23; 32:1a (to גדר), 2b,4a,20–22*,28–30,18f,40(?) (therewith probably Josh. 13:15–19,23–27*,28,29b,32. See Josh. *in loc.*).

14. [An *itinerarium* of the wilderness stations].

33:1–49 (exc. 8f*,14f*,16f*,40,49 [= R]).

15. Moses' death.

Deut. 1:3; 34:1a (to נבו), 5*,7a,8f.

III. Joshua.

1. Crossing the Jordan; passover at Gilgal [Achan's trespass]; the league with Gibeon.

3:4(?); 4:13*,15–17,19; 5:10–12; 7:1,18b,25ba; 9:15b,17–21,27 in part.

2. The inheritance of Reuben and Gad.

13:15–19,23–27*,28,29b,32 (vs. 20–22,29a,30f,33 = R^d).

3. The distribution of the inheritances by lot; Judah's inheritance; a description of the territory of the tribe, giving boundaries, and enumerating the cities and villages.

13:1; 14:1–5; 15:1–12,20–44,48–62 (vs. 45–47 = R, v. 63 = JE inserted by R^d).

4. The inheritance of Manasseh-Ephraim, of Benjamin, and of the other seven tribes; similar tables of boundaries and cities, ending with a colophon.

17:1a,3f,7*,9*,10*; 16:4*,5–9; 18:11a,12–28; 19:1ab–7,8b,10–16,17*, 18–23*,24*,25–31*,32*,33–39*,40*,41–46*,48,51 (17:1b,2,8,11–13; 16:1–3, 10; 18:11b; 19:1aa,8a,9,27 in part, 47,49f = JE. 17:5f = R).

5. The cities of refuge and the cities of the priests and Levites appointed.

20:1(?),2f,6*,7–9; 21:1–40 (41–43 = D²); the portions of ch. 20 omitted are wanting in LXX. Well. and Kuen. consider LXX. more correct here and regard vs. 4f, etc., as late interpolations in a style imitating D. Dill. prefers the Massoretic text and assigns the additions to R^d. The LXX. found them superfluous and so omitted them.

6. The altar built by the transjordanic tribes. Its intention is misunderstood by the rest of Israel and they march against Reuben, Gad and Manasseh; explanation of the Gileadites and peaceful separation of the tribes.

22:9f,13–15,19–21,30f,32a....(vs. 1–6 = D; vs. 7f = R^d including a trace of E in v. 8; vs. 11*,12,24–27,32*,33f = E; vs. 16–20 and 22–29 in their present form = R; the whole chapter thoroughly worked over by R and afterward a second time by R^d).

B. THE EPHRAIMITE NARRATIVE E.

The first demonstrable appearance is in Gen. 20. Probable traces in chs. 15 and 14. Not impossibly 4:17-24, and 6:1-4, belong to E (Dill. III., p. 617).

I. Genesis.

1. [Abram recaptures Lot from Chedorlaomer and is blessed by Melchizedek.]

Ch. 14 = R (on a basis of E (?) exc. vs. 17-20 = R).

2. The promise of Isaac.

15:2* (traces in vs. 1,3,5,6 worked over by J and R).

3. Sarah and Abimelech.

Ch. 20 (exc. v. 18, and ועברים ושפחות in v. 14 = R).

4. Birth of Isaac and expulsion of Hagar and Ishmael.

21:6,8-21.

5. Abraham's covenant with Abimelech at Beer-sheba.

21:22-32a.

6. The sacrifice of Isaac.

22:1,2*,3-10,11*,12f,14*,19 (vs. 15-18 = R).

7. [Abraham's marriage with Keturah.]

25:1-4 (v. 5 = J; v. 6 = R).

8. Birth of Jacob and Esau.

25:25*,27* (fragments).

9. [Isaac in Gerar.]

26:1*,2*,6.

10. The blessing of Isaac; Jacob defrauds Esau of the inheritance.

27:1-45 in part. (Vs. 15,24-27,30a (to אֶת יַעֲקֹב), 35-38 = J. Vs. 21-23,30b,33f = E. 44b = 45aa, one J, the other E. Impossible to carry the analysis further).

11. Flight to Haran; Bethel; Jacob's dream and vow.

28:11f,17-22 (v. 19a(?) J and E; 19b,21b = R).

12. Jacob in Haran; marriage with Leah and Rachel.

29:1,15b-30 (exc. vs. 24,29 = P² and v. 26 = J).

13. Birth of the tribe-fathers.

30:1-3a,6,8,17-24 (exc. 20b,22c,24b[= J],22a[= P²] and 21 [= R or J]).

14. Jacob's service with Laban; he returns from Aram; pursuit of Laban and covenant on Mt. Gilead.

30:26,28 (32-34 "hardly" E's); 31:2,4-17,19f,21*,22-24,26,28-45*,47*, 51-54*; 32:1; (31:10,12, יעקב in v. 45, v. 47 in part, הנה הגל הזה ו and עד הגל הזה ו in vs. 51f, ואת המצבה הזאת in v. 52, and אלהי אביהם in v. 53 = R).

15. The story of Mahanaim and Peniel; encounter with Esau.

32:2f,4* (in part), 14b–22,24,25–32; 33:4*,5,11a (32:33 = R).

16. Jacob's land purchase at Shechem; fulfills his vow at Bethel; death of Deborah and Rachel.

33:19f*; 35:1–4,6b–8,16–19a,20 (v. 6a = P[2], הוא בית אל in v. 6 and הוא בית לחם in 19b, also vs. 21,22a = R).

17. Joseph's prophetic dreams and the envy of his brethren; Reuben seeks to save him from their conspiracy and restore him to his father; he persuades the brethren to cast Joseph into a pit; Midianites pass by, find Joseph, and kidnap him; Reuben returning is in despair at not finding the child; the brethren report his death.

37:5–18a (exc. 5b.8c, ויספר אתו לאחיו in vs. 9,10a [LXX.] = R; vs. 12–14*; מעמק חברון in v. 14 = R or J) 19,20,22,23f*,24,28*,29f, 31f*,34f*,36; also וישמע ראובן in v. 21 (vs. 28c,35b = J; 31f part E, part J).

18. Joseph is brought to Egypt and sold to Potiphar, Pharaoh's head sheriff, who entrusts him with the care of the prison; the dreams of Pharaoh's officers interpreted.

39:4 in part, 6,21 in part; 40:2,3a,4,5a,6–15a,16–23 (39:1 פוטיפר ... הטבחים = R).

19. Joseph interprets Pharaoh's dream, and is made ruler of Egypt.

Ch. 41 (exc. a few traces of J in vs. 14,18–22(?),34, and one part of the following doublets: 30b = 31; 35b = 35a; 41,43b,44 = 40; 49 = 48; 55,56a = 54b.

20. The sons of Jacob go to Egypt to buy food; Joseph meets them roughly and imprisons Simeon on pretence of their being spies; he demands that Benjamin be brought down; Reuben pledges himself for Benjamin's safety.

Ch. 42 (exc. 2a,4b,6, parts of 7, אבל in 10,27,28a*, and 38 [= J]; 28b belongs after v. 35).

21. Joseph reveals himself; his brethren return to fetch Jacob.

43:14*,23c; 45:1–27 (exc. 1a,2,4b,5a,10 in part, 13f = J; vs. 19–21*).

22. Jacob migrates to Egypt.

46:1 in part, 3f,5 in part (1a,5b = J or R); 47:12, parts of 13–26* (13–26 = J on a basis of E, removed by R from after 41:55 and worked over).

23. Jacob blesses Joseph and dies; death of Joseph.

48:1,2a,9a,10b,11f,15f,20 in part, 21f; 50:1–3(?),15–26 (exc. v. 18 and parts of 21.24 [= J]) (in ch. 48 E is expanded by R through the addition of 2b,9b,10a,13f,17–19,20b from J).

II. Exodus.

1. Oppression in Egypt; birth and youth of Moses.

1:6,8–12,15–2:14 (exc. traces of J in 1:10,12,20; 2:14; also 1:21 and parts of 2:6f = J).

2. Moses called at Horeb and commissioned to deliver Israel; revelation of the name Yahweh.

3:1–3*,4b–6,9–16*,18–22*.

3. Moses returns to Egypt with the rod of God; the demand made of Pharaoh.

4:17,18,20b,21,28b,31aα; 5:3f,6–8,10,11a,12–19,20f in part (4:22f = J, removed by R from before 10:28; 6:1 = R).

4. The *five* plagues of Egypt: blood, lice, hail, locusts and darkness.

7:15 in part, 16 in part, 17b.20 in part, 18 in part, 21a,24; 8:16a,21–24a; 9:22,23a,24a,31f,35; 10:8–13a,14a,15 in part, 20,21–27; (in 7:15 אשר נהפך לנחש = R).

5. The destruction of the first-born of Egypt and the exodus.

11:1–3; 12:31–33,37b,38; 13:17–19 (21f*?).

6. The passage through the Red Sea; Miriam's song.

14:5 7 in part(?), 15 in part, 16 in part, 19a, 20 in part, 24 in part, 25a; 15:20f,1–19.

7. [Marah]; water from the rock at Horeb; battle with Amalek; Jethro's visit.

15:22–26 (27 = P[2]); 17:3–6,8–16; 18:1–27 (exc. 2b [= R] and traces of J in 1,(5),9,10; the story last named is probably misplaced).

8. The ten words [and the covenant] at Horeb.

19:2b,3–8*,10–15,16 in part, 17–19*; 20:1–20* (vs. 9–11 = P[2]); then 21–26; 24:3,4 (from ויבן on), 5f,8a,11,12 in part, 13f, and chs. 21–23, viz., the Book of the Covenant, an ancient code incorporated by E. (R removed it from after 24:14, its original position. The following glosses and interpolations by R should be eliminated: 22:20–23,24b,30; 23:13,15,23–25,31b,33).

9. The golden calf; departure from Horeb; the tent of meeting.

31:18b; 32:15 in part, 16–19aα,25–29; 33:1–5 in part (in v. 5 the beginning, to ישראל, then הורידו עדיכם מעליכם), 6*....7–11.

III. Numbers.

1. The departure from Horeb, [Taberah; the manna and the quails in Qibroth Taawah].

10:33a; 11:1–3,7–9,10bα,30–35.

2. Miriam and Aaron rebel; arrival in Kadesh and sending of the spies.

12:1,2 in part, 3a,5 in part, 9-15 (mostly) (v. 16 = R); 13:17b in part, 18,20 in part, 23f,29-31,32 in part; 14:1f in part, 23 in part, 24,25b,39-41 in part, 44 in part (14:11-23 = R).

3. Rebellion of Datham and Abiram; the earth swallows them up.

Traces in 16:1-4 (e. g. 1b, and parts of 2,3f), in 12-15 (e. g. 14ab,15b = E, 14aα,15a = J) and in 25-34 (28f,32a = E, 30f,33a = J).

4. Death of Miriam; water from the rock in Kadesh; embassy to Edom.

20:1b,3a,4f,7,8 (first two words and bα), 9*,10b*,11 (v. 9 = R), 14-19,21.

5. The brazen serpent; Israel in the border of Moab; conquest of the territory of Sihon.

21:4-9 (exc. מהר ההר in v. 4 = R), 12-18a,21-24 (LXX.) (18b-20 and 25-32* = R, from another source [J(?)]; 33-35 has been imported by R^d from Dt. 3:1-4).

6. Balak and Balaam; the involuntary blessing of the prophet hired to curse.

22:2-21 (exc. 3a,4,5a,7a,17f and perhaps ויהבש את אתני in v. 21 [= J]), 36-41; 23:1-26,27f in part(?); 24:25(?) (23:28[27]-30; 24:20-24 = R).

7. The people sin at Baal-peor; Gad and Reuben receive their lot; the cities of Jair.

25:1a,3,5; 32:2a,3,16f (20f in part(?)), 24,34-38 (39,41f(?)).

IV. Deuteronomy.

8. Directions for a sacrificial feast on Ebal; charge to Joshua; [the blessing of Moses].

27:5-7a (vs. 1-3,9f = D¹,4,7b,8 = R^d, 11-26 = R^d and R); 31:14f (vs. 16-23; 32:1-44 = J) and ch. 33 (incorporated by E(?)).

V. Joshua.

In this book the problem of critical analysis is greatly complicated by the introduction of a new element. P² has been extricated with comparative facility and unanimity. JE is still the main residuum, but according to all the critics, greatly expanded and worked over by R^d. Dillmann supposes the author of Deuteronomy to have supplied to his code a historical appendix, which constitutes, therefore, an independent source, taken up by R^d and combined with P² and JE. The four documents, three of them already united by R, were amalgamated and worked over by him. Kuen., Well., Bud., Kitt. attribute these Deuteronomic additions to D² or R^d, the writer who incorporated Deuteronomy with JE and provided it with a historical introduction and appendix. The result is, in the opinion of all, such an obliteration of the characteristics of J and E by R[d], or so thorough an incorporation of them into D², that they are only traceable with difficulty and in a few passages.

Dillmann assigns the following passages to JE in Josh. 1-12: Chs. 2-8:26 (27-30, 31b(?)); ch. 9 for the most part (9:3-9a,11-15a,16,22f); 10:1-11,16-27; 11:1,5-9. From this must be subtracted a verse or two for P² (see P² below) and some minor contributions of D and R[d].

The portions assigned to D by Dill. in Josh. 1-12 are as follows: In general chs. 1-3f; 5:1; 8:32,34f; 10:12-14,28-43; 11:10-23. From P² come only 3:4 in part(?); 4:13 in part, 15-17,19; 5:10-12; 7:1,18b,25 in part; 9:15b,17-21, 27 in part.

In chs. 13-24 P² predominates. Dill. assigns to it 13:15-19,23-27a,28,29b,32; 14:1-5; 15:1-12,20-44,48-62; 16:4 in part, 5-9; 17:1a,3f,7 in part, 9 in part, 10 in part; 18:1,11a, 12-28, ch. 19 for the most part; 20:2f,6 in part, 7-9; 21:1-40; 22:9f,13-15,19-21,30f,32a. This portion removed, the parts assignable to D according to Dill. are 13:1,7; 18:10b; 21:41-22:6 and ch. 23. This element also being removed there remains for JE 14: 6-15 in part; 15:13-19; 16:1-3,10; 17:1-18 in part; 18:2-10,11b; traces in ch. 19 (specifically 19:39f); much of ch. 22 and ch. 24 for the most part.

1. Crossing the Jordan; the people circumcised by Joshua at Gilgal; the "rolling away" of the reproach of Egypt.

3:12; 4:1a,4f,7b,9; 5:2f (exc. שוב and שנית in v. 2 [= R[d]]), 8f (vs. 4-7 = R[d], cf. LXX.).

2. The capture of Jericho.

(5:13-15 = E or J) 6:1 (E or J, 4 in part*, 5f,7b,8f*,13*,15*,16a (17-19 = E or J), 20b (21-25 = E or J) (touches in 3f,11,14f = R; vs. 2,17b, 18 and 27 and the continued blowing of trumpets, 4,8f,13 = R[d]).

3. The capture of Ai and covenant with the Gibeonites.

8:10-12,14 in part, 16 in part, 17 in part, 18,20b,26,30,31b; 9:3-27 (exc. 6b,7,9 in part, 10,14f,16 in part, 17-21,24f,27). (Ch. 7 for the most part = J. 8:1f,7b,8a,22b,27-29 and traces in 3,11,15,21,24; also 9:1f,9 in part, 10,24f,27 in part = R[d]; 8:13 and ירד כנטורת in v. 19 = R).

4. The battle of Gibeon.

10:1-11,16-27 (vs. 12-14,15,28-43 = D; vs. 8 and 25 and 1,2,6,7,19,24, 26f in part = R[d]).

5. Settlement in the land, and inheritances of the tribes; Caleb receives Hebron; the house of Joseph obtain a double portion; they invade Gilead.

14:6-15*; 15:13(?); 16:1-3(?); one of the two stories in 17:14-18 (14f = 16:14 in part, 17f); 19:49f; 22:8*.

6. Conclusion of E's history; Joshua's charge to the people at Shechem; the history briefly reviewed and Israel pledged to the service of Yahweh; Joshua's death and burial.

Ch. 24 (exc. 1f in part, 6-8 in part, 17-19 in part, 10f in part, 13 in part, 26a,31 = R and R[d]).

C. THE JUDÆAN(?) NARRATIVE J.

I. Genesis.

1. The beginning of the world ; paradise ; the woman's transgression and the curse.

2:4b–3:24 (exc. אלהים after יהוה *passim ;* 3:20 and perhaps 2:10–15 = R).

2. Adam's descendants [Cain and Abel(?)] ; a seven-linked genealogy, the last link branching into three ; the song of Lamech ; [a fragmentary ten-linked genealogy ending with Noah and his three sons(?)].

4:1–16 (misplaced(?) ; חוה v. 1 = R), 17–24,25f ; 5:29 (J follows in 17–24 an older source, possibly E).

3. The sons of God and the daughters of men ; corruption of the earth.

6:1–8 (exc. וגם אחרי־כן v. 4, מאדם....השמים and בראתי in v. 7 = R) ; J rests in 6:1–4, as also in 4:17–24, upon an older source, possibly E.

4. [The deluge of forty days ; rescue of Noah and his family in the ark ; sacrifice of Noah and promise of Yahweh.]

7:1f,3 in part, 4f,7*,10,12,16b,17,22*,23* ; 8:2b,3a,6–12,13b,20–22 (R = 7:3a,7 in part, 8f,22f in part).

5. [The peopling of the earth from the sons of Noah] ; Noah's vine culture and prophetic song concerning Shem, Japheth and Canaan.

9:20–27,18f ; 10:8,10–12,13–19,21,25–30 (9:20–27 is from a special source. 10:9,24 and perhaps 14 in part and ואדמה וצבים in v. 19 = R).

6. The tower of Babel and the dispersion ; Abram and his kindred.

11:1–9,28b–30 (exc. באור כסדים = R).

7. Abram called from his home ; his journey with Lot, halting at Shechem and Bethel ; separation from Lot and settlement at Mamre.

12:1–4a,6–9 ; 13:2,5,7–11a,12 last clause, 13–18 (13:3f and ולט עמו in v. 1 = R).

8. Yahweh's covenant with Abram.

Traces in ch. 15 worked over by R ; specifically, v. 4,9–18* (exc. 12–16 = R) ; R = v. 7f ; R^d(?) = vs. (16) 19–21.

9. The birth of Ishmael.

16:2,4–14 ; 25:18b.

10. Visit of three heavenly ones to Abram at Mamre ; promise of Isaac ; punishment of Sodom and Gomorrah ; origin of Moab and Ammon.

18:1–19:38 (exc. 19:29 = P²).

11. Birth of Isaac; [Abram's sojourn with the Philistines(?)]; news of the descendants of Nahor; Abram sets his house in order; the steward sent to the Nahorites to bring a wife for Isaac.

21:1a.2a,7,32b-34; 22:20-24; 25:5,11b,18a; ch. 24 (exc. v. 62 and שרה אמו in v. 67a, and v. 67b = R).

12. Isaac in Gerar; [Abimelech takes Rebekah]; the wells of the *Negeb;* controversy with the Philistines and covenant at Beer-sheba; birth and youth of Esau and Jacob.

26:1b, first three words of v. 2,3a,7-14,16f,19-33; (the first three words of v. 1, v. 2 from ויאמר on, v. 6 = E; 3b-5 = Rd; מלבד.... אברהם in 1a, and vs. 15 and 18 = harmonistic interpolations of R); 25:21-34 (exc. 26c = P[2] and traces of E in vs. 25 and 27).

13. The blessing of Isaac; Jacob supplants Esau.

27:1-45 = JE and is composite, but only partially separable into J and E; J = vs. (7),15,(20),24-27,30a (to את יעקב), 35-38 and 44b or 45aα and other portions not extricable, cf. E *supra).*

14. Jacob's flight to Haran; [the theophany at Bethel;] his marriages and service with Laban.

28:10,13-16,19a,(21b),(19b,21b = R); 29:2-15a,26,31-35; 30:3b,4f,7f (4a and 9b R(?)),9-16,20b,22c,24b (v. 21 = R or J; 22aα = P[2](?)), 25-43 (exc. 26,28 = E).

15. Jacob's return from Aram-Naharaim; pursuit of Laban; covenant on Mt. Gilead.

31:1,3,21 in part, 25,27*,46*,48*-50 (46b,48a = R, from J elsewhere; v. 47 gloss, or perhaps from E elsewhere).

16. The story of Mahanaim and Peniel; [Jacob wrestles with a divine being and receives a blessing and a new name;] crosses the Jabbok at Peniel and meets Esau in peace.

32:4-14a,23; 33:1-16 (exc. 4*,5,11a = E; 32:33 = R).

17. Succoth; Shechem and the rape of Dinah; [Israel's departure; immorality of Reuben; the descendants of Esau].

33:17,18b; 34:2b,3,5,7,11-13,19,25*,26,30f; 35:21(?); 36:2f,10,13,16-18, 20-28(?) (these parts of ch. 36 removed by R from before 32:4. 33:18a; 34:1a,2a,4,6,8-10,15(14)-17,20-24 = P[2]; v. 25b; 35:21(?),22a; 36:1,2a(?) and other portions of ch. 36 = R).

18. Joseph Israel's favorite; his brethren hate him and conspire to kill him; Judah interposes and, as a caravan of Ishmaelites passes by, suggests that they sell him; the Ishmaelites bring Joseph to Egypt.

37:2b,3f,18b,21*,23 and 24 in part, 25-27,28 in part, 31f in part, 33,34f in part (cf. E's part *supra).*

6

19. The origin of Judah's families; his Canaanite affinities and wicked sons.

Ch. 38.

20. Joseph is bought of the Ishmaelites by "an Egyptian;" he is slandered by his master's wife and imprisoned.

39:1 (exc. the portion identical with 37:36 [= R from E]), 2f,4 in part, 5f,7–20,21 in part, 22f.

21. Joseph made lord of Egypt; the famine.

40:1.3b,5b,15b; and traces in 41:14,18–22(?), v. 34,30b or 31,35b or 35a,41,43b,44 or v. 40,49 or 48,55,56a or 54b.

22. Joseph's brethren come to buy food; returning, at the lodging place, they find their money in their sacks; the food consumed, they make a second visit; Judah becomes surety for Benjamin.

42:2a,4b,6, parts of 7, אכל in v. 10,27,28a; 43:1–3; 42:38; 43:4–13, 15–23ab,24–34.

23. Joseph's hospitality; the cup hidden in Benjamin's sack; the brethren brought back; Judah offers himself for Benjamin.

Ch. 44.

24. Joseph reveals himself and sends for his father; Israel goes down to Egypt; is met by Joseph in Goshen; Joseph and five of his brethren petition Pharaoh for leave to occupy Goshen.

45:1a,2,4b,5a,10 in part, 13f,28; 46:28–47:5a,6b.

25. [Joseph's administration in Egypt during the famine; Israel fed.] **47**:12–26,27 in part.

26. Jacob's charge to Joseph; [blessing of Ephraim and Manasseh]; blessing of all the sons; death and burial in Canaan; [Joseph's continued kindness].

47:29–31; 48:2b,9b,10a,13f,17–19,20b; 49:1b–27 (incorporated), 33 in part; 50:(1–3(?)),4–11,14,(18a,21 in part(?)).

II. Exodus.

1. Israel in Egypt; birth and youth of Moses; his flight to Midian and marriage there; the theophany at Sinai; Moses commissioned to deliver Israel and equipped with signs for the people and for Pharaoh.

Traces in 1:10,12,20; v. 21; 2:6f in part, and a trace in v. 14; vs. 15–22; 3:3 in part, 4a,7f,16 in part, 17; 4:1–16 (in 2:18 insert חבב בן before רעואל).

2. Moses returns to Egypt; struggle with Yahweh at the lodging place and circumcision of Moses' son; he [meets Aaron and] reports to the elders of Israel; Moses and the elders go to petition Pharaoh.

2:23ab; 4:19,20a.22–26,27–29a,30,31 in part; 5:1f,5,9,11b,21–23 in part (6:1 = R; 4:22f misplaced).

3. The seven plagues of Egypt: the water turned to blood; frogs; flies; murrain of cattle; hail; locusts; death of the first-born.

7:14,16,25,26–29; 8:4–11a,16–28 (exc. 16a,21–24a = E); 9:1–7,13,(14–16 = R),17–21,23b,24b,25a,26–30,34b; 10:1a,(1b,2,3a = R),3b–7,13b,14b, 15a,16–19,28f; 11:4–8; 12:29f,34–36,38f.

4. The exodus; [laws of *mazzoth*, passover, and the first-born;] departure under guidance of the pillar of fire and cloud, and passage through the Red Sea.

12:21–28; 13:3–16,21f*; 14:5–7 in part, 9 in part, 10–14,19b,20 in part, 21b,24a,25b,27 in part, 30f.

5. [Manna given;] water from the rock at Massa-Meribah.

16:3 in part, 4f,15a,19f in part, 21,25–30.35a (all, however, removed from before Num. 11 and worked over by R or R^d); 17:2,7.

6. The theophany to the people at Sinai; [the covenant before the mount; Moses goes up and remains forty days in the mount; idolatry of the people; Moses' intercession]; renewal [celebration] of the covenant.

19:3–6 in part, 9,11 in part (13b(?)), 16 in part, 18 in part, 20–22,25 (20:18 in part, 20 in part(?)); 24:1f,4aא,7,8b,9f,11 in part, 12 in part, 18b; 32:1–14,19–24,30·34* (35 = R); 33:1–5*,12–23*; 34:1–28; (19:23f = R; 34:10–27 was removed by R from after 24:2. After 34:9 followed originally 33:14–17, then 34:28. Vs. 11–26 are a mere extract from the Book of the Covenant). The traces (of J(?)) in ch. 18 and 24: 3–8 are neglected in III., p. 624.

III. Numbers.

1. Departure from Sinai; Hobab goes with Israel as guide; the Mosaic formula at the moving or resting of the ark; Kibroth-hattaawah; Israel lusts for flesh; seventy elders appointed.

10:29–32....33b,35f; 11:4–6,10* (exc. ‏מאד יהוה אף ויחר‎ = E), 11–29 (the two stories of the murmuring for flesh and the elders, not originally together, united by R).

2. [Rebellion of Miriam and Aaron; Kadesh; spies sent out; the people's murmuring and attack on Amalek.]

Traces in ch. 12 (vs. 2,4f,9 in part); 13:17–20 in part (cf. E), 22,27f; 14:1b,2 in part, 3f(?),8f,28(?),30,39–45 (exc. 39 in part, 41 in part, 44 in part = E).

3. [Rebellion of Dathan and Abiram ; Edom's opposition(?)].

16:1b,2–4 in part, 12–15 in part, 25–34 in part (see E *in loc.*) ; 20:20(?).

4. Attack of the king of Arad (misplaced) ; [perhaps a fragment of a list of encampments ; conquest of territory in Moab].

21:1–3,18b–20(?),25–32(?).

5. Balak and Balaam ; Israel blessed by the prophet of Yahweh.

22:3a,4,5a,7a,17f, ויחבש את אתני in v. 21(?),22–34,35a ; 24:1–18 (19) ; (22:35b [= 21b] ; 23:28[27]–30 ; 24:20[19]–24 = R).

6. Trespass of Israel with the Moabite women ; Gad and Reuben's settlement in the trans-Jordanic district (inheritance of the sons of Machir and Jair misplaced) ; warning to extirpate Canaanite idols.

25:1b,2,4 (32:5–13,20f in part, 23 25–27,31)* ; perhaps 32:39,41f ; 33: 52f,55f.

IV. Deuteronomy.

1. [Warning to Israel by Moses before his death and song of Moses] ; Moses' death.

31:14f (traces), 16–23 ; 32:1–44 ; 34:1b,4.

V. Joshua.*

1. [Israel crosses the Jordan] ; the monument in Gilgal of stones from Jordan ; appearance of the captain of Yahweh's host to Joshua].

4:3bc,6,7a,8,10*,11*,20* ; 5:13–15.

2. The capture of Jericho [and trespass and punishment of Achan].

6:3*,7a,10,11*,14,15a,16b,20aa, (3f,11,14f = R, 2,17b,18,27 and parts of 4,8f,13 = Rd) ch. 7* (exc. vs. 24f [= Rd] and traces of R).

3. The capture of Ai.

8:3–9,14 in part, 15f,17 in part, 19–22a,23–25 ; (8:1f,7b,8a,22b,27–29 and traces in vs. 3,11,15,21,24 = Rd ; v. 13, and כנטות ירו in v. 19 = R).

4. The covenant with the Gibeonites ; Israel deceived ; the Gibeonites enslaved.

9:6b,7,14,15aa, 16 in part (vs. 1f,9 in part, 10,24f,27 in part = Rd).

5. The occupation of the land ; settlement of Caleb and Othniel ; the Jebusites ; Gezer ; the cities which held out against Manasseh ; the Danites capture Laish ; traces of a description of the inheritances.

18:2–10,11b(?) (or = E ; v. 7 = Rd) ; 15:13*,14–19 ; 15:63 ; 16:10 ; 17: 12f ; 19:47 ; the portions of chs. 16f and 19 excluded from P².

---

* For the general analysis of Joshua in Dill. see under E, p. 78.

6. [Dismissal of Reuben and Gad]; a summary of the conquest of their several portions of territory by the tribes independently.

Irrecoverable traces of J underlying ch. 22. Judg. 1 for the most part.

II. PRIESTLY AND "PROPHETIC" CODES IN THE HEXA-TEUCH.

The Law of Holiness, P¹.

Leviticus 17-26, and kindred passages.

The earliest fragment held by any of the critics to belong to this primitive priestly code is

1. [a Sabbath ordinance.]

Ex. 31:13ac,14a (a "resemblance" to P¹ is suggested by Dill. in Ex. 6:6-8; 12:12b and 29:46; the fragment in 31:13f introduced by R).

2. [The law of sin-offerings, in trespasses against God and against one's neighbors.]

Lev. 5:1-6.21-24a (in II.. p. 373f, P¹, or at least some source prior to.. P², is recognized as lying at the basis of Lev. 2 [the law of meal-offerings], 5:1-7,21-26 [as above + vs. 7 and 24b-26], and chs. 6 and 7 [the law of the six kinds of offering]. In the later volume only 5:1-6,21-24a is ascribed to P¹; chs. 6 and 7 contain ancient *toroth*, possibly P¹'s, in the recension of P³).

2. [The law of clean and unclean beasts: defilement by eating and from the touch.]

Fragments incorporated with P² in Lev. 11:1-23,41-47 (11:24-40 and the basis of the rest of the chapter belongs to P². In II., p. 480f, 11: 1-23,41-44a = P¹j; 11:24-40 and 44b-47 chiefly from P¹ in the recension of P². This view is modified in III., pp. 633 and 639f).

4. [(?)Laws concerning uncleanness; uncleanness after childbirth; leprosy.]

The phrase אִישׁ אִישׁ in Lev. 15:2 leads Dillmann to infer that the ancient *toroth* lying at the basis of chs. 12-15 may have been derived from P¹ in the recension of P², or P³, especially in ch. 13f.

5. The blood of beasts; slaughtering of animals to be at the central sanctuary; sacrifices to satyrs, or to any God but Yahweh forbidden; the blood is the life, is sacred, and must not be eaten; the blood of beasts taken in hunting to be poured on the ground and covered; eat-

ing of animals torn of beasts or dying of disease makes unclean till evening.

Lev. 17 (exc. vs. 4–6,7–9,13,15 = P², or were worked over by him).

6. The law of prohibited degrees; different kinds of immorality and the sacrifice of children to Molech forbidden: a *torah* introduced and terminated by a special exhortation.

Lev. 18.

7. A version of the Ten Words and a Code in seven parts.

Lev. 19:1–8,9–18,19f,23–37 (21f, or 20–22 = R.. Traces of P² in vs. 2a,8b,34a,35b).

8. The worship of Molech forbidden; the penalty for cursing parents; prohibition of various forms of impurity; a warning against the impurity of the Canaanites and prohibition of witchcraft.

Lev. 20 (exc. traces of P² in vs. 2,13,27b).

9. Heathen mourning rites and immorality forbidden; directions for "the priest great above his brethren;" a blemish debars from the officiating priesthood.

Lev. 21 (exc. traces of P² in vs. 10,17 and 21–24).

10. The cleanness of priests and their families; offerings must be unblemished; animals for sacrifice must not be killed before the eighth day.

Lev. 22 (exc. P² in vs. 3f,10–13,25).

11. The law of the feast of *mazzoth*, of Pentecost, and of tabernacles.

Lev. 23:9–20 (traces of P² in vs. 11–14), 22,39–43 (P² in v. 39), (vs. 1–8,21,23–38,44 = P²).

12. The penalty of blasphemy and bloodshed; the *lex talionis.*

Lev. 24:15–23 (exc. vs. 16 and 23, and traces in v. 22 = P²); vs. 1–14 also = P².

13. The sabbatical year [and year of jubilee]; idols and *maççebhoth* forbidden.

Lev. 25:18–22, and traces throughout the chapter; 26:1f (25:1–7,8–17,23–55 = P² on a basis of P¹).

14. A paraenetic conclusion to the "Law of Holiness" by the compiler: promises of blessing in case of obedience, and of plagues and curses in case of disobedience; the captivity foretold; the land to lie fallow during the exile and "enjoy her Sabbaths;" repentance in the land of captivity will restore Yahweh's favor; colophon to the code.

Lev. 26:3–46.

15. [(?)The law of the ordeal for jealousy; the water of bitterness mixed with the dust of the sanctuary conveying a curse.]

Num. 5:11–31(?) (a " resemblance " to P¹ in Num. 3:13).

16. [The holy trumpets; fringes, cords and borders to be worn upon the garment; (?)the heave-offering of the first dough.]

Num. 10:9f; 15:38(37)–41 and perhaps vs. 18(17)–21.

The Code of the Priestly Lawbook, P².

Exodus 25—Numbers 36.

1. The pattern shown in the mount; directions to Moses for the construction of the tabernacle and its furniture.

a) A contribution to be made by the people for the purposes of the sanctuary.

Ex. 25:1–9.

b) The pattern of the ark of the covenant and the cherubim; of the table of shew-bread; of the golden candlestick; conclusion of the section.

Ex. 25:10–22,23–30,31–38,39,40 (v. 37 misplaced(?)).

c) Details for the construction of the tabernacle; for the veil and the furniture.

Ex. 26:1–30,31–37.

d) The pattern of the altar; of the fore-court of the tabernacle.

Ex. 27:1–8,9–19 (vs. 20,21 = R from P² elsewhere).

2. Aaron and his sons appointed to the priesthood.

a) The priestly garments; the ephod; the breast-plate; the mantle; the frontlet, tunic, turban and girdle.

Ex. 28:1–5,6–14,15–30,31–35,36–40.

b) [Directions for the investiture of Aaron and his sons; linen breeches.]

Ex. 28:41–43.

3. Directions for the consecration and installation of Aaron and his sons in the priest's office.

Ex. 29:1–35.

4. [An atonement for the altar; an epilogue promising the divine presence in the tent of meeting.]

29:36f,43–46 (vs. 38–42 = R, from P² in Num. 28; in III., p. 636, from Num. 8).

5. [The divine appointment of Bezalel and Oholiab to the workmanship.]

31:1–6 (30:1–10(?),11–16; 31:12–17 = R, from elsewhere in P², including a trace of P¹ in 31:12–17. The rest, viz., 30:17–21,22–28; 31:7–11 = P³).

6. Moses receives the tables of the testimony and descends from Sinai; [his shining face.]

Ex. 31:18a; 32:15a; 34:29–32 (34:33–35 = R).

7. Execution of the directions given to Moses; the cloud fills the sanctuary.

According to the critics Ex. 35–40 is nearly, or quite, all P^3. Of our authorities Dill. alone traces a nucleus of P^2 in 35:1-3,4f,20f; 36:2–6; 40:1f,34–38, and the basis of Num. 9:15–23 and of Num. 7. Well. and Kuen. assign the entire mass to P^3. With regard to Lev. 1–8 there is equal harmony. Well. and Kuen. assign all of chs. 1–7 to P^3 and all but the basis of ch. 8. Dill. admits (III., p. 641) that Lev. 1–7 in its present form and present position cannot belong to P^2 and further admits the working over P^2 has received in ch. 8. The laws of different kinds of offerings in Lev. 1–7 were inserted by P^3, but they contain, beside the fragments of P^1 already noted (5:1-6,21–24a), some truly ancient *toroth* (e. g. 6:2–6), and in general there are no special reasons for denying that chs. 1–3 were derived from P^2. Ch. 4 is a late substitute for P^2's law, now perhaps found in Num. 15:22–31, whereas Lev. 5:14–19 seems to be from P^2 and derived from the position now occupied by the late substitute Num. 5:5–10. The proper position for these fragments Dill. holds to be approximately that now occupied by Num. 7, where the fragment Num. 8:1–4 still remains *in situ*.

a) [A Sabbath ordinance; the free-will offering taken; the work committed to Bezalel and Oholiab.]

Ex. 35:1-3,4f,20f; 36:2–6.

b) [The tabernacle erected and occupied; the oblations of the princes of the tribes; the golden candlestick, its pattern, and the provision for lighting; oil required; the shew-bread; the lamp lighted]; the cloud on the tabernacle as the signal for marching and encamping

Ex. 40:1f,34–38; the basis of Num. 7:1–89 (specifically v. 89); Ex. 25:37; 27:20f; 37:20f; Lev. 24:1–9; Num. 8:1–4; the basis of Num. 9:15–23 (Num. 7 and 9:15–23 in its present form = P^3; the rest = fragments scattered by R).

8. Aaron and his sons consecrated to the priesthood.

Lev. 8*.

9. The inauguration of the ritual; Aaron offers the first sacrifices and blesses the people.

Lev. 9.

10. The sacrilege and death of Nadab and Abihu; [directions to

Aaron, Eleazar and Ithamar]; the priests' dues of the meal offerings to be consumed beside the altar.

Lev. 10:1-5,6-11,12-15 (vs. 8-11 abbreviated by R; vs. 16-20 = R).

11. Fragments of a code of laws concerning offerings, ritual, and ceremonial cleanness, the whole now displaced by Lev. (11) 12-15 (a collection of laws concerning cleanness assigned by all the critics to P³).

a) [The continual burnt offering.]

Ex. 29:38-42.

b) [The law of burnt offerings from the herd, from the flock, of fowls; meal offerings burnt; the same baked; the same of first fruits; peace offerings from the herd; from the flock; from the goats.]

Lev. 1:1-9,10-13,14-17; 2:1-3,4-13,14-16; 3:1-5,6-11,12-17.

c) [The law of sin offering; of trespass offering.]

Num. 15:22-31 (v. 31*); Lev. 5:14-19 (each of these passages is duplicated by P³, the former in Lev. 4, the position formerly occupied by Num. 15:22-31, the latter in Num. 5:5-10; Lev. 5:1 6[7],21-24a[26] = P¹; vs. 7[8]-13,20[24b-26] = R, or P²).

d) [Conclusion of P²'s law of offerings: the meal offerings which must accompany different kinds of burnt offering.]

Num. 15:1-16.

e) [The law of cleanness: beasts that may and may not be eaten; uncleanness from the touch of certain beasts' carcasses; creeping things abominable; colophon.]

Lev. 11:24-40,44b-47 and the basis of the rest of the chapter, Num. 5:1-4 (Lev. 6f,11, except the portions just indicated, and 12-15 are from the hand of P³, who presents herein ancient *toroth* worked over in the place of P²'s law, which in the case of Num. 5:1-4 was displaced by Lev. 12-15).

12. How and when the holy place shall be entered; the ritual of atonement for Aaron and his house; for the sanctuary and people; the goat for Azazel; the day of atonement appointed.

Lev. 16 (abbreviated by R after vs. 2 and 28 to transform it from a general direction for the purification of the sanctuary when accidentally defiled, to a periodical ceremony. From R come also the glosses קדש בגדי הקדש and הם בגדי in vs. 4 and 32).

13. The appointment and ritual of the sacred feasts: passover; *mazzoth;* new-year (ecclesiastical); the day of atonement; tabernacles.

Lev. 23:1-8,21,23-38,44 and traces in vs. 11-14 and 39. (For fragments of P² in chs. 17-22 see under P¹, p. 85).

14. The law of blasphemy on the occasion of cursing in the camp.
Lev. 24:10–14,16,23, and a trace in v. 22.

15. [The sabbatical year; the year of jubilee; the redemption of inheritances; regulations for the conveyance of real estate; usury; the Hebrew must not be enslaved: if sold to a foreigner, he must be redeemed by the next of kin.]
Lev. 25:1–7,8–17,23–31,35–55 = P^2 on a basis of P^1 (vs. 32–34 = P^3).

16. [The law of vows; the redemption of persons dedicated; of cattle; of a house; of a field; the firstling already dedicated; no devoted thing may be redeemed; redemption of the tithe; colophon.]
Lev. 27.

17. Directions for the taking of a census of the people; results of the census; [the order of marching and encampment].
Num. 1.   (Ch. 2 an interpolation by P^3, the material drawn from P^2 and originally standing in Num. 10:13–28.)

18. [The *toledoth* of Aaron and Moses; the Levites assigned to Aaron and his sons as servants of the sanctuary; the census of the Levites.]
Num. 3:1–39 (vs. 32 and 36 worked over, and vs. 24–26,29–31,36 38 taken from ch. 4; vs. 40–51 = P^3).

19. [Directions to number the sons of Kohath; census of the three families of Levi, Kohath, Gershon and Merari.]
Num. 4:1–3,34–48 (vs. 4–33,49 = P^3).

20. [The consecration of the Levites.]
Num. 8:5–10,13b,14,12,13a,15a,20,22.   (Vs. 11,15b–19,21,23–26 = P^3. Num. 5:1–4; 6:22–27, the basis of ch. 7 and 8:1–4 are fragments of P^2 belonging in a different connection and have already been assigned to their original position [according to Dill.].   Num. 5:5–10 = P^3 [corresponding to P^2 in Lev. 5:14–19]; 5:11–31; 6:1–21 = P^3 on a basis of ancient *toroth*.)

21. [An after-passover for the ceremonially unclean.]
A brief notice underlying Num. 9:1–14 (vs. 15–23 = P^2 belonging in a different connection; see v. 7b).

22. Directions concerning the silver trumpets; the journey resumed from Sinai.
Num. 10:1–4,6b,8 (v. 9f = P^1; vs. 5,6a,7 from the hand [P^2 or R] which incorporated v. 9f), 11f (vs. 13–28 = P^3).

23. [Stoning of the Sabbath-breaker.](?)
Num. 15:32–36(?) (this passage perhaps = P^3; the priestly elements of chs. 11–14 are given in the preceding article; 15:1–16,22–30 are

fragments of the displaced law of offerings of P^2; v. 31 = R; vs. 17–21 = P^1).

24. Rank and functions of the priests and Levites; the priests' dues; tithes for the Levites; the tithe of the tithe a heave-offering.

Num. 18 (exc. v. 16 [= R]). (Chs. 16 and 17—mutiny of Korah; plating of the altar with the censers of Korah's company; the plague arrested by Aaron's intercession; budding of Aaron's rod—are treated in the preceding article; 17:6-28 is unanimously assigned to P^2.)

25. Directions for the distribution of the inheritances; boundaries of Canaan; a prince from each tribe appointed to divide the inheritances.

Num. 33:50f,54; 34:1-15 (vs. 13-15*), 16-29 (33:52f,55f = J). (Num. 19:1-33:49 has been treated in the preceding article, with exception of the four legal chapters, 19 and 28-30. These four chapters are unanimously assigned to P^3, with the qualification in Dillmann's case that ch. 19 has a basis of ancient *toroth* like those underlying Lev. 6f; chs. 26f (P^2) and 31 (P^3) are not readily separable from the legislative group at the end of Numbers, but have already been considered in the former article.)

26. Appointment of the cities of the Levites, and the cities of refuge; the law of asylum for the cities of refuge.

Num. 35.

27. Final adjustment of the inheritance of females; the daughters of Zelophehad marry cousins; [colophon].

Num. 36

The Code of the "Prophetic" Hexateuch.*

Deuteronomy.

Deuteronomy spontaneously divides itself into two parts, a) the code, properly so-called, chs. 12-26, and b) the chapters preceding and following this nucleus of legislative material, which serve the purpose of

---

* In speaking of Deuteronomy as "the" code of the "prophetic" portion of the Hexateuch, it must be premised that the expression is not literally applicable. Deuteronomy, according to all the critics, is the work of an author later than either J or E, and in the sense of separate origin may be said to be independent of the "prophetic" authors, but in the matter of literary material "independent" is the last word to use. The work not only occupies the stand-point of J E, but professedly and intentionally reproduces what in some respects has a better claim to the title: "the code of the 'prophetic' Hexateuch," viz., the "Book of the Covenant" (Ex. 20-23. See preceding article), which according to Kuenen occupied in the original document of E the same relative position which Deuteronomy subsequently obtained in the Hexateuch. If we pass over thus the claims of the Book of the Covenant it is merely because D, from his position of literary dependence upon both J

connecting it with the Hexateuch history. As there is practically no disagreement among the critics concerning the former division it will be needless to discuss it in detail. It consists of

a) Laws addressed to the people for their guidance after the occupation of Canaan, concerning: a single place of worship; the blood of beasts shed elsewhere than at the altar; false gods, and enticement to worship them by prophet or fellow-citizens; the idolatrous city to be devoted; heathen mourning rites and the eating of unclean beasts forbidden; tithes for the sanctuary, and hospitality for the Levite; the year of release; compassion for the poor and the enslaved; firstlings; passover, the feast of weeks, and tabernacles; the administration of justice; [idolatry and a blemished sacrifice forbidden;] the priests a court of appeal in the administration of justice; [the king's conduct;] provision for the Levites; heathen practices forbidden; the prophet to be the guide in religious matters; manslaughter and the cities of refuge; removal of the ancient landmark forbidden; the law of testimony and *lex talionis;* military provisions; exemption from military duty; mitigation of the severities of war and siege, except against Canaanites; expiation of untraceable bloodshed; management of domestic affairs; bodies of executed criminals must be promptly buried; various regulations of social life; treatment of mutilated persons and foreigners; cleanness in the camp; various humane regulations; divorce; brief injunctions for justice, humanity and morality in various spheres; the levirate; impure action and fraud forbidden; vengeance must be taken on Amalek; gratitude to God inculcated in the offering of first-fruits; the tithe of the third year for the Levite, stranger, widow, and orphans; a prayer and confession and form of sacred covenant.

Deut. 12-26 (16:21-17:7 perhaps belongs after 12:31 and was misplaced by R^d).

b) The historical introductions and appendices to the code of D (chs. 1-11,27-34). With regard to these introductions and appendices there is also but slight difference of opinion; all the critics are agreed that the more original introduction to the code is chs. 5-11, and all but Well. attribute it to the same hand as chs. 12-26 (Del. also might per-

---

and E for historical and legal material alike, deserves to represent the "prophetic" law in contrast with the priestly. His version of the code, Ex. 20-23, although freely expanded, and in some particulars modified, is yet in the spirit a thoroughly faithful reproduction of what the author regards as the *torah* of Moses, viz., the writings already designated as "prophetic." These statements are in accordance with the unanimous opinions of the critics.

haps be excepted, who considers the basis of chs. 12-26 Mosaic; see (x.)). A second introduction is formed by 1:6-4:40. ·

1. [A few words to designate the place of Moses' declaration of the law in the general history; Israel reminded of the departure from Horeb; of the appointment of officers to assist Moses; of Kadesh-barnea and the sending of the spies; of the murmuring of the people and their presumptuous attack upon the Amorites; of the journey by the way of the Red Sea and peaceful passage through Edom; of the similar treatment of Moab, and of the generation which died in the wilderness; of the capture of the territory of Sihon king of the Amorites, and the battle of Jahaz; of the capture of Bashan from Og, and settlement of Reuben, Gad and half-Manasseh there; of Moses' forewarning of his death, and the direction to give a charge to Joshua; an appeal to the people to obey the law now to be given; a reminder of Baal-peor and Horeb, and forewarning against the corrupt worship of the Canaanites; disobedience will be followed by exile, but sincere repentance in captivity will regain the favor of God, and bring to his remembrance the covenant, as when he brought them out of Egypt.]

Deut. 1:6-4:40* (exc. 2:10-12,20-23; 3:10f,13b,14 = R^d from D; also 1:1f,4f; 4:41-43 = R^d from D; 1:3 = P²).

2. [(Superscription of the code); Moses rehearses the Ten Words of the covenant, and the story of the theophany at Horeb; exhortation to keep the commandment; to love Yahweh; to be faithful to his worship; to observe the law and teach it to the children; the total destruction of the Canaanites and of the instruments of their worship enjoined; faithful observance of the commandment to be pure from Canaanitism will ensure the all-powerful help of Yahweh; exhortation to remember God's dealing and to beware of vain glorying; exhortation to humility in view of the fact that their position as God's chosen people is not due to their own righteousness; the incidents of the golden calf, of Taberah, Massah and Kibroth-hattaawah recalled as examples of their unworthiness; (the story of the renewal of the covenant and the departure from Horeb recalled;) a renewed exhortation to love and obey Yahweh supported by reference to the wonders in Egypt and at the Red Sea, and the death of Dathan and Abiram; a blessing promised for obedience; the blessing and curse to be set before the people on Ebal and Gerizim, as they enter the land.]

Deut. 4:44-11:32 (exc. 4:44-49; 5:5,23; 6:3; 7:22; 9:4,20; 10:19 = R^d; 9:25-10:11 belongs in the introduction and was removed thence by R^d; 11:29-31 was removed by him from D¹'s appendix).

3. [A hortatory conclusion to the code; the blessings in detail which
will follow obedience; the curses in detail which will follow disobedience; colophon to the code.]

Deut. 27:9f; 28:1–68* (27:1–3 = R[d] from D elsewhere [see below];
vs. 5–7a = E; 4,7b,8,11–13,14–26 = R[d]; 4:1–40 and 11:29–31 belong
after ch. 26 and were removed by R[d]).

4. [Direction to write the law upon plastered stones; Moses fore-
warns the people of his death and encourages them under leadership
of Joshua to pursue the conquest; he writes the law and delivers it to
the priests; he makes a final farewell address; an adjuration to all the
assembly to abhor strange gods, and warning against the wrath of Yahweh; a promise that when the curse has been realized true repentance
in exile will bring restoration; the law is brought near, that its observance may be their life; Moses' death and burial.]

Deut. 27:1b–3 (instead of 1a [= R[d]] read ויצו משה את־הזקני
ישראל); 31:1–8,9–13,24–26a,28f; 32:45–47; 28:69–30:20 in part, and
traces in 34:(1b)5f,11f; (28:69–30:20 is an expansion by R[d] of an original address by D[1], of which 30:11–20 and traces in ch. 4 are preserved
intact; 31:14f,23 = E; 16–22 = J; 26b,27 and 30 = R[d]; 32:1–44 = J;
vs. 48–52 = P[2]; ch. 33 = a poem incorporated by E; 34:1a [to נבו],
v. 5 in part, 7a,8f = P[2]; ויראהו....הארץ in v. 1b and v. 4 = J;
v. 10 = E; last four words of v. 1, vs. 2f,7b of uncertain origin).

PART II.

The text of Genesis in the Revised Version, presented in varieties of type to exhibit the Theory of Documentary Sources; with notes explanatory of the phenomena of redaction, and critical marginal references.

ABBREVIATIONS

AND

TYPOGRAPHICAL INDICATIONS.

J. **Judaean prophetic writer, circ. 800 B. C., in this type.**

E. Ephraimite prophetic writer, circ. 750 B. C., in this type.

P. *Author of the Priestly legal-historical work, circ. 450 B. C., in this type.*

J². **Editorial additions to J in this type, or smaller.**

E² and **JE.** Editorial additions to E and to JE in this type, or smaller.

R. *Editorial additions to P and to JEP in this type, or smaller.*

Words supplied enclosed in [   ]. Displaced material between — —. Missing material indicated by [. . . .]. Cf.—compare; Ct. contrast; f. following verse; ff. following verses. (1), (2), (3), etc., refer to Appendix II. Hebrew notes.

PART II.

The First Book of Moses, Commonly Called Genesis.

(P) *In the beginning 'God created the heaven and the earth.* 1
And the earth was 'waste and void ; and darkness was upon the 2
face of the 'deep : and the spirit of God moved upon the face of
the waters. And God said, Let there be light, and there was 3
light. And God saw the light, that it was good, and God 'divided 4
the light from the darkness. And God called the light Day, and 5
the darkness he called Night. And there was evening and there was
morning, one day.

And God said, Let there be a 'firmament in the midst of the 6
waters, and let it divide the waters from the waters. And God 7
made the firmament, and divided the 'waters which were under the
firmament from the waters which were above the firmament : and
it was so. And God called the firmament Heaven. And there 8
was evening and there was morning, a second day.

And God said, Let the 'waters under the heaven be gathered 9
together unto one place, and let the dry land appear : and it was
so. And God called the dry land Earth ; and 'the gathering to- 10
gether of the waters called he Seas : and God saw that it was
good. And God said, Let the earth put forth grass, herb yielding 11
seed, [and] fruit tree bearing fruit 'after its kind, wherein is
the seed thereof, upon the earth : and it was so. And the earth 12

¹Ex. 6: 2f. ²Jer. 4: 23; Is. 34: 11. ³49: 25; Dt. 33: 13. ⁴Job. 26: 10; 38: 19f. ⁵Am.
9: 6; Job 26: 10; 37: 18. ⁶7: 11; 8: 2. ⁷Job 38: 16. ⁸Ex. 7: 19. ⁹vv. 12, 21; 6: 20; 7: 14.

* The formula : " These are the generations of." forms the title to each one of the
ten sections into which the Priestly Law-book is divided, in that portion (Genesis)
which relates to the patriarchal period. This unbroken analogy makes it highly
probable on the documentary theory that the title now found in Gen. ii. 4a originally preceded Gen. i. 1, and was removed by the compiler of P and JE to the end
of the section. The awkward form of the sentence, Gen. i. 1, confirms this idea,
some of the best Hebrew scholars maintaining that the first Hebrew word is properly a construct (" in the beginning of "). The author offers the conjecture that
originally the title read, ii. 4a, " These are the generations of the heavens and the
earth in the beginning of their creation. i. 1, God created," etc. (2)

(97)   7

*brought forth grass, herb yielding seed after its kind, and tree bear-
ing fruit, wherein is the seed thereof, after its kind ; and God saw*

13 *that it was good.   And there was evening and there was morning,
a third day.*

14 *And God said, Let there be* [10]*lights in the firmament of the heaven
to divide the day from the night ; and let them be for signs, and*

15 *for seasons, and for days and years : and let them be for lights in
the firmament of the heaven to give light upon the earth : and it*

16 *was so.   And God made the two great lights ; the greater light to
rule the day, and the lesser light to rule the night :* [he made] *the*

17 *stars also.   And God set them in the firmament of the heaven to*

18 *give light upon the earth, and to* [11]*rule over the day and over the
night, and to divide the light from the darkness ; and God saw*

19 *that it was good.   And there was evening and there was morning,
a fourth day.*

20 *And God said, Let the waters bring forth abundantly the moving
creature that hath life, and let fowl fly above the earth in the open*

21 *firmament of heaven.   And God created the great sea-monsters,
and every living creature that moveth, which the waters brought
forth abundantly, after their kinds, and every winged fowl after*

22 *its kind : and God saw that it was good.   And God blessed them,
saying, Be fruitful, and multiply, and fill the waters in the seas,*

23 *and let fowl multiply in the earth. · And there was evening and
there was morning, a fifth day.*

24 *And God said, Let the earth bring forth the living creature
after its kind, cattle, and creeping things, and beast of the earth*

25 *after its kind : and it was so.   And God made the beast of the
earth after its kind, and the cattle after their kind, and every thing
that creepeth upon the ground after its kind : and God saw that it*

26 *was good.   And God said, Let us make man* [12]*in our own image,
after our likeness : and let them have dominion over the fish of
the sea, and over the fowl of the air, and over the cattle, and over
all* the earth, and over every creeping thing that creepeth upon*

27 *the earth.* [13]*And God created man in his own image, in the image*

[10]Jud. 5:20; Job 38:7.   [11]Jer. 31:35.   [12]5:3; 9:6.   [13]5:1-3; Dt. 4:32.

*Read with Syr. instead of "all," *every beast of,* as the context demands. "Beast
of the earth" means wild beast in distinction from "cattle," i. e. domestic animals. (3)

of God created he him ; *male and female created he them.* [*And* 28
*God blessed them : and God said unto them, Be fruitful, and
multiply, and replenish the earth, and subdue it ; and have dominion over the fish of the sea, and over the fowl of the air, and over
every living thing that moveth upon the earth. And God said,* 29
*Behold, I have given you every herb yielding seed, which is upon
the face of all the earth, and every tree, in the which is the fruit
of a tree yielding seed*]*to you it shall be for meat : and to every* 30
*beast of the earth, and to every fowl of the air, and to every thing
that creepeth upon the earth, wherein there is life,* [*I have given*]
every *green herb for meat : and it was so. And God saw every* 31
*thing that he had made, and, behold, it was very good. And there
was evening and there was morning, the sixth day.*

And the heaven and the earth were finished, and all the host of 2
them. And on the seventh day God finished his work which he 2
had made ; * *[1]and he rested on the seventh day from all his work
which he had made. And God blessed the seventh day, and hal-* 3
*lowed it : because that in it he rested from all his work which God
had created and made.*

—[2]*These are the generations of the heaven and of the earth when* 4
(J) they were created.—† [. . . .] **In the day that Yahweh**‡

[14] 6:19; ct. 7:2.   [15] Cf. 9:2ff; ct. 3.18.   [16] 6:11.   [1] Ex. 31:17.   [2] 5:1; 6:9; 10:1; 11:10, 27, etc.

* From this statement, which seems not quite to agree with the representation of the context in its present form ; from the seven-fold repetition of the formula of approval, verses 4, 10, 12, 18, 21, 25, 31, and a few other phenomena, Wellhausen and some other important authorities infer that Gen. i. 1–ii. 4a is not exactly in its original shape, but has been adapted by the Priestly Writer to serve as the basis for his first legal enactment, ii. 3. The original, according to this theory, may have presented the creation of man as the culminating work of the seventh day. See Bud. I. pp. 470ff., and my article in *Hebraica*, April, 1891.

† Insert before i. 1. See note *in loc.*

‡ In the matter of the transliteration of the Hebrew consonants Y (J) H W (V) H, which is all that the original text affords, the present writer follows the plan of the American revisers, who give the personal name of Israel's God. Instead, however, of using the intrusive vowels e o a, derived from the word *'edonay*,—" Lord," superstitiously substituted by the rabbis for the sacred name, and actually retained by the English committee in preference to the original, the present work follows the example of the majority of modern critical works in the interest of self-consistency, the verdict of scholarship being in favor of short a and e as the original vowels used when the name of Israel's God was pronounced. The vowel sounds were similar to those occurring in the name of the city Calneh, Gen. x. 10.

5 'God* 'made earth and heaven. And no plant of the field was yet in the earth, and no herb of the field had yet sprung up: for Yahweh God had not caused it to rain upon the earth, and there was not a man to

6 till the ground; but there went up a mist from the earth, and watered the whole face of the ground.

7 And Yahweh God 'formed man of the dust of the ground, 'and breathed into his nostrils the breath of

8 life; and man became a living soul. And Yahweh God planted a 'garden eastward, in Eden; and there

9 he put the man whom he had formed. And out of the ground made Yahweh God to grow every tree that is pleasant to the sight, and good for food; the tree of life also† in the midst of the garden,—and the tree

10 of the knowledge of good and evil.—And a river went out of Eden to water the garden; and from thence it was parted, and

11 became four heads. The name of the first is Pishon; that is it which compasseth the whole land of ᵇHavilah, where there is

12 gold; and the gold of that land is good: there is ᵉbdellium and

13 onyx stone. And the name of the second river is Gihon: the

14 the same is it that compasseth the whole land of ᵗᵒCush. And the name of the third river is Hiddekel: that is it which goeth

15 in front of Assyria. And the fourth river is Euphrates. And Yahweh God took the man, and put him into the garden of Eden to

16 dress it and to keep it.‡ And Yahweh God commanded the

ᵃ4:26. ᵇCt. v. 4a and i:i. ᵉCt. i:24. ᵉ7:22. ᵗ13:10. ᵉ10:7, 29; 25:18, etc. ᵉNum. 11:7. ¹ᵒ10:6ff.

*The insertion of this word after Yahweh here and throughout the second and third chapter is regarded as due to harmonistic redaction. A Hebrew had no more need to write God after Yahweh than a Greek to write it after Zeus, or a Roman after Jupiter. Were it not for the purpose of indicating that the *Elohim*, "God" of ch. I. and the Yahweh of ch. II. were identical, or for some other special reason, "Yahweh God" would doubtless have seemed as meaningless to the Hebrew reader as "Zeus God" to the Greek. Inasmuch, however, as the interpolation may have preceded the union of P and JE, and even that of J and E, it is indicated in the type of J².

†The clause, "the tree of life also," is perhaps due to very early supplementary redaction. In this case the last clause of the verse and this should exchange places. See note to iii. 22.

‡Verses 10-15 are supposed to be due to very early supplementary redaction. A considerable amount of material of this kind is found in the J document, (e. g. iv. 2-16a, xii. 10-20, xiii. 14-17, xviii. 22-33) where the incongruity of the material with its context seems to indicate diversity of authorship, at the same time that the ma-

man, saying, Of every tree of the garden thou mayest
freely eat: but of the tree of the knowledge of good and 17
evil,* thou shalt not eat of it: for in the day that thou
eatest thereof thou shalt surely die.

And Yahweh God said, It is not good that the man 18
should be alone; I will make him an help meet for
him. And out of the ground Yahweh God ¹¹formed 19
every beast of the field, and every fowl of the air; and
brought them unto the man to see what he would call
them: and whatsoever the man called every living
creature, that was the name thereof. And the man 20
gave names to all the cattle, and to the fowl of the
air, and to every beast of the field; but for man there
was not found an help meet for him. And Yahweh 21
God caused a ¹²deep sleep to fall upon the man, and he
slept; and he took one of his ribs, and closed up the
flesh instead thereof: and the rib, which Yahweh God 22
had taken from the man, made he a woman, and

terial is obviously written to fit the place and cannot stand alone. (So e. g. iv. 1–16a).
The material is therefore redactional rather than primitive. But on the other hand,
these passages have no harmonistic purpose and betray no knowledge of E or P.
More significant still, their *formal* characteristics (style and language) are identical with that of their more primitive context. The agreement is in fact remarkable.
Only in their religious and doctrinal ideas there is generally a clear advance upon
the usual standpoint of J¹, and as already said, they differ in context from the incorporating material. One of the difficult problems of criticism is to account for
these phenomena. The passages may be accounted for as interpolations due to didactic or supplementary interest (J²), or the incongruities of material may be accounted for as due to the author of our actual J document inserting remarks and
comments of his own into the material which he takes from a still older—doubtless
poetic—source, which he reduces to a continuous prose narrative and thus colors
with his own style and language. On this theory (Dillman's) J himself is really a
J². Other phenomena seem to indicate that these additions date from a period after
the original ballads and traditions had been reduced to something like the form of
J, and it is undeniable that many of a similar character (cf. xxxii. 10–13, referring
apparently both to J and E passages, and Ex. xxxii. 13—Dill—J—referring to Gen.
xxii. 16—Dill—R) are subsequent to the union of J and E. In the present volume
a smaller type appropriate to secondary elements of the J document has been
adopted, but the reader is left to form his own opinion as to whether this secondary material is secondary to the history as a whole or only secondary as compared
with the *sources* of J. The most important J² section will be found in Appendix I.,
separated for special study.

¹¹1 : 24. ¹²15 : 12.

*Read " which is in the midst of the garden," cf. iii. 3.

23 brought her to the man. And the man said, This is
now [13]bone of my bones, and flesh of my flesh: she shall
be called Woman, because she was taken out of man.
24 [14]Therefore shall a man leave his father and his
mother, and shall cleave unto his wife: and they
25 shall be one flesh.* And they were both [15]naked, the
man and his wife, and were not ashamed.

3   Now the serpent was more subtil than any beast of
the field which Yahweh God had made. And he said
unto the woman, Yea, hath God† said, Ye shall not
2 eat of any tree of the garden? And the woman said
unto the serpent, Of the fruit of the trees of the gar-
3 den we may eat: but of the fruit of the tree which is
in the midst of the garden, God hath said, Ye shall
not eat of it, neither shall ye touch it, lest ye die.
4 And the serpent said unto the woman, Ye shall not
5 surely die: for God doth know that [1]in the day ye eat
thereof, then your eyes shall be opened, and ye shall
6 be [2]as God, knowing good and evil. And when the woman saw that the tree was good for food, and that it
was a delight to the eyes, and that the tree was to be
desired to make one wise, she took of the fruit thereof, and did eat; and she gave also unto her husband
7 with her, and he did eat. And the eyes of them both
were opened, and they knew that they were naked;
and they sewed fig leaves together, and made them-

[13]29:14; 37:27. [14]10:9; 19:22. [15]3:7. [1]2:4, 17. [2]v. 22; Dt. 1:39.

*It is the practice of this supposed author, J, to introduce frequent ætiological
narratives, accounting for various phenomena such as the pains of childbirth, iii. 16,
the custom among Israelites of abstaining from a certain sinew, xxxii. 32, frequent
etymologies, etc. The analogy of xxxii. 32 and other passages suggests therefore
that in the verbs of v. 24 the Hebrew imperfect should be rendered in English by
the present, not the future.

†God (Heb. *Elohim*) is used by J in place of Yahweh where a special reason exists
for avoiding the personal name, as when a heathen is speaking, Jud. i. 7; or when
one who is personating the rôle of a heathen speaks, Gen. xliii. 29, or is addressed,
xliv. 16; or if the word is used appellatively as in Ex. ix. 28, " voices of God," i. e.
thunders; or if there is a purpose to conceal the identity of the divine visitant,
Gen. xxxii. 27-30. Here the serpent is either not supposed to know the personal
name of God, or else it is deemed unsuitable to put the divine Name in the mouth
of a beast.

selves aprons. And they heard 'the voice* of Yahweh 8
God walking in the garden 'in the cool of the day: and
the man and his wife hid themselves 'from the presence of Yahweh God amongst the trees of the garden.
And Yahweh God called unto the man, and said unto 9
him, Where art thou? And he said, I heard thy voice 10
in the garden, and I was afraid, because I was naked:
and I hid myself. And he said, Who told thee that 11
thou wast naked? Hast thou eaten of the tree, whereof I commanded thee that thou shouldest not eat?
And the man said, The woman whom thou gavest to be 12
with me, she gave me of the tree, and I did eat. And 13
Yahweh God said unto the woman, 'What is this thou
hast done? And the woman said, The serpent beguiled
me, and I did eat. And Yahweh God said unto the ser- 14
pent, Because thou hast done this, 'cursed art thou
above all cattle, and above every beast of the field;
upon thy belly shalt thou go, and °dust shalt thou eat
all the days of thy life; and I will put enmity between 15
thee and the woman, and between thy seed and her
seed: it shall bruise thy head, and thou shalt bruise
'his heel. Unto the woman he said, I will greatly mul- 16
tiply thy sorrow and thy conception; in sorrow thou
shalt bring forth children; ¹⁰and thy desire shall be
to thy husband, and he shall rule over thee. And 17
unto Adam† he said, Because thou hast hearkened unto the voice of thy wife, and hast eaten of the tree,
of which I commanded thee, saying, Thou shalt not
eat of it: "cursed is the ground for thy sake: in toil
shalt thou eat of it all the days of thy life; thorns 18
also and thistles shall it bring forth to thee; and 19

³II. Sam. 5:24; I. Kings 14:6. ⁴18:1; 24:63. ⁵4:16. ⁶4:10; 12:8. ⁷4:11; 5:29;
9:25. ⁸Mic. 7:17; Is. 65:25. ⁹49:17. ¹⁰30:15. Ct. 4:7. ¹¹5:29.

* The marginal rendering (R. V.) "sound" is alone correct.

†The Hebrew permits either translation, "Adam" or "the man." Translators
with iv. 25 and v. 2 in view have supposed a proper name, but if the work of J
is considered by itself it will be seen that "the man" is anonymous, or if he has a
name it is not Adam—*homo*, but Ish=*vir*. Cf. ii. 23.

[12]thou shalt eat the herb of the field; in the sweat of thy face shalt thou eat bread, till thou return unto the ground; for out of it wast thou taken: for dust 20 thou art, and unto dust shalt thou return.—And the man called his wife's name Eve, because she was the 21 mother of all living.—And Yahweh God made for Adam and for his wife coats of skins, and clothed them.

22   And Yahweh God said, Behold, the man is become [13]as one of us, to know good and evil; and now, [14]lest he put forth his hand, and take also of the tree of life, and eat, and live for ever: 23 —therefore Yahweh God sent him forth from the garden of Eden, to till the ground from whence he was 24 taken.—   So he drove out the man; and he placed at the east of the garden of Eden the [15]Cherubim, and the flame of [16]a sword which turned every way, to keep the way of the tree of life.*

4   And the man [1]knew Eve his wife; and she conceived, and bare Cain, and said, I have gotten a man with [the 2 help of] Yahweh.   And again she bare his brother Abel.

[12]Cf. 2:9, 16. Ct. 1:29.   [13]II. Sam. 14:17, 20.   [14]11:6f.   [15]Ez. 28:14ff; Ps. 18:11. [16]Ez. 10:1-22.   [1]Vv. 17, 25; 19:5, 8; 24:16, etc.

* Verse 20 is misplaced, since it not only comes in very *malàpropos*, but can have absolutely no significance until after iv. 1.   Let the order be iii. 19, 23, 21 (vi. 3?), iv. 1, iii. 20.—Verses 23 and 24 each begin in Hebrew with the simple conjunction "and" which makes the duplication more apparent.   The conflicting reasons for the expulsion (vs. 23, that the man may become the slave of the soil according to vv. 17-19 instead of living on the spontaneously produced fruits of the garden; vs. 24, that the usurpation of the divine prerogative of wisdom may not be increased by the further acquisition of immortality) is supposed by Budde, I. (chapters I. and II.) to be due to the introduction of the tree of life, which seems to him to be the cause of various confusions and to give to the otherwise solemn pronouncing of sentence an appearance of mere action in self-defense, or jealousy.   The threat seems unfulfilled and perhaps impossible of fulfilment.   Budde proposes to remedy all this by regarding the verses 22 and 24 and the clause "the tree of life also," ii. 9, which produces ambiguity in the allusions of iii. 1ff, as due to supplementation from Assyro-Babylonian legend, perhaps from the same period as the interpolation ii. 10-15 and the great Flood-interpolation.   The verse vi. 3, in rather loose connection with its present context, he thinks was removed from between iii. 21 and 23, supplying thus the singular absence of the threatened penalty of ii. 17.   In the latter he would read, "tree which is in the midst of the garden," in accordance with iii. 3, instead of "tree of the knowledge of good and evil."   He obtains thus a perfectly smooth connection, but the conjecture is a bold one and is only provisionally adopted. "Adam," vs. 21, should of course be "the man."   Cf. note on vs. 17.

And [2]Abel was a keeper of sheep, but* Cain was [3]a tiller of
the ground. And in process of time it came to pass, that 3
Cain brought of the fruit of the ground an offering unto Yahweh.
And Abel, he also brought of the firstlings of his flock and of the 4
fat thereof. And Yahweh had respect unto Abel and to his offering: but unto Cain and to his offering he had not respect. And 5
Cain was very wroth, and his countenance fell. And Yahweh said 6
unto Cain, Why art thou wroth? and why is thy countenance
fallen? If thou doest well, [4]shalt thou not be accepted? and if 7
thou doest not well, sin coucheth at the door: [5]and unto thee shall
be his desire, and thou shalt rule over him. And Cain told† Abel 8
his brother [. . .]. And it came to pass, when they were in the
field, that Cain rose up against Abel his brother, and slew him.
And Yahweh said unto Cain, Where is Abel thy brother? And he 9
said, I know not: am I my brother's keeper? And he said, [6]What 10
hast thou done? the voice of thy brother's blood [7]crieth unto me
from the ground. And now cursed art thou from the ground, 11
which hath [8]opened her mouth to receive thy brother's blood from
thy hand; when thou tillest the ground, it shall not henceforth 12
yield unto thee her strength, [9]a fugitive and a wanderer shalt
thou be in the earth. And Cain said unto Yahweh, My punish- 13
ment is greater than I can bear. Behold, thou hast [10]driven me 14
out this day from the face of the ground; [11]and from thy face shall
I be hid; and I shall be a fugitive and a wanderer in the earth;
and it shall come to pass, that whosoever findeth me shall slay me.
And Yahweh said unto him, Therefore whosoever slayeth Cain, 15
[12]vengeance shall be taken on him sevenfold. And Yahweh appointed a sign for Cain, lest any finding him should smite him.

[13]And Cain went out from the presence of Yahweh,‡ and 16
dwelt in the land of Nod, on the east of Eden. And 17
Cain knew his wife; and she conceived, and bare
Enoch: and he builded a city, and called the name of
the city, after the name of his son,‖ Enoch. And unto 18
Enoch was born Irad: and Irad begat Mehujael: and

[2]Ct. v. 20. [3]3:23; v. 12. [4]32:20. [5]Ct. 3:16. [6]3:13; 12:8, etc. [7]18:20f; 19:13;
Ex. 3:9. [8]Num. 16:30. [9]V. 16. Ct. v. 17. [10]3:24. [11]3:8. [12]Ct. v. 24. [13]3:8.

* Heb. "and."   † Heb. "said to."

‡ The passage, iv. 2–16a, is regarded as the work of early supplementation. In
verses 7, 15, and elsewhere, the obvious connection with J in chap. iii. is fully
recognized, but held to indicate not identity but diversity of authorship, the author
of iv. 7, 15, misconceiving the older passages, iii. 16; iv. 24.

‖ Read perhaps with Budde, "his own name." Cf. the successive steps of civiliza-
tion II. 19; III. 7, 21; iv. 26b, 17, 20–22.

Mehujael begat Methushael; and Methushael begat
19 Lamech. "And Lamech took unto him two wives: the
name of the one was Adah, and the name of the other
20 Zillah. And Adah bare Jabal: "he was the father of
21 such as dwell in tents and [have] cattle. And his
brother's name was Jubal: he was the father of all
22 such as handle the "harp and pipe. And Zillah, "she
also bare Tubal-cain, the forger* of every cutting instrument of brass and iron: "and the sister of Tubal-
23 cain was Naamah. And Lamech said unto his wives:

Adah and Zillah, hear my voice;
Ye wives of Lamech, hearken unto my speech :
For I have slain a man for wounding me,
And a young man for bruising me :†
24   "If Cain shall be avenged sevenfold.
Truly Lamech seventy and sevenfold. [. . .]
25   "And Adam knew his wife again; and she bare a son, and called
his name Seth: For, [said she,] "God hath appointed me another
26 seed instead of Abel; for Cain slew him. And to Seth, to him
also there was born a son; and he called his name Enosh: then
"began men to "call upon the name of Yahweh.‡   [. . .]

---

[14]10:25. [15]10:21; 11:29; 19:37f. Ct. v. 2. [16]31:27. [17]V. 26; 10:21; 19:38; 22:20, 24.
[18]36:22. [19]Ct. v. 15 and 5:31. [20]Ct. vv. 1, 17. [21]V. 26. Ct. v. 1. [22]10:8. Ct. vv. 1-5.
[23]12:7, 8; 13:4; 21:33; 26:25, etc.

*The text is certainly corrupt. A literal translation would be, "the forger of
every artificer," etc. Tubal (cf. Tubal x. 2=Tibareni, a tribe noted for metallurgy)
should probably be deprived of the suffix "cain," of doubtful meaning and wanting
in LXX. Budde would read after "Tubal"—"and Lamech became an artificer of
brass and iron." He rejects the last clause of the verse. (4)

†Or, "I will slay a man for a wound [done] to me, and a child for a bruise [done]
to me." So Kautzsch and Socin, Budde, Wellhausen, Dillmann and others. The
life of the "child" ("young man" is scarcely true to the Hebrew) and of the "man"
is the penalty Lamech proposes to exact by means of his superior weapons for a
greater or less injury inflicted on himself. He multiplies thus the powers of his
ancestor Cain eleven-fold.

‡Read with LXX. "He began (i. e. was the first) to call," etc. Cf. vs. 20 and x. 8.
With iv. 25 begins the section of the J document known to critics as the Flood-
interpolation, and supposed to be due to supplementation of the earlier narrative
from Assyro-Chaldæan sources. The Assyrian Creation and Deluge legends were
brought to light by Geo. Smith (Chald. Acc. of Genesis, London, 1876). The dominant critical theory regards this material as having been grafted upon the older
Hebrew tradition by means of a new genealogy starting from Adam and containing
ten names in correspondence with the Assyro-Babylonian story. The only changes

(P) [1]*This is the book of the generations of Adam.* [2]*In the day* **5**
that God created man, in the likeness of God made he him ; [3]*male* **2**
*and female created he them ; and blessed them, and called their
name Adam, in the day when they were created.   And Adam* **3**
lived an hundred and thirty years, and begat [a son] in [4]*his own
likeness, after his image ; and called his name* [5]*Seth : and the* **4**
*days of Adam after he begat Seth were eight hundred years : and
he begat sons and daughters.   And all the days that Adam lived* **5**
were nine hundred and thirty years : and he died.

And Seth lived an hundred and five years, and [6]*begat Enosh :* **6**
and Seth lived after he begat Enosh eight hundred and seven **7**
years, and begat sons and daughters : and all the days of Seth **8**
were nine hundred and twelve years : and he died.

And Enosh lived ninety years, and begat [7]*Kenan ; and Enosh* **9–10**
*lived after he begat Kenan eight hundred and fifteen years, and
begat sons and daughters : and all the days of Enosh were nine* **11**
hundred and five years : and he died.

[8]*And Kenan lived seventy years, and begat Mahalalel :* **12**
and Kenan lived after he begat Mahalalel eight hundred and **13**
forty years, and begat sons and daughters : and all the days of **14**
Kenan were nine hundred and ten years : and he died.

And Mahalalel lived sixty and five years, and begat Jared : **15**
and Mahalalel lived after he begat Jared eight hundred and **16**
thirty years, and begat sons and daughters : and all the days of **17**
Mahalalel were eight hundred ninety and five years : and he died.

And Jared lived an hundred sixty and two years, and begat **18**
Enoch : and Jared lived after he begat Enoch eight hundred **19**
years, and begat sons and daughters : and all the days of Jared **20**
were nine hundred sixty and two years : and he died.

And Enoch lived sixty and five years, and begat Methuselah : **21**

[1]2:4; 6:9, etc. [2]1:26. [3]1:27. Ct. 2:18ff. [4]V. 1; 1:26. [5]4:25. Ct. 4:1ff. [6]4:26.
[7]4:1. [8]Ct. 4:17–23.

required for the insertion were the borrowing of Noah's name (originally, according to Gen. ix. 20ff, an agricultural hero, discoverer of the vine and ancestor of the
peoples of Palestine) for the new rôle of flood-hero and world-ancestor, and insertion of two new links in the genealogy of verses 17, 18. The other names of J's
genealogy may be regarded as having been altered at the same time by the interpolator to the form they now present in ch. v., or this alteration may be due to P.
See Appendix I.

22 *and Enoch [9]walked with God after he begat Methuselah three*
23 *hundred years, and begat sons and daughters : and all the days*
24 *of Enoch were three hundred sixty and five years : and Enoch*
   *walked with God : [10]and he was not ; for God took him.**
25   *And Methuselah lived an hundred eighty and seven years, and*
26 *begat Lamech : and Methuselah lived after he begat Lamech*
   seven hundred eighty and two years, and begat sons and daughters :
27 *and all the days of Methuselah were nine hundred sixty and nine*
   years : and he died.
28   *And Lamech lived an hundred eighty and two years, and begat*
29 (J) [. . .] a son : and he called his name Noah, saying,
   [11]"This same shall comfort us for our work and for
   the toil of our hands, because of [12]the ground which
30 (P) Yahweh hath cursed.† *And Lamech lived after he begat*
   Noah five hundred ninety and five years, and begat sons and
31 *daughters : and all the days of Lamech were seven hundred*
   seventy and seven years : and he died.
32   *And Noah was five hundred years old : and Noah begat Shem,*
   Ham, and Japheth.

[9]6 : 9, Ct. 24 : 40. [10]37 : 30 ; 42 : 13, 36. [11]9 : 20. [12]3 : 17.

*Budde thinks the divergences from the regular formula of P in verses 22*a* and 24 to rest upon data afforded by the genealogy of the Flood interpolator. He also gives reasons for preferring the numerical readings of the Samaritan text in this chapter, in this opinion being supported by the best authorities. The numbers according to the Sam. are as follows ·

	Year of first son.	Years of further life.	Years at death.	Year of death, A. M.
Adam	130	800	930	930
Seth	105	807	912	1042
Enosh	90	815	905	1140
Kenan	70	840	910	1235
Mahalalel	65	830	895	1290
Jared	'62	785	847	1307
Enoch	65	300	365	887
Methuselah	67	653	720	1307
Lamech	53	600	653	1307
Noah	500	450	950	1657

The year 1307 A. M., in which all the latter half of the patriarchs perish except Enoch and Noah, is the year of the Flood.

† From the critical point of view vs. 29 is a fragment of J's genealogy which originally introduced ix. 20–27 where the fulfilment of the prediction is found. On this basis translate literally "from the ground." It is the same ground cursed by Yahweh iii. 17ff, which is now to produce the cheering and comforting vine. Cf. Prov. xxxi. 6f Jer. xvi. 7 ; Ps. cxiv. 15, etc.

(J) And it came to pass, when men began to multiply 6 on the face of the ground, and daughters were born unto them, that ¹the sons of God saw the daughters 2 of men that they were fair; and they took them wives of all that they chose.—And Yahweh said, ²My 3 spirit shall not strive with man for ever, for that he also is flesh: yet shall his days be ³an hundred and twenty years.—The Nephilim were in the earth in those 4 days, and also after that, when the sons of God ⁴came in unto the ⁵daughters of men, and they bare children to them: the same were the ⁶mighty men which were of old, the ⁷men of renown.* [. . .] And Yahweh saw 5 that the wickedness of man was great in the earth, and that ⁸every imagination of the thoughts of his heart was only evil continually. And it ⁹repented Yahweh that he had made man on the 6 earth, and it ¹⁰grieved him at his heart. And Yahweh said, I will 7 ¹¹destroy man whom I have created from the face of the ground; both man, and beast, and creeping thing, and fowl of the air;† for it repenteth me that I have made them. But Noah ¹²found grace in the eyes of 8 Yahweh. [. . .]

> (P) ¹³*These are the generations of Noah. Noah was a right-* 9 *eous man,* [*and*] *perfect in his generations: Noah* ¹⁴*walked with God. And Noah begat three sons, Shem, Ham, and Japheth.* 10 *And the earth was corrupt before God, and the earth was filled* 11 *with violence. And God saw the earth, and, behold, it was cor-* 12 *rupt; for* ¹⁵*all flesh had corrupted his way upon the earth.*

And God said unto Noah, The end of all flesh is come before 13 *me; for the earth is filled with violence through them; and, be-* *hold, I will destroy them with the earth. Make thee an ark of* 14 *gopher wood: rooms shalt thou make in the ark, and shalt pitch* *it within and without with pitch. And this is how thou shalt* 15 *make it: the length of the ark three hundred cubits, the breadth*

¹3:22; Job 1:6; 2:1. ²2:7. ³Dt. 34:7. ⁴16:2; 30:3; 38:8. ⁵11:5. ⁶10:8f. ⁷Num. 16:2. ⁸8:21. ⁹Ex. 32:12, 14. Ct. Num. 23:19. ¹⁰34:7. ¹¹7:23. Ct. v. 13. ¹²18:3; 19:18; 30:27; 32:5; 33:8, 10, 15, etc. ¹³2:4; 5:1, etc. ¹⁴5:22. ¹⁵Vv. 13, 17, 19, etc.

* In verse 3 translate as in Part III. See Rev. Ver. margin. The verse is perhaps taken from after iii. 19 or 21. See note *in loc.* In verse 4 I have deviated from previous analyses. See *Hebraica*, April, 1891. (5)

† The words in small type, vs. 7, are attributed on linguistic grounds to late supplementary redaction.

16 *of it fifty cubits, and the height of it thirty cubits.   A light shalt
thou make to the ark, and to a cubit shalt thou finish it upward ;
and the [16]door of the ark shalt thou set in the side thereof ; with*
17 *lower, second, and third stories shalt thou make it.   And I, behold, I do bring the flood of waters upon the earth, to [17]destroy all
flesh, wherein is the breath of life, from under the heaven ; every*
18 *thing that is in the earth shall die.   But I will [18]establish my covenant with thee ; and thou shalt come into the ark, [19]thou, and thy*
19 *sons, and thy wife, and thy sons' wives with thee.   And of every
living thing of all flesh, [20]two of every sort shalt thou bring into
the ark, to keep them alive with thee; they shall be male and female.*
20 [21]*Of the fowl after their kind, and of the cattle after their kind,
of every creeping thing of the ground after its kind, two of every*
21 *sort shall come unto thee, to keep them alive.   And take thou unto
thee of all food that is eaten, and gather it to thee : and it shall be*
22 *for food for thee, and for them.   [22]Thus did Noah; according to
all that God commanded him, so did he.*

7   (J) And Yahweh said unto Noah, Come thou and all thy house into
the ark ; for thee have I seen righteous before me in this genera-
2 tion. Of every [1]clean beast thou shalt take to thee seven and
seven, [2]the male and his female; and of the beasts that are not
3 clean two, the male and his female; of the fowl also of the air,
seven and seven, male and female:* to keep seed alive upon the face
4 of all the earth. For yet seven days, and [3]I will cause it to rain
upon the earth forty days and forty nights; and every living
thing that I have made will I [4]destroy from off the face of the
5 ground. And Noah did according unto all that Yahweh commanded him.

6   (P) [5]*And Noah was six hundred years old when the flood of*
7 (J) *waters was upon the earth.*   And Noah went in, and his sons,
and his wife, and his sons' wives with him, into the ark, because of
8 the waters of the flood. Of clean beasts, and of beasts that are not
9 clean, and of fowls, and of every thing that creepeth upon the ground, there

[16]Ct. 8:13.   [17]7:15. Ct. 7:2.   [18]9:8ff.   [19]7:7; 8:15f. Ct. 7:1.   [20]7:15f. Ct. 7:2.
[21]1:21.   [22]7:5, 9, 16; Ex. 7:6, 20, etc.   [1]Ct. 6:19f.   [2]Ct. 6:19.   [3]Vv. 10, 12, 23; 8:6.
Ct. vv. 11, 24; 8:3-5.   [4]6:7; v. 23.   [5]12:4; 17:1, etc.

*The expression "the male and his female" of vs. 2 is by no means the same as
"male and female" vv. 3 and 9. The former means literally "the man and his
wife" (German *Maennchen und Weibchen*). The latter is the equivalent of the
English "male and female," but occurs exclusively in passages assigned to P and
the later literature. Hence the assignment of the clause in vv. 3 and 9 to R.

went in two and two unto Noah into the ark, male and female,* as God† 10
commanded Noah. And it came to pass after the *seven days, that
(P) the waters of the flood were upon the earth. *In the six* 11
hundredth year of Noah's life, in the second month, on the seven-
teenth day of the month,‡ on 'the same day were all "the fountains of
the great deep broken up, and the windows of heaven were opened.
(J) *And the rain was upon the earth forty days and forty nights. 12
(P) *In the* [10]*selfsame day entered* [11]*Noah, and Shem, and Ham, and* 13
Japheth, the sons of Noah, and Noah's wife, and the three wives
of his sons with them, into the ark ; they, and [12]*every beast after* 14
its kind, and all the cattle after their kind, and every creeping thing
that creepeth upon the earth after its kind, and every fowl after
its kind, every bird of every sort. And they went in unto Noah 15
into the ark, [13]*two and two of all flesh wherein is the breath of life.*
And they that went in, went in male and female of all flesh, as 16
(J) (P) *God commanded him:*—and Yahweh shut him in.‖—*And* 17
(J) *the flood was forty days§ upon the earth ;* and the waters increased, and bare up the ark, and it was lift up above the earth.
(P) *And the waters prevailed, and increased greatly upon the earth ;* 18
and the ark went upon the face of the waters. And the waters 19
prevailed exceedingly upon the earth ; and all the high mountains
that were under the whole heaven were covered. [14]*Fifteen cubits* 20
upward did the waters prevail ; and the mountains were covered.
And all flesh died that moved upon the earth, both fowl, and cat- 21
tle, and beast, and every creeping thing that creepeth upon the
(J) *earth, and every man :*—all in whose nostrils was the breath 22
of the spirit of life, of all that was in the dry land, died.—And every 23

[6]V. 4. [7]V. 13; 17:23, 26; Ex. 12:41; 19:1. [8]1:2, 6f. [9]V. 4. [10]V. 11, etc. [11]6:18;
vv. 7, 8, 15f. Ct. 7:1. [12]6:20; 1:21. [13]6:17. [14]Cf. 6:15; 8:4.

* Harmonistic redaction. Cf. the " two of each " in vv. 9 and 15 with " sevens " of
vs. 2, and see note to vs. 3.

† Sam. Targ. Vulg. (the latter resting no doubt on LXX. MSS.) have " Yahweh."—
After vs. 9 insert the clause, " and Yahweh shut him in," vs. 16.

‡ I. e. 40 days and 7 days from the first day of the 600th year. Cf. iii. 13 and vii. 4.
P is here apparently dependent on J².

‖ Necessarily removed by the redactor from after vs. 9.

§ Harmonistic redaction.

living thing was destroyed* which was upon the face of the
ground, both man, and cattle, and creeping thing, and fowl of the heaven; and
they were destroyed from the earth: and Noah only was left, and they
24 (P) that were with him in the ark. *And the waters prevailed
upon the earth an hundred and fifty days.*

8   *And God remembered Noah, and every living thing, and all the
cattle that were with him in the ark: and God made a wind to
2 pass over the earth, and the waters assuaged; the fountains also
(J) of the deep and the windows of heaven were stopped, —*and the
3 rain from heaven was restrained; and the waters returned from
(P) off the earth continually;†—*and after an 'hundred and
4 fifty days the waters decreased.   And the ark rested in the seventh
month, on the seventeenth day of the month, upon the mountains of
5 Ararat.   And the waters decreased continually until the tenth
month: in the tenth month, on the first day of the month, were the
6 (J) tops of the mountains seen.*   And it came to pass at the end
of ²forty days, that Noah opened the window of the ark which he
7 had made: and sent forth a raven, and it went forth to and fro,
8 until the waters were dried up from off the earth. [. . .] And he
sent forth a dove from him, to see if the waters were abated from
9 off the face of the ground; but the dove found no rest for the sole of
her foot, and she returned unto him to the ark, for the waters
were on the face of the whole earth: and he put forth his hand,
10 and took her, and brought her in unto him into the ark.   And he
stayed yet other seven days;‡ and again he sent forth the dove
11 out of the ark; and the dove came in to him at eventide; and, lo,
in her mouth an olive leaf pluckt off: ³so Noah knew that the
12 waters were abated from off the earth.   And he stayed yet other
seven days; and sent forth the dove; and she returned not again
13 (P) unto him any more. *And it came to pass in the six hundred
and first year, in the first month, the first day of the month, the
(J) waters were dried up from off the earth:* and Noah removed

---

¹7:24. ²7:4, 12. ³Ct. 8:15.   .

*Read " He (i. e. Yahweh) blotted out every living thing " with margin (R. V.),
and insert vs. 22 after "face of the ground" in 23*a*. " The spirit of " after " the
breath of," vs. 22, is probably a late gloss.

† Insert after 6*a*. " That " (vs. 6) and " and " (vs. 2) represent the same Hebrew
conjunction.

‡ " Yet other " implies the former existence of the clause, " And he stayed seven
days " before vs. 8.

the 'covering * of the ark, and looked, and, behold, the face of the
(P) ground was dried. [. . .] *And in the second month, on* 14
the seven and twentieth day of the month, was the earth dry.

And God spake unto Noah, saying, Go forth of the ark, 15–16
thou, and thy wife, and thy sons, and thy sons' wives with thee.
Bring forth with thee every living thing that is with thee of all 17
flesh, both fowl, and cattle, and every creeping thing that creepeth
upon the earth ; that they may breed abundantly in the earth, and
'be fruitful, and multiply upon the earth. And Noah went forth, 18
and his sons, and his wife, and his sons' wives with him : every 19
beast, every creeping thing, and every fowl, whatsoever moveth up-
on the earth, 'after their families, went forth out of the ark.
(J) And Noah 'builded an altar unto Yahweh, and took of every 20
clean beast, and of every clean fowl, and offered burnt offerings
on the altar. And Yahweh smelled the sweet savour; and Yahweh 21
said in his heart, I will not again curse the ground any more
for man's sake, for that 'the imagination of man's heart is evil
from his youth; neither will I again smite any more every thing
living, as I have done. While the earth remaineth, seedtime and 22
harvest, and cold and heat, and summer and winter, and day and
(P) night shall not cease. [. . .] † *And 'God blessed Noah and* 9
his sons, and said unto them, Be fruitful, and multiply, and re-
plenish the earth. And the fear of you and the dread of you 2
shall be upon every beast of the earth, and upon every fowl of the
air ; with all wherewith the ground teemeth, and all the fishes of
the sea, into your hand are they delivered. Every 'moving thing 3
that liveth shall be food for you ; as the green herb have I given
you all. But flesh with the life thereof, [which is] the blood 4
thereof, shall ye not eat. And surely your blood, [the blood] of 5
your lives, will I require ; at the hand of every beast will I re-
quire it : and at the hand of man, even at the hand of every man's
brother, will I require the life of man. Whoso sheddeth man's 6
blood, by man shall his blood be shed : for 'in the image of God

⁴Ct. 6:16. ⁵1:22, 28, etc. ⁶10:5, 20, 31, etc. ⁷12:8; 13:18, etc. ⁸6:5. ¹1:22, 28, etc.
²Cf. 1:29. ³1:26f; 5:1-3.

* Strictly "cover" or "roof." Both writers avoid the word for ship, that rendered "ark" meaning box or chest ; but the conception is apparently more primitive here than in vi. 14ff.

† Supply perhaps the story of the bow as token of the covenant, cf. ix. 11ff.

7 *made he man.   And you, 'be ye fruitful, and multiply ; bring
forth abundantly in the earth, and multiply therein.*   ·

8   *And God spake unto Noah, and to his sons with him, saying,*

9 *'And I, behold, I establish my covenant with you, and with your*

10 *seed after you ; aud with every living creature that is with you,
the fowl, the cattle, and every beast of the earth with you ; of all*

11 *that go out of the ark, even every beast of the earth.   And 'I will*
*establish my covenant with you ; neither shall all flesh be cut off
any more by the waters of the flood ; neither shall there any more*

12 *be a flood to destroy the earth.   And God said, This is the token
of the covenant which I make between me and you and every living*

13 *creature that is with you, for perpetual generations : I do set my
bow in the cloud, and it shall be 'for a token of a covenant between*

14 *me and the earth.   And it shall come to pass, when I bring a*

15 *cloud over the earth, that the bow shall be seen in the cloud, and I
will remember my covenant, which is between me and you and
every living creature of all flesh ; and the waters shall no more*

16 *become a flood to destroy all flesh.   And the bow shall be in the
cloud ; and I will look upon it, that I may remember the everlasting covenant between God and every living creature of all flesh*

17 *that is upon the earth.   And God said unto Noah, This is the
token of the covenant which I have established between me and all
flesh that is upon the earth.*

18 (J)   And 'the sons of Noah, that went forth of the ark, were Shem,

19 and Ham, and Japheth: and Ham is the father of Canaan.*   These three

4 1 : 28 ; v. 1.   5 6 : 18 ; 17 : 2, 4, 7, 10. etc.   6 V. 9.   7 17 : 11 ; v. 17.   8 6 : 8 ; 7 : 1. Ct. 5 : 32 ;
6 : 10 ; 7 : 13.

* The last clause of vs. 18 is attributed to harmonistic redaction.   Verses 18 and 19
are regarded as the caption to the Flood-interpolator's table of nations in ch. x., by
which Noah appears as ancestor of the world's population.   After the separation of
the documentary analysis is effected, however, the ancient fragment which knows
him as an agricultural hero, discoverer of the vine, IX. 20–27, appears to stand in a
connection which represents him as father only of the tribes of Canaan, the country of the vine, Shem=the Hebrew .stock, Japheth=the Philistines, or perhaps
Phœnicians, and Canaan=the Canaanites.   "Ham, the father of," in vs. 22, appears
thus as a harmonistic gloss, identical with that under consideration, both being
designed to reconcile vs. 24 with vs. 18.   In support of this view it is urged that vs. 25
with its curse upon *Canaan* as the wrong-doer, and especially its expression "his
brethren," proves that " Ham " has no place in the original story, though of course,
as representative of African races, very necessary to the character of Noah as a
world-ancestor.   It being necessary to introduce this story, if at all, *after* the Flood,
the supposed Flood-interpolator if he wished to preserve it would be obliged to

were the sons of Noah: and of these was the whole earth [9]over-
spread.

—And Noah [10]began to be an husbandman, and plant- 20
ed a vineyard: and he drank of the wine, and was 21
[11]drunken; and he was uncovered within his tent.
◂And Ham, the father of* Canaan, saw the nakedness of 22
his father, and told his two brethren without. And 23
Shem and Japheth took a garment, and laid it upon
both their shoulders, and went backward, and covered
the nakedness of their father; and their faces were
[12]backward, and they saw not their father's nakedness. And Noah awoke from his wine, and knew what 24
his youngest † son had done unto him. And he said, 25

   Cursed be Canaan;
[13]A servant of servants shall he be unto his brethren.

[14]And he said, 26
Blessed be Yahweh, the God of Shem:
And let Canaan be his servant.
God enlarge Japheth, 27 .
And let him dwell in the tents of Shem;
And let Canaan be his servant.‡—

(P) *And Noah lived after the flood three hundred and fifty* 28

[9]10:25; 11:1. [10]4:26; 10:8. [11]43:34. [12]12:8; 13:3; 35:21; 49:11. [13]V. 26f. Jos.
9:27; 17:18; Jud. 1:28ff: [14]26:22.

adopt the expedient of introducing the harmonistic clauses here and in vs. 22. The
theory affords thus at least a possible explanation of the inappropriateness of the
story in its present connection. Observe that Noah's sons are married and have
familes according to viii. 18; ix. 18f (J²) and that they are over 100 years old according to vs. 32; xi. 10f. (P).

*See note to vs. 18.—In vs. 20 read "And Noah was (became) an husbandman and
began (i. e. was the first) to plant a vineyard." Cf iv. 2, 17 ("was a city builder")
20–22, 26; x. 9, 8.

† The Hebrew is identical with 1 Sam. xvi. 11; xvii. 14, excluding the translation
"younger" (R. V. margin). The ground for the marginal reading is the fact that
Ham according to the composite Pentateuch is the second and not the youngest
son. But the analysis shows the reference to be not really to Ham in this passage
but to *Canaan*.

‡Insert after v. 29.—Read "their servant" in vs. 26f. The Canaanite is doubly
enslaved. Reduced first by Israel to taskwork he becomes subsequently "servant
of servants" to the Philistine (Phœnician?). "God" vs. 27, if original, was used as
more appropriate in speaking of a people to whom the Deity would not be known by
his personal name; if altered, this was doubtless the ground for change. (6)

29 *years.   And all the days of Noah were nine hundred and fifty
    years : and he died.*

10   ¹*Now these are the generations of the sons of Noah, Shem*
    (J) *Ham and Japheth :*—and ²**unto them were sons born after
    the flood.** *—[. . .]

2   (P) ³*The sons of Japheth ; Gomer, and Magog, and Madai,*
3 *and Javan, and* ⁴*Tubal, and Meshech, and Tiras.   And the sons*
4 *of Gomer ; Ashkenaz, and Riphath, and Togarmah.   And the*
    sons of Javan ; Elishah, and Tarshish, Kittim, and Dodanim.
5 ⁵*Of these were the isles of the nations divided in their lands,* [. . .]
    every one after his tongue ; after their families, in their nations.
6 *And the sons of Ham ; Cush, and Mizraim, and Put, and Ca-*
7 *naan.   And the sons of Cush ; Seba, and* ⁶*Havilah, and Sabtah,*
    and Raamah, and Sabteca : and the sons of Raamah ; ⁶*Sheba,*
8 (J) *and* ⁶*Dedan.*   **And Cush begat Nimrod: he began to be a**
9 **⁷mighty one in the earth.—He was a mighty hunter be-**
    fore Yahweh: ⁸wherefore it is said, Like Nimrod a
    mighty hunter before Yahweh.†— And the beginning of
10 **his kingdom was ⁹Babel, and Erech, and Accad, and Calneh, in**
11 **the land of Shinar.   Out of that land he went forth into Assyria,**
12 **and builded Nineveh, and Rehoboth-Ir, and Calah, and Resen be-**
13 **tween Nineveh and Calah (the same is the great city).   And Miz-**
    raim begat Ludim, and Anamim, and Lehabim, and Naphtuhim,
14 **and Pathrusim, and Casluhim (whence went forth the Philistines),**
    and Caphtorim. ‡

15–16   **And Canaan ¹⁰begat Zidon his firstborn, and Heth ; ¹¹and**
17–18 the Jebusite, and the Amorite, and the Girgashite ; and the Hivite, and the
    Arkite, and the Sinite ; and the Arvadite, and the Zemarite, and the Hamathite :
    and afterward were the families of the Canaanite spread abroad.|
19 ¹²**And the border of the Canaanite was from Zidon, ¹³as thou**

¹2 : 4, etc.   ²4 : 18, 26. Vv. 21, 25.   ³Vv. 6, 22. Ex. 6 : 14ff.   ⁴4 : 22.   ⁵Vv. 20, 31.   ⁶Ct. 28f ;
25 : 3.   ⁷6 : 4.   ⁸2 : 24, etc.   ⁹Ct. 11 : 1–9.   ¹⁰22 : 21.   ¹¹15 : 19ff.   ¹²V. 30.   ¹³13 : 10 ; 25 : 18.

*The last clause of vs. 1 is considered by Kautzsch and Socin to be taken from J's
interpolator. If so its original position must have been between ix. 19*a* and 19*b*. Or
else we may consider ix. 18, 19 to be due to R entire.

†The Hebrew gives reason to think that verse 9 is not now in its original position.
Budde conjectures for it a position after vi. 4. (7)

‡Amos ix. 7 would lead us to expect the relative clause at the end of the verse.
It is perhaps a gloss introduced at the wrong place from the margin.

|Verse 18*b* is in the present connection incomprehensible to the critical mind, since
"the families of the Canaanites" *are* those just enumerated. The analysis traces,

goest toward Gerar, unto Gaza; as thou goest toward Sodom and
(P) Gomorrah and Admah and Zeboiim, unto Lasha. [14]*These 20
are the sons of Ham, after their families, after their tongues, in
their lands, in their nations.*

(J) And [15]unto Shem, **the father of all the children of 21
Eber,** * the elder brother of Japheth, to him also were child-
(P) ren born.   [. . .] *The sons of Shem ; Elam, and [16]Asshur, 22
and Arpachshad, and Lud, and Aram.   And the sons of [17]Aram ; 23
[17]Uz, and Hul, and Gether, and Mash.* And Arpachshad begat 24
Shelah; and Shelah begat Eber.† And unto Eber were born two 25
sons: the name of the one was Peleg; for in his days was the earth
[18]divided; and his brother's name was [19]Joktan. And Joktan be- 26
gat Almodad, and Sheleph, and Hazarmaveth, and Jerah; and 27
Hadoram, and Uzal, and Diklah; and Obal, and Abimael, and 28
[19]Sheba; and Ophir, and [20]Havilah, and Jobab: all these were the 29
sons of Joktan. And their dwelling was from Mesha, as thou goest 30

[14]Vv. 5, 31.   [15]V. 1.   [16]Ct. 25:3.   [17]Ct. 22:21.   [18]11:1–9.   [19]25:3.   [20]V. 7.

however, in many places the hand of a redactor who delights in introducing these
lists of Canaanitish tribes at every practicable point (cf. xv. 19–21, Ex. iii. 8, 17, etc.).
If 16–18*a* were due to this supplementing redaction, intended perhaps to give the
usual number of 12 Palestinian tribes, 18*b* forms a very good connection after vs. 15.

* This clause—or rather the words, "all the children of"—is by many critics
regarded as a harmonistic interpolation connected with vs. 24 (see note following),
the insertion of two generations between Shem and Eber necessitating a change
from "father of Eber." But the original cannot have read "father of Eber," for
no writer would say, "And to Shem, also, the father of Eber, were born sons:
Eber," etc. On the other hand, the evidence against vs. 24 is as conclusive as critical evidence can be, and the clause in question is at least superfluous if not incongruous here. The phenomena may be accounted for by supposing J[2] to be enriched
here, as in vs. 9 and probably elsewhere (cf. vs. 25 with xi. 1–9) in this table, from his
primitive source. With this idea the form of the clause corresponds. Cf. iv. 20f;
xi. 29; xix. 37f.

† Verse 24 introduces two generations, apparently to make the number correspond with the previous genealogies of J[2] and P (ten generations and a triad).
Without it there are, as in J[1] generally (cf. iv. 17–24), seven and a triad. With it
Terah becomes the tenth (by counting both termini, or by the addition of Cainan
[LXX.]) from Shem, as Noah is tenth from Adam. The question arises whether
the interpolation is due to R or to J[2]. In favor of the former is the fact that were
the verse not here R would be compelled to insert it from xi. 12ff. On the other
hand we observe : first, as in the case of the previous genealogy, iv. 17–26, it is J[2]
(iv. 25f.) who has done the work of expanding in advance of P ; and second, if R
were transcribing from xi. 12ff he would doubtless use the word there employed for
"begat," viz., *holid*, the causative, or *Hiphil* form of the verb *yalad*, "to bear."
This P invariably uses, apparently regarding the *Qal* or indicative form, *yalad*,
which J uses, as a gross solecism. It is the latter which is twice used in vs. 24.
Hence the assignment of this verse (against other critics) to J[2] ; with the assumption, of course, that it was preceded by the substance of 22f.

31 (P) **toward Sephar, the mountain of the east.** [. . .] *These
are the sons of Shem, after their families, after their tongues,
in their lands, after their nations.*

32   *These are the families of the sons of Noah, after their generations, in their nations : and of these were the nations divided in
the earth after the flood.*

11   (J) **And the whole earth was of one 'language and
2 of one speech. And it came to pass, as they journeyed 'east, that they found a plain in the land of
3 'Shinar; and they dwelt there. And they said one to
another; 'Go to, let us make brick, and burn them
thoroughly. And they had brick for stone, and slime
4 had they for mortar. And they said, Go to, let us
build us a city, and a tower, whose top [may reach]
unto heaven, and let us make us 'a name; lest we be
scattered abroad upon the face of the whole earth.
5 And Yahweh 'came down to see the city and the tower,
6 which the children of men builded. And Yahweh
said, Behold, they are one people, and they have all
one language; and this is what they begin to do; and
now 'nothing will be withholden from them, which
7 they propose to do. Go to, 'let us go down and there
confound their language, that they may not under-
8 stand one another's speech. [. . .] So Yahweh 'scattered them abroad from thence upon the face of all
9 the earth: and they left off to build the city. "Therefore was the name of it called Babel; because Yahweh did there confound the language of all the earth :
and from thence did Yahweh scatter them abroad upon the face of all the earth.**

10 (P) *"These are the generations of Shem. "Shem was an hun-
11 dred years old, and begat Arpachshad two years after the flood:* * *and
Shem lived after he begat Arpachshad five hundred years, and
begat sons and daughters.*

[1]Ct. 10:5, 20, 31f. [2]2:8; 12:8. [3]10:10. [4]Vv. 4, 7; 38:16; Ex. 1:10. [5]6:4. [6]18:21;
Ex. 3:8. [7]3:22. [8]3:22; 18:2. [9]Ct. ch. 10. [10]2:24; 10:9, etc. [11]2:4, etc. [12]Ch. 5.
* This clause is incompatible with the chronology (cf. vii. 11 ; ix. 28) and is probably
due to supplementation.

And Arpachshad lived five and thirty years, and begat Shelah : 12
and Arpachshad lived after he begat Shelah four hundred and 13
three years, and begat sons and daughters.

And Shelah lived thirty years, and begat Eber ; and Shelah 14–15
lived after he begat Eber four hundred and three years, and begat
sons and daughters.

And Eber lived four and thirty years, and begat Peleg : and 16–17
Eber lived after he begat Peleg four hundred and thirty years,
and begat sons and daughters.

And Peleg lived thirty years, and begat Reu : and Peleg 18–19
lived after he begat Reu two hundred and nine years, and begat
sons and daughters.

And Reu lived two and thirty years, and begat Serug : and 20–21
Reu lived after he begat Serug two hundred and seven years, and
begat sons and daughters.

And Serug lived thirty years, and begat Nahor : and Serug 22–23
lived after he begat Nahor two hundred years, and begat sons and
daughters.

And Nahor lived nine and twenty years, and begat Terah : 24
and Nahor lived after he begat Terah an hundred and nineteen 25
years, and begat sons and daughters.

And Terah lived seventy years, and begat Abram, Nahor, and 26
Haran.

[13]*Now these are the generations of Terah. Terah begat Abram,* 27
(J) *Nahor, and Haran ; and Haran begat Lot.* **And Haran** 28
died in the presence of his father Terah in the [14]**land**
of his nativity, [15]**In Ur of the Chaldees.*** **And Abram and** 29

[13]2 : 4, etc.   [14]24 : 7. Ct. 48 : 6.   [15]15 : 7. Ct. 24 : 4, 7.

* The great Flood interpolation is supposed to end at about this point, where the
genealogy of Abram from Shem, the Flood survivor, coincides with that from Shem
the brother of Japheth and Canaan. Ur of the Chaldees is a name which cannot
belong to the earlier form of the text, since Haran (xxiv. 4, 7) in Aram Naharaim, and not Ur Chasdim in southern Babylonia, was Abram's fatherland ; and
would naturally be the land of Haran's nativity. So Chesed, father of the Chasdim
or Chaldees in Gen. xxii. 22, is *nephew* to Abraham. Hence the strong disposition
among critics to regard "Ur Chasdim" as a last trace of the Assyro-Babylonian
material at the point of interweaving. It is urged that Ur Chasdim is as exactly in
place in a story of Noah the hero of a Babylonian flood story as it is out of place in
the geographical relations of "Noah the husbandman" and his Palestinian descendants.

Nahor took them wives: the name of Abram's wife was Sarai; and the name of Nahor's wife, [16]Milcah, the daughter of Haran, the father of Milcah, and the
30 father of Iscah.   And Sarai was [17]barren; she had no
31 (P) child.   *And Terah took Abram his son, and Lot the son of Haran, his son's son, and Sarai his daughter in law, his son Abram's wife; and they went forth with them* from Ur of the Chaldees, to go into [18]the land of Canaan; and they came unto*
32 *Haran, and dwelt there.   And the days of Terah were two hundred and five years: and Terah died in Haran.*

12⟨ (J) Now Yahweh said unto Abram, Get thee out of thy country, and from thy kindred, and from thy father's house, unto [1]the land that I will shew thee:
2 and [2]I will make of thee a great nation, and I will bless thee, and make thy name great; and be thou
3 a blessing: and [3]I will bless them that [4]bless thee, and him that curseth thee will I curse: and in thee shall
4 all the families of the earth be blessed.†   So Abram went, as Yahweh had spoken unto him; and Lot went (P) with him: —*and Abram was seventy and five years old*
5 *when he departed out of Haran.‡—*[5]*And Abram took Sarai his wife, and Lot his brother's son, and all their substance that they had gathered, and the souls that they had gotten in Haran; and they went forth to go into* [6]*the land of Canaan; and into the land*
6 (J) *of Canaan they came.*   And Abram passed through the land unto the place of Shechem, unto the [8]oak of Moreh.‖   [9]And the Canaanite was then in the land.
7 And Yahweh appeared unto Abram, and said; [10]Unto

[16]22:20ff.   [17]15:2.   [18]Ct. 12:1.   [1]Num. 10:30.   [2]Ct. 11:31.   [3]Ex. 32:10; Num. 14:12.
[4]27:29; Num. 24:9.   [5]28:14. Cf. 48:20; Jer. 23:22. Ct. 18:18; 22:18; 26:4.   [6]31:18;
36:7; 46:6.   [7]11:31.   [8]35:4; Jos. 24:26.   [9]13:7; 24:3, 37.   [10]15:7.

* Translate with Sam. LXX. Vulg. "and brought them forth."

† Or "bless themselves," i. e. invoke a blessing.   Cf. Gen. xlviii. 20.

‡ Insert after 5*b*.

‖ I. e. "Soothsayer's oak," cf. Jud. iv. 5, "the palm tree of Deborah," and ix. 37,
"the augur's oak."   To *ham-maqom*, "the place," vs. 6, B. Stade gives the specific
sense "the sacred place," i. e. shrine, or *bamah*, of Shechem.   Cf. II Kings v. 11.
(Heb.) and note to xxviii. 11.

thy seed will I give this land: "and there builded he
an altar unto Yahweh, who appeared unto him.   And 8
he "removed from thence unto the mountain on the
east of Beth-el, and pitched his tent, having Beth-el
on the west, and Ai on the east: and "there he builded
an altar unto Yahweh, and "called upon the name of
Yahweh.   And Abram journeyed, going on still toward the South. *   9

¹⁵And there was a ¹⁶famine in the land: and Abram went down 10
into Egypt to sojourn there; for the famine was sore in the land.
And it came to pass, when he was come near to enter into Egypt, 11
that he said unto Sarai his wife, ¹⁷Behold now, I know that thou
art ¹⁸a fair woman to look upon: and it shall come to pass, when 12
the Egyptians shall see thee, that they shall say, This is his wife:
and they will kill me, but they will save thee alive.   Say, I pray 13
thee, thou art my sister: that it may be well with me for thy sake,
and that my soul may live because of thee.   And it came to pass, 14
that, when Abram was come into Egypt, the Egyptians beheld the
woman that she was very fair.   And the princes of Pharaoh saw 15
her, and praised her to Pharaoh: and the woman was taken into
Pharaoh's house.   And he entreated Abram well for her sake: 16
¹⁹and he had sheep, and oxen, and he-asses, and manservants, and
maidservants, and she-asses, and camels.   And Yahweh plagued 17
Pharaoh and his house † with great plagues because of Sarai Abram's
wife.   And Pharaoh called Abram, and said, ²⁰What is this that 18
thou hast done unto me? why didst thou not tell me that she was
thy wife?   Why saidst thou, She is my sister? so that I took her 19
to be my wife: now therefore behold thy wife, take her, and go
thy way.   And Pharaoh gave men charge concerning him; and 20
they ²¹brought him on the way, and his wife, and all that he had.

And Abram went up out of Egypt, he, and his wife, and all that he had, and 13
Lot with him, into the South.   And Abram was very rich in cat- 2
tle, in silver, and in gold.   And he went on his journeys from the 3

¹¹v. 8. Ct. 33:20. Jos. 24:1, 26. ¹²26:22. ¹³Ct. 35:7. ¹⁴4:26, etc. ¹⁵Cf. chh. 20
and 26. ¹⁶26:1. ¹⁷16:2; 18:27, 31; 19:2, 8, 19; 27:2. ¹⁸Ct. 12:4; 17:17. ¹⁹30:43; 32:5.
²⁰3:13; 4:10. ²¹18:16.

* Xii. 9 and xiii. 3f form the seams by which the story of the rape of Sarai is supposed to have been connected with the J narrative at this point, the latter verses
bringing us back to the scene and circumstances of xii. 8.   The story itself is quite
in the style of J, and although it duplicates the story of Gen. xxvi., very probably
belongs to this author.   Critics who take this view insert it at some point subsequent to the separation of Lot, since the story itself seems to ignore him.

† From its position (Heb. after " plagues ") this clause appears to be an editorial
adaptation to xx. 17f.   The plagues here referred to are supposed by most critics
to be those related in a different tradition in Ex. vi.ff.

South even to Beth-el, unto [1]the place where his tent had been [2]at the beginning,

4 between Beth-el and Ai; unto the place of the altar, which he had made there [3]at

5 the first: and [1]there Abram called on the name of Yahweh. **And Lot also, which went with Abram, had flocks, and herds, and**

6 **(P) tents.** *[2]And the land was not able to bear them, that they* **(J)** *might dwell together : for their substance was great,* **so that**

7 **they could not dwell together. And there was a 'strife between the herdmen of Abram's cattle and the herdmen of Lot's cattle: 'and the Canaanite and the**

8 **Perizzite dwelled then in the land. And Abram said unto Lot, Let there be no strife, I pray thee, between me and thee, and between my herdmen and thy herd-**

9 **men; for we are brethren. Is not the whole land before thee? separate thyself, I pray thee, from me : if [thou wilt take] the left hand, then I will go to the right; or if [thou take] the right hand, then I will**

10 **go to the left. And Lot lifted up his eyes, and beheld all the Plain of Jordan, that it was well watered every where, 'before Yahweh destroyed Sodom and Gomorrah, like 'the garden of Yahweh, like the land of**

11 **Egypt, as 'thou goest unto Zoar.* So Lot chose him all the Plain of Jordan; and Lot journeyed east:**

12 **(P)** *and they separated themselves the one from the other. Abram dwelled in the land of Canaan, and Lot dwelled in the cities of*

13 **(J)** *the Plain,* **and 'moved his tent as far as Sodom.—Now the men of Sodom were wicked and sinners against**

14 **Yahweh exceedingly.—And Yahweh said unto Abram, after that Lot was separated from him, [10]Lift up now thine eyes, and look from the place where thou art, northward and southward**

15 **and eastward and westward: for all the land which thou seest, to**

16 **thee will I give it, and to thy seed for ever. And I will make thy seed as the dust of the earth : so that if a man can number the**

17 **dust of the earth, then shall thy seed also be numbered. Arise,**

---

[1]12:8. [2]Cf. 41:21; 43:18, 20. Ct. 1:1. [3]Cf. 36:7. Ct. v. 7 and ch. 27. [4]26:20.
[5]12:6, etc. [6]Ch. 19. [7]2:8. [8]10:19, 30. [9]V. 18. [10]12:2, 7; 28:14; 15:18.

* We must either read Zoan (Tanis on the eastern frontier of Egypt, Num. xiii. 22) or omit the preceding clause. Zoar on the barren promontory projecting into the Dead Sea could hardly be compared to the garden of Yahweh (i. e. Eden) and was not on the way to Egypt. Zoar is here given as the southern limit of the fertile land. Read "until thou comest unto Zoar." Cf. xix. 20-22 and x. 19, 30.

walk through the land in the length of it and in the breadth of
it; for unto thee will I give it.*   And Abram ''moved 18
his tent, and came and dwelt ''by the oaks† of Mamre,
which are in Hebron, and built there an altar unto
Yahweh.

(R) *And‡ it came to pass in the days of Amraphel king of Shi-* 14
nar, Arioch king of Ellasar, Chedorlaomer king of Elam, and
Tidal king of Goiim, that they made war with Bera king of Sod- 2
om, and with Birsha king of Gomorrah, Shinab king of Admah,
and Shemeber king of Zeboiim and the king of Bela (the same is
Zoar).   All these joined together in the vale of Siddim (the same 3
is the Salt Sea).   Twelve years they served Chedorlaomer, and in 4
the thirteenth year they rebelled.   And in the fourteenth year 5
came Chedorlaomer, and the kings that were with him, and smote
the Rephaim in Ashteroth-karnaim, and the Zuzim in Ham, and
the Emim in Shavehkiriathaim, and the Horites in their mount 6
Seir, unto El-paran, which is by the wilderness.   And they re- 7
turned, and came to En-mishpat (the same is Kadesh), and smote
all the country of the Amalekites, and also the Amorites, that
dwelt in Hazazontamar.   And there went out the king of Sodom, 8
and the king of Gomorrah, and the king of Admah, and the king
of Zeboiim, and the king of Bela (the same is Zoar); and they set
the battle in array against them in the vale of Siddim; against 9
Chedorlaomer king of Elam, and Tidal king of Goiim, and Am-
raphel king of Shinar, and Arioch king of Ellasar; four kings
against the five.   Now the vale of Siddim was full of slime pits; 10
and the kings of Sodom and Gomorrah fled, and they fell there,
and they that remained fled to the mountain.   And they took all 11
the goods of Sodom and Gomorrah, and all their victuals, and

¹¹v. 12.   ¹²18:1.

* Verses 14-17 are generally regarded as due to supplementary interpolation,
partly on the ground of style, partly because ch. xv. (J and E) seems to show an
unconsciousness of such a promise having already preceded it.   From the critical ·
standpoint it takes the place of ch. xv., now deferred by the insertion of xiv., but
which originally followed immediately upon vs. 18 and formed the contrast to Lot's
unblessed appropriation of the *Kikkar.*   The repetition of the subject "Lot" in vs.
11*a* is explained when verses 14-17 are dropped, as forming a contrast.   Read, "So
Lot .   . but Abram."—Insert vs. 13 after xviii. 16.

† Originally perhaps, a singular referring to the sacred tree of Hebron near the
altar.   Cf. "the tree" xviii. 4 and LXX. singular *passim.*

‡ The dominant school of criticism regards this chapter as a "*midrash*" of late
Babylonian origin.   The date in the period of a Babylonian monarch is urged in
support of this view, as well as other singularities of style, language and subject
matter.

12 *went their way. And they took Lot, Abram's brother's son, who*
13 *dwelt in Sodom, and his goods, and departed. And there came*
   one that had escaped, and told Abram the Hebrew; now he dwelt
   by the [1]oaks of Mamre the Amorite, brother of [3]Eshcol, and brother
14 *of Aner; and these were confederate with Abram. And when*
   Abram heard that his brother was taken captive, he led forth his
   trained men, born in his house, three hundred and eighteen, and
15 *pursued as far as [3]Dan. And he divided himself against them by*
   night, he and his servants, and smote them, and pursued them
16 *unto Hobah, which is on the left hand of Damascus. And he*
   brought back all the goods, and also brought again his brother
17 *Lot, and his goods, and the women also, and the people. And the*
   king of Sodom went out to meet him, after his return from the
   slaughter of Chedorlaomer and the kings that were with him, at
18 *the vale of Shaveh (the same is the King's Vale). And [4]Melchize-*
   dek king of [5]Salem brought forth bread and wine: and he was
19 *priest of God Most High. And he blessed him, and said, Blessed*
20 *be Abram of God Most High,* possessor of heaven and earth: and*
   blessed be God Most High, which hath delivered thine enemies in-
21 *to thy hand. And he gave him a [6]tenth of all. And the king of*
   Sodom said unto Abram, Give me the persons, and take the goods
22 *to thyself. And Abram said to the king of Sodom, I have lift up*
   mine hand unto Yahweh, God Most High, possessor of heaven and
23 *earth, that I will not take a thread nor a shoelatchet nor aught*
   that is thine, lest thou shouldest say, I have made Abram rich:
24 *save only that which the young men have eaten, and the portion*
   of the men which went with me; Aner, Eshcol,† and Mamre, let
   them take their portion

15 (E) After these things the word of Yahweh came unto
   Abram in a [2]vision, saying, Fear not, Abram: I am thy
2 (J) shield, [and] thy exceeding great reward.‡   —And

[1]13:18. [2]Num. 13:23. [3]Ct. Jud. 18:29. [4]Jos. 10:1. [5]Ps. 76:3. [6]28:22. [1]22:1, 20;
39:7; 40:1; 48:1. [2]46:2, and v. 5. Ct. v. 8ff.

* The expression, "Blessed be — of" —, found nowhere else in Scripture in this
form, has been recently discovered by Sayce in the inscription of some Semitic
pilgrims to Egypt of the age of Jeremiah, of whom one subscribes himself "Servant
of Nebo." The only certainty regarding the inscription is the fact that the writers
were of the time of the Exile and were Semites but not Hebrews, with some probability that they came from Mesopotamia. (See *Hebraica* for July, 1890.)

† Cf. Num. xiii. 24.

‡ In xv. 1ff the analysis is very difficult and results are put forward with diffi-
dence. Still the evidence for the presence of E afforded by the form of theophany
(communications from the Deity in E are received in visions of the night. See
Num. xii. 6 (E)), and by the language, is among the critics generally accepted

Abram said, 'O Lord Yahweh, what wilt thou give me,
(E) seeing I go childless, and he that shall be possessor 3
of my house is Dammesek Eliezer*?—And Abram said,
(J) Behold, to me thou hast given no seed :—† and, lo, one
born in my house is mine heir. And, behold, the word 4
of Yahweh came unto him, saying, This man shall not
be thine heir; but he that shall come forth out of
(E) thine own bowels shall be thine heir. And he 5
brought him forth abroad, and said, Look now toward
heaven, and tell the 'stars, if thou be able to tell them :
and he said unto him, So shall thy seed be. [. . .]
(J) And he 'believed in Yahweh ; and he counted it to 6
him for righteousness.‡—And he said unto him, I am 7
Yahweh that 'brought thee out of 'Ur of the Chaldees,
to give thee this land to inherit it. And he said, O 8
'Lord Yahweh, whereby shall I know that I shall inherit it? And he said unto him, Take me an heifer 9
of three years old, and a she-goat of three years old,
and a ram of three years old, and a turtle-dove, and
a young pigeon. And he took him all these, and di- 10
vided them in the midst, and laid each half over

³18:27-32; Ex. 4:10, 13; 34:9. ⁴v. 1. Ct. 8ff. ⁵Ex. 14:31. ⁶15:1. ⁷11:28. ⁸v. 2.

as conclusive, while the simultaneous narration of two episodes, one of which,
the covenant to give the land, is transacted during the day, and the other, the
promise of a son, during the night, contributes to make the duplicate character
of the text apparent. Josh. xxiv. 1ff (E) refers to a story of Abraham's call differ-
ing from chaps. xii.ff, and on this ground the existence of an E story corresponding
to J, xii.-xv., is assumed by the critics *a priori.* The chapter being admittedly
difficult and uncertain in the details of analysis, the author has proceeded independently, referring the reader for authorities to the tables of *Hebraica* iv. (1888) and
for the evidence in support of his own analysis to *Hebraica* for October, 1890.—
"The word of Yahweh," vs. 1, for which in E we should expect "Elohim" (cf.
xx. 8) is explained as assimilated by R to vs. 4.

*In vs. 2 read Eliezer of Damascus with margin R. V. The rendering of the
Chaldee and Syriac versions, however, is only an attempt to make sense out of a
text perhaps corrupt, certainly confused by a punning collocation of *ben-mesek*,
"possessor," and *Dammesek*, "Damascus." All that is clear is that the servant's
name was Eliezer, whereas in ch. xxiv. (J) he appears simply as "Abraham's
servant."

†Critics invert the order of 2b and 3a.

‡Insert 1-6 after 7-18.—The impression one naturally receives that this verse
forms the conclusion of the narrative of J (cf. Ex. xiv. 31 [J]) is probably correct.
See the article above referred to.

11 against the other : but the birds divided he not.   And the birds of prey came down upon the carcases, and
12 (E) Abram drove them away.   And when the sun was going down, [9]a deep sleep fell upon Abram : and, lo, an horror of great
13 darkness fell upon him.   And he said unto Abram, Know of a surety that thy seed shall be a stranger in a land that is
14 not theirs, and shall serve them. [. . .] and they shall afflict them [10]four hundred years ; and also that nation, whom they shall serve, will I judge : and afterward shall they come out with great
15 [11]substance.   But thou shalt go to thy fathers in peace ; thou
16 shalt be buried in a good old age.   And in the [12]fourth generation they shall come hither again : for the iniquity
17 (J) of the [13]Amorite is not yet full.*   And it came to pass, that, when the sun went down, and it was dark, behold a [14]smoking furnace,† and a flaming torch that
18 [15]passed between these pieces.   In that day Yahweh made a covenant with Abram, saying, Unto thy seed have I given this land, from the river of Egypt unto
19 the great river, the river Euphrates: the [16]Kenite, and
20 the Kenizzite, and the Kadmonite, and the Hittite, and the Periz-
21 zite, and the Rephaim, and the Amorite, and the Canaanite, and the Girgashite, and the Jebusite.‡
16   (P) (J) *Now [1]Sarai Abram's wife bare him no children :* and [. . .] she had an handmaid, [2]an Egyptian, whose
2 name was Hagar.   And Sarai said unto Abram, Behold now, Yahweh hath restrained me from bearing ;

[9]2:21.   [10]Cf. Ex. 12:40. Ct. v. 16.   [11]12:5; 13:6, etc.   [12]Ex. 6:16ff. Ct. v. 14.   [13]Num. 21:21; Jos. 24:8, 12.   [14]Ex. 13:21; 19:18.   [15]Jer. 34:18f. Ct ch. 17.   [16]Ex. 3:8, 17; 13:5; 23:20, 28; 33:2, etc.   [1]Ct. 11:30.   [2]12:16. Ct. 21:21.

* Verses 12-16 introduce a new subject not connected with that of vv. 8-11, the formal conveyance of the land by covenant to Abram (cf. Jer. xxxiv. 18f). They seem even discordant among themselves unless the four generations of vs. 16 can be supposed to equal the four hundred years of vs. 13. On this account and because of the style and language ("Amorite" is used by E where J employs "Canaanite") critics regard these verses as interpolated. It is difficult, however, to assign an adequate motive for interpolation unless a part of the material at least is derived from one of the sources (E). As between 12 and 17, vs. 17, which resumes the thread of vs. 12, may perhaps be due to R in the portion which duplicates vs. 12, and 12, 17b, be the true J portion ; this however is immaterial, as the sense is identical.

† "Smoke as from a furnace," Kautzsch and Socin. Cf. Gen. xix. 28 and Ex. xix. 18 (J).

‡ Supplementary redaction. See note on x. 16ff.

go in, I pray thee, unto my handmaid; it may be that
I shall 'obtain children by her. And Abram heark-
(P) ened to the voice of Sarai. *And Sarai Abram's wife* 3
took Hagar the Egyptian, her handmaid, after Abram had dwelt
ten years in the 'land of Canaan, and gave her to Abram her hus-
(J) *band to be his wife.* And he went in unto Hagar, and 4
she conceived: and when she saw that she had conceived, her mistress was despised in her eyes. 'And 5
Sarai said unto Abram, 'My wrong be upon thee: I
gave my handmaid into thy bosom; and when she saw
that she had conceived, I was despised in her eyes:
'Yahweh judge between me and thee. But Abram 6
said unto Sarai, Behold, thy maid is in thy hand; do
to her that which is good in thine eyes. And Sarai
dealt hardly with her, and she fled from her face.
And the angel of Yahweh found her by a fountain of 7
water in the wilderness, by the 'fountain in the way
to Shur. And he said, Hagar, Sarai's handmaid, 8
whence camest thou? and whither goest thou? And
she said, I flee from the face of my mistress Sarai.
(JE) And the angel of Yahweh said unto her, Return to thy mistress, 9
and 'submit thyself under her hands. And the angel of Yahweh 10
said unto her, I will greatly multiply thy seed, that it shall not be
(J) numbered for multitude.* And the angel of Yahweh said 11
unto her, Behold, thou art with child, and shall bear
a son; and thou shalt call his name Ishmael, because
Yahweh hath heard thy affliction. And he shall be 12

²30:3. ⁴12:5. ⁵Ct. 21:9ff. ⁶27:13. ⁷31:53; Ex. 5:21. ⁸V. 14; 20:1; 25:18. ⁹Ct. v. 11.

* From the critical standpoint verses 9, 10, are a harmonistic interpolation of JE
designed to make possible a combination of J's story of the expulsion of Hagar
with E's, ch. xxi., of Hagar and Ishmael. In order to be able to include both narratives it would become necessary after the first expulsion, to bring Hagar back
again, and to omit the account of Ishmael's birth, which, vs. 11f, in the opinion of
critics, requires us to assume followed originally after vs. 14. The evidence for considering vs. 9f harmonistic is found in the different attitude assumed toward Hagar
from that of the context. There (vs. 11) Yahweh is represented as coming to the
rescue of Hagar to deliver her from unjust treatment. To say that Yahweh has
heard her affliction is equivalent to a promise of deliverance, whereas the angel in
vs. 9 commands submission. Moreover the repetition of the subject and consequent
dislocation of the angel's communication is very striking. Cf. 9a, 10a, 11a. Verse
10 may be considered even an independent interpolation. Cf. xiii. 16.

[as] a wild-ass among men ; his hand [shall be] against
every man, and every man's hand against him ; and
¹⁰he shall dwell in the presence of all his brethren.*
13 And she called the name of Yahweh that spake unto
her, Thou art a God that seeth : for she said, Have I
14 even here looked after him that seeth me? "Wherefore the well was called Beer-lahai-roi ; behold, it is
15 (P) between Kadesh and Bered. [. . .]† *And Hagar
bare Abram a son : and Abram called the name of his son, which*
16 *Hagar bare, Ishmael.   And Abram was fourscore and six years
old, when Hagar bare Ishmael to Abram.*

17   ¹*And when Abram was ninety years old and nine, Yahweh‡ appeared to Abram, and said unto him, I am ²God Almighty ; walk
2 before me, and be thou perfect.   And I will make my covenant
3 between me and thee, and will multiply thee exceedingly.   And
4 Abram fell on his face : and God talked with him, saying, As
for me, behold, my covenant is with thee, and thou shalt be the*

¹⁰25 : 18. ¹¹2 : 24, etc. ¹Cf. ch. 9. ²Ex. 6 : 2.

* Kautzsch and Socin translate. *Er soll allen seinen Verwandten auf den Nacken
sitzen.*

† Wellhausen suggests a plausible reading for 13*b*, the text in its present shape
being unintelligible, and translates, " And she called the name of Yahweh that
spake unto her El-roi : (" God of vision "—in the passive sense) for she said, " I have
seen God and live after my seeing." (8)
The name of the well (*beer*) according to the original (vowelless) text of the
Hebrew, is L H I R ' I, and the vowels supplied in the mind of the narrator were
certainly those which afford the translation "living one who sees." But in Jud. xv.
9ff we have found (p. 14) this word L H I supplied with the vowels e. i. to form the
word "jawbone" or "cliff." If these are the true vowels the sense of the name
Beer-lehi-roi is " Well of the conspicuous cliff," or " Well of Lookout Rock." But
it is also suggested by Wellhausen that instead of R ' I we should read R ' I,
in which case the translation would be " Well of the antelope's jawbone" (cf.
Strabo's *Onugnathos* and the Well of the ass's jawbone in Jud. xv. 9ff), and the mis-
understanding of the name would be accounted for through the extinction of the
antelope and consequent obsolescence of the word. The conjectures are, of
course, occasioned by the difficulty of supposing a well to go by the name, " Well
of the living one who sees," if indeed the Hebrew be not more insupposable than
the English. (8)

‡ On account of Ex. vi. 2ff critics consider it impossible to suppose that P violated
here and in xxi. 1*b* his otherwise unbroken use of *Elohim*, " God, ' or *El Shaddai*,
" God Almighty," especially as the personal name here would be in discordance
with the first words of address immediately following. The same alteration is
assumed to have taken place here, which the evidence of Sam. Targ. and Vulg. goes
to show took place in vii. 9.

father of a multitude of nations. Neither shall thy name any 5
more be called Abram, but thy name shall be Abraham : for the
father of a multitude of nations have I made thee. And I will 6
make thee exceeding fruitful, and I will make nations of thee,
and kings shall come out of thee. And I will establish my cove- 7
nant between me, and thee and thy seed after thee throughout their
generations for an everlasting covenant, to be a God unto thee and
to thy seed after thee. And I will give unto thee, and to thy seed 8
after thee, the land of thy sojournings, all the land of Canaan, for
an everlasting possession ; and I will be their God. And God 9
said unto Abraham, And as for thee, thou shalt keep my covenant,
thou, and thy seed after thee throughout their generations. This 10
is my covenant, which ye shall keep, between me and you and thy
seed after thee ; every male among you shall be circumcised. And 11
ye shall be circumcised in the flesh of your foreskin ; ʰand it shall
be a token of a covenant betwixt me and you. And he that is eight 12
days old shall be circumcised among you, every male throughout
your generations, he that is born in the house, or bought with money
of any stranger, which is not of thy seed. He that is born in thy 13
house, and he that is bought with thy money, must needs be circum-
cised : and my covenant shall be in your flesh for an everlasting
covenant. And the uncircumcised male who is not circumcised in 14
the flesh of his foreskin, that soul shall be cut off from his people ;
he hath broken my covenant.

And God said unto Abraham, As for Sarai thy wife, thou shalt 15
not call her name Sarai, but Sarah shall her name be. And I 16
will bless her, and moreover I will give thee a son of her : yea, I
will bless her, and she shall be [a mother of] nations ; ᵏkings of
peoples shall be of her. Then Abraham fell upon his face, and 17
ᵇlaughed, and said in his heart, Shall a child be born unto him that
is an hundred years old? and shall Sarah, that is ninety years old,
bear? And Abraham said unto God, Oh that Ishmael might live 18
before thee! And God said, Nay, but Sarah thy wife shall bear 19
thee a son ; and thou shalt call his name Isaac : ᶜand I will estab-
lish my covenant with him for an everlasting covenant for his seed
after him. And as for Ishmael, I have heard thee : behold, I 20

ᵃ9:12f. ᵇ35:11. ᶜCt. 18:12ff. ᵈVv. 2, 4, 7, 11, 13, 21.

9

*have blessed him, and will make him fruitful, and will multiply
him exceedingly ; [7]twelve princes shall he beget, and I will make*
21 *him a great nation.   But my covenant will I establish with Isaac,
which Sarah shall bear unto thee [8]at this set time in the next year.*
22 *And he left off talking with him, and [9]God went up from Abra-*
23 *ham.   And Abraham took Ishmael his son, and all that were born
in his house, and all that were bought with his money, every male
among the men of Abraham's house, and circumcised the flesh of
their foreskin [10]in the selfsame day, as God had said unto him.*
24 *And Abraham was ninety years old and nine, when he was cir-*
25 *cumcised in the flesh of his foreskin.   And Ishmael his son was
[11]thirteen years old, when he was circumcised in the flesh of his*
26 *foreskin.   In the selfsame day was Abraham circumcised, and*
27 *Ishmael his son.   And all the men of his house, those born in the
house, and those bought with money of the stranger, were circumcised with him.*

18   (J) And Yahweh appeared unto him by the 'oaks* of
Mamre, as he sat in the tent door [2]in the heat of the
2 day; and he lift up his eyes and looked, and, lo, three
men stood over against him: and when he saw them,
[3]he ran to meet them from the tent door, and bowed
3 himself to the earth, and said, 'My lord, [5]if now I
have found favour in thy sight, pass not away, I pray
4 thee, from thy servant: let now a little water be
fetched, and wash your feet, and rest yourselves un-
5 der [6]the tree: and I will fetch a morsel of bread, and
comfort ye your heart; after that ye shall pass on:
[7]forasmuch as ye are come to your servant.   And they
6 said, So do, as thou hast said.   And Abraham hastened into the tent unto Sarah, and said, Make ready
quickly three measures of fine meal, knead it, and
7 make cakes.   And Abraham ran unto the herd, and
fetched a calf tender and good, and gave it unto the
8 servant; and he hasted to dress it.   And he took but-

[7]25:16.   [8]21:2.   [9]35:13.   [10]7:11, 13.   v. 26.   [11]Ct. 21:9, 14, 15, 16.   [1]13:18.   [2]3:8.
[3]24:17; 29:13; 33:4.   [4]32:5, 18, etc.   Cf. 19:2ff.   [5]19:19; 30:27; 32:5; 33:8, 10, etc.
[6]v. 8.   Ct. v. 1.   [7]19:8; 33:10; 38:26; Num. 10:31; 14:43.   Ct. 41:39.

* Better, perhaps, "oak."   Cf. vv. 4 and 8 and note on Gen. xiii. 18.

ter, and milk, and the calf which he had dressed, and set it before them; and he stood by them under the tree, and they did eat. And they said unto him, 9 Where is Sarah thy wife? And he said, Behold, in the tent. And he said, [8]I will certainly return unto 10 thee when the season cometh round; and, lo, Sarah thy wife shall have a son. And Sarah heard in the tent door, which was behind him. Now Abraham and 11 Sarah were [9]old, [and] well stricken in age; it had ceased to be with Sarah after the [10]manner of women. And [11]Sarah laughed within herself, saying, After I 12 am waxed old shall I have pleasure, my lord being old also? And Yahweh said unto Abraham, Wherefore 13 did Sarah laugh, saying, Shall I of a surety bear a child, which am old? Is any thing too hard for Yah- 14 weh? At the set time I will return unto thee, when the season cometh round, and Sarah shall have a son. Then Sarah denied, saying, I laughed not; for she 15 was afraid. And he said, Nay; but thou didst laugh.*

And the men rose up from thence, and [12]looked to- 16 ward Sodom: and Abraham went with them [13]to bring them on the way. And Yahweh said, Shall I hide from Abra- 17 ham that which I do: seeing that Abraham shall surely become 18 a great and mighty nation, and all the [14]nations of the earth shall be blessed in him? For I have known him, to the end that he 19 may command his children and his household after him, that they may keep the way of Yahweh, to do justice and judgement; to the end that Yahweh may bring upon Abraham that which he hath spoken of him.† And Yahweh said, Because [15]the cry 20

[8]21:1. [9]24:1; 21:7. [10]Ct. 31:35. [11]Ct. 17:17; 21:6f, 9; 26:8. [12]19:27f; Num. 21:20. [13]12:20. [14]Cf. 22:18; 26:4. Ct. 12:3; 28:14. [15]4:10 13:13.

*The name Isaac has given rise to many etymologizing stories which seek in various ways to connect it with the stem Ç H Q "to laugh." Thus in xvii. 17 (P), "Abram laughed;" here (J), "Sarah laughed." In (E) xxi. 6*a* Sarah says "God hath prepared laughter for me," and so names the child *Yiçhaq*; but the same author has a further play upon the name in verse 9 of the same chapter. Xxi. 6*b* seems, further, to be a different version (J) from 6*a* (E) of the sense of Sarah's utterance ("Everyone will laugh *at* me"), and (J) has still a third play upon the name in xxvi. 8. This reduplication is one of the indications which point to a collection of popular traditions as the ultimate source of J and E.

† Didactic interpolation.

of Sodom and Gomorrah is great, and because their
21 sin is very grievous; "I will go down now, and see
whether they have done altogether * according to the
cry of it, which is come unto me; and if not, I will
22 know. And the men turned from thence, and went
toward Sodom: but Abraham stood yet before Yahweh.†
23 And Abraham drew near, and "said, Wilt thou consume the right-
24 eous with the wicked? Peradventure there be fifty righteous
within the city: wilt thou consume and not spare the place for
25 the fifty righteous that are therein? That be far from thee to do
after this manner, to slay the righteous with the wicked, that so
the righteous should be as the wicked; that be far from thee:
26 shall not the Judge of all the earth do right? And Yahweh said,
If I find in Sodom fifty righteous within the city, then I will spare
27 all the place for their sake. And Abraham answered and said,
Behold now, I have taken upon me to speak unto [18]the Lord, which
28 am but [19]dust and ashes: peradventure there shall lack five of the
fifty righteous: wilt thou destroy all the city for lack of five?
And he said, I will not destroy it, if I find there forty and five.
29 And he spake unto him yet again, and said, Peradventure there
shall be forty found there. And he said, I will not do it for the
30 forty's sake. And he said, Oh let not the Lord be angry, and I will
speak: peradventure there shall thirty be found there. And he
31 said, I will not do it, if I find thirty there. And he said, Behold
now, I have taken upon me to speak unto the Lord: peradventure
there shall be twenty found there. And he said, I will not destroy
32 it for the twenty's sake. And he said, Oh let not the Lord be angry, and I will speak yet but this once: peradventure ten shall be
found there. And he said, I will not destroy it for the ten's sake.

[16]11:5, 7; Ex. 3:8.   [17]Cf. Ex. 32:11ff; Num. 14:13ff. Ct. v. 21.   [18]15:2, 8; vv. 30ff;
Ex. 4:10, 13.   [19]2:7.

* The word "cry" as used by J has a special sense. Oppression or evil doing,
apart from any protest or appeal of the oppressed, besieges the divine ear with its
clamor. Abel's blood, iv. 10, Hagar's wrong, xvi. 11, Israel's oppression, Ex. iii. 7,
produce a "cry," and Yahweh comes down to intervene. Accordingly, "cry" in
vs. 21 is something more than "report" or "scandal," and Olshausen's conjectural
reading "all" instead of "altogether" is to be commended. Yahweh cannot doubt
the "cry," he comes down to see whether they have "all" gone astray, not to see
whether he was "altogether" right in his apprehension of the facts. The conjecture
relieves vs. 21 of an unnecessary load of anthropomorphism. (9)

† One of the few textual amendments which Jewish tradition brings to light is
afforded in vs. 22b. The present reading, violating the requirement of the context,
is enumerated among the *tiqqunei sopherim* or "corrections of the scribes" for an
original "Yahweh stood still before Abraham," which was rejected as irreverent.

And Yahweh went his way, as soon as he had left communing with 33
Abraham:* and Abraham returned unto his place.

'And the two angels† came to Sodom at even; and 19
Lot sat in the gate of Sodom: and Lot saw them, and
'rose up to meet them; and he bowed himself with
his face to the earth; and he said, Behold now, my 2
lords, turn aside, I pray you, into your servant's
house, and tarry all night, and wash your feet, and
ye shall rise up early, and go on your way. And they
said, Nay; but we will abide in the street all night.
And he urged them greatly; and they turned in unto 3
him, and entered into his house; and he made them
a feast, and did bake unleavened bread, and they did
eat. But before they lay down, the men of the city, 4
[even] the men of Sodom, compassed the house round,
both young and old, all the people 'from every quarter; and they called unto Lot, and said unto· him, 5
Where are the men which came in to thee this night?

¹Cf. Jud. 19. ²18:1ff. ³47:21.

*Some of the best critics regard vv. 22*b*-33*a* as a didactic interpolation designed
to relieve the appearance of wholesale, undiscriminating slaughter of whole cities.
By means of it, it is made clear that *all* the inhabitants of the *Kikkar* were vicious,
therefore "the Judge of all the earth" did right. Evidence for regarding the passage as interpolated is found partly in the contrast in the conception of Abraham's
relation to Yahweh; the familiar terms of the first part of the chapter, and the reverence of address here (cf. vs. 27); but mainly in its premature assumption that
Yahweh intends to *destroy* the cities (cf. vs. 23 with vs. 21), really a consequence of
ch. xix.—It is significant that the *basis* of chh. xviii.f is characterized by an extreme
anthropomorphism (vs. 8, 20ff) like that of the older parts of J in chh. i.-xi. If Wellhausen's conjecture (see note following) as to ch. xix. is correct, the story in its
original form would be intolerable to any of the biblical writers. In any case,
these chapters present to the eye of all critics the appearance of having undergone
systematic modification for the elevation of the original material to meet a higher
religious standpoint. In favor of regarding J, the author of the history, as himself
the modifier, is (*a*) the distinctive color of style and language in vv. 23-33, which is
indistinguishable from J's, and (*b*) the frequent recurrence of poetic words and
phrases in the older material (cf. e. g. xii. 3 with xxvii. 29, Num. xxiv. 9), as if J as a
whole were not so much a composition as a prose version of ancient poems. Cf.
note on ii. 10-15, and see Part III.

†Read "the men" (cf. xviii. 22*a*; xix. 10, 12, 16; ct. vs. 15). Yahweh is certainly
regarded by the story itself, vv. 17, 21ff, as present at Sodom. The introduction of
xviii. 22ff stands connected with a series of alterations, as in vs. 13. Wellhausen
(*Compos.* p. 27f) calls attention to evidence for an original form of the story in
which Yahweh appears alone (cf. xviii. 3, 10, 17; xix. 10, 17f).

bring them out unto us, that we may 'know them.
6 And Lot went out unto them to the door, and shut
7 the door after him.   And he said, I pray you, 'my
8 brethren, do not so wickedly.   Behold now, I have
two daughters which have not known man; let me, I
pray you, bring them out unto you, and do ye to them
as is good in your eyes: only unto these men do nothing; 'forasmuch as they are come under the shadow
9 of my roof. And they said, Stand back. And they
said, This one fellow came in to sojourn, and he will
needs be a judge: now will we deal worse with thee,
than with them.   And they pressed sore upon the
10 man, even Lot, and drew near to break the door. But
the men put forth their hand, and brought Lot into
11 the house to them, and shut to the door. And they
smote the men that were at the door of the house with
blindness, both small and great: so that they wearied
12 themselves to find the door. And the men said unto
Lot, Hast thou here any besides? son in law, and thy
sons,* and thy daughters, and whomsoever thou hast
13 in the city; bring them out of the place: for we will
destroy this place, because 'the cry of them is waxen
great before Yahweh; and Yahweh hath sent us to destroy
14 it.   And Lot went out, and spake unto his sons in law,
which married his daughters, and said, Up, get you
out of this place; for Yahweh will destroy the city.
But he seemed unto his sons in law as one that mocked.
15 And when the morning 'arose, then the angels hastened Lot, saying, Arise, take thy wife, and thy two
daughters which are here; lest thou be consumed in
16 the 'iniquity of the city. But he lingered; and the
men laid hold upon his hand, and upon the hand of
his wife, and upon the hand of his two daughters:
Yahweh being merciful unto him: and they brought
17 him forth, and set him without the city.   And it

'4:1, etc. '29:4. '18:5, etc. '18:20f. '32:24, 26. '4:13.

* Read "thy sons-in-law." Cf. vs. 14. (10)

came to pass, when they brought them forth abroad, that he said, Escape for thy life : look not behind thee, neither stay thou in all the Plain; escape to the mountain, lest thou be consumed. And Lot said unto 18 them, Oh, not so, my lord : behold now, thy servant 19 hath [10]found grace in thy sight, and thou hast magnified thy mercy, which thou hast shewed unto me in saving my life; and I cannot escape to the mountain, lest evil overtake me, and I die : behold now, this city 20 is near to flee unto, and it is a little one : Oh, let me escape thither, (is it not a little one?) and my soul shall live. And he said unto him, See, I have [11]accepted thee concerning this thing also, that I will not overthrow the city of which thou hast spoken. Haste 22 thee, escape thither; for I cannot do any thing till thou be come thither. [12]Therefore the name of the city was called Zoar. [13]The sun was risen upon the 23 earth when Lot came unto Zoar. Then Yahweh rained 24 upon Sodom and Gomorrah brimstone and fire from Yahweh out of heaven; and he overthrew those cities, 25 and all the Plain, and all the inhabitants of the cities, and that which grew upon the ground. [. . . .] But 26 his wife looked back from behind him, and she became a pillar of salt. And Abraham gat up early in the 27 morning to [14]the place where he had stood before Yahweh : and he looked toward Sodom and Gomorrah, and 28 toward all the land of the Plain, and beheld, and, lo, the smoke of the land went up [15]as the smoke of a furnace.

(P)—*And it came to pass, when God destroyed the cities of the* 29 *Plain, that God remembered Abraham, and sent Lot out of the midst of the overthrow, when he overthrew the cities in the which Lot dwelt.*—*

(J) And Lot went up out of Zoar, and dwelt in the 30 mountain, and his two daughters with him; for he

[10]18:3, etc. [11]4:7; 32:20. [12]2:24, etc. [13]32:31. [14]18:16, 22. [15]15:17; Ex. 19:18.

* Verse 29 should perhaps be inserted after xiii. 12*a*.

feared to dwell in Zoar: and he dwelt in a cave, he and
31 his two daughters. And the [16]firstborn said unto the
[16]younger, Our father is old, and there is not a man
in the earth to come in unto us after the manner of
32 all the earth: come, let us make our father drink
wine, and we will lie with him, that we may preserve
33 seed of our father. And they made their father drink
wine that night: and the firstborn went in, and lay
with her father; and he knew not when she lay down,
34 nor when she arose. And it came to pass on the morrow, that the firstborn said unto the younger, Behold,
I lay yesternight with my father: let us make him
drink wine this night also; and go thou in, and lie
with him, that we may preserve seed of our father.
35 And they made their father drink wine that night also:
and the younger arose, and lay with him; and he knew
36 not when she lay down, nor when she arose. Thus
were both the daughters of Lot with child by their
37 father. And the firstborn bare a son, and called his
name Moab· [17]the same is the father of the Moabites
38 unto this day. And the younger; she also bare a son,
and called his name Ben-ammi: [17]the same is the father of the children of Ammon unto this day.*

20   (E) [1]And Abraham journeyed from thence toward the
land of the South, and dwelt [2]between Kadesh and Shur;
2 and he sojourned in Gerar. And Abraham said of Sarah
his wife, She is my sister: and Abimelech king of Gerar
3 sent, and took Sarah. [. . .] But [3]God came to Abim-

[16]Cf. 29:26. Ct. 29:16f.   [17]4:20f, etc.   [1]Ct. 12:10ff; ch. 26.   [2]16:14.   [3]Vv. 6:11, 13, 17.
etc.; Ex. 3:13f. Ct. 4:1, etc.

*The passage, xix. 30–38, is a repulsive exhibition of the malignant wit of the
people, exercised upon the names of the kindred tribes Ammon and Moab, the first
by a punning etymology being derived from *ben-ammi*, "son of my people," and
the second, in an equally forced derivation, from *mai*, "water," or the preposition
min, "from," and *ab*, "father."—The implied contrast in feeling toward Moab and
Ammon with that of previous chapters (cf. Dt. ii. 9 and 19), is sufficient to prove
a diverse origin for the traditions, the present saga perhaps reflecting the exasper-
ated feeling of Israel during the Syrian wars (II. Kings xiii. 20; Amos i. 13; Dt.
xxiii. 3) but does not warrant the assumption of diverse authorship. See note to
xviii. 33.

elech [4]in a dream of the night, and said to him, Behold, thou art but a dead man, because of the woman which thou hast taken ; for she is a man's wife. Now Abimelech 4 had not come near her : and he said, Lord, wilt thou slay even a righteous nation ? Said he not himself unto me, 5 She is my. sister ? and she, even she herself said, He is my brother : in the integrity of my heart and the innocency of my hands have I done this. And God said unto him 6 [5]in the dream, Yea, I know that in the integrity of thy heart thou hast done this, and I also withheld thee from sinning against me : therefore suffered I thee not to touch her. Now therefore restore the man's wife ; for [6]he is a 7 prophet, and he shall pray for thee, and thou shalt live : and if thou restore her not, know thou that thou shalt surely die, thou, and all that are thine. And Abimelech 8 rose early in the morning, and called all his servants, and told all these things in their ears : and the men were sore afraid. Then Abimelech called Abraham, and said unto 9 him, What hast thou done unto us? and wherein have I sinned against thee, that [7]thou hast brought on me and on my kingdom a great sin ? thou hast done deeds unto me that ought not to be done. And Abimelech said unto 10 Abraham, What sawest thou, that thou hast done this thing? And Abraham said, Because I thought, Surely the 11 fear of God is not in this place ; and they will slay me for my wife's sake. And moreover she is [7]indeed my sister, 12 the daughter of my father, but not the daughter of my mother; and she became my wife: and it came to pass, when 13 [8]God caused me to [9]wander from my father's house, that I said unto her, This is thy kindness which thou shalt shew unto me ; at every place whither we shall come, say of me, He is my brother. And Abimelech [10]took sheep and oxen, 14 and menservants and womenservants, and gave them unto Abraham, and restored him Sarah his wife. And Abimelech 15 said, Behold, my land is before thee : dwell where it pleas-

[4]15:1 ; 21 : 12, 14 ; 22 : 1, 3 ; 28 : 12 ; 31 : 10, 24 ; 37 : 5, 9, 19 ; 40 ; 41 ; 46 : 2 ; Num. 12 : 6. [5]Num. 12 : 6. [6]Ex. 32 : 21. [7]Jos. 7 : 20. Ct. 18 : 13. [8]Jos. 24 : 2f. [9]37 : 15. [10]Cf. 21 : 27. Ct. 12 : 16.

16 eth thee.   And unto Sarah he said, Behold, I have given
thy brother a thousand pieces of silver : behold, it is for
thee a covering of the eyes to all that are with thee ; and
17 in respect of all thou art righted.   And Abraham prayed
unto God : and God healed Abimelech, and his wife, and
18 his ''maidservants ; and they bare children.   For Yahweh
had fast closed up all the wombs of the house of Abimelech, because
of Sarah Abraham's wife.*

21   **(J) And Yahweh visited Sarah 'as he had said,**
2 (P) (J) *and Yahweh did unto Sarah 'as he had spoken.*   **And
Sarah conceived, and bare Abraham 'a son in his old**
3 (P) **age,** *at the 'set time of which God had spoken to him.   And
Abraham called the name of his son that was born unto him,*
4 *whom Sarah bare to him, Isaac.   And Abraham circumcised his
son Isaac when he was eight days old, 'as God had commanded*
5 *him.   And Abraham was an hundred years old, when his son*
6 (E) *Isaac was born unto him.*   And Sarah said, God hath
(J) made me to 'laugh :—**every one that heareth will**
7 **'laugh with me.†—And she said, Who would have said
unto Abraham, that Sarah should give children suck?
for I have borne him 'a son in his old age.**
8   (E) And the child grew, and was weaned : and Abraham made a great feast on the day that Isaac was weaned.
9 'And Sarah saw the son of Hagar the Egyptian, which
10 she had borne unto Abraham, mocking.‡   Wherefore she
said unto Abraham, Cast out this bondwoman and her son:

---

¹¹21:10-13; 30:3; 31:33; Ex. 2:5, etc. Ct. v. 14; 16:2-8; 30:7-18, etc. ¹18:10ff;
²17:16, 21. ³V. 7; 37:3; 44:20. ⁴17:21. ⁵17:12, 19. ⁶Ct. 17:17; 18:12; v. 9; 26:8. ⁷Ct.
16:4ff and 25:9.

* Ch. xxi. affords evidence both of abbreviation and retouching.   Yahweh in vs.
18 in contrast to *Elohim*, used universally by E previous to Ex. iii. 13 for the same
reason that P uses it previous to Ex. vi. 2, calls attention to the content of vs. 18,
which appears to be a substitute *post eventum* for something omitted between
verses 2 and 3 to which vv. 6 and 17 also refer.   The second clause of vs. 14 similarly
appears from the language (J alone uses *shiphcah*, "maidservant," E always
'amah, cf. vs. 17) to be interpolated.   Cf. xxi. 27, and note to xxi. 25.

† Translate, perhaps, "will laugh *at* me" (Job. v. 22 ; xxix. 7, 18, 22 ; Ps. lix. 9) ;
and transpose the clause, as suggested by Budde (*Urgeschichte* p. 224), to the middle
of vs. 7.   For the repeated plays upon the name Isaac, cf. note to xviii. 15.

‡ From the same stem as Isaac. Cf. note to xviii. 15.—Translate with margin
(R. V.) "playing" (xxvi. 8 ; Ex. xxxii. 6 ; Jud. xvi. 25, etc.).

for the son of this bondwoman shall not be heir with my son, even with Isaac. And the thing was very grievous in 11 Abraham's sight on account of his son. And God said un- 12 to Abraham, Let it not be grievous in thy sight because of the lad, and because of thy bondwoman ; in all that Sarah saith unto thee, hearken unto her voice ; for in Isaac shall thy seed be called. And also of the son of the bondwoman 13 will I make a nation, because he is thy seed. [8]And Abra- 14 ham rose up early in the morning, and took bread and a bottle of water, and gave it unto Hagar, putting it on her shoulder, and the child,* and sent her away : and she departed, and wandered in the wilderness of [9]Beer-sheba. And the water in the bottle was spent, and she cast the 15 child under one of the shrubs. And she went, and sat her 16 down over against him a good way off, as it were a bow-shot : for she said, Let me not look upon the death of the child. And she sat over against him, and lift up her voice, and wept.† And God heard the voice of the lad : [10]and the 17 angel of God called to Hagar out of heaven, and said unto her, What aileth thee, Hagar? fear not; for God hath heard the voice of the lad where he is. Arise, lift up the 18 lad, and hold him in thine hand ; for I will make him a great nation. And God opened her eyes, and she saw a 19 well of water ; and she went, and filled the bottle with water, and gave the lad drink. [. . .] And God was 20 with the lad, and he grew ; and he dwelt in the wilderness, and became an archer.‡ And he [11]dwelt in the wilder- 21

[8]V. 12 ; 22 : 1, 3, etc. [9]V. 27ff ; 22 : 19. [10]Cf. 22 : 11. Ct. 16 : 7. [11]16 : 12 ; 25 : 18.

*LXX. have, "and put the child upon her shoulder," etc. The present Massoretic text is unhebrew and is supposed by critics to be due to late correction suggested by the fact that according to the chronology of P (cf. xvii. 25) Ishmael must have been 17 or 18 years old at this time. The author, E, has of course in mind a very little child. Cf. vv. 15, 18, and note following.

† Verse 16*b* suggests further evidence of alteration for harmonistic purposes. LXX. have, "Therefore she sat down over against him. And *the child* lifted up its voice and wept." Cf. vs. 17*a*, "God heard the voice *of the lad*." Hence the etymology *yishma-el* — "God hears." Ct. xvi. 11.

‡ Kautzsch and Socin translate "became an archer, a bowman." After vs. 19 JE has omitted, "And she called his name Ishmael," or the equivalent (cf. vs. 17), on account of xvi. 11. (11)

ness of Paran : and his mother took him a wife out of the land of Egypt. [. . .]

22   ¹²And it came to pass at that time, that Abimelech and Phicol the captain of his host spake unto Abraham, saying,
23 God is with thee in all that thou doest : now therefore swear unto me here by God that thou wilt not deal falsely with me, nor with my son, nor with my son's son : but according to the kindness that I have done unto thee, thou shalt do unto me, and to the land wherein thou hast so-
24–25 journed. And Abraham said, I will swear. And Abraham reproved Abimelech because of the well of water, which Abimelech's servants had violently taken away.*
26 And Abimelech said, I know not who hath done this thing: neither didst thou tell me, neither yet heard I of it, but to-
27 day. ¹³And Abraham took sheep and oxen, and gave them
28 unto Abimelech ; and they two made a covenant. And Abraham set seven ewe lambs of the flock by themselves.
29 And Abimelech said unto Abraham, What mean these
30 seven ewe lambs which thou hast set by themselves? And he said, These seven ewe lambs shalt thou take of my hand, that it may be a witness unto me, that I have digged
31 (J) this well.† —¹⁴**Wherefore he called that place Beer-**
32 **sheba ; ¹⁵because there they sware both of them. So they made a covenant at Beer-sheba : and Abimelech**

¹²26 : 26ff.   ¹³20 : 14.   ¹⁴2 : 24, etc.   ¹⁵26 : 31.

* Verse 25 obviously refers to something now omitted originally parallel to xxvi. 19ff. This account of ch. xx.f (E), is in fact so remarkably similar to that of ch. xxvi. as to suggest the objection to the analysis, " No compiler would permit materials so incongruous, or mutually exclusive, to stand side by side : the analysis proves too much." In weighing this objection the reader's attention is called to the case of Tatian's Diatessaron cited in ch. I. and to the article of Prof. Moore's there referred to. It is also to be observed that while JE permits chaps. xx.f and xxvi. to stand so near together with scarcely more of difference than the appearance of Abraham in the principal role in one case and Isaac in the other, verse 25 and the determinative prefix *eth* in vs. 28 ("*the* seven ewe lambs ") bear witness to a process of abbreviation which ch. xx.f has undergone, apparently to remove too great coincidence or conflict.

† According to verse 30 the ceremony at "the Well of the *Seven* " is a certification of Abraham's right to the well, the digging of which we must suppose was related in the omitted portions. In ch. xxvi. the well, on the contrary, is merely a witness to the covenant, the fact of the treaty of friendship with Abimelech being brought into the foreground and commemorated by the name, " Well of the *Oath*."

rose up, and Phicol the captain of his host, and [16]they returned into the land of the Philistines. And [Abra- 33 ham] planted a tamarisk tree in Beer-sheba, [17]and called there on the name of Yahweh, the Everlasting (E) God.— And Abraham sojourned in the land of the 34 Philistines many days.*

[1]And it came to pass after these things, that God did 22 [2]prove Abraham, and said unto him, [3]Abraham ; and he said, Here am I. And he said, Take now thy son, thine 2 only son, whom thou lovest, even Isaac, and get thee into the land of [4]Moriah,;† and offer him there for a burnt offering upon one of the mountains which I will tell thee of. And 3 Abraham [5]rose early in the morning, and saddled his ass, and took two of his young men with him, and Isaac his son ; and he clave the wood for the burnt offering, and rose up, and went unto the place of which God had told him. On the third day Abraham lifted up his eyes, and 4 saw the place‡ afar off. And Abraham said unto his 5 young men, Abide ye here with the ass, and I and the lad will go [6]yonder ; and we will worship, and come again to you. And Abraham took the wood of the burnt offering, 6 and laid it upon Isaac his son ; and he took in his hand the fire and the knife ; and they went both of them together. And Isaac spake unto Abraham his father, and said, [7]My 7 father: and he said, Here am I, my son. And he said, Behold, the fire and the wood : but where is the lamb for a burnt offering? And Abraham said, [8]God will provide 8 himself the lamb for a burnt offering, my son : so they

[16]26:1, 26. [17]4:26, etc. [1]15:1, etc. [2]Ex. 16:4; 20:20. [3]Vv. 7, 11 ; 27:1, 18; 31:11; 37:13; 46:2f; Ex. 3:4. [4]II. Chron. 3:1. [5]V. 1. Cf. 20:8; 21:14. [6]31:37; Ex. 2:12; Num. 23:15. [7]Vv. 1, 11 ; 27:1, 18, etc. [8]V. 14.

* In vs. 33 supply Isaac instead of " Abraham " of the revisers and transpose vv. 31–33 with xxvi. 33. For this new analysis and the conjectural readings of xxii. 2 and 14 consult my article before referred to in *Hebraica*, April, 1891.

† " Moriah " is regarded by all critics as a late alteration connected with the Jehovistic verses of this chapter. Read " the Negeb " as in xx. 1 ; xxiv. 62; Num. xiii. 29.

‡ Some conspicuous place with a well-known altar. Cf. vs. 9, " the altar there," an expression scarcely to be accounted for as " *the requisite* altar." (Kautzsch and Socin.)

9 went both of them together.   And they came to the place
which God had told him of ; and Abraham built the altar
there, and laid the wood in order, and bound Isaac his son,
10 and laid him on the altar, upon the wood.   And Abraham
stretched forth his hand, and took the knife to slay his son.
11 And the angel of Yahweh* called unto him out of heaven,
and said, 'Abraham, Abraham : and he said, Here am I.
12 And he said, Lay not thine hand upon the lad, neither do
thou anything unto him : for now I know that thou [10]fear-
est God, seeing thou hast not withheld thy son, thine only
13 son, from me.   And Abraham lifted up his eyes, and looked,
and behold, behind [him] a ram caught in the thicket by
his horns : and Abraham went and took the ram, and offered him up for a burnt offering in the stead of his son.
14 And Abraham called the name of that place Yahweh-jireh:
as it is said to this day, In the mount of Yahweh it shall be
15 (JE) provided.   And the angel of Yahweh called unto Abraham a
16 second time out of heaven, and said, By myself have I sworn, saith
Yahweh, Because thou hast done this thing, [11]and hast not withheld
17 thy son, thine only son : that in blessing I will bless thee, and in
multiplying I will multiply thy seed [12]as the stars of the heaven, and as
[13]the sand which is upon the sea shore ; and thy seed shall possess
18 the gate of his enemies ; and in thy seed shall all the [14]nations of the
19 (E) earth be blessed ; because thou hast obeyed my voice.†   So
Abraham returned unto his young men, and they rose up
and went together to [15]Beer-sheba ; and Abraham dwelt
at [16]Beer-sheba.
20   (J) [10]And it came to pass after these things, [. . .] that‡

[9]Vv. 1, 7, etc.   [10]20:11.   [11]V. 12.   [12]15:5.   [13]Ct. 13:16.   [14]18:18 ; 26:4. Ct. 12:3 ; 28:14.
[15]21:27ff.   [16]15:1 ; 22:1, etc.

* "Yahweh" is accounted for by assimilation of vs. 11 to vs. 15.   Cf. xxi. 17.

† Apart from the use of Yahweh in the passage 14*b*-18, the reintroduction of the
angel, as by afterthought, is to the critic an almost certain mark of interpolation.
The little word *'odh* "again," "the second time" in such connection (cf. xxxv. 9 ;
Josh. v. 2-9) has a suspicious character. The object of the assumed interpolation of
the chapter is, of course, the adaptation to the Judæan point of view of a narrative of northern origin, transmitted to us through Judæan hands. In vs. 14 read
"El-roi" and "God" for Yahweh-jireh and Yahweh. See *Hebraica*, April, 1891,
and cf. Heb. note (12).—Verses 15-18 are of the usual didactic character (cf. xiii.
14-17 ; xv. 13-16 ; xviii. 18f), but while mainly reproducing the blessing of Abram,
xii. 1-3, substitute "nations" for the "families" of xii. 3.

‡ Hebrew, "and."

it was told Abraham, saying, Behold, [17]Milcah, [18]she also hath borne children unto thy brother Nahor: [19]Uz 21 his firstborn, and Buz his brother, and [20]Kemuel the father of Aram; and Chesed, and Hazo, and Pildash, 22 and Jidlaph, and Bethuel. [21]And Bethuel begat Re- 23 bekah: these eight did Milcah bear to Nahor, Abraham's brother. And his concubine, whose name was 24 Reumah, [22]she also bare Tebah, and Gaham, and Tahash, and [23]Maacah.*

(P) [1]*And the life of Sarah was an hundred and seven and* 23 *twenty years: these were the years of the life of Sarah. And* 2 *Sarah died in Kiriath-arba (the same is Hebron), in the land of Canaan. And Abraham came to mourn for Sarah, and to weep for her. And Abraham rose up from before his dead, and spake* 3 *unto the [2]children of Heth, saying, I am a stranger and a sojour-* 4 *ner with you: [3]give me a possession of a buryingplace with you, that I may bury my dead out of my sight. And [3]the children of* 5 *Heth answered Abraham, saying unto him, Hear us, my lord:* 6 *thou art a mighty prince among us: in the choice of our sepulchres bury thy dead; none of us shall withhold from thee his sepulchre, but that thou mayest bury thy dead. And Abraham* 7 *rose up, and bowed himself to the people of the land, even to the children of Heth. And he communed with them, saying, If it be* 8 *your mind that I should bury my dead out of my sight, hear me, and intreat for me to Ephron the son of Zohar, that he may give* 9 *me the cave of Machpelah, which he hath, which is in the end of his field; for the full price let him give it to me in the midst of you for a possession of a buryingplace. Now Ephron was sitting* 10

[17]11:29. [18]V. 24; 4:4, 22, 26; 10:21; 19:38. [19]Ct. 10:15, 23. [20]Ct. 10:22f. [21]24:4, 10, 24. [22]Dt. 3:14; Jos. 12:5; 13:11, 13. [1]25:7, 17, etc. [2]Vv. 5, 7, 10, 16, 18, 20; 25:10; 49:32. Ct. 12:6, etc. [3]49:29f. Ct. 33:19; Jos. 24:32.

* The significance of this brief genealogical table is not apparent in the present condition of the text. Eliminate however the non-J portions, and verse 20 comes into immediate connection with Sarah's unexpected fruitfulness in xxi. 7 on the one hand, while on the other this table of the twelve tribes of north Semitic stock, including the genealogy of Rebekah, stands immediately before the list of twelve tribes of south Semitic stock (Keturites) in xxv. 1-5. This latter passage, however, is supposed to have preceded ch. xxiv. on account of the apparent reference in xxiv. 36 to xxv. 5. The story of Isaac's marriage with Rebekah then followed a few lines after Rebekah's genealogy.

*in the midst of the children of Heth : and Ephron the Hittite
answered Abraham in the audience of the children of Heth, even*
11 *of all that went in at the gate of his city, saying, Nay, my Lord,
hear me : the field give I thee, and the cave that is therein, I give
it thee ; in the presence of the sons of my people give I it thee :*
12 *bury thy dead.   And Abraham bowed himself down before the*
13 *people of the land.   And he spake unto Ephron in the audience of
the people of the land, saying, But if thou wilt, I pray thee, hear
me : I will give the price of the field ; take it of me, and I will*
14 *bury my dead there.   And Ephron answered Abraham, saying*
15 *unto him, My lord, hearken unto me : a piece of land worth 'four
hundred shekels of silver, what is that betwixt me and thee ? bury*
16 *therefore thy dead.   And Abraham hearkened unto Ephron ; and
Abraham weighed to Ephron the silver, which he had named in
the audience of the children of Heth, four hundred shekels of*
17 *silver, current [money] with the merchant.   So the field of Ephron, which was in Machpelah, which was before Mamre, the
field, and the cave which was therein, and all the trees that were
in the field, that were in all the border thereof round about, were*
18 *made sure unto Abraham for a possession in the presence of the
children of Heth, before all that went in at the gate of his city.*
19 *And after this, Abraham buried Sarah his wife in the cave of
the field of Machpelah before Mamre (the same is Hebron), in*
20 *the land of Canaan.   And the field, and the cave that is therein,
were made sure unto Abraham for a possession of a buryingplace by the children of Heth.*

24   (J) 'And Abraham was old, [and] well stricken in
age : and Yahweh had blessed Abraham in all things.
2 And Abraham said unto 'his servant, the elder of his
house, that ruled over all that he had, 'Put, I pray
3 thee, thy hand under my thigh : and I will make thee
swear by Yahweh, the God of heaven and the God of
earth, that thou shalt not take a wife for my son of
the daughters of the Canaanites, 'among whom I
4 dwell : but thou shalt go unto 'my country, and to my
5 kindred, and take a wife for my son Isaac.   And the

'33:19.   '18:11.   'Ct. 15:2f.   '47:29.   '12:6, Ct. 23:7.   '12:1ff.

servant said unto him, Peradventure the woman will
not be willing to follow me unto this land: must I
needs bring thy son again unto the land from whence
thou camest? And Abraham said unto him, Beware 6
thou that thou bring not my son thither again. Yah- 7
weh, the God of heaven, that 'took me from my father's house, and from the land of my nativity, and
that spake unto me, and that sware unto me, saying,
Unto thy seed will I give this land : he shall send his
angel before thee, and thou shalt take a wife for my
son from thence. And if the woman be not willing to 8
follow thee, then thou shalt be clear from this my
oath ; only thou shalt not bring my son thither again.
And the servant put his hand under the thigh of 9
Abraham his master, and sware to him concerning
this matter. And the servant took ten camels, of the 10
camels of his master, and departed ; 'having all goodly things of his master's in his hand: and he arose,
and went* to Mesopotamia † unto the city of Nahor.
And he made the camels to kneel down without the 11
city by the well of water at the time of evening, the
time that women go out to draw water. And he said, 12
O Yahweh, the God of my master Abraham, 'send me,
I pray thee, good speed this day, and shew kindness
unto my master Abraham. Behold, I stand by the 13
fountain of water ; and the daughters of the men of
the city come out to draw water : and let it come to 14
pass, that the damsel to whom I shall say, Let down
thy pitcher, I pray thee, that I may drink ; and she

⁵12:1ff. ⁶V. 2. ⁷27:20.

*The superfluous "and departed" may be a mere anticipation of 10*b*, to be
eliminated with LXX. So Kautzsch and Socin.

†The reading (R. V. margin), Aram Naharaim, i. e. Aram of the two rivers (in the
Amarna tablets, *Naharina*), is alone correct. It has only an etymological resemblance to "Mesopotamia." The region of Harran (xxvii. 43; xxviii. 10, cf. xl. 31) is
meant, between the Euphrates and Chaboras, and by no means that of "Ur of the
Chaldees" between the Euphrates and Tigris." P has "Paddan-aram" (xxv. 20;
xxxi. 18, etc.) or Plain of Aram. Both the rivers and the plain are those of *Syria*
(Aram) and not of Assyria, still less of Babylonia.

shall say, Drink, and I will give thy camels drink
also: let the same be she that thou hast appointed for
thy servant Isaac; and thereby shall I know that thou
15 hast shewed kindness unto my master. And it came
to pass, before he had done speaking, that, behold,
[8]Rebekah came out, who was born to Bethuel the son
of Milcah, the wife of Nahor, Abraham's brother,
16 with her pitcher on her shoulder. And the damsel
was [9]very fair to look upon, a virgin, neither had any
man [10]known her: and she went down to the fountain,
17 and filled her pitcher, and came up. And the servant ran to meet her, and said, Give me to drink, I
18 pray thee, a little water of thy pitcher. And she
said, Drink, my lord: and she hasted, and let down
19 her pitcher upon her hand, and gave him drink. And
when she had done giving him drink, she said, I will
draw for thy camels also, until they have done drink-
20 ing. And she hasted, and emptied her pitcher into
the [11]trough, and ran again unto the well to draw, and
21 drew for all his camels. And the man looked sted-
fastly on her; holding his peace, to know whether
Yahweh had made his journey [12]prosperous or not.
22 And it came to pass, as the camels had done drinking,
that the man took a golden ring of half a shekel
weight, and two bracelets for her hands of ten shekels
23 weight of gold; and said, Whose daughter art thou?
tell me, I pray thee. Is there room in thy father's
24 house for us to lodge in? And she said unto him, I
am [8]the daughter of Bethuel the son of Milcah, which
25 she bare unto Nahor. She said moreover unto him,
We have both straw and provender enough, and room
26 to lodge in. And the man bowed his head, and wor-
27 shipped Yahweh. And he said, Blessed be Yahweh,
the God of my master Abraham, who hath not forsaken [13]his mercy and his truth toward my master:

[8]22:23; 11:29. [9]12:11. [10]4:1; 19:5, 8. [11]29:3; 30:38. [12]Vv. 40, 42, 56; 39:2f, 23.
[13]V. 49; 32:11; 47:29; Ex. 34:6; Jos. 2:14.

as for me, Yahweh hath led me in the way to the
house of my master's brethren. And the damsel ran, 28
and told her mother's house according to these words.
And Rebekah had a brother, and his name was Laban: 29
—and Laban ran out unto the man, unto the fountain.— And it came to pass, when he saw the ring, 30
and the bracelets upon his sister's hands, and when he
heard the words of Rebekah his sister, saying, Thus
spake the man unto me;* that he came unto the man;
and, behold, he stood by the camels at the fountain.
And he said, Come in, "thou blessed of Yahweh, 31
wherefore standest thou without? for I have prepared the house, and room for the camels. And the 32
man came † into the house, and he ungirded the camels; and he gave straw and provender for the camels,
and water to wash his feet and the men's feet that
were with him. And there was set meat before him 33
to eat: but he said, I will not eat, until I have told
mine errand. And he said, Speak on. And he said, 34
I am Abraham's servant. And Yahweh hath blessed 35
my master greatly; and he is become great: and he
hath given him "flocks and herds, and silver and gold,
and menservants and maidservants, and camels and
asses. And Sarah my master's wife bare a son to my 36
master when she was old: "and unto him hath he
given all that he hath. "And my master made me 37
swear, saying, Thou shalt not take a wife for my son
of the daughters of the Canaanites, in whose land I
dwell; but thou shalt go unto my father's house, and 38
to my kindred, and take a wife for my son. And I 39
said unto my master, Peradventure the woman will
not follow me. And he said unto me, Yahweh, before 40
whom I walk, will send his angel with thee, and prosper thy way; and thou shalt take a wife for my son

[13]26:29. [14]12:16; 13:2; 30:43; 32:5. [15]Cf. 25:5. [16]Vv. 3-8.

* The true position of 29*b* would seem to be between 30 *a* and *b*.

† Read with Vulg., "And he [Laban] brought," etc.

41 of my kindred, and of my father's house: then shalt
   thou be clear from my oath, when thou comest to my
   kindred;* and if they give her not to thee, thou shalt
42 be clear from my oath. [17]And I came this day unto
   the fountain, and said, O Yahweh, the God of my
   master Abraham, if now thou do prosper my way
43 which I go: behold, I stand by the fountain of water;
   and let it come to pass, that the maiden which cometh forth to draw, to whom I shall say, Give me, I
44 pray thee, a little water of thy pitcher to drink; and
   she shall say to me, Both drink thou, and I will also
   draw for thy camels: let the same be the woman
   whom Yahweh hath appointed for my master's son.
45 And before I had done speaking in mine heart, behold, Rebekah came forth with her pitcher on her
   shoulder; and she went down unto the fountain, and
   drew: and I said unto her, Let me drink, I pray thee.
46 And she made haste, and let down her pitcher from
   her shoulder, and said, Drink, and she made the
47 camels drink also: so I drank, and she made the camels drink also. And I asked her, and said, Whose
   daughter art thou? And she said, The daughter of
   Bethuel, Nahor's son, whom Milcah bare unto him;
   and I put the ring upon her nose, and the bracelets
48 upon her hands. And I bowed my head, and worshipped Yahweh, and blessed Yahweh, the God of my
   master Abraham, which had led me in the right way
   to take me my master's brother's daughter for his
49 son. And now if ye will [18]deal kindly and truly with
   my master, tell me: and if not, tell me; that I may
50 [19]turn to the right hand, or to the left. Then Laban
   and Bethuel † answered and said, The thing proceedeth

[17]Vv. 12–14. [18]47:29. [19]13:9.

* Kautzsch and Socin point out that some phrase equivalent to, " And they give
thee a wife for Isaac," must be supplied here.

†" And Bethuel" is perhaps interpolated here, as verses 28, 53 and 55 would lead
us to suppose Laban alone to be the head of the house.

from Yahweh : we cannot speak unto thee bad or good.
Behold, Rebekah is before thee, take her, and go, and 51
let her be thy master's son's wife, as Yahweh hath
spoken.   And it came to pass, that, when Abraham's 52
servant heard their words, he bowed himself down to
the earth unto Yahweh.   And the servant brought 53
forth jewels of silver, and jewels of gold, and raiment,
and gave them to Rebekah : he gave also to her brother and to her mother precious things.   And they 54
did eat and drink, he and the men that were with him,
and tarried all night; and they rose up in the morning, and he said, Send me away unto my master.   And 55
her brother and her mother said, Let the damsel abide
with us [a few] days, at the least ten ; after that she
shall go.   And he said unto them, ²⁰Hinder me not, 56
seeing Yahweh hath prospered my way ; send me away
that I may go to my master.   And they said, We will 57
call the damsel, and inquire at her mouth.   And they 58
called Rebekah, and said unto her, Wilt thou go with
this man?   And she said, I will go.   And they sent 59
away Rebekah their sister, and her ²¹nurse, and Abraham's servant, and his men.   And they blessed Re- 60
bekah, and said unto her, Our sister, be thou [the
mother] of thousands of ten thousands, and let thy
seed possess the gate of those which hate them.   And 61
Rebekah arose, and her damsels, and they rode upon
the camels, and followed the man: [. . .] and the
servant took Rebekah, and went his way.*   And Isaac 62

²⁰32 : 4 ; 34 : 19.   ²¹Ct. 35 : 8.

*In vs. 61 something has almost certainly been omitted.   To the eye of
the Hebrew scholar vs. 61*a* cannot tolerate 61*b* after it, especially after vs. 59.
Moreover, from the standpoint of the analysis, it is certain that J related
somewhere in ch. xxiv. the death of Abraham.   Verses 1ff form the death-bed
scene (cf. xlvii. 29), and after this chapter Abraham appears no more.   Also the
servant reports to *Isaac* as his master, and calls him so expressly in vs. 65.   The
notice of Abraham's death, however, would have to be stricken out when xxv. 7ff
was incorporated.   This notice Kautzsch and Socin think came after 61*a* as follows :
" And they came to Hebron and found Abram dead ;" then 61*b*, "and the servant
took Rebekah and came to . . . . . ."   Perhaps 61*b* should be completed by
drawing to it the first word of vs. 62 (Isaac).   We should have then, with the addition

came from the way of "Beer-lahai-roi; for he dwelt
63 in the land of the South. And Isaac went out to med-
itate in the field "at the eventide: and he lifted up
his eyes, and saw, and, behold, there were camels
64 coming. And Rebekah lifted up her eyes, and when
65 she saw Isaac, she lighted off the camel. And she
said unto the servant, What man is this that walketh
in the field to meet us? And the servant said, It is
my master: and she took "her veil, and covered her-
66 self. And the servant told Isaac all the things that
67 he had done. And Isaac brought her into *his mother
Sarah's* tent, and took Rebekah, and she became his
wife, and he loved her: and Isaac "was comforted
after *his mother's* death.*

25   —And Abraham took another wife, and her name
 2 was Keturah. And she bare him Zimran, and 'Jokshan, and *Medan,* and Midian, and Ishbak, and Shuah.
 3 And Jokshan begat 'Sheba, and Dedan. And the sons
of Dedan were Asshurim, and Letushim, and Leum-
 4 mim. And the sons of Midian; Ephah, and Epher,
and Hanoch, and Abida, and Eldaah. 'All these were
 5 the children of Keturah. 'And Abraham gave all
 6 (R) that he had unto Isaac.†—   *But unto the sons of the* ⁵con-

²²25:11. ²³3:8. ²⁴38:14, 19. ²⁵37:35; 38:12. ¹Ct. 10:26. ²Ct. 10:7, 28. ³9:19;
10:29. ⁴24:36. ⁵Ct. 16:3; V. 1.

of a single letter after 6*b*, "*to* Isaac: and he went by the way of Beer-lahai-roi
(LXX. "through the wilderness"); for *he* (emphatic, i. e. Isaac) dwelt in the land of
the South." The repetition of Isaac as subject both in 62 and 63 is thus avoided. (13)

 * The Hebrew form of the word "tent" (absolute, not construct) shows that it
originally stood alone, and not in construction, as here, with a genitive. As the
words, "his mother Sarah's," thus appear to be spurious, and the whole chapter
suggests, as already mentioned, the death, not of Sarah, but of Abraham, Wellhausen attributes this gloss and the alteration of "father's" to "mother's" in
vs. 67 to R, who wished to harmonize with P, and had chap. xxiii in mind.

 † Xxv. 1-5 has been referred to as displaced from its original position. In fact, it
is hardly less incongruous after the relation of Abram's death (see note preceding)
than after the repeated allusions to his extreme old age and hopelessness of posterity
which fill the preceding chapters, especially in P. Verse 5 in particular relates,
as we have seen, an incident which Abram's servant relates as having already
transpired in xxiv. 36. For this verse, with the fragment 11*b*, which perhaps goes
with it, the most probable position would seem to be after xxiv. 1. Verses 1-4 must
of course have preceded xxiv. 1, and they find in fact an appropriate context be-

cubines, which Abraham had, Abraham gave gifts : and he sent them away from
(P) *Isaac his son, while he yet lived, eastward, unto the east country.** *⁶And* 7
these are the days of the years of Abraham's life which he lived,
an hundred threescore and fifteen years. And Abraham gave up 8
the ghost, and died in a good old age, an old man, and full [of
years] ; and was gathered to his people. *⁷And Isaac and Ishmael* 9
his sons buried him in the cave of Machpelah, in the field of Eph-
ron the son of Zohar the Hittite, which is before Mamre ; the 10
field which Abraham purchased of the children of Heth : there
was Abraham buried, and Sarah his wife. And it came to pass 11
after the death of Abraham, that God blessed Isaac his son :

(J) **⁸and Isaac dwelt by Beer-lahai-roi.†**

(P) *⁹Now these are the generations of Ishmael, Abraham's son,* 12
whom Hagar the Egyptian, Sarah's handmaid, bare unto Abra-
ham : ¹⁰and these are the names of the sons of Ishmael, by their 13
names, according to their generations : the firstborn of Ishmael,
Nebaioth ; and Kedar, and Adbeel, and Mibsam, and Mishma, 14
and Dumah, and Massa ; Hadad, and Temah, Jetur, Naphish, 15
and Kedemah : these are the sons of Ishmael, and these are their 16
names, by their villages, and by their encampments ; twelve princes
according to their nations. *⁸And these are the years of the life of* 17
Ishmael, an hundred and thirty and seven years : and he gave up

(J) *the ghost and died ; and was gathered unto his people.* **—And** 18
they dwelt from ¹¹Havilah unto Shur that is before
Egypt, as thou goest toward Assyria; ¹²he abode in the
presence of all his brethren.‡—

⁶V. 17; 35:28f, etc.   ⁷49:31.   ⁸24:62.   ⁹2:4, etc.   ¹⁰36:10, 40; 46:8.   ¹¹2:11, etc.
¹²16:12.

tween xxii. 24 and xxiv. 1. Dillmann would prefer to place vv. 1–4 before ch. xviii.

* Dillmann gives reasons (Gen. ⁵, p. 305) for attributing xxv. 6 to late redaction.
According to both J and E, Hagar is more than a "concubine" and Keturah is even
a "wife." Hagar's son, according to both, is already long since settled in the
"east country." If spurious, the object of the verse is certainly to point out the
inferiority of the Abrahamic 12 tribes just enumerated (Medan, vs. 2, is probably a
mere explanatory gloss to Midian, for the two are interchangeable : cf. xxvii. 36) to
Isaac's descendants.

† The true position of 11b is a difficult question. Perhaps it stands best after all
where it is, i. e. directly after ch. xxiv.

‡ Verse 18 is a veritable *crux.* It has certainly a relation to xvi. 12, and is supposed by Wellhausen to be taken from that connection. It applies of course to the
people (Ishmael), of whom it is there predicted that " he shall dwell over against all

19 (P) [13]*And these are the generations of Isaac, Abraham's son ;*
20 *Abraham begat Isaac : and Isaac was forty years old when he took Rebekah, the daughter of Bethuel the* [14]*Syrian of Paddan-aram, the sister of Laban the* [14]*Syrian, to be his wife.* [. . .]
21 (J) —And Isaac [15]intreated Yahweh for his wife, because she was [16]barren : and Yahweh was intreated of
22 him, and Rebekah his wife conceived. And the children struggled together within her ; and she said, If it be so, wherefore do I live? And she went to [17]in-
23 quire of Yahweh. And Yahweh said unto her,
Two nations are in thy womb,
And two peoples shall be separated even from thy
    bowels :
And the one people shall be stronger than the other
    people ;
And the elder shall serve the younger.
24 [18]And when her days to be delivered were fulfilled, be-
25 hold, there were twins in her womb. And the first came forth [19]red,* all over like an hairy garment ; and
26 they called his name Esau. And after that came forth his brother, and his hand [20]had hold on Esau's heel : (P) and his name was called Jacob : *and Isaac was three-*
27 (J) *score years old when she bare them.* And the boys grew :

[13]2:4, etc.   [14]Cf. 10:23. Ct. 22:20ff.   [15]Ex. 8:4, 5, 24-26; 9:28, etc.   [16]11:30; 29:31.
[17]26:23-25   [18]38:27ff.   [19]V. 30.   [20]Ct. 27:36.

his brethren."—The phrase, "as thou goest toward Assyria," is meaningless and almost certainly corrupt; probably a mere dittograph. Cf. Well. iv., p. 22 note. This chapter seems in fact a critic's limbo for fragments left over by the compilers.

* A play upon Edom, " red." Budde (Urg. p. 217 n. 2) conjectures some word like *seir*, "hirsute," which would really correspond with the succeeding clause, or else a word corresponding to the name Esau ("rough") given in the latter part of the verse. The objection is that the superseding of an appropriate word by an inappropriate one is not usual. The present word, *edumni*, on the contrary, if original, may be regarded as a trace of E's parallel account, which in the story of Jacob and Esau is almost identical, and seems to imply that in E the name Edom was given from the color of the skin at birth. Possibly the expression, "upright man," of vs. 27, which gives the translators so much trouble, may also be derived from E ; J could scarcely think of attributing to Jacob a character of simple uprightness and integrity ; but how to reconcile this with E's story, the leading feature of which is still Jacob's duplicity, it is hard to see. J had perhaps only : "And Esau was . . . a man of the field, but Jacob was a dweller in tents." Cf. Gen. iv. 20.

and Esau was a cunning hunter, a man of the field;
and Jacob was a plain man, dwelling in tents. ²⁷Now 28
Isaac loved Esau, because he did eat of his venison:
and Rebekah loved Jacob. And Jacob sod pottage: 29
and Esau came in from the field, and he was faint:
and Esau said to Jacob, Feed me, I pray thee, with 30
that same red [pottage]; for I am faint: therefore
was his name called Edom. And Jacob said, ²⁸Sell me 31
this day thy birthright. And Esau said, Behold, I am 32
at the point to die: and what profit shall the birthright do to me? And Jacob said, Swear to me this 33
day; and he sware unto him: and he sold his birthright unto Jacob. And Jacob gave Esau bread and 34
pottage of lentils; and he did eat and drink, and rose
up, and went his way: so Esau despised his birthright.*—

¹And there was a famine in the land, ²beside the first 26
famine that was in the days of Abraham. And Isaac went
unto Abimelech king of the Philistines unto Gerar.
(JE) And Yahweh appeared unto him, and said, ³Go not 2
down into Egypt; dwell in the land which I shall tell thee of:
(J) sojourn in this land, and I will be with thee, and 3
(JE) will bless thee; for unto thee, and unto thy seed, I will
give all these lands, and I will establish ⁴the oath which I sware unto
Abraham thy father ; and I will multiply thy seed as the stars of 4
heaven, and will give unto thy seed all these lands ; and in thy seed
shall all the ¹nations of the earth be blessed ; because that Abraham 5
⁵obeyed my voice, and kept my charge, my commandments, my stat-
(J) utes, and my laws.† And Isaac dwelt in Gerar: and 6, 7

²¹27:5, 7. ²²27:36. Cf. 43:33; 48:13ff; 49:3. ¹Ct. ch. 20f. ²12:10ff. ³Ct. vv. 1*b*, 3*a*.
⁴22:17f. Ct. 12:3. ⁵18:19; Ex. 15:25f; Dt. 11:1.

* Of course xxv. 21ff, with its story of Rebekah, long barren, then giving birth to
twins who grow to maturity, cannot originally have preceded xxvi., in which she
appears as the young and attractive wife of Isaac. The positions must be reversed ;
xxv. 11*b* should be followed by xxvi. 1–33, then xxv. 21ff. Thus the place of Isaac's
"intreating of Yahweh" is made plain, viz., Beersheba.

† Ch. xxvi. affords an instructive study of the supposed methods of the interpolator. ·
The second clause of verse 1 is regarded as an explanation made necessary by the
interpolation of Gen. xii. 10ff. At the same time the clause and the passage it refers
to must precede in date the union of J and E, since otherwise it would be not Gen.
xii. 10ff which required explanation, but the much nearer and more closely parallel

the men of the place asked him of his wife; [6]and he
said, She is my sister: for he feared to say, My wife;
lest, [said he], the men of the place should kill me for
8 Rebekah: because [7]she was fair to look upon. And it
came to pass, when he had been there a long time,
that Abimelech king of the Philistines looked out at
a window, and saw, and, behold, Isaac was [8]sporting
9 with Rebekah his wife. And Abimelech called Isaac,
and said, Behold, of a surety she is thy wife: and how
saidst thou, She is my sister? And Isaac said unto
10 him, Because I said, Lest I die for her. And Abimelech said, What is this thou hast done unto us? one
of the people might lightly have lien with thy wife,
and thou shouldest have brought guiltiness upon us.
11 And Abimelech charged all the people, saying, He
that toucheth this man or his wife shall surely be
12 put to death. And Isaac sowed in the land, and found
in the same year an hundredfold: and Yahweh blessed
13 him. [9]And the man waxed great, and grew more and
14 more until he became very great: and he had [10]posses-
sions of flocks, and possessions of herds, and a great
15 (JE) household: and the Philistines envied him. Now
all the [11]wells which his father's servants had digged in the days of
Abraham his father, the Philistines had stopped them, and filled
16 (J) them with earth.* **And Abimelech said unto Isaac, Go**

[6]12:10ff; 20:1ff. [7]24:16. Ct. 25:21ff. [8]21:9. [9]8:3, 5; 12:9; 24:35; 48:19. [10]47:17f.
[11]21:25ff.

incident, Gen. xx. Verses 2*b*, 4, 5, and all but the first clause of 3 would show
didactic interpolation of a very common kind, exhibiting the style of the Deuteronomist, especially in vs. 5.

* Harmonistic interpolation. On the composite authorship theory the editor had
already incorporated the story of Abraham digging and naming these very wells
(xxi. 22ff (E)), or if he had omitted some, he preserved one at least (Beersheba).
To permit the story of Isaac's digging and naming the same wells the only possible
expedient was that some one should fill them with earth. The Philistines accordingly
(who, however, according to xxi. 25 (E) and xxvi. 20f (J) are more eager to appropriate
the wells than to destroy them) are brought in by JE to do this service. The interpolator betrays himself, however, in the endeavor, in vs. 18, to meet the difficulty of
identity of names. True he states that Isaac " called their names after the names
by which his father had called them ;" but this contradicts the verses immediately
following, according to which Isaac gave them names suggested by the events occurring now in his own time.

from us; for thou art much mightier than we. And 17
Isaac departed thence, and encamped in the valley of
(JE) Gerar, and dwelt there. And Isaac digged again [12]the 18
wells of water, which they had digged in the days of Abraham his
father; for the Philistines had stopped them after the death of Abraham : [13]and he called their names after the names by which his father
(J) had called them.* And Isaac's servants digged in the 19
valley, and found there a well of springing water.
[14]And the herdmen of Gerar strove with Isaac's herd- 20
men, saying, The water is ours: and he called the
name of the well Esek; because they contended with
him. And they digged another well, and they strove 21
for that also: and he called the name of it Sitnah.
And he removed from thence, and digged another 22
well; and for that they strove not: and he called the
name of it Rehoboth; and he said, For now Yahweh
hath made room for us, and we shall be fruitful in
the land. And he went up from thence to Beer-sheba. 23
[15]And Yahweh appeared unto him the same night, and 24
said, I am the God of Abraham thy father: fear not,
for I am with thee, and will bless thee, and multiply
thy seed for my servant Abraham's sake. [16]And he 25
builded an altar there, and called upon the name of
Yahweh, and pitched his tent there: and there Isaac's
servants digged a well. [17]Then Abimelech went to 26
him from Gerar, and Ahuzzath his friend, and Phicol
the captain of his host. And Isaac said unto them, 27
Wherefore are ye come unto me, seeing ye hate me,
and have sent me away from you? And they said, 28
[18]We saw plainly that Yahweh was with thee: and we
said, Let there now be an oath betwixt us, even betwixt
us and thee, and let us make a covenant with thee;
that thou wilt do us no hurt, as we have not touched 29
thee, and as we have done unto thee nothing but good,
and have sent thee away in peace: [19]thou art now the

[12]21 : 25ff. [13]Ct. vv. 20ff. [14]21 : 25. [15]12 : 1ff. [16]12 : 7; 4 : 26, etc. [17]Ct. 21 : 22. [18]30 : 27.
[19]24 : 31.

* Harmonistic interpolation. See note preceding.

30 blessed of Yahweh. And he made them a feast, and
31 they did eat and drink. And they rose up betimes in
the morning, and sware one to another: and Isaac
sent them away, and they departed from him in peace.
32 And it came to pass the same day, that Isaac's servants came, and told him concerning the well which
they had digged, and said unto him, We have found
33 (E) water.*   —And he called it Shibah : therefore the
name of the city is Beer-sheba unto this day.†—

34   (P) [20]*And when Esau was forty years old he took to wife*
[21]*Judith the daughter of Beeri the Hittite, and* [21]*Basemath the*
35 *daughter of Elon the Hittite : and they were a grief of mind un-*
to Isaac and to Rebekah.

27 (J) And it came to pass, that when Isaac was old, [1]and
his eyes were dim, so that he could not see,‡ [. . .]
(E) he called Esau his elder son, and said unto him, [2]My
2 son : and he said unto him, Here am I.   And he said, Be-
3 hold now, I am old, I know not the day of my death.   Now
(J) therefore take, I pray thee, thy weapons, thy quiver and thy bow, and go out to the field, and take me
4 (E) venison ; and make me savoury meat, such as I love,
(J) and bring it to me, that I may eat ; [. . .] [3]that my

[20]Cf. 27:46; 28:9. Ct. ch. 27.   [21]Ct. 36:1ff.   [1]48:10ff.   [2]22:1, 7, 11, etc.   [3]Vv. 19, 25, 31.

* Insert here xxi. 31–33.

† Insert after xxi. 30.

‡There is no analysis of ch. xxvii. which pretends to be more than tentative.
J and E are here so nearly identical and so closely interwoven as to make an exact
separation impossible. The most critics feel sure of is that both J and E related
the same story of the usurpation of Jacob, for the story is referred to in Gen. xxxii.
3ff. by J, and xxxv. 1 by E, and that the two accounts are here combined, J's turning
upon the deception of Isaac through the smell of the perfumed holiday garments
Rebekah has put upon Jacob (cf. vs. 15 with 24–27), and E's upon his deception by the
sense of touch, the goat's-hair covering of neck and hands suggesting to Isaac the
hairy arms and neck of Esau. (Cf. verses 11–14, 16, with 21–23). A few other doublets
(30a–30b, 44b–45a), some allusions to portions otherwise determined (29b—xii. 3;
Num. xxiv. 9; vs. 36—xxv. 29ff) and a few linguistic marks (Yahweh, verses 7, 20, 27;
Elohim vs. 28; E's formula of address in verses 1 and 18—cf. xxii. 1, 7, 11; xxxi. 11,
etc.—; " His eyes were dim," etc.—cf. xlviii. 10; Dt. xxxiv. 7, and in contrast I. Sam.
iv. 15; I. Kings xiv. 4;—a Hebrew word characteristic of E in verses 13 and 30) are all
the clews which have been suggested for guidance in the analysis of this difficult
chapter. For details of the tentative analysis herewith presented the reader is
referred to my article in *Hebraica* for Jan., 1891.

(E) **soul may bless thee** before I die. And Rebekah heard 5
(J) when Isaac spake to Esau his son. [. . .] **And Esau
went to the field to hunt for venison, and to bring it.
And Rebekah spake unto Jacob her son, saying, Be-** 6
hold, I heard thy father speak unto Esau thy brother,
(E) **saying, Bring me venison,** and ⁴make me savoury 7
(J) meat, that I may eat, and bless thee **—before Yahweh**
(E) [. . .]— before my death. Now therefore, my son, 8
⁵obey my voice according to that which I command thee.
Go now to the flock, and fetch me from thence two good 9
kids of the goats ; and I will make them savoury meat for
thy father, such as he loveth : and thou shalt bring it to 10
thy father, that he may eat, so that he may bless thee before his death. And Jacob said to Rebekah his mother, 11
Behold, ⁶Esau my brother is a hairy man, and I am a smooth
man. My father peradventure will ⁷feel me, and I shall 12
seem to him as a deceiver ; and I shall bring a curse upon
me, and not a blessing. And his mother said unto him, 13
Upon me be thy curse, my son ; only obey my voice, and
go fetch me them. And he went, and fetched, and brought 14
them to his mother : and his mother made savoury meat,
(J) such as his father loved. **And Rebekah took the** 15
**goodly raiment* of Esau her elder son, which were
with her in the house, and put them upon Jacob her**
(E) **younger son** [. . .]: and she put the skins of the 16
kids of the goats upon his hands, and upon the smooth of
his neck : and she gave the savoury meat and the bread, 17
which she had prepared, into the hand of her son Jacob.
And he came unto his father, and said, ⁸My father : and he 18
(J) said, Here am I ; [. . .] **who art thou, my son?
And Jacob said unto his father, I am Esau thy first-** 19
**born ; I have done according as thou badest me : arise,
I pray thee, sit and eat of my venison, that thy soul
may bless me. And Isaac said unto his son, How is it** 20

⁴vv. 4, 10, 14, 17, 31.　⁵vv. 13, 43.　⁶25 : 25.　⁷v. 21f ; 31 : 34, 37 ; Ex. 10 : 21.　⁸22 : 1, 7, 11,
etc. v. 2.

* *Perfumed* festal garments. W. R. Smith *Religion of the Semites*, p. 433. Cf. vs.
27. Jud. xiv. 12f.

that thou hast found it so quickly, my son? And he
said, Because Yahweh thy God 'sent me good speed.
21 (E) And Isaac said unto Jacob, Come near, I pray thee,
that I may [10]feel thee, my son, whether thou be my very
22 son Esau or not. And Jacob went near unto Isaac his father; and he felt him, and said, The voice is Jacob's voice,
23 but the hands are the hands of Esau. And he discerned
him not, because his hands were hairy, as his brother
24 (J) Esau's hands: [11]so he blessed him. And he said, Art
25 thou my very son Esau? And he said, I am. And he
said, Bring it near to me, and I will eat of my son's
venison, that my soul may bless thee. And he brought
it near to him, and he did eat: and he brought him
26 wine, and he drank. And his father Isaac said unto
27 him, Come near now, and kiss me, my son. And he
came near, and kissed him: and he smelled the smell
of [12]his raiment, and blessed him, and said,

> See the smell of my son
> Is as the smell of a field which Yahweh hath
> blessed :

28 (E) And God give thee of [13]the dew of heaven
> And of the fatness of the earth,
> And plenty of corn and wine:

29 (J) Let peoples serve thee,
> And nations bow down to thee:

(E) [14]Be lord over thy brethren,
> And let thy mother's sons bow down to thee :

(J) [15]Cursed be every one that curseth thee,
> And blessed be every one that blesseth thee.

30 And it came to pass, as soon as Isaac had made an end
(E) of blessing Jacob, and Jacob was yet scarce gone out
(J) from the presence of Isaac his father, [. . .] that
31 (E) Esau his brother came in from his hunting. And
he also made savoury meat, and brought it unto his father;
(J) and he said unto his father, [16]Let my father arise,

*9 24:12.   10V. 12, etc.   11Ct. vv. 24-27.   12V. 15.   13V. 39.   14V. 37.   15 12:3; Num. 24:9.
16V. 18f.*

and eat of his son's venison, that thy soul may bless me. And Isaac his father said unto him, Who art thou? 32 And he said, I am thy son, thy firstborn, Esau. And 33 Isaac trembled very exceedingly, and said, Who then is he that hath taken venison and brought it me, and I have eaten of all before thou camest, and have (E) blessed him? yea, [and] he shall be blessed. When 34 Esau heard the words of his father, he cried with an exceeding great and bitter cry, and said unto his father, Bless me, even me also, O my father. And he said, Thy brother came 35 (J) with guile, and hath taken away thy blessing. And he 36 said, Is not he rightly named Jacob? for he hath supplanted me these two times: he took away my birthright; and, behold, now he hath taken away my bless- (E) ing. And he said, Hast thou not reserved a blessing for me? And Isaac answered and said unto Esau, Behold, 37 [17]I have made him thy lord, and all his brethren have I given to him for servants; and with corn and wine have I sustained him: and what then shall I do for thee, my son? And Esau said unto his father, Hast thou but one blessing, 38 my father? [18]bless me, even me also, O my father. And Esau lifted up his voice, and wept. And Isaac his father 39 answered and said unto him,

    Behold, of the fatness of the earth shall be thy dwelling,
    And of the dew of heaven from above;
    And by thy sword shalt thou live, and thou shalt serve 40
       thy brother;
    And it shall come to pass when thou shalt break loose,
    That thou shalt shake his yoke from off thy neck.

(J) And Esau hated Jacob because of the blessing 41 (E) wherewith his father blessed him: [...] and Esau said in his heart, The days of mourning for my father are at hand; then will I slay my brother Jacob. And the 42 words of Esau her elder son were told to Rebekah; and she sent and called Jacob her younger son, and said unto him, Behold, thy brother Esau, as touching thee, doth com-

[17]v. 29. [18]v. 34.

43 fort himself, [purposing] to kill thee.   Now therefore, my
   son, obey my voice; and arise, [19]flee thou to Laban my
44 brother to Haran; and tarry with him [20]a few days, until
45 (J) thy brother's fury turn away; **until thy brother's
   anger turn away from thee, and he forget that which
   (E) thou hast done to him**: then I will send, and fetch
   thee from thence: why should I be [21]bereaved of you both
   in one day?*

46 (R) *And Rebekah said to Isaac, I am weary of my life because of the daughters of Heth: if Jacob take a wife of the daughters of Heth, such as these, of the*
28 (P) *daughters of the land, [22]what good shall my life do me?†   And Isaac
   called Jacob, and [1]blessed him, and charged him, and said unto
   him, Thou shalt not take a wife of the daughters of Canaan.*
 2 *Arise, go to Paddan-aram, to the house of Bethuel thy mother's
   father; and take thee a wife from thence of the daughters of*
 3 *Laban thy mother's brother.   And [2]God Almighty bless thee, and
   make thee fruitful, and multiply thee, that thou mayest be a com-*
 4 *pany of peoples; and give thee the blessing of Abraham, to thee,
   and to thy seed with thee; that thou mayest inherit the land of thy*
 5 *sojournings, which God gave unto Abraham.   And Isaac sent
   away Jacob, and he went to Paddan-aram unto Laban, son of
   Bethuel the Syrian, the brother of Rebekah, Jacob's and Esau's*
 6 *mother.   Now Esau saw that Isaac had blessed Jacob and sent
   him away to Paddan-aram, to take him a wife from thence; and
   that as he blessed him he gave him a charge, saying, Thou shalt*
 7 *not take a wife of the daughters of Canaan; and that Jacob
   obeyed his father and his mother, and was gone to Paddan-aram:*
 8 *and Esau saw that [3]the daughters of Canaan pleased not Isaac*
 9 *his father; and Esau went unto Ishmael, and took unto the wives*

[19]35:1.   [20]29:20.   [21]42:36; 43:14.   [22]25:22.   [1]27:23-45.   [2]Ex. 6:3.   [3]26:34f.

*The notice of Isaac's death, which on the Documentary Theory followed the
death-bed scene of this chapter (cf. vs. 41b), would of course have to be omitted, as
in the case of Abraham, for harmonistic reasons. (See Gen. xxxv. 29.) In verses
41-45 it is impossible to decide as between J and E, and the more unnecessary as the
meaning is identical. The division adopted is merely provisional. Cf., however,
vs. 43a with vv. 8 and 13 and Ex. xviii. 19.

†Assigned to R for linguistic reasons mainly. Cf. xxv. 22. (See Dillmann, Gen. 5,
in loc.) The matter is, perhaps, superfluous, but introduced apparently to resume
connection with xxvi. 34f.

which he had, 'Mahalath the daughter of Ishmael Abraham's son, the sister of Nebaioth, to be his wife. [. . .]

(J) And Jacob went out from 'Beer-sheba, and went 10 (E) toward* Haran. And he lighted upon a certain 11 place,† and tarried there all night, because the sun was set ; and he took one of the stones of the place, and put it under his head, and lay down in that place to sleep. And 12 he °dreamed, and behold a ladder set up on the earth, and the top of it reached to heaven : and behold the angels of **(J)** God ascending and descending on it. **—And, behold, 13 Yahweh stood 'above it, and said, 'I am Yahweh, the God of Abraham thy father, and the God of Isaac: the land whereon thou liest, to thee will I give it, and to thy seed ; and thy seed shall be as the dust of the 14 earth, and thou shalt 'spread abroad to the west, and to the east, and to the north, and to the south : '°and in thee and in thy seed shall all the families of the (JE) earth be blessed.** ''And, behold, I am with thee, and 15 will keep thee whithersoever thou goest, and will bring thee again into this land ; for I will not leave thee, until I have done that which I **(J)** have spoken to thee of. **And Jacob awaked out of his 16 sleep, and he said, ''Surely Yahweh is in this place ; (E) and I knew it not.‡—** And he was afraid, and said, 17

⁴25:25. ⁵26:23. ⁶20:3, etc. ; 35:1. ⁷18:2 ; 24:13. ⁸26:24 ; 12:7 ; 13:15f. ⁹30:30, 43 ; Ex. 1:12. ¹⁰12:3. ¹¹Cf. v. 20. ¹²Ex. 2:14.

* Or, " came unto."

†See note to Gen. xii. 6. If, as historical criticism maintains, the narratives of Genesis are the local traditions of the various shrines of Beer-sheba, Shechem, etc., "*the* place " (Heb. vs. 11) would of course refer to the well-known sanctuary of Bethel (cf. Amos vii. 12f.), with its immemorial stone pillar, black with the anointing oil of countless pilgrims, and its sacred tree (Gen. xxxv. 8 ; cf. 1 Sam. x. 3 ; Amos iv. 4 ; v. 5.).

‡ In vs. 13 read " beside him " according to the (R. V.) margin.—It would be easy with Kuenen and some other critics to consider vv. 13-16 and 19 as simple interpolations of JE like xiii. 14-17 ; xxii. 15-18 and others, but the language of vs. 14 is strongly characteristic of J (cf. xii. 3 ; xxx. 30), and quite in contrast with JE (xxii. 18 and xxvi. 4). There is also a characteristic primitiveness of thought in vs. 16 which it is difficult to attribute to an interpolator. Vs. 15, however, is obviously related to vs. 20f., and must therefore on this theory be attributed to JE. This analysis by no means ignores the important arguments of Kuenen. Hex. pp. 147 and 243. The evidence from Hos. xii. 4, and we may add, from P even, in xxxv. 15, points to a derivation of the "*pillar* " (not the altar, cf. Gen. xii. 8) in Bethel from the occasion of a theophany to Jacob *after* his return from Aram Naharaim, as J's version. If this view

I I

How dreadful is this place ! this is none other but the house
18 of God, and this is the gate of heaven.   And Jacob rose up
early in the morning, [13]and took the stone that he had put
under his head, and [14]set it up for a pillar, and poured oil
19 (J) upon the top of it.   —[15]And he called the name of
that place Beth-el: *but the name of the city was Luz at the first.**—
20 (E) [16]And Jacob vowed a vow, saying, If God will be with
me, and will keep me in this way that I go, and will give
21 me bread to eat, and raiment to put on, so that I come
again to my father's house [17]in peace, then shall Yahweh be
22 my God, and this stone, which I have set up for a pillar,
shall be God's house : and of all that thou shalt give me I
will surely give the tenth unto thee.

29   Then Jacob went on his journey, and came to [1]the land
2 (J) of the children of the east. [. . .] [2]And he looked,
and behold a well in the field, and, lo, three flocks of
sheep lying there by it; for out of that well they
watered the flocks: and [3]the stone upon the well's
3 mouth was great.   And thither were all the flocks
gathered : and [4]they rolled the stone from the well's
mouth, and watered the sheep, and put the stone
4 again upon the well's mouth in its place.   And Jacob
said unto them, 'My brethren, whence be ye?   And
5 they said, Of Haran are we.   And he said unto them,
Know ye Laban the son of Nahor?   And they said,
6 We know him.   And he said unto them, 'Is it well
with him?   And they said, It is well: and, behold,
7 Rachel his daughter cometh with the sheep.   And he
said, Lo, it is yet high day, neither is it time that the
cattle should be gathered together: water ye the
8 sheep, and go and feed them.   And they said, 'We
cannot, until all the flocks be gathered together, and

[13]35:14f. [14]31:45; 33:20; 35:20, etc. [15]Ct. 35:6f. [16]31:13. [17]33:18 (?) [1]Ct. 28:7, 10.
[2]Cf. 24:11ff; Ex. 2:16ff. [3]V. 10. [4]19:7. [5]43:27.

be adopted, vv. 13, 14, 16 and 19 (cf. xxxv. 7 E) must be considered displaced by JE
from the context of xxxv. 14. See the author's article in *Hebraica*, July, 1891, entitled, Notes on the analysis of Genesis xxxii.-l.

* See note preceding, and cf. xxxv. 7. Insert after xxxv. 14.

'they roll the stone from the well's mouth; then we water the sheep. While he yet spake with them, 9 Rachel came with her father's sheep; for 'she kept them. And it came to pass, when Jacob saw Rachel 10 the daughter of Laban his mother's brother, and the sheep of Laban his mother's brother, that Jacob went near, and 'rolled the stone from the well's mouth, and watered the flock of Laban his mother's brother. And Jacob kissed Rachel, and 'lifted up his voice, and 11 wept. And Jacob told Rachel that he was her father's 12 brother, and that he was Rebekah's son: and she ran and told her father. And it came to pass, when La- 13 ban heard the tidings of Jacob his sister's son, that '°he ran to meet him, and embraced him, and kissed him, and brought him to his house. And he told Laban all these things. And Laban said to him, 14 (E) Surely thou art "my bone and my flesh. [...] And he abode with him the space of a month. And Laban said 15 unto Jacob, Because thou art my brother, shouldest thou therefore serve me for nought? tell me, what shall thy '²wages be? And Laban had two daughters: the name of 16 the elder was Leah, and the name of the "younger was Rachel. And Leah's eyes were tender; but Rachel was 17 '⁴beautiful and well favoured. And Jacob ·loved Rachel; 18 and he said, I will serve thee seven years for Rachel thy younger daughter. And Laban said, It is better that I 19 give her to thee, than that I should give her to another man: abide with me. And Jacob served seven years for 20 Rachel; and they seemed unto him but '⁵a few days, for the love he had to her. And Jacob said unto Laban, Give 21 me my wife, for my days are fulfilled, that I may go in unto her. And Laban gathered together all the men of 22 the place, and made a feast. And it came to pass in the 23 evening, that he took Leah his daughter, and brought her (P) to him; and he went in unto her. *And Laban gave* 24

⁶V. 10.   ⁷Ex. 2:16.   ⁸32:25.   ⁹45:14; 46:29.   ¹⁰33:4; 18:2; 24:17.   ¹¹2:23; 37:27.   ¹²31:7, 41. Ct. 30:28, 32f; 31:8.   ¹³Ct. 19:31; V. 26f.   ¹⁴Ct. 12:11; 24:16; 26:7.   ¹⁵27:44.

Zilpah his handmaid unto his daughter Leah for an handmaid.

25 (E) [. . .] And it came to pass in the morning that, behold, it was Leah : and he said to Laban, What is this thou hast done unto me ? did not I serve with thee for Rachel ?
26 (J) wherefore then hast thou beguiled me ? [. . .] **And Laban said, "It is not so done in our place, to give**
27 (E) **the "younger before the firstborn. Fulfil the week*** of this one, and we will give thee the other also for the service which thou shalt serve with me yet seven other
28 years. And Jacob did so, and fulfilled her week, and he
29 (P) gave him Rachel his daughter to wife. *And Laban gave to Rachel his daughter Bilhah his handmaid to be her hand-*
30 (E) *maid.* [. . .] And he went in also unto Rachel, and he loved also Rachel more than Leah, and served with him yet seven other years. [. . .]
31   (J) **And Yahweh saw that Leah was hated, "and he**
32 **opened her womb: "but Rachel was barren. "And Leah conceived, and bare a son, and she called his name Reuben; for she said, Because Yahweh hath looked upon my affliction; for now my husband will**
33 **love me. "And she conceived again, and bare a son; and said, Because Yahweh hath heard that I am hated, he hath therefore given me this [son] also :**
34 **and she called his name Simeon. "And she conceived again, and bare a son; and said, Now this time will my husband be joined unto me, because I have borne him three sons : "therefore was his name called† Levi.**
35 **"And she conceived again, and bare a son : and she said, This time will I praise Yahweh : "therefore she called his name Judah ; and she left bearing. [. . .]**
30   (E) And when Rachel saw that she bare Jacob no children, Rachel envied her sister ; and she said unto Jacob,
2 Give me children, or else I die. And Jacob's anger was kindled against Rachel : and he said, 'Am I in God's

---

¹⁶34:7. ¹⁷Ct. v. 16. ¹⁸30:22. ¹⁹11:30; 25:21. ²⁰4:1, 17, etc. ²¹3:24, etc. ¹50:19.

* I. e. the week of wedding festivities.

* Read with LXX. Sam. Syr., " she called." Cf. verses 3², 33, 35.

stead, who hath withheld from thee the fruit of the womb?
And she said, Behold my 'maid Bilhah, go in unto her; 3
(J) that she may 'bear upon my knees : **and I also may**
'obtain children by her. And she gave him Bilhah her 4
handmaid to wife : and Jacob went in unto her. [. . .]
(E) And Bilhah conceived, and bare Jacob a son. And 5–6
Rachel said, God hath judged me, and hath also heard my
voice, and hath given me a son : therefore called she his
(J) (E) name Dan. **And Bilhah Rachel's handmaid** con- 7
(J) ceived again, and **bare Jacob a second son. [. . .]**
(E) And Rachel said, With mighty wrestlings have I 8
wrestled with my sister, and have prevailed : and she
(J) called his name Naphtali. [. . .] **When Leah saw** 9
that she had left bearing, she took Zilpah her hand-
maid, and gave her to Jacob to wife. And Zilpah 10
Leah's handmaid bare Jacob a son. And Leah said, 11
Fortunate! and she called his name Gad. And Zilpah 12
Leah's handmaid bare Jacob a second son. And Leah 13
said, Happy am I! for the daughters will call me
happy : and she called his name Asher. And Reuben 14
went in the days of wheat harvest, and found man-
drakes in the field, and brought them unto his mother
Leah. Then Rachel said to Leah, Give me, I pray
thee, of thy son's mandrakes. And she said unto her, 15
Is it a small matter that thou hast taken away my
husband? and wouldest thou take away my son's man-
drakes also? And Rachel said, Therefore 'he shall lie
with thee to-night for thy son's mandrakes. And 16
Jacob came from the field in the evening, and Leah
went out to meet him, and said, Thou must come in
unto me; for I have surely 'hired thee with my son's
mandrakes. And he lay with her that night. [. . .]
(E) And God hearkened unto Leah, and she conceived, 17
and bare Jacob a fifth son. And Leah said, God hath given 18
me my hire, because I gave my handmaid to my husband :

²20:17; 21:10, 12f. Ct. 16:2, 5, etc., and vv. 4, 9ff. ³50:23. ⁴16:2. ⁵Ct. v. 17. ⁶Ct.
v. 18.

19 and she called his name Issachar.   And Leah conceived
20 again, and bare a sixth son to Jacob.   And Leah said, God
(J) hath endowed me with a good dowry ;* [. . .] **now
will my husband dwell with me, because I have borne**
21 **him six sons ; and she called his name Zebulun.   And
afterwards she bare a daughter, and called her name**
22 (E) **Dinah.** [. . .]† **And** God **remembered Rachel,** [7]**and**
23 (J) God hearkened to her, **and** [8]**opened her womb.**   And
(E) she conceived, and bare a son : and said, God hath
24 taken away‡ my reproach : and she called his name Joseph,
(J) [. . .] **saying, Yahweh add to me** [9]**another son.**
25 **And it came to pass, when Rachel had borne Joseph,
that Jacob said unto Laban, Send me away, that I
may go unto** [10]**mine own place, and to my country.**
26 (E) **Give me my wives** and my children,| for whom I have
served thee, and let me go : for thou knowest my service
27 (J) wherewith I have served thee.   **And Laban said unto
him,** [11]**If now I have found favour in thine eyes,
[tarry : for] I have** [12]**divined that Yahweh hath blessed**
28 (E) **me for thy sake.**   And he said, Appoint me thy wages,
29 (J) and I will give it. [. . .]   **And he said unto him,
Thou knowest how I have served thee, and how thy**
30 **cattle hath fared with me.   For it was little which
thou hadst before I came, and it hath** [13]**increased unto a multitude ; and Yahweh hath blessed thee whithersoever I turned : and now when shall I provide for**
31 **mine own house also?   And he said, What shall I give
thee?   And Jacob said, Thou shalt not give me aught :
if thou wilt do this thing for me, I will again feed**

---

[7]V. 17.   [8]29 : 31.   [9]35 : 18.   [10]29 : 26.   [11]18 : 3, etc.   [12]44 : 15.   [13]28 : 14, etc.

* Heb. *Zebed.*   Verse 20 contains two etymologies for Zebulun.   According to the
analysis, R seems to have generally selected the more felicitous of the two, but
sometimes to afford both (cf. 23f), and is not averse to presenting still a third in
many cases (cf. ch. xlix.).

† Perhaps vs. 21. is R's.

‡ Heb. *Asaph.*   Verse 24*b* (J) derives the name from *yasaph*, "add to."

| "Whom" is feminine, hence the "children" are here interpolated.

(E) thy flock [. . .] and keep it.*   I will pass through 32
all thy flock to-day, ¹⁴removing from thence every speckled
and spotted one, and every black one among the sheep,
and the spotted and speckled among the goats : and [of
such] shall be my hire.   So shall my righteousness an- 33
swer for me hereafter, when thou shalt come concerning
my hire that is before thee : every one that is not speckled
and spotted among the goats, and black among the sheep,
that [if found] with me shall be counted stolen.† [. . .]
(J) And Laban said, Behold, I would it might be ac- 34
cording to thy word.   And he removed that day the 35
he-goats that were ¹⁵ringstraked and spotted, and all
the she-goats that were speckled and spotted, every
one that had white in it, and all the black ones among
the sheep, and gave them into the hand of his sons :
and he set three days' journey betwixt himself and 36
Jacob : and Jacob fed the rest of Laban's flocks.   And
Jacob took him rods of fresh poplar, and of the al-
mond and of the plane tree ; and peeled white strakes
in them, and made the white appear which was in the
rods.   And he set the rods which he had peeled over 38
(E) against the flocks ¹⁶in the gutters in the watering
troughs where the flocks came to drink ; and they con-
(J) ceived when they came to drink. [. . .] **And the** 39
flocks conceived before the rods, and the flocks

¹⁴31 : 8.   ¹⁵Ct. 31 : 8–10.   ¹⁶Ex. 2 : 16.

* The Hebrew has, " feed thy flock, keep it," with no conjunction.   Kautzsch and
Socin regard the second word as simply a parallel furnished by the other source
(E) to the first.   According to these authors, " R took it up in order to lose no shade
of meaning."

† The latter part of ch. xxx. presents confessedly an incompletely solved problem
of analysis.   For this reason the author departs from the view of critics presented
in the tables of *Hebraica* iv. 4 (July, 1888), and submits an original analysis, for the
evidence in support of which the reader is referred to the above-quoted article in
Hebraica for July, 1891.   The basis of analysis must of course be in any event the
story of E as retold by Jacob in xxxi. 5–12 and again in verses 38–42.   The main
point of difference between the narrative here presupposed and the form of the story
afforded by ch. xxx. is, as all critics recognize, that Jacob does not outwit Laban by
his own cunning, but quietly submits to repeated over-reaching from Laban, who
continually " changes his wages."   His deliverance is due solely to divine intervention on behalf of an *ish tam* or " man of simple integrity" (xxv. 27).   Cf. xxxi. 7.

brought forth [17]ringstraked, speckled, and spotted.
40 (E) **And Jacob separated the lambs,** and set the faces of
the flocks toward the [18]ringstraked and all the black in the
(J) flock of Laban ; [. . .] **and he put his own droves**
41 **apart, and put them not unto Laban's flock. And it
came to pass, whensoever the stronger of the flock
did conceive, that Jacob laid the rods before the eyes
of the flock [19]in the gutters, that they might conceive**
42 **among the rods; but when the flock were feeble, he
put them not in: so the feebler were Laban's, and the**
43 **stronger Jacob's.   And the man [20]increased exceedingly, and [21]had large flocks, and maidservants and
menservants, and camels and asses.**

31   **And** [*] **he heard the words of Laban's sons, saying,
Jacob hath taken away all that was our father's ; and
of that which was our father's hath he gotten all this**
2 (E) **glory.** [1]And Jacob beheld the countenance of Laban,
3 (J) and, behold, it was not toward him as beforetime. [2]And
Yahweh said unto Jacob, Return unto the land of thy fathers,
4 (E) **and to thy kindred ; and I will be with thee.** And Jacob
sent and called Rachel and Leah to the field unto his flock,
5 and said unto them, I see your father's countenance, that it
is not toward me as beforetime ; but the God of my father
6 hath been with me. [3]And ye know that with all my power
7 I have served your father. And your father hath deceived
me, and [4]changed my wages ten times ; but God [5]suffered
8 him not to hurt me. If he said thus, The speckled shall
be thy wages ; then all the flock bare speckled : and if he
said thus, The ringstraked shall be thy wages : then bare

[17]Ct. 31 : 8-10. [18]31 : 8. [19]Ex. 2 : 16. [20]28 : 14 ; 30 : 30, etc. [21]32 : 4. [1]V. 5. [2]32 : 9. [3]30 : 26.
[4]Ct. 30 : 35ff. Cf. Num. 14 : 22. [5]20 : 6.

[*] For the present independent analysis of ch. xxxi. see *Hebraica* for July, 1891, and
for the general form of previous analyses chapter III. Wellhausen I., p. 428, rejects
verses 10 and 12 on the ground that " I am the God of Bethel " can only come first
in the theophany, and that the verses 10 and 12 introduce a subject matter foreign
to that of vs. 13, one which could not have been presented at the same time, but
necessarily, according to the story, months, if not years, previously. Verse 3 is regarded as an interpolation supplying a higher motive for Jacob's flight than that of
vs. 1. It must, however, be as early as xxxii. 10, which itself, however, is subsequent
to the union of J and E. See note *in loc.*

all the flock ringstraked. [6]Thus God hath taken away 9
(JE) the cattle of your father, and given them to me. And 10
it came to pass at the time that the flock conceived, that I lifted up
mine eyes, and saw in a dream, and, behold, the he-goats which
leaped upon the flock were ringstraked, speckled, and grisled.
(E) [7]And the angel of God said unto me in the dream, 11
(JE) [8]Jacob : and I said, Here am I. And he said, Lift up 12
now thine eyes, and see, all the he-goats which leap upon the flock
are ringstraked, speckled, and grisled : for I have seen all that Laban
(E) doeth unto thee. I am the God of Beth-el, where thou 13
anointedst a pillar, where thou vowedst a vow unto me :
now arise, get thee out from this land, and return unto the
land of thy nativity. And Rachel and Leah answered and 14
said unto him, Is there yet any portion or inheritance for
us in our father's house ? Are we not counted of him stran- 15
gers ? for he hath sold us, and hath also quite devoured
[9]our money. For all the riches which God hath taken 16
away from our father, that is ours and our children's : now
then, whatsoever God hath said unto thee, do. Then Ja- 17
cob rose up, and set his sons and his wives upon the camels ;
(P) and he carried away all his cattle, [10]*and all his substance* 18
which he had gathered, the cattle of his getting, which he had
gathered in Paddan-aram, for to go to Isaac his father unto the
(E) *land of Canaan.* Now Laban was gone to shear his 19
sheep: and Rachel stole the teraphim that were her father's.
And Jacob [11]stole away unawares to Laban the Syrian, in 20
that he told him not that he fled. So he fled with all that 21
(J) he had ; **and he rose up, and passed over the river,**
(E) and set his face toward the mountain of Gilead.

And it was told Laban on the third day that Jacob was 22
fled. And he took his brethren with him, and pursued 23
after him seven days' journey ; [12]and he overtook him in
the mountain of Gilead. And God came to Laban the 24
Syrian[13]in a dream of the night, and said unto him, Take
heed to thyself that thou speak not to Jacob either good
(J) or bad. **And Laban came up with Jacob. Now Ja-** 25

[6]Ct. 30·42. [7]20:3, etc. [8]22:1, etc. [9]29:18, 27 ; Ex. 21:35. [10]12:5; 36:6. [11]v. 26.
Ct. v. 27. [12]v. 25a. [13]15:1; 20:3, etc.

cob had pitched his tent in the mountain : [. . .] and
Laban with his brethren pitched in the mountain of
26 (E) **Gilead.** [. . .] And Laban said to Jacob, What hast
thou done, that thou hast [14]stolen away unawares to me,
and carried away my daughters as captives of the sword?
27 (J) **Wherefore didst thou flee secretly, and** [15]**steal
away from me; and didst not tell me, that I might
have sent thee away with mirth and with songs, with**
28 (E) **tabret and with harp;** and hast not suffered me to
kiss my sons and my daughters? now hast thou done fool-
29 ishly.   It is in the power of my hand to do you hurt : but
the God of your father spake unto me yesternight, saying,
Take heed to thyself that thou speak not to Jacob either
30 good or bad.   And now, [though] thou wouldest needs be
gone, because thou sore longedst after thy father's house,
31 (J) [yet] wherefore hast thou stolen my gods? **And Jacob
answered and said to Laban, Because I was afraid: for
I said, Lest thou shouldest take thy daughters from**
32 (E) **me by force.** [. . .]* With whomsoever thou findest thy gods, he shall not live : before our brethren discern
thou what is thine with me, and take it to thee. For Jacob
33 knew not that Rachel had stolen them.   And Laban went
into Jacob's tent, and into Leah's tent, and into the tent of the
two maidservants ; but he found them not.   And he went out
34 of Leah's tent, and entered into Rachel's tent. Now Rachel
had taken the teraphim, and put them in the camel's furniture, and sat upon them.   And Laban [16]felt about all the
35 tent, but found them not.   And she said to her father, Let
not my lord be angry that I cannot rise up before thee ; for
[17]the manner of women is upon me.   And he searched, but
36 (J) found not the teraphim.   **And Jacob was wroth, and
(E) chode with Laban:** [. . .] and Jacob answered
and said to Laban, What is my trespass? what is my sin,
37 that thou has hotly pursued after me?   Whereas thou hast
felt about all my stuff, what hast thou found of all thy

[14]V. 26. Ct. v. 27. [15]Ct. v. 20. [16]27:12, 21f. [17]Ct. 18:11.
* The missing words, " And he said," are found in LXX.

household stuff? Set it here before my brethren and thy
(J) brethren, that they may judge betwixt us two. **This 38
twenty years have I been with thee; thy ewes and thy
she-goats have not [18]cast their young, and the rams of
thy flocks have I not eaten. That which was torn of 39
beasts I brought not unto thee; I bare the loss of it;
of my hand didst thou require it, whether stolen by
day or stolen by night. Thus I was; in the day the 40
drought consumed me, and the frost by night; and**
(E) my sleep fled from mine eyes.* These twenty years 41
have I been in thy house; [19]I served thee fourteen years
for thy two daughters, and six years for thy flock: and
[20]thou hast changed my wages ten times. Except the God 42
of my father, the God of Abraham, and the Fear of Isaac,
had been with me, surely now hadst thou sent me away
empty. God hath seen mine affliction and the labour of
(J) my hands, and rebuked thee yesternight. **And Laban 43
answered and said unto Jacob, [21]The daughters are
my daughters, and the children are my children, and
the flocks are my flocks, and all that thou seest is
mine: and what can I do this day unto these my
daughters, or unto their children which they have
borne? And now come, let us make a covenant, I and 44
thou; [. . .] and let it be for a [22]witness between me .**
(E) and thee. And Jacob [23]took a stone, and set it up 45
(J) for a pillar. **And Jacob said unto his brethren, 46
Gather stones; and they took stones, and made an**
(E) heap: [24]and they did eat there by the heap.—[25]And 47
Laban called it Jegar-sahadutha: but Jacob called it
(J) Galeed.— **And Laban said, This heap is witness 48
between me and thee this day. —Therefore was the 49
name of it called Galeed: and [. . .] Mizpah,† for he**

[18]Ex. 23:26. Cf. 27:45; 42:36; 43:14. [19]29:18, 27. [20]Vv. 7-9. [21]V. 31. [22]V. 48f.
[23]28:18, etc. [24]V. 54. [25]Vv. 5, 48f.

* Vv. 36a, 38-40 may equally well be assigned to E.

† LXX. have *Massêpha*, midway between *maççebah*, "pillar" (i. e. the stone dolmen
so frequent in E and forming part of the earlier worship (Is. xix. 19), but forbidden
after the period of Josiah), and *mizpah*, "watch-tower." This curious phenomenon
suggests the possibility of an original play upon the words *maççebah* and *mizpah*.

said, Yahweh watch between me and thee, when we are
50 absent one from another.— If thou shalt afflict my
daughters, and if thou shalt take wives besides my
daughters, no man is with us; see [26]God is witness be-
51 (E) twixt me and thee. And Laban said to Jacob, Behold this heap, and behold the pillar, which [27]I have set betwixt
52 me and thee. This heap be witness, and the pillar be witness,
that I will not pass over this heap to thee, and that thou
shalt not pass over this heap and this pillar unto me, for harm.
53 [28]The God of Abraham, and the God of Nahor, the God of
their father, judge betwixt us. And Jacob sware by the
54 Fear of his father Isaac. [29]And Jacob offered a sacrifice
in the mountain, and called his brethren to eat bread : and
they did eat bread, and tarried all night in the mountain.
55 [30]And early in the morning Laban rose up, and kissed his sons
and his daughters, and blessed them : and Laban depart-
32 ed, and returned unto his place. And Jacob went on his
2 way, and the angels of God met him. [1]And Jacob said
when he saw them, This is God's host : and he called the
name of that place Mahanaim.

3   (J) And Jacob sent messengers before him to Esau
his brother unto the land of Seir ;—the field of Edom.—
4 And he commanded them, saying, Thus shall ye say
unto my lord Esau; Thus saith thy servant Jacob, I
5 have sojourned with Laban, and stayed until now : and
[2]I have oxen, and asses [and] flocks, and menservants
and maidservants : and I have sent to tell my lord,
6 [3]that I may find grace in thy sight. And the messengers returned to Jacob, saying, We came to thy
brother Esau, and moreover he cometh to meet thee,
7 and [4]four hundred men with him. Then Jacob was
greatly afraid and was distressed : and he divided the
people that was with him, and the flocks, and the
8 herds, and the camels, into [5]two companies;* and he

[26]Ct. v. 44.   [27]Ct. v. 46.   [28]Vv. 42, 37.   [29]Ex. 18:12.   [30]20:8; 21:14; 22:3; 28:18.
[1]Vv. 7, 10.   [2]12:16; 30:43.   [3]18:3, etc.   [4]33:1.   [5]Ct. v. 1f.

* Heb. *Mahanaim*. The word is strictly the dual of *mahaneh*, "camp" or "company." The etymology of verses 1 and 2 (E) regards it simply as a plural, or

said, If Esau come to the one company, and smite it, then the company which is left shall escape. [. . .] (JE) And Jacob said, O God of my father Abraham, and God of my 9 father Isaac, O Yahweh, which [6]saidst unto me, Return unto thy country, and to thy kindred, and I will do thee good : I am not 10 worthy of the least of all [7]the mercies, and of all the truth, which thou hast shewed unto thy servant ; for with my staff I passed over this [8]Jordan ; and now I am become [9]two companies. Deliver me, I 11 pray thee, from the hand of my brother, from the hand of Esau ; for I fear him, lest he come and smite me, the mother with the children. And thou [10]saidst, I will surely do thee good, and make thy 12 seed as the sand of the sea, which cannot be numbered for multiude.*

(E) (J) And he lodged [11]there † that night ; and took of 13 that which he had with him a [12]present for Esau his brother; two hundred [13]she-goats and twenty he-goats, 14 two hundred ewes and twenty rams, thirty milch cam- 15 els and their colts, forty kine and ten bulls, twenty she-asses and ten foals. And he delivered them 16 into the hand of his servants, every [14]drove by itself, and said unto his servants, Pass over before me, and put a space betwixt drove and drove. And he com- 17 manded the foremost, saying, When Esau my brother meeteth thee, and asketh thee, saying, Whose art

[6]31:3. [7]47:29. [8]Ct. v. 22. [9]Vv. 1f, 7. [10]22:17. Ct. 13:16; 28:14. [11]V. 2. [12]Vv. 18, 20f; 33:10. Ct. 33:11. [13]31:38. [14]29:2f, 8; 30:40; v. 19; 35:21.

perhaps more exactly as a singular, the ending *aim* being understood as an Aramaic locative ending corresponding to the *am* of the Moabite stone. According to Wellhausen (Comp. d. Hex., p. 45 [434], note) this is correct and would denote an exacter knowledge of Aramaic forms on the part of E than of J. Dillmann, however, regards Mahanaim as taken by both J and E for a dual, the *two* hosts of xxxii. 2 being Jacob's and "God's."

* For a great number of reasons verses 9-12 are regarded as due to didactic interpolation. It is claimed that the writer shows himself unmindful of the real scene, which must be, not only according to vs. 22, but by relation to Mahanaim and Penuel, the ford, not of Jordan, as he has it, vs. 10, but Jabbok. Verse 12 also refers to xxxi. 3, a verse of doubtful authenticity, and the tone and coloring recall the frequent so-called Deuteronomic (didactic) interpolations. (Cf. Gen. xviii. 23ff, xxvi. 3ff, etc.) But the conclusive reason against vv. 9-12 is the reference in vs. 12 to xxviii. 14, which, however, appears to have been made from memory, and combines phrases derived from xvi. 10 and xxii. 17, *both* JE. Hence the close similarity of the style (vs. 10) in this case is insufficient to establish the Jahvistic authorship.

† "There" may refer to vs. 2, or to the passage, "Therefore he called the name of the place Mahanaim," which, we must suppose, was omitted from J after vs. 8 for harmonistic reasons. In the latter case the critics are right in assigning this clause to J.

thou? and whither goest thou? and whose are these
18 before thee? then thou shalt say, [They be] thy servant Jacob's; it is a present sent unto my lord Esau:
19 and, behold, [15]he also is behind us. And he commanded also the second, and the third, and all that
followed the droves, saying, On this manner shall ye
20 speak unto Esau, when ye find him; and ye shall say,
Moreover, behold, thy servant Jacob is behind us.
For he said, I will appease him with the present that
goeth before me, and afterward I will see his face;
21 peradventure he will [16]accept me. So the present
passed over before him* and he himself lodged that
night in the company.†
22   And he rose up that night, and took his two wives,
and his two handmaids, and his eleven children, [...]
23 (E) and passed over the ford of [17]Jabbok. [...] —And
(J) he took them,‡—and sent them over the stream, and
24 sent over that he had. [18]And Jacob was left alone;

[15]4:22, 26, etc.   [16]4:7; I. Sam. 25:35.   [17]Ct. v. 10.   [18]Cf. Ex. 4:24ff.

* In spite of the universal opinion of critics, which sees in vv. 13*b*-20 a parallel of E
to J's vv. 3-13*a*, I am driven by the unmistakable linguistic marks, and especially
by the reference in xxxiii. 8-10 (cf. vs. 20 above), where the language is still more
positively J's, to assign vv. 3-21*a* to this writer. See my article, Notes on the
Analysis of Gen. xxxii.-l. in *Hebraica* for July, 1891. The comparison of the
"present" (literally "offering"), which "goes before" the suppliant to "appease"
the Deity and induces him to "accept" (literally "lift up the face of," cf. Gen. iv. 7)
the worshipper in vs. 20 is an elaborate preparation for the etymology of xxxiii. 10.
Jacob will see Esau "as one seeth the face of God" (*Peni el*), i. e. with a *minchah* or
peace-offering.

† Wellhausen translates this word as a proper noun, "in Mahaneh," connecting
this with E's etymology of the name ("God's host," v. 2), which, in his opinion,
treats it as a singular.

‡ The clause, "and he took," should doubtless precede "and passed over."
"Them" must, of couse, be due to JE since we have here two substantially identical
statements, and in each source the object of the verb must have been explicitly
given. Supply "his people." The equivalent phrase in vs. 22 is linguistically
characterized as J's.—I am indebted to Prof. Moore for the suggestion that vs. 30 is
perhaps E's. The linguistic form is in fact characteristic of E. Cf. e. g. xxxiii. 17*b*
(J). The verse, however, cannot be understood as referring to the incident narrated
in the context, but rather to some theophany parallel to it in E. This wrestling
story gives in fact the aetiology of Jabboq ("wrestler") and of Israel, not of Peniel,
and J's etymology of Peniel (or rather Penuel, cf. vs. 31) follows later (xxxiii. 8-10),
his story of Jabboq and Israel ending at vs. 29.

and there wrestled [19]a man with him until the [20]break-
ing of the day. And when he saw that he [21]prevailed 25
not against him, he touched the hollow of his thigh;
and the hollow of Jacob's thigh was strained, as he
wrestled with him. And he said, Let me go, for the 26
day [20]breaketh. And he said, I will not let thee go,
except thou bless me. And he said unto him, What 27
is thy name? And he said, Jacob. And he said, Thy 28
name shall be called no more Jacob, but [22]Israel: for
thou hast striven with God* and [with] men, and hast
prevailed. And Jacob asked him, and said, Tell me, 29
I pray thee, thy name. And he said, Wherefore is it
that thou dost ask after my name? And he blessed
(E) him there. [. . .] [23]And Jacob called the name of 30
the place Peniel: for, [said he], I have seen God face to
(J) face, and my life is preserved.† [. . .] And the sun 31
rose upon him as he passed over Penuel, and he halt-
ed upon his thigh. [24]Therefore the children of Israel 32
eat not the sinew of the hip which is upon the hollow
of the thigh, unto this day: because he touched the
hollow of Jacob's thigh in the sinew of the hip.‡

And Jacob lifted up his eyes, and looked, and, be- 33
hold, Esau came, and with him [1]four hundred men.

[19]18:2; 19:5. [20]19:15; v. 26. [21]29:8-10. [22]Ct. 35:10. [23]28:19; 32:2. Ct. 33:17.
[24]2:24; 10:9, etc. [1]32:6.

* The use of Elohim here is perfectly in accord with J's practise elsewhere (cf.
note to Gen. iii. 1.) In the contrasted expression, "God and men," it would be used
(cf. Jud. ix. 9, 13) even were there not the additional exigencies of the etymology
(*Isra-el*) and the concealment of the *name*, vs. 29. The fact that J from this point on
(in chapters xxxiii. and xxxiv. R seems to have altered to "Jacob" on account of
xxxv. 10) uses "Israel," while E continues to employ "Jacob," establishes the
fact that this story belongs really to the former. See, however, the article,
Hebraica, July, 1891, above cited.

† The reference is probably to a theophany of E corresponding to the Jabboq-
Israel story of J. Possibly some of the material of vs. 11f may have been derived
from the missing account of Peniel in E.

‡ Dillmann, who regards verses 25-31 as E, finds a ground for rejecting vs. 32 as
R's in the fact that its style and language are akin to J. If, however, the foregoing
passage, with which it is connected in subject-matter, be assigned to J, as above,
the references given (Dill., Gen. 5, *in loc.*) to the J passages, x. 9, xix. 37f, xxxvi. 33.
which are the only argument I find advanced against the genuineness of the verse,
prove simply the contrary. Cf. in addition Gen. ii. 24 note.

And he divided the children unto Leah, and unto
2 Rachel, and unto the two handmaids. And he put
the handmaids and their children foremost, and Leah
and her children after, and [2]Rachel and Joseph hinder-
3 most. And he himself passed over before them, and
bowed himself to the ground seven times, until he
4 came near to his brother. And Esau [3]ran to meet him,
(E) and embraced him, and fell on his neck, and kissed
5 him : and they wept. And he lifted up his eyes, and saw
[4]the women and the children; and said, Who are these
with thee? And he said, The children which God hath
6 (J) graciously given thy servant. [...] [5]Then the handmaids came near, they and their children, and they
7 bowed themselves. And Leah also and her children
came near and bowed themselves: and after came
Joseph near and Rachel, and they bowed themselves.
8 And he said, What meanest thou by [6]all this company
which I met? And he said, [7]To find grace in the sight
9 of my lord. And Esau said, I have enough; my
10 brother, let that thou hast be thine. And Jacob said,
Nay, I pray thee, [8]if now I have found grace in thy
sight, then [9]receive my present at my hand : [10]foras-
much as I have seen thy face, as one seeth the [10]face
11 (E) of God, and thou wast pleased with me. Take, I
pray thee, my [11]gift that is brought to thee ; because [12]God
hath dealt graciously with me, and because I have enough.
12 (J) And he urged him, and he took it.[*] And he said, Let
us take our journey, and let us go, and I will go be-
13 fore thee. And he said unto him, My lord knoweth
that the children are tender, and that the flocks and
herds with me give suck ; and if they overdrive them
14 one day, all the flocks will die. Let my lord, I pray
thee, pass over before his servant: and I will lead on
softly, according to the pace of the cattle that is be-

[2]29:30f. [3]18:2, etc. [4]Ct. v. 6f. [5]Vv. 1-3. [6]32:13-21. [7]18:3, etc.; 32:6. [8]32:20.
[9]18:5; 19:8, etc. [10]Ct. 32:30. [11]Ct. v. 10, etc. [12]V. 5.

[*] Referring to the story of which a trace appears to remain in xxxii. 3. For the
above analysis, see notes on chap. xxxii. and cf. *Hebraica* VII. 4.

fore me and according to the pace of the children,
until I come unto my lord unto [13]Seir. And Esau said, 15
Let me now leave with thee some of the folk that are
with me. And he said, what needeth it? let me [14]find
grace in the sight of my lord. So Esau returned that 16
day on his way unto Seir. And Jacob journeyed to 17
Succoth, and built him an house, and made booths for
his cattle: [15]therefore the name of the place is called
Succoth. [. . .]

(E) And Jacob came [16]in peace to the city of Shechem, 18
which is in the land of Canaan, [17]*when he came from Paddan-aram;** *
and encamped before the city. [18]And he bought the parcel 19
of ground, where he had spread his tent, at the hand of
the children of Hamor, Shechem's father, for an hundred
pieces of money. [19]And he erected there† an altar, and 20
called it El-elohe-Israel. [. . .]

And ‡ [1]Dinah the daughter of Leah, which she bare un- 34
to Jacob, went out to see [2]the daughters of the land. [. . .]
(J) And Shechem the son of Hamor [3]the Hivite, [4]*the* 2

[13]32:3. [14]18:3, etc.; 32:6. [15]2:24, etc. [16]28:21. [17]35:9. [18]Jos. 24:32. Ct. ch. 23.
[19]35:7. [1]21:9. [2]27:46. [3]Ct. 23:10, etc. [4]17:20; 23:6.

* Verse 18 appears to have been supplemented by R, since "Paddan-aram" is
employed by P and R exclusively (cf. xxxv. 9, P; and Josh. xxiv. 32, E). Wellhausen offers the conjecture "to Shechem" for "in peace to," but cf. xxviii. 21. (14)

† The verb *naçab*, "to erect," is not used of the "building" of an altar, but is the
regular term for "setting up" a *maççebah* or pillar of stone, and contains in fact the
same radical. Hence we must either assume the omission of two words meaning
"a pillar and built" at this point, or, more probably, take *mizbeach*, "altar," to be
a correction for *maççebah*, "pillar," a change historical criticism accounts for by
the fact that the maççebah in the seventh century came to be regarded by the
orthodox party as an idolatrous abomination, a radical iconoclasm taking the place
of the earlier policy of *Umdeutung*, or accommodation to Yahweh worship. (Cf.
Hos. iii. 4, Is. xix. 19 and the numerous passages in JE, Gen. xxviii. 18; xxxv. 14, 20;
Ex. xxiv. 4; Josh. iv. 4-8, 20; xxiv. 26, etc., with Ex. xxiii. 24; xxxiv. 13; Num.
xxxiii. 52; Dt. xii. 3; and ct. Dt. xvi. 21f; Lev. xxvi. 1f.)

‡ The assignment of the secondary element of ch. xxxiv. to E in the above analysis is in accordance with the reasoning of Cornill in his *Beitrag* on the analysis of
this chapter in the *Ztschr, f. a. Wiss.* xi. 1. In regard to the J element, and the
separation of parts, critics are practically agreed. But there are strong objections
to E as author of the secondary element, both in the character of the story compared with the rest of this document, in the subsequent references (xxxv. 5 and
xlviii. 22), and in the language, which exhibits frequent traces of R. On the whole,
the objections to E seem to be outweighed by the considerations urged by Cornill
and by Wellhausen (iv. p. 312ff).

(E) *prince of the land,* **saw her; and he took her,** and lay
3 (J) **with her, and humbled her.   And his soul 'clave
unto —Dinah the daughter of Jacob,— and he loved**
4 (E) **the damsel,** 'and spake kindly unto the damsel.   And
Shechem spake unto his father Hamor, saying, Get me this
5 (J) damsel to wife.   **Now Jacob heard** *that he had defiled
Dinah his daughter:* **and his sons were with his cattle in
the field: and Jacob held his peace until they came.**
6 (E) And Hamor the father of Shechem went out unto
7 (J) Jacob to commune with him.   **And the sons of Jacob
came in from the field when they heard it: and the
men 'were grieved, and they were very wroth, because
he had wrought folly in Israel in lying with Jacob's**
8 (E) **daughter;** 'which thing ought not to be done.   And
Hamor communed with 'them, saying, The soul of my son
Shechem longeth for your daughter : I pray you give her
9 unto him to wife.   And make ye marriages with us ; give
your daughters unto us, and take our daughters unto you.
10 And ye shall dwell with us : and '°the land shall be before
you : dwell and trade ye therein, *and get you possessions therein.*
11 (J) **And Shechem said unto her father and unto her
brethren, ''Let me find grace in your eyes, and what**
12 **ye shall say unto me I will give.   Ask me never so
much dowry and gift, and I will give according as ye
shall say unto me : but give me the damsel to wife.**
13 (JE) And the sons of Jacob answered Shechem and Hamor his father
with ''guile, and spake, because * he had defiled Dinah their sister,

⁵2 : 24.   ⁶50 : 21.   ⁷45 : 5.   ⁸29 : 26.   ⁹Ct. v. 6.   ¹°20 : 15.   ¹¹6 : 8; 18 : 3, etc.   ¹²27 : 35.

* Verse 13 gives evidence of editorial treatment in the redundant, " and said "
(cf. A. V.) and otherwise.   It combines apparently elements from both narratives,
which, however, can scarcely be sundered out.   The gap in J at this point leaves
it uncertain what condition was imposed upon Shechem.   There are very serious
difficulties in the way of supposing it to have been circumcision, for infant circumcision in this author (J) is apparently first instituted by Zipporah, Ex. iv. 24ff,
in place of the primitive rite of marital circumcision, but it does not become universal until Josh. v. 2–9 (omit the harmonistic interpolations " again " and " the second
time," vs. 2 and vv. 4–7).   In this element of the narrative it is only a family incident
which is related, and whatever condition was imposed it must have been, according
to the tenor of the story, something for Shechem alone to fulfil (marital circumcision?).
Cf. vs. 19.   Cornill suggests that the dowry was a " parcel " of land.   Cf. xxxiii. 19 (E)
and l. 5 (J).   In this case, " with guile," vs. 13, doubtless an original expression of J,

(E) and said unto them, We cannot do this thing, to give our 14
sister to one that is uncircumcised ; for that were a reproach unto us : only on this condition will we consent un- 15
to you : if ye will be as we be, *that* ¹³*every male of you be circumcised:*
then will we give our daughters unto you, and we will take 16
your daughters to us, and we will dwell with you, and we
will become one people.   But if ye will not hearken unto 17
us, to be circumcised ; then will we take our daughter, and
we will be gone.   And their words pleased Hamor, and 18
(J) Shechem Hamor's son.   **And the young man** ¹⁴**de-** 19
ferred not to do the thing, because he had delight in
Jacob's daughter : and he was honoured above all the
(E) **house of his father.**   And Hamor and Shechem his 20
son came unto the gate of their city, and communed with
the men of their city, saying, These men are peaceable 21
with us ; therefore let them dwell in the land, and trade
therein ; for, behold, the land is large enough for them ;
let us take their daughters to us for wives, and let us give
them our daughters.   Only on this condition will the men 22
consent unto us to dwell with us, to become one people, if
every male among us be circumcised, as they are circumcised.
¹⁵*Shall not their cattle and their substance and all their beasts be ours ?* only 23
let us consent unto them, and they will dwell with us.
And unto Hamor and unto Shechem his son hearkened 24
all that went out of the gate of his city ; and *every male* was
circumcised, all that went out of the gate of his city.   And 25
it came to pass on the third day, when they were sore, [. . .]
(J) **that two of the sons of Jacob,** ¹⁶**Simeon and Levi,**
(E) **Dinah's brethren, took each man his sword,** and
(J) came upon the city unawares, ¹⁷*and slew all the males.*   **And** 26
they slew Hamor and Shechem his son with the edge
of the sword, and took Dinah out of Shechem's house,
(E) **and went forth.**   The sons of Jacob came upon the 27
slain, and spoiled the city, *because they had defiled their sister.*   They 28

¹³17:10. ¹⁴24:56; 32:5. ¹⁵36:6; Jos. 14:4. ¹⁶49:5f. ¹⁷Num. 31:7–9.

would apply to the conduct of Simeon and Levi in accepting a dowry when they intended to take revenge.

took their flocks and their herds and their asses, and that
which was in the city, and that which was in the field ; and
29 all their wealth, and all their little ones and their wives,
(J) took they captive **and spoiled,** *even* **all that was in**
30 **the house. And Jacob said to Simeon and Levi, Ye
have troubled me, to make me** [18]**to stink among the
inhabitants of the land, among** [19]**the Canaanites and
the Perizzites : and, I being few in number, they will
gather themselves together against me and smite me ;**
31 **and I shall be destroyed, I and my house. And they
said, Should he deal with our sister as with an harlot ?*** [. . .]
35   (E) And God said unto Jacob, Arise, go up to Beth-el,
and [1]dwell there : and make there an altar unto God, who
[2]appeared unto thee when thou [3]fleddest from the face of
2 Esau thy brother Then Jacob said unto his household,
and to all that were with him, Put away the [4]strange gods
that are among you, and [5]purify yourselves, and change
3 your garments : and let us arise, and go up to Beth-el ; and
[6]I will make there an altar unto God, who answered me in
the day of my distress, and was with me in the way which
4 I went. And they gave unto Jacob all the strange gods
which were in their hand, and the rings which were in
their ears ; and Jacob hid them under [7]the oak which was
5 by Shechem.   And they journeyed : [8]and a great terror
was upon the cities that were round about them, [9]and they
6 (P) did not pursue after the sons of Jacob.†   [10]*So Jacob
came to Luz, which is in the land of Canaan,* [11]*(the same is Beth-el)*,
7 (E) [. . .] he and all the people that were with him.
And he built there an altar, and called the place [12]El-beth-
el : because there God was revealed unto him, when he

[18]Ex. 5:21. [19]13:7. [1]Ct. v. 16. [2]28:11ff. [3]27:43ff. [4]31:19 ; Jos. 24:20, 23. [5]Ex.
19:10. [6]28:20-22. [7]Jos. 24:26. [8]30:8. [9]34:25ff. [10]28:10ff. [11]V. 15. [12]33:20. Ct. v. 15.

*The work of R in ch. xxxiv. is doubtless even more drastic than would appear
from the above division of the text. Enough, however, of resemblance to E can be
made out to make the presence of this writer probable.

† The reasons assigned for considering vs. 5 due to R seem to the author inade-
quate.

fled from the face of his brother. And [13]Deborah Re- 8
bekah's nurse died, and she was buried below Beth-el under
[14]the oak : and the name of it was called Allon-bacuth.

(P) *[15]And God appeared unto Jacob again, when he came from* 9
Paddan-aram, and blessed him. —[16]And God said unto him, Thy 10
name is Jacob : thy name shall not be called any more Jacob, but
Israel shall be thy name : and he called his name Israel.— And 11
God said unto him, [17]I am God Almighty : [18]be fruitful and mul-
tiply ; a nation and a company of nations shall be of thee, and kings
shall come out of thy loins ; and the land which I gave unto Abra- 12
ham and Isaac, to thee will I give it, and to thy seed after thee will I
give the land. [19]And God went up from him in the place where he spake 13
(J) *with him.* * And Jacob set up a pillar in the place 14
where he spake with him, a pillar of stone: and he
poured out a drink offering thereon, and poured oil
(P) thereon.† *And Jacob called the name of the place where* 15
(J) *God spake with him, [20]Beth-el.* And they journeyed 16
from Beth-el; and there was still some way to come
to Ephrath : and Rachel travailed, and she had hard
labour. And it came to pass, when she was in hard 17
labour, that the midwife said unto her, Fear not: for
now thou shalt have [21]another son. And it came to 18
pass, as her soul was in departing (for she died), that
she called his name Ben-oni: but his father called
(E) him Benjamin. And Rachel died, and was buried in 19
the way to Ephrath (the same is Beth-lehem). And Jacob set 20
up a pillar upon her grave : the same is the Pillar of
(J) Rachel's grave unto this day. And Israel journeyed, 21
and spread his tent beyond the tower of Eder. And 22
it came to pass, while Israel dwelt in that land, that

[13]Ct. 24 : 59. [14]Jud. 4 : 5 ; 13 : 40. [15]I. Sam. 8 : 3f. [16]Ct. 32 : 27ff. [17]Ex. 6 : 2f. [18]17 : 6,
16. [19]17 : 22. [20]Ct. 28 : 19. [21]30 : 23. Ct. vv. 24 and 26.

* Verses 9–13 seem to present an unusual amount of redactional work. "In the
place where he spake with him" is probably a dittograph from vs. 14, as appears from
a comparison of xvii. 22 ; but the last clause of vs. 12 seems to be due to supplementary redaction. Of much more importance is the apparent interference of vs. 10
between vv. 9 and 11. The verse is attributed by all critics to P, but would appear to
have been derived originally from between 12 and 13, or from some other connection.

† See note to xxviii. 16.

**"Reuben went and lay with Bilhah his father's con-
cubine : and Israel heard of it.*** [. . .]

23   (P) *Now the sons of Jacob were twelve : the sons of Leah ;
Reuben, Jacob's firstborn, and Simeon, and Levi, and Judah, and*
24 *Issachar, and Zebulun : the sons of Rachel ; Joseph and Ben-*
25 *jamin : and the sons of Bilhah, Rachel's handmaid ; Dan and*
26 *Naphtali : and the sons of Zilpah, Leah's handmaid ; Gad and
Asher : these are the sons of Jacob, which were born to him* "*in*
27 *Paddan-aram. And Jacob came unto Isaac his father to Mamre,
to Kiriath-arba (the same is Hebron), where Abraham and Isaac*
28 *sojourned.* "*And the days of Isaac were an hundred and four-*
29 *score years. And Isaac gave up the ghost, and died, and was
gathered unto his people, old and full of days ; and Esau and
Jacob his sons buried him.*

36   (R) ¹*Now these are the generations of Esau (the same is Edom).*
 2 *Esau took his wives of the daughters of Canaan ;* ²*Adah the
daughter of Elon the Hittite, and Oholibamah the daughter of*
 3 *Anah, the daughter of Zibeon the Hivite ; and Basemath Ishmael's*
 4 *daughter, sister of Nebaioth. And Adah bare to Esau Eliphaz ;*
 5 *and Basemath bare Reuel ; and Oholibamah bare Jeush, and Jalam, and Korah :* ³*these are the sons of Esau, which were born un-*

²²49 : 3.   ²³Ct. v. 18.   ²⁴25 : 8f.   ¹V. 9.   ²Ct. 26 : 34 ; 28 : 9.   ³35 : 26.

* The analysis of J E in vv. 16–22 is abandoned by K. and S. Other critics assign 16–20
to E, noting apparent traces of J. The evidence for the above analysis will be found
in *Hebraica* VII. 4 (1891). The main argument for J as narrator of these "journey-
ings" is the command to "dwell there" (at Bethel) in vs. 1 (E, cf. vs. 16*a*, J), but
cf. also 17*b* with xxx. 24*b* (J), and "for she died," vs. 18, with "and Rachel died,"
vs. 19.—"Tower of the flock" (*Eder*) in vs. 21 Well. considers an allusion by R to
Jerusalem (cf. Micah iv. 8) ; but Dillmann translates, "on the further side of a watch
tower." Verse 22 may possibly be an anticipatory explanation of xlix. 3, which is
supposed to allude to the ancient Arab practise perpetuated in Reuben, prevalent
perhaps among the neighboring Moabites and Ammonites (Gen. xix. 30ff), and
alluded to in II. Sam. xvi. 22 and I. Kings ii. 22. Such suppositions, however, of the
insertion of matter of fact, to serve as the basis of subsequent reference, are in the
highest degree precarious. The author has, therefore, retained 21f as J's (cf.
"Israel" with "Jacob" vs. 20), though willing to admit the probability of alteration, especially abbreviation, by R.—Textual and the higher criticism come practically into contact in vs. 19, which exhibits an interesting phenomenon. The gloss
("the same is Bethlehem") betrays its late origin by its mistaken explanation. The
grave of the ancestress of Joseph and Benjamin was shown before the Exile, not in
the midst of Judah, but on the boundary between these two tribes. That the "Ephrath" here referred to was not Bethlehem, but a town of Ephraim (i. e. "Ephrath-
ite"), in the neighborhood of Bethel, as the context here demands, and in such a
position as above stated to be probable, is made certain by I. Sam. x. 2ff, "by
Rachel's sepulchre in the border of Benjamin by Zelzah," and by Jer. xxxi. 15.

(P) *to nim in the land of Canaan.** 'And Esau took his wives,* 6
and his sons, and his daughters, and all the souls of his house, and
his cattle, and all his beasts, and all his possessions, which he had
gathered in the land of Canaan; and went into a land† away
from his brother Jacob. 'For their substance was too great for* 7
them to dwell together; and the land of their sojournings could
not bear them because of their cattle. And Esau dwelt in mount 8
Seir: Esau is Edom. '*And these are the generations of Esau the* 9
(R) *father of the Edomites in mount Seir: these are the names* 10
of Esau's sons; Eliphaz the son of Adah the wife of Esau, Reuel
the son of Basemath the wife of Esau. And the sons of Eli- 11
phaz were Teman, Omar, Zepho, and Gatam, and Kenaz. And 12
Timna was concubine to Eliphaz Esau's son; and she bare to
Eliphaz Amalek: these are the sons of Adah Esau's wife. And 13
these are the sons of Reuel; Nahath, and Zerah, Shammah,
and Mizzah: these were the sons of Basemath Esau's wife.
And these were the sons of Oholibamah the daughter of Anah, 14
the daughter of Zibeon, Esau's wife: and she bare to Esau
Jeush, and Jalam, and Korah. These are the dukes of the sons of 15
Esau: the sons of Eliphaz 'the firstborn of Esau; duke Teman,
duke Omar, duke Zepho, duke Kenaz, ⁸duke Korah, duke Gatam, 16
duke Amalek: these are the dukes that came of Eliphaz, in the
land of Edom; these are the sons of Adah. And these are the 17
sons of Reuel Esau's son; duke Nahath, duke Zerah, duke Sham-
mah, duke Mizzah: these are the dukes that came of Reuel in the
land of Edom; these are the sons of Basemath Esau's wife. And 18
these are the sons of Oholibamah Esau's wife; duke Jeush, duke
Jalam, duke Korah: these are the dukes that came of Oholibamah
the daughter of Anah, Esau's wife. These are the sons of Esau, 19
and these are their dukes: the same is Edom.

These are the sons of Seir the Horite, the inhabitants of the 20
land; Lotan and Shobal and Zibeon and Anah, and Dishon and
Ezer and Dishan: these are the dukes that came of the Horites, 21
the children of Seir in the land of Edom. And the children of 22

⁴12:5, etc. ⁵13:6. Ct. ch. 27; 32:3, etc. ⁶2:4, etc. ⁷25:13; 35:23. ⁸Ct. vv. 14, 18.

* Xxxvi. 1–5 is a passage completely in the style of P, even to the wording of the
title (cf. vs. 9), but impossible to assign to P on account of xxvi. 34f and xxviii. 9. In
vs. 2 read "son" according to (R. V.) margin, and for "Hivite," Horite (cf. vv. 20
and 24). See note to vs. 30.

† The Hebrew of vs. 6b shows that after the word "land" the proper name of the
land "Seir," has fallen out. Xxxvii. 1 probably preceded vs. 6 in its original
position. Vs. 8b presents a different shade of meaning from vs. 9, and is regarded
as a gloss

Lotan were Hori and Hemam; [9]and Lotan's sister was Timna.
23 *And these are the children of Shobal; Alvan and Manahath and*
24 *Ebal, Shepho and Onam.   And these are the children of Zibeon;*
   Aiah and Anah: this is Anah who found the hot springs in the wil-
25 *derness, as he fed the asses of Zibeon his father.   And these are the*
   children of Anah; Dishon and Oholibamah the daughter of Anah.
26 *And these are the children of Dishon; Hemdan and Eshban and*
27 *Ithran and Cheran.   These are the children of Ezer; Bilhan and*
28 *Zaavan and Akan.   These are the children of Dishan; Uz and*
29 *Aran.   These are the dukes that came of the Horites; duke Lotan,*
30 *duke Shobal, duke Zibeon, duke Anah, duke Dishon, duke Ezer,*
   duke Dishan: these are the dukes that came of the Horites, ac-
   *cording to their dukes in the land of Seir.**

31   **(J) And these are the kings that reigned in the land
     of Edom, before there reigned any king over the chil-**
32 **dren of Israel.   And Bela the son of Beor reigned in**
33 **Edom; and the name of his city was Dinhabah.   And
     Bela died, and Jobab the son of Zerah of Bozrah**
34 **reigned in his stead.   And Jobab died, and Husham
     of the land of the Temanites reigned in his stead.**
35 **And Husham died, and Hadad the son of Bedad, who
     smote Midian in [10]the field of Moab, reigned in his**
36 **stead: and the name of his city was Avith.   And Ha-
     dad died, and Samlah of Masrekah reigned in his**
37 **stead.   And Samlah died, and Shaul of Rehoboth by**
38 **the River reigned in his stead.   And Shaul died, and
     Baal-hanan the son of Achbor reigned in his stead.**
39 **And Baal-hanan the son of Achbor died, and Hadar
     reigned in his stead: and the name of his city was
     Pau; and his wife's name was Mehetabel, the daugh-**
40 **(P) ter of Matred, the daughter of Me-zahab.** *And
     these are the names of the dukes that came of Esau, according to
     their families, after their places, by their names; duke Timnah,*

[9]V. 12; 4:22.   [10]32:4; Num. 21:20.

* Vv. 10–30 are assigned to R, according to the conviction of many critics that they,
as well as vv. 2–5a, contain at least material derived from J, especially vs. 24; but
in despair of discovering any clew to disentangle the threads.   The material has
apparently been recast by the redactor who so exactly imitates the style of P in vs.
1–5.—Cf. Part III.—In vs. 27 read Jaakan according to (R. V.) margin on account of
Num. xxxiii. 31f.

duke Alvah, duke Jetheth ; duke Oholibamah, duke Elah, duke 41
Pinon ; duke Kenaz, duke Teman, duke Mibzar ; duke Mag- 42–43
diel, duke Iram : these be the dukes of Edom, according to their
habitations in the land of their possession.   This is Esau the
father of the Edomites. *

—And Jacob dwelt in the land of his father's sojournings, in **37**
the land of Canaan.†— [1]*These are the generations of Jacob.* **2**
(E) *Joseph, being seventeen years old,* [. . .] was feeding the
flock with his brethren ; and he was a lad with the sons of
Bilhah, and with the sons of Zilpah, his father's wives : and Joseph
brought the evil report of them unto their father.‡
(J) Now [2]**Israel loved Joseph more than all his chil-** **3**
dren, because he was [3]**the son of his old age: and he**
made him a coat of many colours.‖   And his brethren **4**
saw that their father loved him more than all his breth-
ren; and they hated him, and could not speak peace-
(E) ably unto him.   And Joseph dreamed a dream, and **5**
he told it to his brethren : and they hated him yet the more.§
And he said unto them, Hear, I pray you, this dream which **6**
I have dreamed : for, behold, we were binding sheaves in **7**
the field, and, lo, my sheaf arose, and also stood upright ;
and, behold, your sheaves came round about, and made
obeisance to my sheaf.   And his brethren said unto him, **8**
Shalt thou indeed reign over us ? or shalt thou indeed have
dominion over us ?   And they hated him yet the more for his

[1]*2 :24,* etc.   [2]*32 :28.*   [3]*21 :2; 44 :20.*

* The last part of ch. xxxvi. affords better ground for analysis, but even 31–39
must be considered of uncertain origin. Vv. 40–43 are regarded by all critics as
certainly from P.

† Insert after xxxvi. 8.

‡ The clause in brevier type is supposed to have been inserted to remove the
reproach implied in the clause following from the sons of Leah, i. e. Reuben,
Simeon, Levi and Judah.

‖ Read " long sleeved tunic " with (R. V.) margin, and cf. II. Sam. xiii. 18ff.

§ From the critical standpoint verse 5*b* betrays an acquaintance with vs. 4 and
anticipates vs. 11, besides giving it a twist toward the conception of J. Possibly E
might have had a statement of this hatred after vs. 2, but even in this case it should
not appear until his brethren have heard the subject-matter of the dream. The
LXX. would, therefore, be right in omitting the clause. The same judgment applies
to vs. 8*b,* where " dreams " (plural) anticipates vs. 9.

9 dreams, and for his words.* And he dreamed yet another
dream, and told it to his brethren, and said, Behold, I have
dreamed yet a dream ; and, behold, the sun and the moon
10 and eleven stars made obeisance to me. And he told it to his
father, and to his brethren ;† and his father rebuked him, and
said unto him, What is this dream that thou hast dreamed ?
Shall I and thy mother and thy brethren indeed come to
11 bow down ourselves to thee to the earth? And his brethren 'envied him ; but his father kept the saying in mind.
12 **(J) And his brethren went to feed their father's flock**
13 **in Shechem.   And Israel said unto Joseph, Do not**
thy brethren feed the flock in Shechem? come, and I
(E) will send thee unto them. [. . .] And he said to
14 him, 'Here am I. And he said to him, Go now, see whether
it be well with thy brethren, and well with the flock ;
(J) and bring me word again. **So he sent him out of**
15 **(E) the vale of Hebron,‡ and he came to Shechem.** And
a certain man found him, and, behold, he was 'wandering
in the field : and the man asked him, saying, What seekest
16 thou ? And he said, I seek my brethren : tell me, I pray
17 thee, where they are feeding [the flock]. And the man
said, They are departed hence : for I heard them say, Let
us go to Dothan. And Joseph went after his brethren,
18 and found them in Dothan. And they saw him afar off,
(J) and before he came near unto them, they con-
19 **(E) spired against him to slay him.** And they said
20 one to another, Behold, this 'dreamer cometh. Come now
therefore, and let us slay him, and cast him into one of the
pits, and we will say, 'An evil beast hath devoured him :
21 **(J) and we shall see what will become of his dreams. And**

⁴30:1; Ct. v. 3f. ⁵22:1, 7, etc. ⁶21:14. ⁷vv. 5-11. ⁸v. 33. Ct. 44:28.

* See note preceding.

† Supplementary redaction. A part of 9a is repeated and the "father" included,
as the following, "his father rebuked him," may have seemed to require a special
statement that "his father" also was informed. So Wellhausen *et al.*

‡ Critics seriously question whether Hebron was the place originally mentioned
here.

Reuben* heard it, and delivered him out of their hand ;
(E) and said, Let us not take his life.   And Reuben 22
said unto them, Shed no blood ; cast him into this pit that
is in the wilderness, but ⁹lay no hand upon him : that he
might deliver him out of their hand, to restore him to his
(J) father.   **And it came to pass, when Joseph was** 23
(E) **come unto his brethren,** [. . .] that† they strip
(J) Joseph of his coat, **the coat of many colours that**
(E) **was on him**; and they took him, and cast him into 24
the pit : and the pit was empty, there was no water in it.
(J) And they sat down to eat bread : ¹⁰**and they lifted up** 25
their eyes and looked, and, behold, a travelling com-
pany of Ishmaelites came from Gilead, with their
camels bearing ¹¹**spicery and balm and myrrh, going**
to carry it down to Egypt.   And Judah said unto his 26
brethren, What profit is it if we slay our brother and
conceal his blood?   Come, and let us sell him to the 27
Ishmaelites, and let not our hand be upon him ; for
he is our brother, ¹²**our flesh.   And his brethren**
(E) **hearkened unto him.**   And there passed by Midian- 28
ites, merchantmen : and ¹³they drew and lifted up Joseph
(J) out of the pit, ¹⁴**and sold Joseph to the Ishmaelites**
(E) **for twenty pieces of silver.**   And they brought
Joseph into Egypt.   And Reuben ¹⁵returned unto the pit ; 29
and, behold, Joseph was not in the pit ; and ¹⁶he rent his
clothes.   And he returned unto his brethren, and said, 30
The child is not ; and I, whither shall I go?   And they 31
took Joseph's coat, and killed a he-goat, and dipped the
(J) coat in the blood ; **and they sent the coat of many** 32
(E) **colours,** [. . .] and they brought it to their father ;
and said, This have we found : know now whether it be thy
son's coat or not.   And he knew it, and said, It is my son's 33
(J) coat ; ¹⁷an evil beast hath devoured him ; **Joseph is**

⁹22:12.   ¹⁰33:1.   ¹¹43:11.   ¹²2:23; 29:14.   ¹³40:15. Ct. 45:4.   ¹⁴45:4. Ct. 40:15.
¹⁵v. 22. Ct. v. 27.   ¹⁶v. 20.   ¹⁷44:28.

* Supposed to have been altered in conformity with the following verse from
" Judah," who in J is always spokesman.   Reuben is introduced as if for the first
time in the next verse.   † Heb. " And."

34 (E) **without doubt torn in pieces.**   And Jacob rent his garments, and put sackcloth upon his loins, and mourned

35 (J) for his son many days.   **And all his sons and all his daughters rose up to comfort him; but he refused [18]to be comforted; and he said, [19]For I will go down to the grave to my son mourning.**   And his father wept for

36 (E) him.   And the [20]Midianites sold him into Egypt unto Potiphar, an officer of Pharaoh's, the captain of the guard.*

38   (J) —And it came to pass at that time, that Judah went down from his brethren, and turned in to a cer-

2 tain Adullamite, whose name was Hirah.   And Judah saw there a daughter of a certain Canaanite whose name was Shua; and he took her, and went in unto

3 her.   And she conceived, and bare a son; and he†

4 called his name Er.   And she conceived again, and

5 bare a son; and she called his name Onan.   And she yet again bare a son, and called his name Shelah: and

6 he‡ was at Chezib, when she bare him.   And Judah took a wife for Er his firstborn, and her name was

7 Tamar.   And Er, Judah's firstborn, was wicked in

8 the sight of Yahweh, and Yahweh slew him.   And Judah said unto Onan, Go in unto thy brother's wife, and perform the duty of an husband's brother unto

9 her, and raise up seed to thy brother.   And Onan knew that the seed should not be his; and it came to pass, when he went in unto his brother's wife, that he spilled it on the ground, lest he should give seed

10 to his brother.   And the thing which he did was evil

11 in the sight of Yahweh: and he slew him also.   Then said Judah to Tamar his daughter in law, Remain a

[18]24:67; 38:12.   [19]42:38.   [20]V. 28*a*. Ct. 25, 28*b*; 39:1.

*The slight divergences from the usual analyses of ch. xxxvii. in verses 28 and 32f are based upon the statements in xl. 15 (E) in contrast with xlv. 4f (J) in regard to the means of Joseph's being brought down to Egypt, and of xliv. 28 (J) in regard to Israel's utterance.   Verses 29–31, 32*b, c, d*, 33*a* (E), represent the dismay of Reuben and the brothers at finding Joseph gone from the pit as perfectly genuine and their assumption of his death as real.   Cf. xlii. 13 and 22 (E).

† Read "she called" with Sam. and Targ. Jon.

‡ Read "and she" with LXX.

widow in thy father's house, till Shelah my son be
grown up; for he said, Lest he also die, like his brethren. And Tamar went and dwelt in her father's house.
[1]And in process of time Shua's daughter, the wife of 12
Judah, died; and Judah [2]was comforted, and went up
unto his sheepshearers to Timnah, he and his friend
Hirah the Adullamite. And it was told Tamar, say- 13
ing, Behold, thy father in law goeth up to Timnah to
shear his sheep. And she put off from her the gar- 14
ments of widowhood, and covered herself with her
veil, and wrapped herself, and sat in the gate of
Enaim, which is by the way to Timnah; for she saw
that Shelah was grown up, and she was not given unto him to wife. When Judah saw her, he thought her
to be an harlot; for she had covered her face. And 16
he turned unto her by the way, and said, [3]Go to, I
pray thee, let me come in unto thee: for he knew not
that she was his daughter in law. And she said,
What wilt thou give me, that thou mayest come in
unto me? And he said, I will send thee a kid of the 17
goats from the flock. And she said, Wilt thou give
me a pledge, till thou send it? And he said, What 18
pledge shall I give thee? And she said, Thy signet
and thy cord, and thy staff that is in thine hand. And
he gave them to her, and came in unto her, and she
conceived by him. And she arose, and went away, 19
and put off her veil from her, and put on the garments of her widowhood. And Judah sent the kid of 20
the goats by the hand of his friend the Adullamite, to
receive the pledge from the woman's hand: but he
found her not. Then he asked the men of her place, 21
saying, Where is the harlot that was at Enaim by the
way-side? And they said, There hath been no harlot
here. And he returned to Judah, and said, I have 22
not found her; and also the men of the place said,
There hath been no harlot here. And Judah said, 23

[1]26:8. [2]24:67. [3]11:3.

Let her take it to her, lest we be put to shame: behold, I sent this kid, and thou hast not found her.

24 And it came to pass about three months after, that it
was told Judah, saying, Tamar thy daughter in law
hath played the harlot; and moreover, behold, she is
with child by whoredom.   And Judah said, Bring her

25 forth, and ⁴let her be burnt.   When she was brought
forth, she sent to her father in law, saying, By the
man whose these are, am I with child: and she said,
Discern, I pray thee, whose are these, the signet, and

26 the cords, and the staff.   And Judah acknowledged
them, and said, She is more righteous than I, ⁵foras-
much as I gave her not to Shelah my son.   And he

27 ⁶knew her again no more.   ⁷And it came to pass in the
time of her travail, that, behold, twins were in her

28 womb.   And it came to pass, when she travailed, that
one put out a hand: ⁸and the midwife took and bound
upon his hand a scarlet thread, saying, This came out

29 first.   And it came to pass, as he drew back his hand,
that, behold, his brother came out: and she said,
Wherefore hast thou made a breach for thyself? there-

30 fore his name was called Perez.   And afterward came
out his brother, that had the scarlet thread upon his
hand: and his name was called Zerah.*—

39   And Joseph was brought down to Egypt; and Potiphar, an officer of Pharaoh's, the captain of the guard,† an Egyptian, bought him of the hand of the ¹Ishmaelites,

⁴Ct. Lev. 20:10; Dt. 22:23ff. ⁵18:5, etc. ⁶4:1, etc. ⁷25:24ff. ⁸35:17. ¹37:25ff.
Ct. 37:36.

* It is difficult to find a position in the narrative of Genesis as we now have it
where ch. xxxviii. would appear less inappropriately than in its present position,
though it is now quite impossible to reconcile with the context. We may suppose
perhaps that originally it stood after xxxv. 22. Cf. the beginning of this verse with
xxxviii. 1. According to historical criticism the narrative represents a tradition of
Judah separating himself from his brethren, going into the southern district, and
mingling there with the Canaanitish tribes, and anticipates thus the story of the
settling of this region by Judah in alliance with the Kenites, Kenizzites and Jerach-
meelites, after the Exodus, very much as Gen. xii. 1off is supposed to anticipate the
story of Egyptian oppression, plagues, deliverance and occupation of Canaan.

   In vv. 29 and 30 read " she called " with Sam. and Syr.

† Harmonistic redaction. Cf. xxxvii. 36.

which had brought him down thither. And Yahweh 2
was with Joseph, 'and he was a prosperous man; and
he was in the house of his master the Egyptian. And 3
his master saw that Yahweh was with him, and that
Yahweh made all that he did to prosper in his hand.
(E) And Joseph 'found grace in his sight 'and he minis- 4
(J) tered unto him : and he made him overseer over his
house, and all that he had he put into his hand. And 5
it came to pass 'from the time that he made him overseer in his house, and over all that he had, that Yahweh 'blessed the Egyptian's house for Joseph's sake;
and the blessing of Yahweh was upon all that he had,
(E) in the house and in the field. And he left all that 6
(J) he had in Joseph's hand; 'and he knew not aught
[that was] with him, save the bread which he did eat.
And Joseph was comely, and well favoured. And it 7
came to pass after these things, that his master's
wife cast her eyes upon Joseph: and she said, Lie
with me. But he refused, and said unto his master's 8
wife, 'Behold, my master knoweth not what is with
me in the house, and he hath put all that he hath into my hand; there is none greater in this house than 9
I; neither hath he kept back any thing from me but
thee, because thou art his wife: how then can I do
this great wickedness, and sin against God?* And it 10
came to pass, as she spake to Joseph day by day, that
he hearkened not unto her, to lie by her, [or] to be
with her. And it came to pass about this time, that 11
he went into the house to do his work; and there
was none of the men of the house there within. And 12
she caught him by his garment, saying, Lie with me:
and he left his garment in her hand, and fled, and got
him out. And it came to pass, when she saw that he 13
had left his garment in her hand, and was fled forth,
that she called unto the men of her house, and spake 14

[2]24:21. [3]6:8, etc. [4]40:4; Ex. 24:13. [5]Ex. 4:10; 5:23; 9:24. [6]30:27. [7]v. 8.
* Elohim because a heathen is addressed. Cf. Gen. iii. 1, note.

unto them, saying, See, he hath brought in an Hebrew
unto us to mock us; he came in unto me to lie with
15 me, and I cried with a loud voice: and it came to
pass, when he heard that I lifted up my voice and
cried, that he left his garment by me, and fled, and
16 got him out. And she laid up his garment by her,
17 until his master came home. And she spake unto
him according to these words, saying, The Hebrew
servant, which thou hast brought unto us, came in
18 unto me to mock me: and it came to pass, as I lifted
up my voice and cried, that he left his garment by
19 me, and fled out. And it came to pass, when his master heard the words of his wife, which she spake unto him, saying, After this manner did thy servant to
20 me; that his wrath was kindled. And Joseph's master took him, and put him into the prison, the place
where the king's prisoners were bound :* and he was there
21 in the prison. But Yahweh was with Joseph, and
ᵇshewed kindness unto him, and gave him favour in
22 the sight of the keeper of the prison. And the keeper
of the prison committed to Joseph's hand all the prisoners that were in the prison; and whatsoever they
23 did there, he was the doer of it. ᶜThe keeper of the
prison looked not to any thing that was under his
hand, because Yahweh was with him; and that which
he did, Yahweh made it to prosper.†

40 (E)(J) ¹And it came to pass after these things, that ‡
the butler of the king of Egypt and his baker offen-
2 (E) ded their lord the king of Egypt. [. . .] And ‖
Pharaoh was wroth against his two officers, against the
chief of the butlers, and against the chief of the bakers.

ᵃ24:12. ᵇV. 5f. ᶜ15:1; 22:1, 20, etc.

* The clauses in brevier type, vv. 10 and 20, are probably explanatory glosses.

† Verses 21-23 are suspected by some critics of alteration by R, or perhaps even of
being interpolated entire, in the interest of harmony between J's representation and
E's. There seems to me to be no sufficient ground for rejecting them in whole or in
part.

‡ Heb. "And." ‖ Heb. "That."

And he put them in ward [2]in the house of the captain of 3
(J) the guard, **[3]into the prison, the place where Joseph
(E) was bound.** [...]   And the captain of the guard 4
charged Joseph with them, and he ministered unto them :
and they continued a season in ward.   And they dreamed 5
a dream both of them, each man his dream, in one night,
**(J) each man according to the interpretation of his
dream, the butler and the baker of the king of Egypt,
(E) which were bound in the prison.** [...] And Joseph 6
came in unto them in the morning, and saw them, and,
behold, they were sad.   And he asked Pharaoh's officers 7
that were with him in ward [4]in his master's house, saying,
Wherefore look ye so sadly to-day?   And they said unto 8
him, We have dreamed a dream, and there is none that
can interpret it.   And Joseph said unto them, [5]Do not interpretations belong to God? tell it me, I pray you.   And 9
the chief butler told his dream to Joseph, and said to him,
In my dream, behold, a vine was before me ; and in the 10
vine were three branches : and it was as though it budded,
[and] its blossoms shot forth ; [and] the clusters thereof
brought forth ripe grapes : and Pharaoh's cup was in my 11
hand ; and I took the grapes, and pressed them into Pharaoh's cup, and I gave the cup into Pharaoh's hand.   And 12
Joseph said unto him, This is the interpretation of it : the
three branches are three days ; within yet three days shall 13
Pharaoh lift up thine head, and restore thee to thine office :
and thou shalt give Pharaoh's cup into his hand, after the
former manner when thou wast his butler.   But have me 14
in thy remembrance when it shall be well with thee, and
shew kindness, I pray thee, unto me, and make mention of
me unto Pharaoh, and bring me out of this house : [6]for in- 15
deed I was stolen away out of the land of the Hebrews :
**(J) and here also have I done nothing that they should
(E) [7]put me into the dungeon.** [...]   When the chief 16
baker saw that the interpretation was good, he said unto
Joseph, I also was in my dream, and, behold, three baskets

[2]37 : 36.   [3]39 : 20ff.   [4]Ct. 39 : 20ff.   [5]41 : 16, 38f.   [6]37 : 28*a*.   Ct. 28*b*.   [7]39 : 20ff.

13

17 of white bread were on my head : and in the uppermost
basket there was of all manner of bakemeats for Pharaoh ;
and the birds did eat them out of the basket upon my
18 head. And Joseph answered and said, This is the inter-
19 pretation thereof : the three baskets are three days ; within yet three days shall Pharaoh ⁹lift up thy head from off
thee, and shall hang thee on a tree ; and the birds shall
20 eat thy flesh from off thee. And it came to pass the third
day, which was Pharaoh's birthday, that he made a feast
unto all his servants : and he lifted up the head of the
chief butler and the head of the chief baker among his
21 servants.* And he restored the chief butler unto his butlership again ; and he gave the cup into Pharaoh's hand :
22 but he hanged the chief baker : as Joseph had interpreted
23 to them. Yet did not the chief butler remember Joseph,
but forgat him.

41 And it came to pass at the end of two full years, that
Pharaoh dreamed : and, behold, he stood by the river.
2 And, behold, there came up out of the river seven kine,
well favoured and fat fleshed ; and they fed in the reed-
3 grass. And, behold, seven other kine came up after them
out of the river, ill' favoured and leanfleshed ; and stood
4 by the other kine upon the brink of the river. And the ill
favoured and leanfleshed kine did eat up the seven well
5 favoured and fat kine. So Pharaoh awoke. And he slept
and dreamed a second time : and, behold, seven ears of
6 corn came up upon one stalk, rank and good. And, behold, seven ears, thin and blasted with the east wind,
7 sprung up after them. And the thin ears swallowed up
the seven rank and full ears. And Pharaoh awoke, and,
8 behold, it was a dream. And it came to pass in the morning that his spirit was troubled ; and he sent and called
for all the magicians of Egypt, and all his wise men thereof : and Pharaoh told them his dream ;† but there was

⁹v. 13.

* With a play upon the double sense of the expression, "lift up the head." Cf.
vv. 13 and 19.

† Read " dreams " with Sam., and cf. last clause of the verse.

none that could interpret them unto Pharaoh. Then spake 9
the chief butler unto Pharaoh, saying, I do remember my
faults this day : [1]Pharaoh was wroth with his servants, and 10
put me* in ward in the house of the captain of the guard,
me and the chief baker : and we dreamed a dream in one 11
night, I and he ; we dreamed each man according to the
interpretation of his dream. And there was with us there 12
a young man, an Hebrew, [2]servant to the captain of the
guard ; and we told him, and he interpreted to us our
dreams ; to each man according to his dream he did interpret. And it came to pass, as he interpreted to us, so it 13
was ; me he restored unto mine office, and him he hanged.
(J) Then Pharaoh sent and called Joseph, **and they** 14
brought him hastily [3]out of the dungeon : [. . .] and
(E) he shaved himself, and changed his raiment, and came
in unto Pharaoh. And Pharaoh said unto Joseph, I have 15
dreamed a dream, and there is none that can interpret it :
and I have heard say of thee, that when thou hearest a dream
thou canst interpret it. And Joseph answered Pharaoh 16
saying, [4]It is not in me : God shall give Pharaoh an answer
of peace. And Pharaoh spake unto Joseph, In my dream, 17
behold, I stood upon the brink of the river : and, behold, 18
there came up out of the river seven kine, fatfleshed and
well favoured ; and they fed in the reed-grass : and, be- 19
hold, seven other kine came up after them, poor and very
ill favoured and leanfleshed, such as I never saw in all the
land of Egypt for badness : and the lean and ill favoured 20
kine did eat up the first seven fat kine : and when they had 21
eaten them up, it could not be known that they had eaten
them ; but they were still ill favoured, as at the beginning.
So I awoke. And I saw in my dream, and, behold, seven 22
ears came up upon one stalk, full and good : and, behold, 23
seven ears, withered, thin, [and] blasted with the east wind,
sprung up after them : and the thin ears swallowed up the 24
seven good ears : and I told it unto the magicians ; but

[1]Ch. 40. [2]37:36; 40:4. Ct. 39:20ff; V. 14*b*. [3]39:20ff; 40:15. Ct. v. 12. [4]40:8; 45:8.
* Read with LXX. and Sam. "them."

25 there was none that could declare it to me. And Joseph
said unto Pharaoh, The dream of Pharaoh is one : what
26 God is about to do he hath declared unto Pharaoh. The
seven good kine are seven years ; and the seven good ears
27 are seven years : the dream is one. And the seven lean
and ill favoured kine that came up after them are seven
years, and also the seven empty ears blasted with the east
28 wind ; they shall be seven years of famine. That is the
thing which I spake unto Pharaoh : what God is about to
29 do he hath shewed unto Pharaoh.   Behold, there come
seven years of great plenty throughout all the land of
30 Egypt : and there shall arise after them seven years of
famine ; and all the plenty shall be forgotten in the land
31 (J) of Egypt ; and the famine shall consume the land ; **and
the plenty shall not be known in the land by reason
of that famine which followeth ; for it shall be very**
32 (E) **grievous.** [. . .]   And for that the dream was
doubled unto Pharaoh twice, it is because the thing is
established by God, and God will shortly bring it to pass.
33 Now therefore let Pharaoh look out a man discreet
34 (J) and wise, and set him over the land of Egypt. **Let
(E) Pharaoh do [this],** and let him appoint overseers
(J) over the land **and take up 'the fifth part of the land
35 of Egypt in the seven plenteous years. And let them
gather all the food of these good years that come,**
(E) and lay up corn under the hand of Pharaoh for food
36 (J) (E) **'in the cities, and let them keep it.** And the
food shall be for a store to the land against the seven years
of famine, which shall be in the land of Egypt ; that the
37 land perish not through the famine. And the thing was
good in the eyes of Pharaoh, and in the eyes of all his ser-
38 vants. And Pharaoh said unto his servants, Can we find
such a one as this, a man in whom the spirit of God is ?
39 And Pharaoh said unto Joseph, 'Forasmuch as God hath
shewed thee all this, there is none so discreet and wise as
40 thou : thou shalt be over my house, and according unto

[5]47:26. [6]47:21. [7]Ct. 18:5, etc.

thy word shall all my people be ruled: only in the throne
(J) will I be greater than thou. **And Pharaoh said unto** 41
**Joseph, [8]See, I have set thee over all the land of Egypt.
And Pharaoh took off his signet ring from his hand,** 42
**and put it upon Joseph's hand, and arrayed him in vest-
ures of fine linen, and put a gold chain about his neck;
and he made him to ride in the second chariot which** 43
**he had; and they cried before him, Bow the knee: and
he set him over all the land of Egypt. And Pharaoh** 44
**said unto Joseph, I am Pharaoh, and without thee
shall no man lift up his hand or his foot in all the land
of Egypt. And Pharaoh called Joseph's name Zaphe-** 45
nath-paneah; and he gave him to wife Asenath the
(P) **daughter of [9]Poti-phera priest of On.** *And Joseph
went out over the land of Egypt. And Joseph was thirty years* 46
old when he stood before Pharaoh king of Egypt. [. . .]
(J) **And Joseph went out from the presence of Pharaoh, and went throughout all the land of Egypt.[ˊ]
And in the seven plenteous years the earth brought** 47
forth by handfuls. And he gathered up all the food 48
**of the seven years which were in the land of Egypt,
and laid up the food [10]in the cities: the food of the
field, which was round about every city, laid he up in**
(E) **the same.** And Joseph laid up corn [11]as the sand of 49
the sea, very much, until he left numbering; for it was
without number. And unto Joseph were born two sons 50
before the year of famine came, which Ásenath the daughter
of Poti-phera priest of On bare unto him. And Joseph called 51
the name of the firstborn Manasseh: For, [said he], God
hath made me forget all my toil, and all my father's house.
And the name of the second called he Ephraim: For God 52
(J) hath made me fruitful in the land of my affliction. **And** 53
the seven years of plenty, that was in the land of
(E) **Egypt, came to an end.** And the seven years of 54
famine began to come, according as Joseph had said: and
there was famine in all lands; but in all the land of

[8]27:27; 31:50; Ek. 33:13. [9]Cf. 37:36. [10]V. 35; 47:21. [11]I. Kings 4:20, 29.

55 (J) Egypt there was bread. And when all the land of
Egypt was famished, the people cried to Pharaoh for
bread : and Pharaoh said unto all the Egyptians, Go
56 unto Joseph ; what he saith to you, do. And the
famine was over all the face of the earth : and Joseph
opened all the storehouses, and sold unto the Egyptians ; and the famine was sore in the land of Egypt.
57 (E) [. . .] And all countries came into Egypt to Joseph
for to buy corn ; because the famine was sore in all the
earth.*

42   Now Jacob saw that there was corn in Egypt, and Jacob
said unto his sons, Why do ye look one upon another?
2 (J) (E) And he said, Behold, I have heard that there is
(J) (E) corn in Egypt : get you down thither, and buy
3 for us from thence ; that we may live, and not die. And
Joseph's ten brethren went down to buy corn from Egypt.
4 But Benjamin, Joseph's brother, Jacob sent not with his
(J) brethren ; for he said, 'Lest peradventure mischief
5 befall him. And the sons of Israel came to buy among
those that came : for the famine was in the land of
6 (E) Canaan. *And Joseph was the governor over the land ;
(J) he it was that *sold to all the people of the land :
(E) and Joseph's brethren came, and bowed down them-
7 (J) selves to him with their faces to the earth. And
Joseph saw his brethren, and he knew them, but
(E) made himself strange unto them, —'and spake
(J) roughly with them ;— and he said unto them,
Whence come ye? And they said, From the land of

¹V. 38 ; 44 : 29. ²41 : 40. ³41 : 56. ⁴V. 30 ; I. Sam. 20 : 10.

* The latter part of ch. xli. is admitted by all critics to present a problem for the
analysis almost impossible of exact solution. Points of general assent are : 1st.
That the groundword of the chapter, especially in the first part relating the
dreams, is E's. 2d. That this narrative of E has been filled out, especially in the
latter part, with material from J. 3d. The presence of P in vs. 46a at least. In support of this view differences are pointed out, consisting mainly in the supplying of
new descriptive terms, in the first and second relation of the dreams ; and redun-
dancies and reduplications in 30f, 33-36, 48f, 54-57. Regarding "Poti-pherah" as a
variant of "Potiphar" and xlvii. 13-26 (J) as exhibiting a contrast in feeling toward
the distress of the famine-stricken people, to xlv. 5b (E), the author submits again
an independent analysis, referring as before to *Hebraica* VII. 4 (1891).

(E) Canaan to buy food.   And Joseph knew his brethren,   8
but they knew not him.   And Joseph remembered [6]the   9
dreams which he dreamed of them,* and said unto them,
[5]Ye are spies; to see the nakedness of the land ye are
come.   And they said unto him, Nay, my lord, but to buy   10
food are thy servants come.   We are all one man's sons;   11
we are true men, thy servants are no spies.   And he said   12
unto them, Nay, but to see the nakedness of the land ye
are come.   And they said, We thy servants are twelve   13
brethren, the sons of one man in the land of Canaan; and,
behold, the youngest is this day with our father, [7]and one
is not.   And Joseph said unto them, That is it that I spake
unto you, saying, Ye are spies : hereby ye shall be proved :
by the life of Pharaoh ye shall not go forth hence, except   15
your youngest brother come hither.   Send one of you, and   16
let him fetch your brother, and ye shall be bound, that
your words may be proved, whether there be truth in you :
or else by the life of Pharaoh surely ye are spies.   [8]And   17
he put them all together into ward three days.   And   18
Joseph said unto them the third day, This do, and live; for
I fear God : if ye be true men, let one of your brethren be   19
bound in your prison house; but go ye, carry corn for
the famine of your houses : and bring your youngest   20
brother unto me; so shall your words be verified, and ye
shall not die.   And they did so.   And they said one to   21
another, We are verily guilty concerning our brother, in
that we saw the distress of his soul, when he besought us,
and we would not hear; therefore is this distress come upon us.   And Reuben answered them, saying, [9]spake I not   22
unto you, saying, Do not sin against child; and ye would
not hear? therefore also, behold, his blood is required.
And they knew not that Joseph understood them; for   23
there was an interpreter between them.   And he turned   24
himself about from them, and wept; and he returned to

[6]37:5-11.   [5]vv. 29-34. Ct. 43:5-7.   [7]37:30.   [8]40:3.   [9]37:22f.

* Insert here the misplaced clause, "and he spake roughly with them," vs. 7.
According to the analysis the "roughness" appears only in E.   Cf. xliii. 7 ; xliv.
19ff (J) with xlii. 30 (E).

them, and spake to them, and took Simeon from among
25 them, and bound him before their eyes.   Then Joseph
commanded to fill their vessels with corn, and to restore
every man's money into his sack, and to give them [10]pro-
visions for the way : and thus was it done unto them.
26 And they laded their asses with their corn, and departed
27 (J) thence.   [11]**And as one of them opened his sack to
give his ass provender in [12]the lodging place, he espied
his money; and, behold, it was in the mouth of his**
28 **sack.   And he said unto his brethren, My money is
restored; and, lo, it is even in my sack: and their
(E) heart failed them, [. . .]** —and they turned trembling one to another, saying, What is this that God hath
29 done unto us?—   And they came unto Jacob their father
unto the land of Canaan, and told him all that had befallen
30 them ; saying, [13]The man, the lord of the land, spake rough-
31 ly with us, and took us for spies of the country.   And we
32 said unto him, We are true men ; we are no spies : we be
twelve brethren, sons of our father ; one is not, and the
youngest is this day with our father in the land of Canaan.
33 And the man, the lord of the land, said unto us, Hereby
shall I know that ye are true men ; leave one of your
brethren with me, and take [corn for] the famine of your
34 houses, and go your way : and bring your youngest brother unto me : then shall I know that ye are no spies, but
that ye are true men : so will I deliver you your brother,
35 and ye shall traffick in the land.   [14]And it came to pass as
they emptied their sacks, that, behold, every man's bundle
of money was in his sack : and when they and their father
36 saw their bundles of money, they were afraid.*   And Jacob

[10]45:21.   [11]43:21. Ct. v. 35.   [12]Ex. 4:24.   [13]Vv. 8ff.   [14]Ct. v. 27; 43:21.

* If E's, verse 28b must be inserted after vs. 35, on the ground that the surprise
and fear depicted in vs. 35 (E) presuppose that the discovery is then a genuine discovery, *for the first time*, of the restored money ; and not one already made "at
the lodging place."   On the same ground 27, 28a are considered the remains of J's
narrative which is reiterated in xliii. 21.   The difficulties which exegetically will be
explained in various ways are accounted for by the analysis as due to the attempt
of JE to preserve as much as possible of two divergent narratives.   These difficulties are not merely that xliii. 21 taken in connection with 27f and compared with vs.

their father said unto them, Me have ye bereaved of my children : Joseph is not, and Simeon is not, and ye will take Benjamin away : all these things are against me. [16]And Reuben spake unto his father, saying, Slay my two 37 sons, if I bring him not to thee : deliver him into my hand, (J) and I will bring him to thee again.—**And he said, My 38 son shall not go down with you; for his brother is dead, and he only is left: if mischief befall him by the way in the which ye go, then shall ye bring down my gray hairs with sorrow to the grave.***—

And the famine was 'sore in the land.   And it came 43 to pass, when they had eaten up the corn which they 2 had brought out of Egypt, their father said unto them, Go again, buy us a little food.   And Judah 3 spake unto him, saying, [2]The man did solemnly protest unto us, saying, Ye shall not see my face except your brother be with you.   If thou wilt send 4 our brother with us, we will go down and buy thee food : but if thou wilt not send him, we will not go 5 down : for the man said unto us, Ye shall not see my face, except your brother be with you.   And 'Israel 6

[16]Ct. 43 :8ff. [1]12 : 10; 47 :4, 13. [2]44 :20-24. [3]32 : 28, etc.

35 compels us to assume a double discovery and a double surprise. If verses 25-35 are to be read as they stand, we must assume—1st, that after one brother had announced the discovery of his money the others restrained all curiosity to open their sacks until arrived at home ; 2d, that only one ass had provender, while the other nine went hungry. Observe *per contra* that in vs. 25 (E) Joseph "gave them provision for the way," which made the opening of the sacks needless. Correspondingly in verses 25 and 35 (E) the money is put "into the sack" to be discovered when they are "emptied" (35), whereas in vs. 27; xliii. 12, 21; xliv. 1, 8 (J), it is put "in the *mouth* of the sack" with the apparent intention that it shall be discovered at the first opening.—In 27a "sack" (Heb. *saq*) is regarded as a substitution by R of E's word for J's (*amtachath*, 27b, 28; xliii. 12, 21-23; xliv. 1-8). '

* Critics discover the original answer to Reuben's offer in xlviii. 14. From their point of view it could not be otherwise than affirmative, because Simeon is waiting in prison in Egypt for release at the appearance of Benjamin. The transposition of this verse from an original position after xliii. 7, and removal of the original affirmative answer xlii. 14 (E) enables JE to introduce both accounts of the offering of suretyship by Reuben (xlii. 37, E) and by Judah (xliii. 8f, J). This process also permitted the postponement of the return to Egypt, and the introduction of xliii. 1ff (J) where in accordance with the account (xliii. 7 ; xliv. 19-23, J) of the friendly reception of the brothers (no imprisonment of Simeon) they quietly wait in Canaan till the exhaustion of their store of food.

said, Wherefore dealt ye so ill with me, as to tell the
7 man whether ye had yet a brother? And they said,
The man asked straitly concerning ourselves, and
concerning our kindred, saying, Is your father yet
alive? have ye [another] brother? and we told him
according to the tenor of these words: could we in
any wise know that he would say, Bring your brother
8 down? 'And Judah said unto Israel his father, Send
the lad with me, and we will arise and go; that we
may live, and not die, both we, and thou, and also
9 our little ones. I will be surety for him; of my hand
shalt thou require him: if I bring him not unto thee,
and set him before thee, then let me bear the blame
10 for ever: for except we had lingered, surely we had
11 now returned a second time. And their father Israel
said unto them, If it be so now, do this; take of the
choice fruits of the land in your vessels, and carry
down the man a present, a little balm, and a little
12 honey, spicery and myrrh, nuts, and almonds: and
take double money in your hand; and the money that
was 'returned in the mouth of your sacks carry again
13 in your hand; peradventure it was an oversight: take
also your brother, and arise, go again unto the man:
14 (E) and 'God Almighty give you mercy before the man,
that he may release unto you your other brother and Benjamin. 'And if I be bereaved of my children, I am bereaved. [. . .]
15   (J) And the men took that present, and they took
double money in their hand, and Benjamin; and rose
up, and went down to Egypt, and stood before Joseph.
16 And when Joseph saw Benjamin with them, he said
to 'the steward of his house, Bring the men into the
house, and slay, and make ready; for the men shall
17 dine with me at noon. And the man did as Joseph
bade; and the man brought the men into Joseph's
18 house. And the men were afraid, because they were

⁴Ct. 42:37. ⁵42:27. Ct. 42:35. ⁶Ex. 3:13. ⁷42:36. ⁸39:4.

brought into Joseph's house; and they said, Because
of the money that was returned in our sacks at the
first time are we brought in; that he may seek occasion against us, and fall upon us, and take us for bondmen, and our asses.   And they came near to the 19
steward of Joseph's house, and they spake unto him
at the door of the house, and said, Oh my lord, we 20
came indeed down at the first time to buy food : [9]and 21
it came to pass, when we came to the lodging place,
that we opened our sacks, and, behold, every man's
money was in the mouth of his sack, our money in
full weight: and we have brought it again in our
hand.   And other money have we brought down in 22
our hand to buy food : we know not who put our
money in our sacks.   And he said, Peace be to you, 23
fear not : your God, and the God of your father, hath
given you treasure in your sacks: I had your money.
(E) (J) [10]And he brought Simeon out unto them.   And 24
the man brought the men into Joseph's house, and
gave them water, and they washed their feet; and he
[11]gave their asses provender.   And they made ready 25
the present against Joseph came at noon: for they
heard that they should eat bread there.   And when 26
Joseph came home, they brought him the present
which was in their hand into the house, and bowed
down themselves to him to the earth.   [12]And he asked 27
them of their welfare, and said, Is your father well,
the old man of whom ye spake? Is he yet alive? And 28
they said, Thy servant our father is well, he is yet
alive. [13]And they bowed the head, and made obeisance.
And he lifted up his eyes, and saw Benjamin his bro- 29
ther, his mother's son, and said, Is this your youngest brother, of whom ye spake unto me?   And he
said, God be gracious unto thee, [14]my son.   And Jo- 30
seph made haste; for his bowels did yearn upon his

[9]42:27; Ex. 4:24.   [10]42:24.   [11]24:32; 42:27.   [12]V. 7. Ct. 45:3.   [13]24:26, 48.   [14]35:17f.
Ct. 46:21.

brother : and he sought where to weep; and he entered
31 into his chamber, and wept there.   And he washed
his face, and came out ; and he refrained himself, and
32 said, Set on bread.   And they set on for him by himself, and for them by themselves, and for the Egyptians, which did eat with him, by themselves: [15]be-
cause the Egyptians might not eat bread with the
Hebrews; for that is an abomination unto the Egyp-
33 tians.   And they sat before him, the first-born according to his birthright, and the youngest according
to his youth : and the men marvelled one with an-
34 other.   And he took [and sent] messes unto them from
before him : but Benjamin's mess was five times so
much as any of theirs.   And they drank, and [16]were
merry with him.

44   And he commanded the steward of his house, saying, Fill the men's sacks with food, as much as they
can carry, and put every man's money [1]in his sack's
2 mouth.   And put my cup, the silver cup, [1]in the
sack's mouth of the youngest, and his corn money.
And he did according to the word that Joseph had
3 spoken.   As soon as the morning was light, the men
4 were sent away, they and their asses.   [And] when
they were gone out of the city, and were not yet
far off, Joseph said unto his steward, Up, follow
after the men; and when thou dost overtake them,
say unto them, Wherefore have ye rewarded evil for
5 good?*   Is not this it in which my lord drinketh, and
whereby he indeed [2]divineth? ye have done evil in so
6 doing.   And he overtook them, and he spake unto
7 them these words.   And they said unto him, Wherefore speaketh my lord such words as these?   God
forbid that thy servants should do such a thing.
8 Behold, the money, which we found [1]in our sacks'
mouths, we brought again unto thee out of the land

[15]46:34.   [16]9:21.   [1]42:27; 43:12, 21. Ct. 42:35.   [2]30:27; V. 15.

* LXX., Syr., and Vulg. supply " Why have ye stolen my silver cup?"

of Canaan: how then should we steal out of thy lord's house silver or gold? With whomsoever of thy ser- 9 vants it be found, let him die, and we also will be my lord's bondmen. And he said, Now also let it be 'ac- 10 cording unto your words: he with whom it is found shall be my bondman: and ye shall be blameless. Then they hasted, and took down every man his sack 11 to the ground, and opened every man his sack. And 12 he searched, [and] began at the eldest, and left at the youngest: and the cup was found in Benjamin's sack. Then they rent their clothes, and laded every man 13 his ass, and returned to the city. And Judah and his 14 brethren came to Joseph's house; and he was yet there: and they fell before him on the ground. And 15 Joseph said unto them, What deed is this that ye have done? know ye not that such a man as I can indeed divine? And Judah* said, What shall we say unto my 16 lord? what shall we speak? or how shall we clear ourselves?† God hath found out the iniquity of thy servants: behold, we are my lord's bondmen, both we, and he also in whose hand the cup is found. And he 17 said, God forbid that I should do so: the man in whose hand the cup is found, he shall be my bondman; but as for you, get you up in peace unto your father.

Then Judah came near unto him, and said, Oh my 18 lord, let thy servant, I pray thee, speak a word in my lord's ears, and let not thine anger burn against thy servant: for thou art even as Pharaoh. 'My lord 19 asked his servants, saying, Have ye a father, or a brother? And we said unto my lord, We have a father, 20 an old man, and a 'child of his old age, a little one; and his brother is dead, and he alone is left of his mother, and his father loveth him. And thou saidst 21 unto thy servants, Bring him down unto me, that I

²30:34. ³43:7. Ct. ch. 42. ⁴37:3.

* Perhaps better, "they said." Cf. vs. 18 and vs. 7.

† Sam. and LXX. insert "since."—For the use of Elohim throughout this J chapter cf. note to Gen. iii. 1.

22 may set mine eyes upon him. And 'we said unto my
   lord, The lad cannot leave his father : for if he should
23 leave his father, his father would die. And thou
   saidst unto thy servants, Except your youngest brother come down with you, ye shall see my face no more.
24 And it came to pass when we came up unto thy servant
25 my father, we told him the words of my lord. 'And
26 our father said, Go again, buy us a little food. And we
   said, We cannot go down : if our youngest brother be
   with us, then will we go down : for we may not see the
   man's face, except our youngest brother be with us.
27 And thy servant my father said unto us, Ye know that
28 my wife bare me two sons : and the one went out from
   me, 'and I said, Surely he is torn in pieces ; and I
29 have not seen him since : 'and if ye take this one also
   from me, and mischief befall him, ye shall bring down
30 my gray hairs with sorrow to the grave. Now therefore when I come to thy servant my father, and the
   lad be not with us ; seeing that his life is bound up in
31 the lad's life ; it shall come to pass, when he seeth
   that the lad is not [with us], that he will die : and thy
   servants shall bring down the gray hairs of thy ser-
32 vant our father with sorrow to the grave. 'For thy
   servant became surety for the lad unto my father,
   saying, If I bring him not unto thee, then shall I bear
33 the blame to my father for ever. Now therefore, let
   thy servant, I pray thee, abide instead of the lad a
   bondman to my lord ; and let the lad go up with his
34 brethren. For how shall I go up to my father, and
   the lad be not with me? lest I see the evil that shall
   come on my father.
45   Then* Joseph could not 'refrain himself before all
      them that stood by him ; and he cried, Cause every

⁵Ct. 42 : 13, 20, 33. ⁶43 : 2f. Ct. 42 : 36f. ⁷37 : 33*b*. ⁸42 : 38. ⁹43 : 9. ¹43 : 31.

* See *Hebraica* VII. 4 (1891) for the evidence in support of the present analysis,
divergent, in verses 9–14, in some degree from accepted theories. Cf. also my
article "JE in the Middle Books of the Pentateuch," *Journal of Bibl. Lit.*, 1890, Part
II., p. 192f.

(E) **man to go out from me.** And there stood no man
with him, while Joseph [2]made himself known unto his
(J) (E) brethren. **And he wept aloud:** and the Egyp- 2
(J) tians heard, **'and the house of Pharaoh heard.**
(E) And Joseph said unto his brethren, I am Joseph, 3
'doth my father yet live?* And his brethren could not
answer him; for they were troubled at his presence.
(J) **And Joseph said unto his brethren, Come near to** 4
me, I pray you. And they came near. And he said,
I am Joseph your brother, whom 'ye sold into Egypt.
(E) **And now be not 'grieved,** nor angry with yourselves, 5
(J) (E) **that 'ye sold me hither:** [. . .] 'for God did
send me before you to preserve life. For these two years 6
hath the famine been in the land: and there are yet five
years, in the which there shall be neither plowing nor
harvest. And God sent me before you to preserve you a 7
remnant in the earth, and to save you alive by a great deliverance. So now it was not you that sent me hither, but 8
God: and he hath made me a father to Pharaoh, and 'lord
of all his house, and ruler over all the land of Egypt.
Haste ye, and go up to my father, and say unto him, Thus 9
saith thy son Joseph, God hath made me lord of all
(J) Egypt: come down unto me, tarry not: —and 'thou 10
shalt dwell in the land of Goshen, and thou shalt be
near unto me, thou, and thy children, and thy child-
ren's children, and 'thy flocks, and thy herds, and
(E) **all that thou hast:—** and there will I "nourish thee; 11
for there are yet five years of famine; lest thou come to
poverty, thou, and thy household, and all that thou hast.
And, behold, your eyes see, and the eyes of my brother 12
Benjamin, that it is my mouth that speaketh unto you.

[2]Num. 12:6. [3]Ct. v. 16. [4]Ct. 43:27; 44:19-34. [5]37:27f. Ct. 40:15. [6]6:6; 34:7; Ex.
1:12. [7]50:20. [8]41:40f. [9]46:28, 34. [10]46:32. Ct. v. 20. [11]47:12; 50:21.

* The question, vs. 3a, presupposes seemingly quite a different kind of interview
from that detailed in ch. xliii., especially in xliii. 27, 28, and in xliv. 18-34 where
Israel is constantly spoken of. If the documentary theory be followed, the natural
inference from this verse would be that the interview in E was brief, and of the
unfriendly character described in xliii. 9-20, 30-34; at least not affording Joseph in-
formation in regard to his father.

13 (J) **And ye shall tell my father of all my glory in Egypt, and of all that ye have seen; and ye shall**
14 **haste and bring down my father hither.** [12]**And he fell upon his brother Benjamin's neck, and wept; and**
15 (E) **Benjamin wept upon his neck.** [. . .] And he kissed all his brethren, and wept upon them : and after that his brethren talked with him.
16   [13]And the fame thereof was heard in Pharaoh's house, saying, Joseph's brethren are come : and it pleased Pha-
17 raoh well, and his servants. And Pharaoh said unto Joseph, Say unto thy brethren, This do ye ; lade your beasts,
18 and go, get you unto the land of Canaan ; and take your father and your households, and come unto me : and I will give you the good of the land of Egypt, and ye shall eat
19 (JE) the fat of the land.   Now thou art commanded, this do ye ; take you wagons out of the land of Egypt for your little ones, and for
20 your wives, and bring your father, and come. Also regard not your
21 stuff ; for the good of all the land of Egypt is yours.   [14]And the sons of
   (E) (JE) Israel did so : and Joseph gave them wagons, according
   (E) to the commandment of Pharaoh,* and gave them [15]provision
22 for the way.   To all of them he gave each man changes of raiment ; but to Benjamin he gave three hundred pieces
23 of silver, and five changes of raiment. And to his father he sent after this manner ; ten asses laden with the good things of Egypt, and ten she-asses laden with corn and
24 bread and victual for his father by the way. So he sent his brethren away, and they departed : and he said unto
25 them, See that ye fall not out by the way.† And they

[12]33:4; 46:29.   [13]Ct. v. 2.   [14]Ct. v. 24.   [15]42:25.

* Supplementary redaction. For the verb translated "thou art commanded," a singular which does not agree with the plural verbs before and after, we might read with Dillmann "command them," but the Sam. and LXX. text, the linguistic marks and the prolepsis of 21*a* lead the critics to consider the passage one of the cases of heightening or retouching of the colors, by R, who is supposed to have exhibited the interest taken by Pharaoh by introducing, or at least materially modifying, vv. 19–21 (except 21*b* and *d*), and of course also xlvi. 5*b*.

† If the revisers are right in their translation of 24*b*, the sense must be a warning against mutual reproaches for the treatment of Joseph. Cf. xlii. 22. But perhaps a better sense might be obtainable if we knew what E related in regard to the second visit to Egypt.

went up out of Egypt, and came into the land of Canaan unto Jacob their father. And they told him, saying, 26 Joseph is yet alive, and he is ruler over all the land of Egypt. And his heart fainted, for he believed them not. And they told him [16]all the words of Joseph, which he had 27 said unto them : and when he saw [17]the wagons which Joseph had sent to carry him, the spirit of Jacob their (J) father revived : **and Israel said, [18]"It is enough ; 28 Joseph my son is yet alive: I will go and see him before I die.**

And Israel took his journey with all that he had, 46 (E) and came to Beer-sheba, and [1]offered sacrifices unto the God of his father Isaac. And God spake unto Israel 2 [2]in the visions of the night, and said, [3]Jacob, Jacob. And he said, Here am I. And he said, I am God, the God of 3 thy father : fear not to go down into Egypt ; for I will there make of thee a great nation : for I will go down with 4 thee into Egypt ; and [4]I will also surely bring thee up again : and Joseph shall put his hand upon thine eyes. (JE) And Jacob rose up from Beer-sheba : [5]and the sons of 5 Israel carried Jacob their father, and their little ones, and their wives, in the wagons which Pharaoh had sent to carry him. (P) [6]*And they took their cattle, and their goods, which they had* 6 *gotten in the land of Canaan, and came into Egypt, Jacob, and all his seed with him : his sons, and his sons' sons with him, his* 7 *daughters, and his sons' daughters, and all his seed brought he with him into Egypt.**

(R) [7]*And these are the names of the children of Israel, which* 8 *came into Egypt, Jacob and his sons; Reuben, Jacob's firstborn. And the sons of Reuben ; Hanoch, and Pallu, and Hezron, and* 9 *Carmi. And the sons of Simeon ; Jemuel, and Jamin, and Ohad,* 10 *and Jachin, and Zohar, and Shaul the son of a Canaanitish woman. And the sons of Levi ; Gershon, Kohath, and Merari.* 11

[16]V. 11. [17]V. 21. [18]46:30. [1]31:54. [2]15:1; 20:3, etc. [3]22:1, 7, etc. [4]15:16. [5]46:19ff. [6]12:5; 31:18; 36:6. [7]Ex. 1:1ff; 6:14ff. Cf. 25:13; 36:10.

* The work of R is traced in the change of Jacob to " Israel," xlvi. 2 (cf. latter part of the verse), and in vs. 5*b* corresponding to xlv. 19f. If, as Dillman thinks, vs. 5 refers to the removal of Jacob from his home, the clause, "and came to Beer-sheba," vs. 1, must also be due to R. In xxxv. 1 (" dwell there "), however, it seems to be implied that Bethel was Jacob's home. Cf. xxxvii. 15ff.

14

12 *And the sons of Judah ; Er, and Onan, and Shelah, and Perez, and Zerah ; but Er and Onan died in the land of Canaan. And the sons*
13 *of Perez were Hezron and Hamul. And the sons of Issachar ;*
14 *Tola, and Puvah, and Iob, and Shimron. And the sons of Zebu-*
15 *lun ; Sered, and Elon, and Jahleel. These are the sons of Leah, which she bare unto Jacob in Paddan-aram, with his daughter Dinah :*
16 *all the souls of his sons and his daughters were thirty and three. And the sons of Gad : Ziphion, and Haggi, Shuni, and Ezbon, Eri,*
17 *and Arodi, and Areli. And the sons of Asher ; Imnah, and Ish- vah, and Ishvi, and Beriah, and Serah their sister : and the sons*
18 *of Beriah ; Heber, and Malchiel. These are the sons of Zilpah, which Laban gave to Leah his daughter, and these she bare unto*
19 *Jacob, even sixteen souls. The sons of Rachel Jacob's wife ;*
20 *Joseph and Benjamin. And unto Joseph in the land of Egypt were born Manasseh and Ephraim, which Asenath the daughter*
21 *of Poti-phera priest of On bare unto him. And the sons of Benja- min ; Bela, and Becher, and Ashbel, Gera, and Naaman, Ehi,*
22 *and Rosh, Muppim, and Huppim, and Ard. These are the sons of*
23 *Rachel, which were born* to Jacob : all the souls were fourteen.*
24 *And the sons of Dan ; Hushim. And the sons of Naphtali ; Jah-*
25 *zeel, and Guni, and Jezer, and Shillem. These are the sons of Bilhah, which Laban gave unto Rachel his daughter, and these*
26 *she bare unto Jacob : all the souls were seven. All the souls that came with Jacob into Egypt, which came out of his loins, besides Jacob's sons' wives, all the souls were threescore and six ;*
27 *and the sons of Joseph, which were born to him in Egypt, were two souls : all the souls of the house of Jacob, which came into Egypt, were [8]threescore and ten.†*

28 **And he sent [8]Judah before him unto Joseph, to shew the way before him‡ unto [9]Goshen; and they**
29 **came into the land of Goshen. And Joseph [11]made ready his chariot, and went up to meet Israel his father, to Goshen; and he presented himself unto him, [12]and fell on his neck, and wept on his neck a**

[8]Ex. 1:5. [9]37:26; 43:3, 8; 44:14, 18. [10]45:10. [11]50:9. [12]33:4; 45:14.

* LXX. Sam. "she bare." Cf. vs. 15.

† According to most critics a late genealogical table not in agreement with P. Ex. i. 5 (cf. vs. 27) and vi. 14ff. Dillmann holds that in order to balance the insertion of 12*b*, Jacob and Dinah are also counted in by R, contrary to the original intention of the table. (Cf. 15*b* with vv. 23 and 25.)

‡ No good sense is obtainable from this clause. If Judah was sent to Joseph he could not have gone "to show the way" which was besides needless. Probably the original sense was "to report his coming." Cf. vs. 29.

good while. And Israel said unto Joseph, [13]"Now let 30
me die, since I have seen thy face, that thou art yet
alive. And Joseph said unto his brethren, and unto 31
his father's house, I will go up, and [14]"tell Pharaoh,
and will say unto him, My brethren, and my father's
house, which were in the land of Canaan, are come
unto me; and the men are shepherds, for they have been 32
keepers of cattle;* and [16]"they have brought their flocks,
and their herds, and all that they have. And it shall 33
come to pass, when Pharaoh shall call you, and shall
say, What is your occupation? that ye shall say, Thy 34
servants have been keepers of cattle from our youth
even until now, [16]"both we and our fathers: that ye
may dwell in the land of Goshen; [17]"for every shepherd
is an abomination unto the Egyptians.

Then Joseph went in and told Pharaoh, and said, 47
My father and my brethren, and their flocks, and their
herds, and all that they have, are come out of the
land of Canaan; and, behold, they are in the land of
Goshen. [1]'And from among his brethren he took 2
five men, and presented them unto Pharaoh. And 3
Pharaoh said unto his brethren, What is your occupation? And they said unto Pharaoh, Thy servants are
shepherds, both we, and our fathers. And they said unto 4
Pharaoh,† To sojourn in the land are we come; for there
is no pasture for thy servants' flocks; for the famine
is sore in the land of Canaan: now therefore, we pray
thee, let thy servants dwell [2]'in the land of Goshen.
(P) *And Pharaoh spake unto Joseph, saying, [3]'Thy father and* 5
thy brethren are come unto thee : the land of Egypt is before thee ; 6
in the best of the land make thy father and thy brethren to dwell ;
(J) in the land of Goshen let them dwell: and if thou
knowest any able men among them, then make them

[13]45:28. [14]Ct. 45:16ff. [15]45:10. [16]4:2. [17]43:32. [1]Ct. v. 7; 46:31ff. [2]45:10; 46:24.
[3]Ct. 46:31.

* Translate "for they were keepers of cattle." According to Kautzsch and Socin,
a gloss intended to justify vs. 34.

† Dittograph from vs. 3.

7 (P) **rulers over my cattle.*** *And Joseph brought in Jacob his father, and set him before Pharaoh: and Jacob blessed Pha-*
8 *raoh. And Pharaoh said unto Jacob, How many are the days*
9 *of the years of thy life? And Jacob said unto Pharaoh, 'The days of the years of my pilgrimage are an hundred and thirty years: few and evil have been the days of the years of my life, and they have not attained unto the days of the years of the life of*
10 *my fathers in the days of their pilgrimage. And Jacob blessed*
11 *Pharaoh, and went out from the presence of Pharaoh. And Joseph placed his father and his brethren, and gave them a possession in the land of Egypt, in the best of the land, in the land of*
12 (E) *Rameses, as Pharaoh had commanded.* [. . .] And Joseph 'nourished his father, and his brethren, and all his father's household, with bread, according to their families.
13   (J) —'And there was no bread in all the land; for the famine was very 'sore, so that the land of Egypt and the land of Canaan fainted by reason of the fam-

⁴25:7. ⁵45:11; 50:21. ⁶41:55ff. ⁷12:10; 41:31; 43:1; v. 4.

* The documentary analysis furnishes in this passage an extraordinary proof of the superiority here of the LXX. text, and is in turn most singularly corroborated by it. Employing the distinctive type of our text, the translation and order of xlvii. 5f (LXX.) are as follows:

J 5. And Pharaoh said unto Joseph, Let them dwell in the land of Goshen, and if thou knowest any able men among them, make them rulers over my cattle.

P 6. *And Jacob and his sons came into Egypt to Joseph; and Pharaoh king of Egypt heard of it. And Pharaoh spake unto Joseph, saying, Thy father and thy brethren are come unto thee; behold, the land of Egypt is before thee; in the best of the land make thy father and thy brethren to dwell.*

If the explanation of this remarkable phenomenon which the analysis suggests be adopted, the conclusion is no less radical than unavoidable. The process of adjustment of P to JE had not ceased at the time of the LXX. translation. The order of clauses has been altered, the clause " And Pharaoh said unto Joseph," at the beginning of vs. 5, essential as it is to the sense of J, and the longer passage, " And Jacob and his sons came into Egypt to Joseph, and Pharaoh king of Egypt heard it," at the beginning of vs. 6, which completes P's story, have been omitted from the text since the period of the LXX.; apparently because of the contradiction involved; for the supposition that this contradiction was *introduced* by the LXX. is incredible.

ine.   And Joseph gathered up all the money that was 14
found in the land of Egypt, and in the land of Canaan,
for the corn which they bought: and Joseph brought
the money into ⁸Pharaoh's house.   And when the 15
money was all spent in the land of Egypt, and in the
land of Canaan, all the Egyptians came unto Joseph,
and said, Give us bread: for why should we die in thy
presence? for [our] money faileth.   And Joseph said, 16
Give your cattle; and I will give you for your cattle,
if money fail.   And they brought their cattle unto 17
Joseph: And Joseph gave them bread in exchange for
the horses, and for the ⁹flocks, and for the herds, and
for the asses: and he ¹⁰fed them with bread in exchange for all their cattle for that year.   And when 18
that year was ended, they came unto him the second
year, and said unto him, We will not hide from my
lord, how that our money is all spent; and the herds of
cattle are my lord's; there is nought left in the sight
of my lord, but our bodies, and our lands: wherefore 19
should we die before thine eyes, ¹¹both we and our
land? buy us and our land for bread, and we and our
land will be servants unto Pharaoh : and give us seed,
that we may live, and not die, and that the land be
not desolate.   So Joseph bought all the land of Egypt 20
for Pharaoh; for the Egyptians sold every man his
field, because the famine was ¹²sore upon them: and
the land became Pharaoh's.   And as for the people, 21
he removed them ¹³to the cities from one end of the
border of Egypt even to the other end thereof.   Only 22
the land of ¹⁴the priests bought he not: for the priests
had a portion from Pharaoh, and did eat their portion which Pharaoh gave them; wherefore they sold
not their land.   Then Joseph said unto the people, 23
Behold, I have bought you this day and your land
for Pharaoh: lo, here is seed for you, and ye shall
sow the land.   And it shall come to pass at the in- 24

⁸45:2. ⁹26:14. ¹⁰33:14. ¹¹46:34. ¹²41:56. Ct. v. 13. ¹³41:35. ¹⁴41:45; Ex. 2:16ff.

gatherings, that ye shall give a fifth unto Pharaoh, and four [15]parts shall be your own, for seed of the field, and for your food, and for them of your house-
25 holds, and for food for your little ones. And they said, Thou hast saved our lives: let us [16]find grace in the sight of my lord, and we will be Pharaoh's serv-
26 ants. And Joseph made it a statute concerning the land of Egypt unto this day, that Pharaoh should have [17]the fifth; only the land of the priests alone be-
27 (P) came not Pharaoh's.*— And Israel dwelt *in the land of Egypt,* in the land of Goshen; [18]*and they gat them possessions therein, and* [19]*were fruitful, and multiplied exceedingly.*

28 *And Jacob lived in the land of Egypt* [20]*seventeen years;* [20]*so the days of Jacob, the years of his life, were an hundred forty and seven*
29 (J) *years.* And the time drew near that Israel must die: and he called his son Joseph, and said unto him, [21]If now I have found grace in thy sight, [22]put, I pray thee, thy hand under my thigh, and [23]deal kindly and
30 truly with me; bury me not, I pray thee, in Egypt: but when I sleep with my fathers, thou shalt carry me out of Egypt, [24]*and bury me in their buryingplace.* And
31 he said, I will do as thou hast said. And he said, Swear unto me: and he sware unto him. [25]And Israel bowed himself upon the bed's head.

48   (E) [1]And it came to pass after these things that one said to Joseph, [2]Behold, thy father is sick: and he took with
2 him [3]his two sons, Manasseh and Ephraim. And one told Jacob, and said, Behold, thy son Joseph cometh unto thee;

[15]43:34. [16]6:6, etc. [17]41:34. [18]Num. 32:30; Jos. 22:9, 19. [19]1:22, etc. [20]v. 9·
[21]6:6, etc. [22]24:2. [23]24:49; 32:11. [24]50:5. [25]48:2. [1]15:1; 22:1, etc. [2]Ct. 47:29.
[3]41:50ff.

* The passage xlvii. 13–26 is generally supposed to be misplaced, and to have been removed from after xli. 56. With this idea the "second year" of vs. 18, compared with the "yet five years of famine" of xlv. 11, would agree very well. However, two years seems a short time for the events of vv. 13–26, and the passage need not necessarily be removed. Portions of E are held by some critics to be discoverable in xlvii. 13–26, though no cogent reasons are offered, and on the other hand, several new make-weights for J may be added to those noted by Dillmann and others. See *Hebraica* VII. 4 (1891).

(J) and 'Israel strengthened himself, and sat upon
(P) the bed. *—And Jacob said unto Joseph, [2]God Almighty* 3
*appeared unto me at Luz in the land of Canaan, and blessed me,
and said unto me, Behold, I will make thee fruitful, and multiply* 4
*thee, and I will make of thee a company of peoples ; and will give
this land to thy seed after thee for an everlasting possession.
[3]And now thy two sons, which were born unto thee in the land of* 5
*Egypt before I came unto thee into Egypt, are mine ; Ephraim
and Manasseh, even as Reuben and Simeon, shall be mine. And* 6
*thy issue, which thou begettest after them, shall be thine ; they
shall be called after the name of their brethren in their inheri-*
(R) *tance.—* [7]*And as for me, when I came from Paddan,* 7
*Rachel died by me in the land of Canaan in the way, when there
was still some way to come unto Ephrath: and I buried her there*
(J) *in the way to Ephrath (the same is Beth-lehem).*—* **And** 8
(E) **Israel beheld Joseph's sons,** and said, [8]Who are
these ? And Joseph said unto his father, They are my 9
(J) sons, whom God hath given me here. **And he said,
Bring them, I pray thee, unto me, and I will bless
them.** [9]Now the eyes of Israel were dim for age, so 10
(E) **that he could not see.** And he brought them near
unto him : and he kissed them, and embraced them. And 11
Israel said unto Joseph, I had not thought to see thy face ;

[4]47:31 ; 49:33. Ct. v. 2a.　[5]35:9ff.　[6]Jos. 14:4; 17:14ff.　[7]35:16ff.　[8]33:5.　[9]27:1, 21f.

* This verse 7, so awkwardly placed, is conjectured by Budde (*Ztschr. f. A. T. W.*
III., 1883) to be a substitute of R for the words, "and Rachel," omitted for harmonistic reasons at the end of xlix. 31. The verse is generally assigned to R upon the
basis of xxxv. 19, and the conjecture that it is a harmonistie modification of P's
original thought, according to which the whole patriarchal family were interred
together in the cave of Machpelah, to conform to E (xxxv. 19), seems very plausible ;
Bruston (*ibid.*, 1887, p. 206ff) suggests that vs. 7 was taken by R from after xlvii. 29
and recast, and in fact the reference of l. 5 seems to indicate an alteration there.
On the other hand, xlix. 29-32 seems to fail of completeness without this "and
Rachel," while Josh. xxiv. 32, compared with Gen. xxxiii. 19 and l. 5, and the
singular reference, Acts vii. 16, suggests to the critic that P may have taken his
account from E's similar story and located it quite differently. The inappropriate
position now occupied by vv. 3-7, especially apparent in the case of vs. 7, is perhaps
to be corrected by transposing this passage to a place after xlix. 28 as its original
one. P's story would then read in the following order, xlix. 1, first clause, 28 (from
"and blessed them "), xlviii. 3-6. The singular, "and as for me," of xlviii. 7 may
perhaps have been taken from xlix. 29, from before "I am to be gathered unto my
people."

12 and, lo, God hath let me [10]see thy seed also. [11]And Joseph
brought them out from between his* knees ; and he bowed
13 (J) himself with his face to the earth. **And Joseph took
them both, Ephraim in his right hand toward Israel's left hand, and Manasseh in his left hand toward Israel's right hand, and brought them near
14 unto him. And Israel stretched out his right hand,
and laid it upon Ephraim's head, who was the
[12]younger, and his left hand upon Manasseh's head,
guiding his hands wittingly; for Manasseh was the
15 (E) [13]firstborn.** And he blessed Joseph, and said, The
God before whom my fathers Abraham and Isaac did walk,
the God which hath fed me all my life long unto this day,
16 [14]the angel which hath redeemed me from all evil, bless
the lads ; and [14]let my name be named on them, and the
name of my fathers Abraham and Isaac ; and let them
17 (J) grow into a multitude in the midst of the earth. **And
when Joseph saw that his father laid his right hand
upon the head of Ephraim, it displeased him: and
he held up his father's hand, to remove it from
18 Ephraim's head unto Manasseh's head. And Joseph
said unto his father, Not so, my father: for this is
the firstborn; put thy right hand upon his head.**
19 [15]And his father refused, and said, I know [it] my
son, I know [it]: he also shall become a people, and
he also shall be great: howbeit his younger brother
shall be greater than he, and his seed shall become a
20 (E) multitude of nations. And he blessed them that
day, saying, In thee shall Israel bless, saying, God make
thee as Ephraim and as Manasseh : and he set Ephraim
21 before Manasseh. [16]And Israel said unto Joseph, Behold,

[10]Ct. v. 10.   [11]V. 15f, 21. Ct. v. 13.   [12]19:31ff; 25:23; 29:26; 43:33. Ct. 29:16, etc.
[13]31:11; 32:2f. [14]21:12. [15]39:8. [16]50:24.

*I. e. Jacob's. In E Joseph brings his sons to his father that he may "see"
them, vs. 11. In J Israel is blind, vs. 10*a*, and the boys are brought to be blessed,
vv. 9*b*, 13f. In E, after the boys have been presented, Joseph brings them out from
between his father's knees in order himself to come there and receive the paternal
blessing. "Israel," vs. 11, is of course to be considered altered from "Jacob"
under the influence of vs. 10.

I die : [17]but God shall be with you, and bring you again unto the land of your fathers. Moreover I have given to 22 thee [18]one portion* above thy brethren, which I took out of the hand of the [19]Amorite [20]with my sword and with my bow. [. . .]

(P) (J) *And Jacob called unto his sons,* and said : Gather 49 yourselves together, that I may tell you that which shall befall you in the latter days.

Assemble yourselves, and hear, ye sons of Jacob; 2
And hearken unto Israel your father.

Reuben, thou art my firstborn, my might, and 3
the beginning of my strength;
The excellency† of dignity, and the excellency of
power.
Unstable‡ as water, thou shalt not have the excel- 4
lency;
Because [1]thou wentest up to thy father's bed :
Then defiledst thou it: he went up to my couch.

Simeon and Levi are brethren; 5
Weapons of violence are their swords.
O my soul, come not thou into their council; 6
Unto their assembly, my glory, be not thou united;
For [2]in their anger they slew a man,
And in their selfwill they houghed an ox.
Cursed be their anger, for it was fierce; 7
And their wrath, for it was cruel:
I will divide them in Jacob,
And scatter them in Israel.

[17]46:4. [18]Ch. 34. [19]15:16; Jos. 24:8. [20]Jos. 24:12. [1]35:22. [2]Ch. 34.

* Read "Shechem," the "portion" of Joseph, i. e. the northern kingdom. A play upon words. Kuenen suggests the reading "*not* with my sword *nor* with my bow," as in Josh. xxiv. 12 (cf. Gen. xxxiii. 19), and accounts for the alteration as harmonistic, to secure agreement with chapter xxxiv.

† For "excellency" read "pre-eminence" (twice). So in vs. 4. This translation of the American committee of revisers is certainly to be preferred in vs. 3f. Reuben is deprived of the right of the firstborn, "the preëminence," on account of his unruly lust, reference to which is also made in xxxv. 22. (See note to that passage.) Simeon and Levi, the next in order of age, are likewise passed over on account of their deed of cruelty. This brings the preëminence to Judah, vs. 8.

‡ For "Unstable" read "Boiling over" and omit the marg.—*Am. Com*

8 Judah, 'thee shall thy brethren praise:
Thy hand shall be on the neck of thine enemies;
Thy father's sons shall bow down before thee.

9 Judah is a lion's whelp;
From the prey, my son, thou art gone up:
'He stooped down, he couched as a lion,
And as a lioness; who shall rouse him up?

10 The sceptre shall not depart from Judah,
Nor the ruler's staff from between his feet,
Until Shiloh come;
And unto him shall the obedience of the peoples be.

11 Binding his foal unto the vine,
And his ass's colt unto the choice vine;
He hath washed his garments in wine;
And his vesture in the blood of grapes:

12 'His eyes shall be red with wine,
And his teeth white with milk.

13 Zebulun shall 'dwell at the haven of the sea:
And he shall be for an haven of ships;
And his border shall be upon Zidon.

14 Issachar is a strong ass,
Couching down between the sheepfolds:

15 And he saw a resting place that it was good,
And the land that it was pleasant;
And he bowed his shoulder to bear,
And became 'a servant under taskwork.

16 'Dan shall judge his people,
As one of the tribes of Israel.

17 Dan shall be a serpent in the way,
An adder in the path,
That biteth the horse's heels,
So that his rider falleth backward.

18 I have waited for thy salvation, O Yahweh.

19 'Gad, a troop shall press upon him:
But he shall press upon their heel.

[2]29:35. [4]Num. 24:9. [5]9:21; 43:34. [6]30:20; Dt. 33:19. [7]Jud. 1:28, 30, etc. [8]30:6.
[9]Ct. 30:11.

Out of Asher his bread shall be fat,   20
And he shall yield royal dainties.
  Naphtali is a hind let loose: 21
He giveth goodly words.*
  Joseph is a fruitful bough,   22
A fruitful bough by a fountain;
His branches run over the wall.
The archers have sorely grieved him,   23
And shot at him, and persecuted him:
But his bow abode in strength,   24
And the arms of his hands were made strong,
By the hands of the Mighty One of Jacob,
(From thence is the shepherd, the stone of Israel),†
Even by the God of thy father, who shall help thee, 25
And by the Almighty, who shall bless thee,
[10]With blessings of heaven above,
Blessings of [11]the deep that coucheth beneath,
Blessings of the breasts, and of the womb.
[12]The blessings of thy father   26
Have prevailed above the blessings of my progeni-
    tors
Unto the utmost bound of the everlasting hills:

[10]27:28. [11]1:2; 7:11. [12]Dt. 33:15f.

*Translate with Dillmann and others, "Naphtali is a slender terebinth. He giveth goodly shoots," with allusion, as in vv. 13 and 17, to the geographical shape of Naphtali, long and slender, and to the heroes of this tribe (Jud. iv. 6). The change in the reading affects only the vowel points.

In vs. 20 read "Asher, his," etc., according to margin. "Out of" is simply the Hebrew suffix *m*, "their," carried over from the preceding word and used as the prefix *m*, "out of," for the following word. Cf. vv. 3, 5, 8, 13, 14, 16, 19, 21, 27.

The last word of vs. 5, and "Shiloh" of vs. 10, present unsolved problems. Wellhausen pronounces vs. 10, from the interruption it causes, to be an interpolation.

† I am indebted to Prof. Geo. F. Moore of Andover, among other kindnesses, for the admirable conjecture which by very slight alteration of the text (see Heb. note 15) affords the following simple rendering of one of the most difficult passages of the Pentateuch:

> "But his bow abode in strength,
> And the arms of his hands were made strong
> By the hands of the mighty one of Jacob,
> By the arms of the Rock of Israel;
> Even by the God of thy father who shall help thee,
> And by the Almighty who shall bless thee."

> They shall be on the head of Joseph,
> And on the crown of the head of him that was
>   separate from his brethren.*

27   Benjamin is as a wolf that ravineth :
> In the morning he shall devour the prey,
> And at even he shall divide the spoil.

28   All these are the twelve tribes of Israel : and this (P) is it that their father spake unto them :† *and blessed them ; every one according to his blessing he blessed them.*

29 [13]*And he charged them, and said unto them, I am to be gathered unto my people : bury me with my fathers in the cave that is in*

30 *the field of Ephron the Hittite, in the cave that is in the field of Machpelah, which is before Mamre, in the land of Canaan,* [14]*which Abraham bought with the field from Ephron the Hittite*

31 *for a possession of a buryingplace :* [15]*there they buried Abraham and Sarah his wife ; there they buried Isaac and Rebekah his*

---

[13]50:12f. Ct. 47:29-31.   [14]Ch. 23.   [15]23:19; 25:9.

* In vs. 26 translate "the blessings of the ancient mountains," etc., according to margin. See Part III. The hegemony of Judah is deduced in this poem as a natural right ; the royal honor of Joseph—the "crowned one" among his brethren —on the other hand, corresponds to the realities of the post-Solomonic period. Altogether the attitude assumed by the poet is that which might be expected from a Judæan to whom the preëminence of Ephraim had become an accepted fact—even a matter for patriotic gratulation.

† The Blessing of Jacob is an incorporated poem of such peculiar characteristics that it is easier to speak of it as a whole than to append the copious notes which would be desirable to each salient part. While not supposed to be strictly the composition of J, it is printed in the type assigned to this author because apparently forming part of his original work. Historical criticism as to the antiquity of the poem need not be entered into, and exegetical notes are not within the sphere of the present work. The numerous word-plays, however, which are a striking characteristic of this and similar poems (cf. e. g. the Blessing of Moses, Dt. xxxiii.), require some explanation to the English reader beside that afforded by the margin. The play upon the verb *hodah,* "praise," in vs. 8, will be generally recognized. The question is whether there is not a further secondary play in *yadhka,* "thy hand." —The same verb, *zabal,* "to dwell," is resorted to in vs. 13 for a play upon the name Zebulun as in ch. xxx. Similarly Dan, vs. 16, is connected, as in ch. xxx., with *din,* "to judge," the figure of the adder in the path being suggested, however, by the geographical position of the tribe on the great caravan route, at the gates of the country. For the word-plays of vs. 19 see Part III.—*Ben phorath* of vs. 22, translated "a fruitful bough," is probably a play upon Ephraim or "Ephrath." With the adoption of Prof. Moore's conjecture the following passage presents no great difficulty. The blessings of heaven above and of the *tehom,* or "great deep" (i. e. the world ocean, the primeval "waters under the earth"—cf. Gen. i. 2 and vii. 11—beneath, are the fertilizing rain and springs, which make Joseph's territory more luxuriant than the mountain slopes. Cf. xxvii. 27f.

wife ; and there I buried Leah : the field and the cave that is* 32
therein, which was purchased from the children of Heth.
(J) *And when Jacob made an end of charging his sons,* [10]*he* 33
(P) **gathered up his feet into the bed, [. . .]** *and*
yielded up the ghost, and was gathered unto his people.

(J) [1]**And Joseph fell upon his father's face, and** 50
wept upon him, and kissed him. And Joseph com- 2
manded his servants the physicians to embalm his
father: and the physicians embalmed Israel. And 3
forty days were fulfilled for him; for so are fulfilled
the days of embalming: and the Egyptians wept for
him threescore and ten days.
And when the days of weeping for him were past, 4
Joseph spake unto the house of Pharaoh, saying, [2]**If**
now I have found grace in your eyes, speak, I pray
you, in the ears of Pharaoh, saying, [3]**My father made** 5
me swear, saying, Lo, I die: in my grave which I
have digged for me in the land of Canaan,† there
shalt thou bury me. Now therefore let me go up,
I pray thee, and bury my father, and I will come
again. And Pharaoh said, Go up, and bury thy fa- 6
ther, according as he made thee swear. And Joseph 7
went up to bury his father: and with him went up
all the servants of Pharaoh, [4]**the elders of his house,**
and all the elders of the land of Egypt, and all 8
the house of Joseph, and his brethren, and his fa-
ther's house: [5]**only their little ones, and their flocks,**
and their herds, they left in the land of Goshen.
And there went up with him both chariots and 9
horsemen: and it was a very great company. And 10
they came to the threshing-floor of Atad, which is
beyond Jordan, and there they lamented with a very
great and sore lamentation: and he made a mourn-
ing for his father seven days. And when [6]**the in-** 11

[10]48:2. [1]33:4; 45:14; 46:29. [2]18:3, etc. [3]47:29. [4]24:2. [5]47:1. [6]12:6. Ct. 15:16;
48:22.
  * Insert "and Rachel." See note to xlviii. 7.
  † Showing alteration of xlvii. 30.

habitants of the land, the Canaanites, saw the mourning in the floor of Atad, they said, This is a grievous mourning to the Egyptians: [7]wherefore the name of it was called Abelmizraim, which is beyond Jordan.*

12 (P) [8]*And his sons did unto him according as he commanded them:*

13 *for his sons carried him into the land of Canaan, and buried him in the cave of the field of Machpelah, which Abraham bought with the field, for a possession of a buryingplace, of Ephron the Hittite, before Mamre.*

14   (J) And Joseph returned into Egypt, he, and his brethren, and all that went up with him to bury his

15 (E) father, after he had buried his father.   And when Joseph's brethren saw that their father was dead, they said, It may be that Joseph will hate us, and will

16 fully requite us all the evil which we did unto him.   And they sent a message unto Joseph, saying, Thy father did

17 command before he died, saying, So shall ye say unto Joseph, [9]Forgive, I pray thee now, the transgression of thy brethren, and their sin, for that they did unto thee evil: and now, we pray thee, forgive the transgression of the servants of the God of thy father.   And Joseph wept

18 when they spake unto him.   And his brethren also went and fell down before his face: and they said, Behold, we

19 be thy servants.   And Joseph said unto them, Fear not:

20 [10]for am I in the place of God?   [11]And as for you, ye meant evil against me; but God meant it for good, to bring to pass, as it is this day, to save much people alive.

21 [12]Now therefore fear ye not: I will nourish you, and your little ones.   And he comforted them, [13]and spake kindly unto them.

22   And Joseph dwelt in Egypt, he, and his father's house:

[7]33:17, etc. [8]49:29f. [9]Ex. 32:31. [10]30:2. [11]45:7f. [12]45:11; 47:12. [13]34:3.

* The evidence of duplicate accounts which Kautzsch and Socin discover in vv. 9-11 is very precarious. If traces of E's narrative are present here, it would scarcely be in the names Abelmizraim and Goren-ha-Atad that they would probably come to the surface. The place of sepulture of the patriarchs in E is Shechem, xxxiii. 19; Jos. xxiv. 32. Verse 10*b* has, however, the appearance of a doublet, and may perhaps be parallel to the preceding half-verse.

(P) (E) *and Joseph lived an hundred and ten years.* And 23 Joseph saw Ephraim's children of the third generation: [14]the children also of Machir the son of Manasseh were [15]born upon Joseph's knees. [16]And Joseph said unto his 24 brethren, I die: but God will surely visit you, and bring you up out of this land unto the land which he sware to Abraham, to Isaac, and to Jacob. [17]And Joseph took an 25 oath of the children of Israel, saying, God will surely visit you, and ye shall carry up my bones from hence. So 26 Joseph died, being an hundred and ten years old: and they embalmed him, and he was put in a coffin in Egypt.

[14]Num. 32:39f.　[15]30:3.　[16]48:21.　[17]Ex. 13:19.

PART III.

———

The Documents J, E and P separately restored in a revised translation, with textual emendations of good authority.

15

PART III.

THE JUDÆAN PROPHETIC NARRATIVE J¹, CIRC. 800 B. C.

STORY OF CREATION AND OF THE GARDEN OF YAHWEH.
THE MAKING OF THE MAN, OF PLANTS, OF
ANIMALS AND OF THE WOMAN.

[. . . When as yet there was neither earth nor heaven but only the limitless abyss (*tehom*), Yahweh set fast the foundations of the earth, and raised up its pillars in the midst of the waters. And over its surface he spread out the dome of the heaven, establishing there the courses of the sun and moon and the stars ; but upon the surface of the earth beneath there was neither motion nor life : all was yet a solitude *] in the day that Yahweh 2— 4b made earth and heaven. And there was yet no plant of 5 the field in the earth, and no herb of the field had yet sprung up, for Yahweh had not caused it to rain upon the earth, and there was not a man to till the ground ; but there went up a mist from the earth, and watered the 6 whole face of the ground. And Yahweh moulded man 7 of the dust of the ground, and breathed into his nostrils breath of life ; and man became a living creature. And Yahweh planted a garden in Eden, in the East ; and 8 there he put the man whom he had moulded. And out 9 of the ground made Yahweh to spring up every tree that is pleasant to the sight, and good for food ; and the tree of the knowledge of good and evil, in the midst of the garden. And Yahweh commanded the man, saying, Of every 16 tree of the garden thou mayest freely eat : but of the tree 17 which is in the midst of the garden, thou shalt not eat : for in the day that thou eatest thereof thou shalt surely die.

---

* Conjecturally restored from indications in the earlier literature (e. g. Gen. xlix. 25 ; 1 Sam. ii. 8 ; Dt. xxxiii. 13, 26 ; Jud. v. 20), and by comparison with the Babylonian cosmogonic myths, a connection with which in even the Eden story has recently come to light.

18   And Yahweh said, It is not good that the man should be
19 alone; I will make him an help to match him. So Yahweh moulded out of the ground every beast of the field,
and every fowl of the air; and brought them unto the man
to see what he would call them: and whatsoever the man
20 called it, that is the name thereof. And the man gave
names to all cattle, and to the fowl of the air, and to every
wild beast; but still for a man he did not find an help to
21 match him. And Yahweh caused a deep sleep to fall
upon the man, and he slept; and he took one of his ribs,
22 and closed up the flesh in its place: and Yahweh built up
the rib which he had taken from the man into a woman,
23 and brought her unto the man. And the man said, This
time, at least, it is bone of my bones, and flesh of my flesh:
she shall be called Ishah (Woman), because she was taken
24 out of Ish (Man). Therefore doth a man leave his father
and his mother, and cleaveth unto his wife: and they
25 become one flesh. And they were both naked, the man
and his wife, and were not ashamed.

THE STORY OF THE TREE OF KNOWLEDGE. HOW EVIL, TOIL AND DEATH CAME TO BE IN THE WORLD.

3   Now the serpent was more subtle than any wild beast
which Yahweh had made. And he said unto the woman,
Hath God indeed said, Ye shall not eat of any tree of the
2 garden? And the woman said unto the serpent, Of the
3 fruit of the trees of the garden we may eat: but of the
fruit of the tree which is in the midst of the garden, God
hath said, Ye shall not eat of it, neither shall ye touch it,
4 lest ye die. And the serpent said unto the woman, Ye
5 shall not die at all: for God doth know that in the day
ye eat thereof, your eyes shall be opened, and ye shall
6 be as gods, knowing good and evil. And when the woman
saw that the tree was good for food, and that it was a delight to the eyes, and that the tree was to be desired to
make one wise, she took of the fruit thereof, and did eat;
and she gave also unto her husband with her, and he did

eat.   And the eyes of them both were opened, and they 7
knew that they were naked ;   and they sewed fig leaves
together, and made themselves girdles.   And they heard 8
the footstep of Yahweh walking in the garden in the evening breeze : and the man and his wife hid themselves from
the presence of Yahweh amongst the trees of the garden.
And Yahweh called unto the man, and said unto him, 9
Where art thou?   And he said, I heard thy footstep in 10
the garden, and I was afraid, because I was naked ; and I
hid myself.   And he said, Who told thee that thou wast 11
naked?   Hast thou eaten of the tree, whereof I commanded thee that thou shouldest not eat?   And the man said, 12
The woman whom thou didst put with me, she gave me
of the tree, and I did eat.   And Yahweh said unto the 13
woman, What is this thou hast done?   And the woman
said, The serpent beguiled me, and I did eat.

   And Yahweh said unto the serpent, Because thou hast 14
done this,

> Cúrsed art thóu from all cáttle,
> From áll the wild béasts of the fiéld ;
> Thou shalt gó on thy bélly,
> And dúst shalt thou éat all thy life's days.

> Hátred I pút between thée and the wóman,   15
> Between thy seed and hér seed ·
> Théy shall stríke at thy héad,
> And thóu shalt stríke at their héel.

Unto the woman he said,   16
> I will múltiply thy páin in concéption ;
> With páin shalt thou bríng forth chíldren ;
> Yet shalt lóng for thy húsband
> And hé shall rúle thee.

And to the man he said, Because thou hast hearkened un- 17
to the voice of thy wife, and hast eaten of the tree of which
I commanded thee, saying, Thou shalt not eat of it,
> Accúrst is the gróund for thy sáke ;
> Eat óf it in tóil all thy life's dáys,

18   Thístles and thórns it shall béar thee ;
      And the hérb of the fiéld be thy fóod.

19   In the swéat of thy fáce eat thy bréad,
      Tíll thou retúrn to the gróund ;
      For from ít wast thou táken :
      For dúst thou árt, and to dúst thou retúrnest.*

23   So Yahweh sent him forth from the garden of Eden, to
21   till the ground from whence he was taken. And Yahweh
      made for the man and for his wife garments of skins and
6—3   clothed them. And Yahweh said, My breath shall not
      prevail in man forever . . . . . (?) he is flesh. Therefore
      his days shall be an hundred and twenty years.

THE STORY OF THE MAN'S DESCENDANTS.
HOW THE ARTS BEGAN.

4—1   And the man knew his wife ; and she conceived and
      bare Cain, and said I have gotten (*Kanithi*) a man with
3—20 the help of Yahweh. And the man called his wife's
      name Eve (*Havvah*, as if from *havah*, "to live"), because
      she was the mother of all living.
4—2*b*, 16*b* And Cain became a tiller of the ground, and dwelt
      in the land of Nod (Wandering), on this side of Eden.
17   And Cain knew his wife, and she conceived and bare
      Enoch : and he became the builder of a city, and he
      called the name of the city after his own name Enoch.
18   And unto Enoch was born Irad : and Irad begat Mehu-
      jael : and Mehujael begat Methushael : and Methushael
19   begat Lamech. And Lamech took unto him two wives ;
      the name of the one was Adah, and the name of the other
20   Zillah. And Adah bare Jabal : he was the progenitor of
21   such as dwell in tents and [have] cattle. And his broth-
      er's name was Jubal : he was the progenitor of all such

---

*The above versification of the text is not intended to imply that the original
poem was of exactly this form. The tonic accent is employed to indicate the rhythm
and number of the Hebrew words where traces seem to remain of rhythm as well
as other characteristics of poetry in the original. The lines and strophes are determined by the sense. So in all subsequent cases.

as handle the harp and pipe.   And Zillah, she also bare 22
Tubal, and he became a smith, a forger of brass and iron :
and the sister of Tubal was Naamah.   And Lamech said 23
unto his wives :

    Ádah and Zíllah, héar my vóice ;
    Ye wíves of Lámech, líst to my spéech :
    For I will sláy a mán for each wóund,
    And a bóy for each brúise.
    If Cáin be avénged sevenfóld,
    Truly séventy and sévenfold Lámech.

THE STORY OF THE DECENDANTS OF JABAL.   HOW
THE CURSE OF TOIL WAS MITIGATED BY
THE DISCOVERY OF THE VINE.

[And Jabal, Lamech's firstborn, begat] a son : and 5—28*b*
he called his name Noah (Comfort), saying,   29

    Cómfort he bríngs for our lábor and tóil,
    Out of the sóil which Yáhweḥ hath cúrsed.

[And Noah begat three sons, Shem Japheth and
Canaan.]

And Noah was the first husbandman to plant a 9—20
vineyard : and he drank of the wine, and was drunken ; 21
and he was uncovered within his tent.   And Canaan saw 22
the nakedness of his father, and told his two brethren
without.   And Shem and Japheth took a mantle and laid 23
it upon both their shoulders, and went backward, and
covered the nakedness of their father ; and their faces
were backward, and they saw not their father's nakedness,   And Noah awoke from his wine, and learned what 24
his youngest son had done unto him.   And he said,   25

    Cúrsed be Cánaan ;
    A sláve's slave be hé to his bréthren.

And he said,   26

    Bléssed of Yáhweh be Shém :
    And let Cánaan be sláve to them bóth.
    Jápheth let Yáhweh enlárge (*japht*),   27
    And let him dwéll in the ténts of Shém ;
    And let Cánaan be sláve to them bóth.

The Story of the Demi-Gods.   How the ancient heroes came into the world.

6   And it came to pass, when men began to multiply on
the face of the ground, and daughters were born unto
2 them, that the sons of God* saw the daughters of men
that they were fair ; and they took them wives of any that
4*b* they chose.   And the sons of God came in unto the
daughters of men, and they bare children to them : the
same were the heroes which were of old, the men of re-
10—9 nown.   [And Naamah (?) bare Nimrod] he became a
hero of the chase before Yahweh : wherefore the saying
is, Like Nimrod a hero of the chase before Yahweh.   [He
went forth into Assyria and builded Nineveh.]

The Story of Babylon.   How the first great empires were founded, and the nations and languages of the world originated

11   Now the whole earth was of one language and of one
2 speech.   And it came to pass, as they journeyed in the
east, that they found a plain in the land of Shinar; and
3 they dwelt there.   And they said one to another, Go to, let
us make brick, and burn them thoroughly.   And they used
the brick for stone, and the bitumen they used for mortar.
4 And they said, Go to, let us build us a city, and a tower,
·whose top may reach unto heaven, and let us make us a
monument, lest we be scattered abroad upon the face of the
5 whole earth.   And Yahweh came down to see the city and
6 the tower, which the children of men builded.   And Yahweh said, Behold, they are one people, and they have all
one language; and this is but the beginning of what they
will do : for now nothing will be impossible for them, what-
7 ever they may purpose to do.   Go to, let us go down, and
there turn their language to babble, that they may not
8 understand one another's speech.   So Yahweh scattered
them abroad from thence upon the face of all the earth:

*I. e. divine beings.   Cf. iii. 5 ; Job ii. 1.

and they left off to build the city. Therefore was the 9
name of it called Babel ; because Yahweh did there turn
to babble (*balal*) the language of all the earth : and from
thence did Yahweh scatter them abroad upon the face of
all the earth.

THE STORY OF THE DESCENDANTS OF SHEM.

[Now Shem was] the father of all the children of 10—21*b*
Eber. [The firstborn of Shem was Eber, and Eber begat a son and called his name Peleg (Division), for in
his days the earth was divided. And Peleg begat Reu :
and Reu begat Serug : and Serug begat Terah : and
Terah begat Abram, Nahor and Haran : and the son of
Haran was Lot.] And Haran died in the presence of 11—28
his father Terah in the land of his nativity. And Abram 29
and Nahor took them wives : the name of Abram's wife
was Sarai ; and the name of Nahor's wife, Milcah, the
daughter of Haran, the father of Milcah, and the father
of Iscah. And Sarai was barren : she had no child. 30

THE STORY OF ABRAM. HOW THE ANCESTOR OF THE HEBREWS CAME FROM ARAM NAHARAIM. THE ALTARS OF SHECHEM AND BETHEL.

Now Yahweh said unto Abram : 12

Get thee oút of thy coúntry,
From fátherland ánd from thy hóme,
To the cóuntry that Í will shéw thee.

And of thée I will máke a great nátion, 2
And will bléss thee and máke thy name gréat ;
And bé thou a bléssing.

Them that bléss thee will Í bless, 3
Them that cúrse thee will Í curse,
And by thée shall all tríbes of the eárth invoke bléss-
ings.

So Abram went, as Yahweh had spoken unto him ; and 4
Lot went with him.

6   And Abram passed through the land unto the place of
Shechem, unto the oak of Moreh (Soothsayer).   And the
7 Canaanite was then in the land.   And Yahweh appeared
unto Abram, and said unto him, Unto thy seed will I give
this land : and there builded he an altar unto Yahweh,
8 who appeared unto him.   And he removed from thence
unto the mountain on the east of Bethel, and pitched his
tent, having Bethel on the west, and Ai on the east : and
there he builded an altar unto Yahweh, and called upon
the name of Yahweh.

THE STORY OF THE DIVISION OF THE LAND.   HOW LOT, THE ANCESTOR OF MOAB AND AMMON, WITHDREW FROM ABRAM.

13—2 Now Abram was very rich in cattle and silver and
5 gold.   And Lot also, which went with Abram, had flocks,
6b and herds, and tents, so that they could not dwell to-
7 gether.   And there arose a strife between the herdmen of
Abram's cattle and the herdmen of Lot's cattle : and the
Canaanite and the Perizzite dwelled then in the land.
8 And Abram said unto Lot, Let there be no strife, I pray
thee, between me and thee, and between my herdmen
9 and thy herdmen : for we are brethren.   Is not the whole
land before thee ? separate thyself, I pray thee, from me :
if [thou wilt take] the left hand, then I will go to the right ;
or if [thou take] the right hand, then I will go to the left.
10 And Lot lifted up his eyes, and beheld all the Plain of
Jordan, that it was well watered every where, before Yahweh destroyed Sodom and Gomorrah, like the garden of
11 Yahweh, till thou come unto Zoar.   So Lot chose him all
12b the Plain of Jordan ; and Lot journeyed east, and moved
18 his tent as far as Sodom.   And Abram moved his tent,
and came and dwelt by the oak of Mamre, which is in
Hebron, and built there an altar unto Yahweh.

THE STORY OF THE COVENANT.   HOW YAHWEH GAVE THE LAND TO ABRAM.

15—7 [And Yahweh appeared unto Abram] and said unto

him, I am Yahweh that brought thee out from thy
fatherland, to give thee this land to inherit it. And 8
he said, O Lord Yahweh whereby shall I know that
I shall inherit it? And he said unto him, Take me an 9
heifer of three years old, and a she-goat of three years
old, and a ram of three years old, and a turtle-dove, and
a young pigeon. And he took him all these, and divided 10
them in the midst, and laid each half over against the
other: but the birds divided he not. And the birds of 11
prey came down upon the carcases, and Abram drove
them away. And it came to pass, that, when the sun 17
went down, and thick darkness had come on, behold
a smoking oven, and a flaming torch that passed between these pieces. In that day Yahweh made a cove- 18
nant with Abram, saying, Unto thy seed have I given this
land, from the river of Egypt unto the great river, the
river Euphrates. And Abram said, O Lord Yahweh, 15—2
what wilt thou give me, seeing I go hence? and, lo, one
born in my house is mine heir. And, behold, the word of 4
Yahweh came unto him, saying, This man shall not be
thine heir; but one that shall come forth out of thine own
bowels shall be thine heir. And he believed in Yahweh; 6
and he counted it to him for righteousness.

THE STORY OF ISHMAEL. HOW THE ISHMAELITES OBTAINED THEIR SEAT. ORIGIN OF THE WELL OF BEER-LAHAI-ROI.

Now [Sarai] had an Egyptian handmaid, whose 16
name was Hagar. And Sarai said unto Abram, Behold 2
now, Yahweh hath restrained me from bearing; go in, I
pray thee, unto my handmaid; it may be that I shall obtain children by her. And Abram hearkened to the voice
of Sarai, and went in unto Hagar, and she conceived: 4
and when she saw that she had conceived, her mistress
was despised in her eyes. And Sarai said unto Abram, 5
My wrong be visited upon thee: I gave my handmaid into thy bosom; and when she saw that she had conceived,

I was despised in her eyes : Yahweh judge between me
6 and thee. But Abram said unto Sarai, Behold, thy maid
is in thy hand ; do to her that which is good in thine eyes.
And Sarai dealt hardly with her, and she fled from her
7 face. And the angel of Yahweh found her by a fountain
of water in the wilderness, by the fountain in the way to
8 Shur.   And he said, Hagar, Sarai's handmaid, whence
camest thou? and whither goest thou? And she said, I
11 am fleeing from the face of my mistress Sarai. And the
angel of Yahweh said unto her :

> Lo thóu art with chíld, and shalt béar a són :
> Íshmael (God hears) cáll thou his náme ;
> For Yáhweh hath héard thy afflíction.

12 And hé shall bé a wild-áss of a mán ;
His hánd against áll, and áll against hím ;
He shall dwéll fronting áll of his bréthren.

13   And she called the name of Yahweh that spake unto
her, El Roi (God visible) : for she said, Have I even seen
14 God, and live after my seeing? Wherefore the well was
called, Beer-lahai-roi (Well of him that seeth me and
liveth) ; behold, it is between Kadesh and Bered.

STORY OF THE PROMISE OF ISAAC. HOW ABRAM RECEIVED
YAHWEH AS HIS GUEST, BUT THE SODOMITES
. USED SHAMEFUL TREATMENT.

18   And Yahweh appeared unto [Abram] by the oak of
Mamre, as he sat in the tent door in the heat of the day ;
2 and he lifted up his eyes and looked, and, lo, three men
stood over against him : and when he saw them, he ran
to meet them from the tent door, and bowed himself to
3 the earth, and said, My lord, if now I have found favour
in thy sight, pass not away, I pray thee, from thy servant :
4 let now a little water be fetched, and wash your feet, and
5 rest yourselves under the tree : and I will fetch a morsel
of bread, and comfort ye your heart ; after that ye shall
pass on : forasmuch as ye are come to your servant. And

they said, So do, as thou hast said.   And Abram hastened 6
into the tent unto Sarai, and said, Make ready quickly
three pecks of fine meal, knead it, and make cakes.   And 7
Abram ran unto the herd, and fetched a calf tender and
good, and gave it unto the servant ; and he hasted to dress
it.   And he took curds, and milk, and the calf which he 8
had dressed, and set it before them ; and he stood by
them under the tree, and they did eat.   And they said 9
unto him, Where is Sarai thy wife ? And he said, Behold,
in the tent.   And he said, I will certainly return unto 10
thee when the season cometh round ; and, lo, Sarai thy
wife shall have a son.   And Sarai heard in the tent door,
which was behind him.   Now Abram and Sarai were 11
old, [and] well stricken in age ; it had ceased to be with
Sarai after the manner of women.   And Sarai laughed 12
within herself, saying, After I am waxed old, shall I have
pleasure, my lord being old also ? And Yahweh said un- 13
to Abram, Wherefore did Sarai laugh, saying, Shall I of a
surety bear a child, now that I am old ? Is any thing too 14
hard for Yahweh ? At the set time I will return unto
thee, when the season cometh round, and Sarai shall have
a son.   Then Sarai denied, saying, I laughed not ; for she 15
was afraid.   And he said, Nay ; but thou didst laugh.

And the men rose up from thence, and looked toward 16
Sodom : and Abram went with them to bring them on
the way.   Now the men of Sodom were wicked and 13—13
sinners against Yahweh exceedingly.   And Yahweh 18—20
said, I hear that the outcry against Sodom and Gomorrah
is great, and that their sin is very grievous ; I will go 21
down now, and see whether they have done altogether
according to the scandal of it, which is come unto me ;
and if not, I will know.   And the men turned from thence, 22
and went toward Sodom : and Abram returned unto his 33*b*
place.

And the men came to Sodom at even ; and Lot sat in **19**
the gate of Sodom : and Lot saw them, and rose up to
meet them ; and he bowed himself with his face to the

2 earth ; and he said, Behold now, my lords, turn aside, I
pray you, into your servant's house, and tarry all night,
and wash your feet, and ye shall rise up early, and go on
your way.   And they said, Nay ; but we will abide in the
3 street all night.   And he urged them greatly ; and they
turned in unto him, and entered into his house ; and he
made them a feast, and did bake unleavened bread, and
4 they did eat.   But before they lay down, the men of the
city compassed the house round, both young and old, all
5 the people from every quarter ; and they called unto Lot,
and said unto him, Where are the men which came in to
thee this night? bring them out unto us, that we may
6 know them.   And Lot went out unto them to the door,
7 and shut the door after him.   And he said, I pray you,
8 my brethren, do not so wickedly.   Behold now, I have two
daughters which have not known man ; let me, I pray
you, bring them out unto you, and do ye to them as is
good in your eyes : only unto these men do nothing ; forasmuch as they are come under the shadow of my roof.
9 And they said, Stand back.   And they said, This one fellow came in to sojourn, and he will needs be a judge :
now will we deal worse with thee, than with them.   And
they pressed sore upon the man, and drew near to break
10 the door.   But the men put forth their hand, and brought
11 Lot into the house to them, and shut(?) the door.   And
they smote the men that were at the door of the house
with blindness, both small and great : so that they wearied
12 themselves to find the door.   And the men said unto Lot,
Hast thou here any besides? thy sons in law and thy
daughters, and whomsoever thou hast in the city ; bring
13 them out of the place : for we will destroy this place,
because the scandal of them is waxen great before Yahweh ;
14 and Yahweh hath sent us to destroy it.   And Lot went out,
and spake unto his sons in law, which were to marry his
daughters, and said, Up, get you out of this place ; for
Yahweh will destroy the city.   But he seemed unto his
15 sons in law as one that mocked.   And when the morning

arose, then the men hastened Lot, saying, Arise, take thy
wife, and thy two daughters which are here; lest thou
be consumed in the punishment of the city. But he lin- 16
gered; and the men laid hold upon his hand, and upon the
hand of his wife, and upon the hand of his two daughters;
Yahweh being merciful unto him: and they brought him
forth, and set him without the city. And it came to pass, 17
when they had brought them forth abroad, that he said,
Escape for thy life; look not behind thee, neither stay
thou in all the Plain; escape to the mountain, lest thou
be consumed. And Lot said unto them, Oh, not so, my 18
lord: behold now, thy servant hath found grace in thy 19
sight, and thou hast magnified thy mercy, which thou hast
shewed unto me in saving my life; and I cannot escape
to the mountain, lest the calamity overtake me, and I die:
behold now, this city is near to flee unto, and it is a little 20
one: Oh, let me escape thither, (is it not a little one?) and
my soul shall live. And he said unto him, See, I have ac- 21
cepted thee concerning this thing also, that I will not overthrow the city of which thou hast spoken. Haste thee, 22
escape thither; for I cannot do any thing till thou be come
thither. Therefore the name of the city was called Zoar.
(Little). The sun was risen upon the earth when Lot 23
came unto Zoar. Then Yahweh rained upon Sodom and 24
upon Gomorrah brimstone and fire from Yahweh out of
heaven; and he overthrew those cities, and all the Plain, 25
and all the inhabitants of the cities, and that which grew
upon the ground. [. . .] But his wife looked back from 26
behind him, and she became a pillar of salt. And Abram 27
gat up early in the morning to the place where he had
stood before Yahweh: and he looked down toward Sodom 28
and Gomorrah, and toward all the land of the Plain, and
beheld, and, lo, the smoke of the land went up as the
smoke of a furnace.

STORY OF THE ORIGIN OF THE MOABITES AND AMMONITES.

And Lot went up out of Zoar, and dwelt in the moun- 30

tain country, and his two daughters with him ; for he feared to dwell in Zoar ; and he dwelt in a cave, he and
31 his two daughters.   And the firstborn said unto the younger, Our father is old, and there is not a man in the earth to come in unto us after the manner of all the earth :
32 come, let us make our father drink wine, and we will lie
33 with him, that we may preserve seed of our father.   And they made their father drink wine that night : and the firstborn went in, and lay with her father ; and he knew
34 not when she lay down nor when she arose.   And it came to pass on the morrow, that the firstborn said unto the younger, Behold, I lay yesternight with my father : let us make him drink wine this night also ; and go thou in, and lie with him, that we may preserve seed of our father.
35 And they made their father drink wine that night also : and the younger arose, and lay with him ; and he knew
36 not when she lay down nor when she arose.   Thus were both the daughters of Lot with child by their father.
37 And the firstborn bare a son, and called his name Moab (as if=Father's seed) : the same is the father of the
38 Moabites unto this day.   And the younger, she also bare a son, and called his name Ben-ammi (as if=Son of my people) : the same is the father of the children of Ammon unto this day.

STORY OF THE BIRTH OF ISAAC.   THE TWELVE TRIBES OF SYRIAN STOCK AND TWELVE SOUTH ARABIAN TRIBES OF ABRAHAMIC STOCK.

21—1, 2 And Yahweh visited Sarai as he had said.   And Sarai conceived and bare Abram a son in his old age.
7 And she said :

    Whó would have sáid unto Ábram,
    Sarái shall béar to thee sóns ?
6b   Will laúgh at me* áll they that héar it ;
7b   For a són of his óld age I báre him.

22—20   And it was told Abram, saying, Behold, Milcah, she

* With a play upon the name Isaac.

also hath borne children unto thy brother Nahor ; Uz his 21
firstborn, and Buz his brother, and Kemuel the father of
Aram ; and Chesed, and Hazo, and Pildash, and Jidlaph, 22
and Bethuel. And Bethuel begat Rebekah : these eight 23
did Milcah bear to Nahor, Abram's brother. And his 24
concubine, whose name was Reumah, she also bare Tebah,
and Gaham, and Tahash, and Maacah.   .

And Abram took another wife, and her name was 25
Keturah. And she bare him Zimran, and Jokshan, and 2
Midian, and Ishbak, and Shuah. And Jokshan begat 3
Sheba, and Dedan. And the sons of Dedan were Asshu-
rim, and Letushim, and Leummim. And the sons of 4
Midian ; Ephah, and Epher, and Hanoch, and Abida, and
Eldaah. All these were the children of Keturah. And 5
Abram gave all that he had unto Isaac. [But unto Ish-
mael also he sent gifts unto the east country], for he dwelt 18
from Havilah unto Shur that is before Egypt (as thou
goest toward Ashur?) ; he dwelt in front of (?) all his
brethren. And Isaac dwelt by Beer-lahai-roi.   11*b*

STORY OF THE DEATH OF ABRAM. HOW A WIFE
WAS BROUGHT TO ISAAC FROM THE
SYRIAN FATHERLAND.

Now Abram was old, and well stricken in age : and 24
Yahweh had blessed Abram in all things. And Abram 2
said unto his servant, the elder of his house, that ruled
over all that he had, Put, I pray thee, thy hand under my
thigh : and I will make thee swear by Yahweh, the God of 3
heaven and the God of the earth, that thou shalt not take
a wife for my son of the daughters of the Canaanites,
among whom I dwell : but thou shalt go unto my country, 4
and to my kindred, and take a wife for my son Isaac. And 5
the servant said unto him, Peradventure the woman will
not be willing to follow me unto this land : must I needs
bring thy son again unto the land from whence thou camest? And Abram said unto him, Beware that thou 6
bring not my son thither again. Yahweh, the God of 7

heaven, that took me from my father's house, and from the land of my nativity, and that spake unto me, and that sware unto me, saying, Unto thy seed will I give this land; he shall send his angel before thee, and thou shalt

8 take a wife for my son from thence. And if the woman be not willing to follow thee, then thou shalt be clear from this my oath; only thou shalt not bring my son

9 thither again. And the servant put his hand under the thigh of Abram his master, and sware to him concerning

10 this matter. And the servant took ten camels, of the camels of his master, for all his master's goods were in his hand. And he arose and went to Aram Naharaim,*

11 unto the city of Nahor. And he made the camels to kneel down without the city by the well of water at the time of evening, the time that women go out to draw

12 water. And he said, O Yahweh, the God of my master Abram, send me, I pray thee, good speed this day, and

13 shew kindness unto my master Abram. Behold, I stand by the fountain of water; and the daughters of the men

14 of the city come out to draw water: and let it come to pass, that the damsel to whom I shall say, Let down thy pitcher, I pray thee, that I may drink; and she shall say, Drink, and I will give thy camels drink also: let the same be she that thou hast appointed for thy servant Isaac; and thereby shall I know that thou hast shewed

15 kindness unto my master. And it came to pass, before he had done speaking, that, behold, Rebekah came out, who was born to Bethuel the son of Milcah, the wife of Nahor, Abram's brother, with her pitcher upon her

16 shoulder. And the damsel was very fair to look upon, a virgin, neither had any man known her: and she went down to the fountain, and filled her pitcher, and came

17 up. And the servant ran to meet her, and said, Give me

18 to drink, I pray thee, a little water of thy pitcher. And she said, Drink, my lord: and she hasted, and let down

* I. e. "River-Syria." By no means Mesopotamia, but the "Plain of Syria," Paddan-aram, as P calls it, near the seat of the Hittite empire. "Naharina" on the monuments of Egypt.

her pitcher upon her hand, and gave him drink. And 19
when she had done giving him drink, she said, I will
draw for thy camels also, until they have done drinking. .
And she hasted, and emptied her pitcher into the trough, 20
and ran again unto the well to draw, and drew for all his
camels. And the man looked steadfastly on her, to know 21
whether Yahweh had made his journey prosperous or
not. And it came to pass, as the camels had done drink- 22
ing, that the man took a golden ring of half a shekel
weight, and two bracelets for her hands of ten shekels
weight of gold ; and said, Whose daughter art thou ? tell 23
me, I pray thee. Is there room in thy father's house for
us to lodge in ? And she said unto him, I am the daugh- 24
ter of Bethuel the son of Milcah, which she bare unto
Nahor. She said moreover unto him, We have both 25
straw and provender enough, and room to lodge in. And 26
the man bowed his head, and worshipped Yahweh. And 27
he said, Blessed be Yahweh, the God of my master
Abram, who hath not forsaken his mercy and his truth
toward my master : as for me, Yahweh hath led me in
the way to the house of my master's brethren. And the 28
damsel ran, and told her mother's house according to
these words. And Rebekah had a brother, and his name 29
was Laban. And it came to pass, when he saw the ring, 30
and the bracelets upon his sister's hands, and when he
heard the words of Rebekah his sister, saying, Thus
spake the man unto me ; that Laban ran out unto the foun- 29*b*
tain, and came unto the man ; and, behold, he stood by the
camels at the fountain. And he said, Come in, thou 31
blessed of Yahweh ; wherefore standest thou without ? for
I have prepared the house, and room for the camels. And 32
he brought the man into the house, and ungirded the camels ; and he gave straw and provender for the camels, and
water to wash his feet and the men's feet that were with
him. And there was set meat before him to eat : but he 33
said, I will not eat, until I have told mine errand. And 34
he said, Speak on. And he said, I am Abram's servant.

35 And Yahweh hath blessed my master greatly ; and he is
become great : and he hath given him flocks and herds,
and silver and gold, and menservants and maidservants,
36 and camels and asses. And Sarai my master's wife bare
a son to my master when she was old : and unto him hath
37 he given all that he hath. And my master made me
swear, saying, Thou shalt not take a wife for my son of
the daughters of the Canaanites, in whose land I dwell ;
38 but thou shalt go unto my father's house, and to my
39 kindred, and take a wife for my son. And I said unto
my master, Peradventure the woman will not follow me.
40 And he said unto me, Yahweh, before whom I walk, will
send his angel with thee, and prosper thy way ; and thou
shalt take a wife for my son of my kindred, and of my
41 father's house : then shalt thou be clear from my oath,
when thou comest to my kindred ; and if they give her
42 not to thee, thou shalt be clear from my oath. And I
came this day unto the fountain, and said, O Yahweh,
the God of my master Abram, if now thou do prosper
43 my way which I go : behold, I stand by the fountain of
water ; and let it come to pass, that the maiden which
cometh forth to draw, to whom I shall say, Give me, I
44 pray thee, a little water of thy pitcher to drink ; and she
shall say to me, Both drink thou, and I will also draw for
thy camels: let the same be the woman whom Yahweh
45 hath appointed for my master's son. . And before I had
done speaking in mine heart, behold, Rebekah came
forth with her pitcher on her shoulder ; and she went
down unto the fountain, and drew: and I said unto her,
46 Let me drink, I pray thee. And she made haste, and
let down her pitcher from her shoulder, and said, Drink,
and I will give thy camels drink also : so I drank, and
47 she made the camels drink also. And I asked her, and
said, Whose daughter art thou ? And she said, The
daughter of Bethuel, Nahor's son, whom Milcah bare
unto him : and I put the ring upon her nose, and the
48 bracelets upon her hands. And I bowed my head, and

worshipped Yahweh, and blessed Yahweh, the God of my master Abram, which had led me in the right way to take my master's brother's daughter for his son. And 49 now if ye will deal kindly and truly with my master, tell me : and if not, tell me ; that I may turn to the right hand, or to the left. Then Laban answered and said, 50 The thing proceedeth from Yahweh : we cannot speak unto thee bad or good. Behold, Rebekah is before thee, 51 take her, and go, and let her be thy master's son's wife, as Yahweh hath spoken. And it came to pass, that, 52 when Abram's servant heard their words, he bowed himself down to the earth unto Yahweh. And the servant 53 brought forth jewels of silver, and jewels of gold, and raiment, and gave them to Rebekah : he gave also to her brother and to her mother precious things. And 54 they did eat and drink, he and the men that were with him, and tarried all night ; and they rose up in the morning, and he said, Send me away unto my master. And 55 her brother and her mother said, Let the damsel abide with us a year, or ten months ; after that she shall go. And he said unto them, Hinder me not, seeing Yahweh 56 hath prospered my way ; send me away that I may go to my master. And they said, We will call the damsel, 57 and inquire at her mouth. And they called Rebekah, 58 and said unto her, Wilt thou go with this man ? And she said, I will go. And they sent away Rebekah their 59 sister, and her nurse, and Abram's servant, and his men. And they blessed Rebekah, and said unto her,

> Of ten thóusands of thóusands be móther, O síster,
> And thy séed posséss the gáte of their fóes.

And Rebekah arose, and her damsels, and they rode 61 upon the camels, and followed the man : [and they came to Beer-sheba, and found Abram dead]. And the ser- 61a vant took Rebekah and went his way through the wilder- 62 ness of Beer-lahai-roi [to] come [unto] Isaac ; for he dwelt in the land of the South (Negeb). And Isaac 63

went out to . . . (?) in the field at the eventide: and he lifted up his eyes, and saw, and, behold, there
64 were camels coming. And Rebekah lifted up her eyes, and when she saw Isaac, she lighted off the camel.
65 And she said unto the servant, What man is this that walketh in the field to meet us? And the servant said, It is my master: and she took her veil, and covered her-
66 self. And the servant told Isaac all the things that he
67 had done. And Isaac brought her into the tent, and took Rebekah, and she became his wife, and he loved her: and Isaac was comforted after his father's death.

THE STORY OF ISAAC AND THE PHILISTINES: HOW REBEKAH WAS TAKEN AND RESTORED, AND THE WELLS OF THE NEGEB WERE DUG.

26 And there was a famine in the land. And Isaac went unto Abimelech king of the Philistines unto Gerar.
2, 3 And Yahweh appeared unto him and said, Sojourn in this
6, 7 land. So Isaac dwelt in Gerar. And the men of the place asked him of his wife; and he said, She is my sister; for he feared to say, My wife; lest, said he, the men of the place should kill me for Rebekah; because
8 she was fair to look upon. And it came to pass, when he had been there a long time, that Abimelech king of the Philistines looked out at a window, and saw, and, behold,
9 Isaac was sporting* with Rebekah his wife. And Abime-lech called Isaac, and said, Behold, of a surety she is thy wife: and how saidst thou, She is my sister? And Isaac
10 said unto him, Because I said, Lest I die for her. And Abimelech said, What is this thou hast done unto us? one of the people might easily have lien with thy wife, and
11 thou shouldest have brought guiltiness upon us. And Abimelech charged all the people, saying, He that touch-eth this man or his wife shall surely be put to death.
12 And Isaac sowed in that land, and found in the same
13 year an hundredfold: and Yahweh· blessed him. And

---

* A play upon the name Isaac.

the man waxed great, and grew more and more until he
became very great: and he had possessions of flocks, and 14
possessions of herds, and a great household: and the
Philistines envied him.   And Abimelech said unto Isaac, 16
Go from us; for thou art much mightier than we.   And 17
Isaac departed thence, and encamped in the valley of
Gerar, and dwelt there.   And Isaac's servants digged in 19
the valley, and found there a well of springing water.
And the herdmen of Gerar strove with Isaac's herdmen, 20
saying, The water is ours: and he called the name of the
well Esek (Contention); because they contended with
him.   And they digged another well, and they strove for 21
that also: and he called the name of it Sitnah (Enmity).
And he removed from thence, and digged another well; 22
and for that they strove not: and he called the name of
it Rehoboth (Room); and he said, For now Yahweh hath
made room for us, and we shall be fruitful in the land.
And he went up from thence to Beer-sheba.   And 23, 24
Yahweh appeared unto him the same night, and said, I
am the God of Abram thy father: fear not, for I am with
thee, and will bless thee, and multiply thy seed for my
servant Abram's sake.   And he builded an altar there, 25
and called upon the name of Yahweh, and pitched his
tent there: and there Isaac's servants digged a well.
Then Abimelech went to him from Gerar, and Ahuzzath 26
his friend, and Phicol the captain of his host.   And Isaac 27
said unto them,

> Whérefore cóme ye to mé,
> Séeing ye béar me háte,
> And have sént me awáy from you?

> And they sáid, We cértainly sáw   28
> That Yáhweh was éver with thée;
> And we sáid, Let there nów be an óath
> On óur part and thíne, bétween us;
> Let us séal a cóvenant with thée:

29 That thóu wilt dó us no húrt,
 As wé have not tóuched thee at áll,
 And as wé have dóne unto thée naught but góod,
 And despátched thee in péace :
 Thou árt now the bléssed of Yáhweh.

30 And he made them a feast, and they did eat and drink.
31 And they rose up betimes in the morning, and sware one
 to another : and Isaac sent them away, and they departed
32 from him in peace. And it came to pass the same day,
 that Isaac's servants came, and told him concerning the
 well which they had digged, and said unto him, We have
 found water.

21—31 Wherefore he called that place Beer-sheba (Well of
32 the Oath); because there they sware both of them. So
 they made a covenant at Beer-sheba: and Abimelech
 rose up, and Phicol the captain of his host, and they
33 returned into the land of the Philistines. And he [Isaac]
 planted a tamarisk tree in Beer-sheba, and called there
 on the name of Yahweh El Elyon.

STORY OF THE ORACLE OF THE TWIN PEOPLES.
THE RIVALRY OF ESAU AND JACOB.

25—21 And Isaac intreated Yahweh for his wife, because
 she was barren : and Yahweh was intreated of him, and
22 Rebekah his wife conceived. And the children struggled
 together within her ; and she said, If it be so, wherefore
 do I live ? And she went to obtain an oracle from Yah-
23 weh. And Yahweh said unto her,

 Two nátions are ín thy wómb,
 And two péoples shall párt from thy bówels :
 And one tríbe shall preváil o'er the óther ;
 And the élder be sláve to the yóunger.

24 And when her days to be delivered were fulfilled, behold,
25 there were twins in her womb. And the first came forth
 [shaggy], all over like an hair (*sear;* connected with Seir)

garment ; and they called his name Esau. And after that 26
came forth his brother, and his hand had hold on Esau's
heel ; and his name was called Jacob (One that takes by
the heel, or supplants). And the boys grew : and Esau 27
became a cunning hunter, a man of the field ; but Jacob
was a smooth (?) man, dwelling in tents. Now Isaac 28
loved Esau, because he did eat of his venison : and Rebekah loved Jacob. And Jacob sod pottage : and Esau 29
came in from the field, and he was faint : and Esau said 30
to Jacob, Feed me, I pray thee, with that same red [pot-
tage] for I am faint : therefore was his name called
Edom (Red). And Jacob said, Sell me this day thy 31
birthright. And Esau said, Behold, I am at the point to 32
die : and what profit shall the birthright do to me ? And 33
Jacob said, Swear to me this day ; and he sware unto
him : and he sold his birthright unto Jacob. And Jacob 34
gave Esau bread and pottage of lentils ; and he did eat
and drink, and rose up, and went his way : so Esau
despised his birthright.

STORY OF THE BLESSING OF ISAAC. HOW JACOB SUPPLANTED
ESAU IN THE INHERITANCE.

And it came to pass, when Isaac was old, and his eyes 27
were dim, so that he could not see [that he called Esau
and said], take, I pray thee, thy weapons, thy quiver and 3
thy bow, and go out to the field, and take me venison ;
and [bring it to me] that my soul may bless thee. 4
And Esau went to the field to hunt for venison, and to 5*b*
bring it. And Rebekah spake unto Jacob her son, say- 6
ing, Behold, I heard thy father speak unto Esau thy
brother, saying, Bring me venison [that I may eat and 7
my soul may bless thee] before Yahweh. And Rebekah 15
took the [perfumed ?] festal garments of Esau her elder
son, which were with her in the house, and put them
upon Jacob her younger son : [and Jacob came and presented himself to his father. And Isaac said] Who art 18*c*
thou, my son ? And Jacob said unto his father, I am 19

Esau thy firstborn ; I have done according as thou badest
me : arise, I pray thee, sit and eat of my vension, that
20 thy soul may bless me. And Isaac said unto his son,
How is it that thou hast found it so quickly, my son?
And he said, Because Yahweh thy God sent me good
24 speed. And he said, Art thou my very son Esau? And
25 he said, I am. And he said, Bring it near to me, and I
will eat of my son's venison, that my soul may bless thee.
And he brought it near to him, and he did eat : and he
26 brought him wine, and he drank. And his father Isaac
said unto him, Come near now, and kiss me, my son.
27 And he came near, and kissed him : and he smelled the
smell of his raiment, and blessed him, and said,

> Ís not the sméll of my són like the sméll of a fíeld
> Which Yáhweh hath wátered with bléssing?
29 Nátions shall bów before thée, and péoples shall serve
>   thee.
> [For in thée all tríbes shall be bléssed].
> Blessing thée shall be bléssing, and cúrsing thee cúrse.

30 And it came to pass, as soon as Isaac had made an end
of blessing Jacob, that Esau his brother came in from
31 his hunting. And he said unto his father, Let my father
arise, and eat of his son's venison, that thy soul may bless
32 me. And Isaac his father said unto him, Who art thou?
33 And he said, I am thy son, thy firstborn Esau. And
Isaac trembled very exceedingly, and said, Who then is
he that hath taken venison, and brought it me, and I
have eaten of all before thou camest, and have blessed
36 him? surely he shall have the blessing. And he [Esau]
said, Is not he rightly named Jacob (Supplanter)? for he
hath supplanted me these two times : he took away my
birthright ; and behold now he hath taken away my blessing.
41   . And Esau was at feud with Jacob because of the blessing wherewith his father blessed him. [And Rebekah
knew it, and when Isaac was dead she called Jacob and

said unto him, Thy brother Esau will seek to kill thee;
for thy father is now dead. Arise, flee to Aram Naharaim,
and abide with my brother Laban] until thy brother's 45
anger turn away from thee, and he forget that which thou
hast done to him ; then I will send and fetch thee from
thence ; why should I be bereaved of you both in one day ?

The Story of Jacob's service with Laban. How his wives were won.

So Jacob went out from Beer-sheba, and went 28—10
unto Haran.

And he looked, and behold a well in the field, and, 29—2
lo, three flocks of sheep lying there by it ; for out of that
well they watered the flocks : and there was a great stone
upon the well's mouth. And all the flocks used to gather 3
there, and then they rolled the stone from the well's
mouth, and watered the sheep, and put the stone again
upon the well's mouth in its place. And Jacob said unto 4
them, My brethren, whence be ye? And they said, Of
Haran are we. And he said unto them, Know ye Laban 5
the son of Nahor? And they said, We know him. And 6
he said unto them, Is it well with him? And they said,
It is well : and, behold, Rachel his daughter cometh with
the sheep. And he said, Lo, it is yet high day, neither 7
is it time that the cattle should be gathered together :
water ye the sheep, and go again and feed them. And 8
they said, We cannot, until all the flocks be gathered
together, and they [i. e. all the shepherds together] roll
the stone from the well's mouth ; then we water the sheep.
While he yet spake with them, Rachel came with her 9
father's sheep; for she kept them. And it came to 10
pass, when Jacob saw Rachel the daughter of Laban
his mother's brother, and the sheep of Laban his
mother's brother, that Jacob went near, and [single-
handed] rolled the stone from the well's mouth, and
watered the flock of Laban his mother's brother. And 11
Jacob kissed Rachel, and lifted up his voice, and wept.

12 And Jacob told Rachel that he was her father's brother,
   and that he was Rebekah's son: and she ran and told
13 her father. And it came to pass, when Laban heard the
   tidings of Jacob his sister's son, that he ran to meet him,
   and embraced him, and kissed him, and brought him to
14 his house. And he told Laban all these things. And
   Laban said to him, Surely thou art my bone and my
   flesh. [And Jacob kept the flock of Laban, and he loved
   Rachel, Laban's younger daughter, and asked her of her
26 father to wife.] And Laban said, It is not so done in
   our place, to give the younger before the firstborn. [If
   thou wilt serve with me . . . years, then I will give
   thee Leah my firstborn and Rachel also. And Jacob did
   so, and Laban gave him his two daughters to wife.]

THE STORY OF THE BIRTH OF THE PATRIARCHS. HOW THE
NAMES OF THE TRIBES OF ISRAEL ORIGINATED.
RIVALRY OF LEAH AND RACHEL.

31   And Yahweh saw that Leah was hated, and he opened
32 her womb: but Rachel was barren. And Leah conceived, and bare a son, and she called his name Reuben:
   for she said, Because Yahweh hath looked upon my
   affliction (*raah beonyi*); for now my husband will love
33 me. And she conceived again, and bare a son; and said,
   Because Yahweh hath heard (*shama*) that I am hated, he
   therefore hath given me this son also. And she called
34 his name Simeon. And she conceived again, and bare a
   son; and said, Now this time will my husband be joined
   (from the root *lavah*) unto me, because I have borne him
35 three sons: therefore she called his name Levi. And
   she conceived again, and bare a son: and she said, This
   time will I praise (from *hodah*) Yahweh: therefore she
   called his name Judah; and she left bearing.
      [And when Rachel saw that she was barren, she said
   unto Jacob, Behold my handmaid Bilhah, go in unto her,]
30—3, 4 that I also may obtain children by her. And she
   gave him Bilhah her handmaid to wife, and Jacob went

in unto her. [And Bilhah conceived and bare a son. And Rachel said, Yahweh hath judged (*dan*) me, therefore she called his name Dan.] And Bilhah Rachel's 7 handmaid bare Jacob a second son. [And Rachel said, ... therefore she called his name Naphtali.] When Leah saw that she had left bearing, she took Zil- 9 pah her handmaid, and gave her to Jacob to wife. And 10 Zilpah Leah's handmaid bare Jacob a son. And Leah 11 said, By [good] Fortune! and she called his name Gad (Fortune). And Zilpah Leah's handmaid bare Jacob a 12 second son. And Leah said, By my [good] luck! for the 13 daughters will say, Thy luck! (*asherē*): and she called his name Asher. And Reuben went in the days of wheat 14 harvest, and found mandrakes in the field, and brought them unto his mother Leah. Then Rachel said to Leah, Give me, I pray thee, of thy son's mandrakes. And she 15 said unto her, Is it a small matter that thou hast taken away my husband? and wouldest thou take away my son's mandrakes also? And Rachel said, Well then, he shall lie with thee to-night for thy son's mandrakes. And 16 Jacob came from the field in the evening, and Leah went out to meet him, and said, Thou must come in unto me; for I have surely hired (*sachar*) thee with my son's mandrakes. And he lay with her that night. [And Leah conceived again and bare a son and called his name Issachar. And she conceived again a sixth time and bare a son, and said], Now will my husband dwell (*zabal*) 20*b* with me, because I have borne him six sons: and she called his name Zebulun.

And Yahweh remembered Rachel, and opened her 22 womb. [And she conceived, and bare a son, and called his name Joseph,] saying, Yahweh add (*joseph*) to me 24*b* another son.

THE STORY OF JACOB'S TRIAL OF CUNNING WITH LABAN.
HOW THE HEBREW WON AWAY THE WEALTH
OF THE SYRIAN SHEPHERD.

And it came to pass, when Rachel had borne Joseph, 25

that Jacob said unto Laban, Send me away, that I may
27 go unto mine own place, and to my country. And Laban
said unto him, If now I have found favour in thine eyes,
[tarry: for] I have learned by divination that Yahweh
hath blessed me for thy sake. And he said unto him,
Thou knowest how I have served thee, and how thy
30 cattle hath fared with me. For it was little which thou
hadst before I came, and it hath increased unto a multitude; and Yahweh hath blessed thee whithersoever
I turned: and now when shall I provide for mine own
31 house also? And he said, What shall I give thee? And
Jacob said, Thou shalt not give me aught: if thou wilt do
this thing for me, I will again feed thy flock. [What-
soever is born to the flock henceforth ringstraked,
speckled or spotted shall be mine; but the white (*laban*)
34 shall be thine.] And Laban said, Behold, I would it
35 might be according to thy word. And he removed that
day the he-goats that were ringstraked and spotted, and
all the she-goats that were speckled and spotted, every
one that had white in it, and all the black ones among the
36 sheep, and gave them into the hand of his sons; and he
set three days' journey betwixt himself and Jacob: and
37 Jacob fed the rest of Laban's flocks. And Jacob took
him rods of fresh poplar, and of the almond and of the
plane tree; and peeled white strakes in them, and made
38 the white appear which was in the rods. And he set
the rods which he had peeled over against the flocks in
39 the watering-troughs. And the flocks rutted before the
rods, and the flocks brought forth ringstraked, speckled,
40 and spotted. And Jacob separated the lambs, and he put
his own droves apart, and put them not unto Laban's
41 flock. And it came to pass, whensoever the stronger of
the flock did rut, that Jacob laid the rods before the
eyes of the flock in the troughs, that they might rut among
42 the rods; but when the flock were feeble, he put them
not in: so the feebler were Laban's, and the stronger
43 Jacob's. And the man increased exceedingly, and had

large flocks, and maidservants and menservants, and camels and asses.

THE STORY OF GILEAD AND MIZPAH. HOW A BOUNDARY WAS FIXED BETWEEN ISRAEL AND ARAM.

And he heard the words of Laban's sons, saying,　　31—1
>Jácob hath táken awáy
>>Áll that wás our fáther's ;
>>And of thát which wás our fáther's
>Hath he gótten him áll this wéalth.

And he rose up and passed over the river (Euphrates). 21
And Laban [pursued after and] came up with Jacob. 25
Now Jacob had pitched his tent in the mountain [of Mizpah], and Laban with his brethren pitched in the mountain of Gilead.　[And Laban said to Jacob:]
>Why didst thou sécretly flée,　　　　　　27
>>And didst stéal awáy from me ;
>>And dídst not téll me ;
>That I might spéed thee with mírth and with sóngs,
>>With tábret and hárp?

And Jacob answered and said unto Laban,　　　31
>Because I féared ; because I sáid,
>Lest thou rób me óf thy dáughters.

And Laban answered and said unto Jacob :　　　43
>The dáughters are míne, and the chíldren are míne,
>The flócks are my flócks, mine is áll that thou séest.
>What nów can I dó unto thése my dáughters ?
>Or únto their chíldren whích they have bórne ?
>And nów come ón, let us stáblish a cóvenant,　　44
>And lét us cast úp a cáirn, I and thóu :
>It shall bé for a wítness betwéen me and thée.

So he [Laban] said unto his brethren, Gather stones ; and 46
they took stones and made a cairn, and they did eat [the

48 covenant meal] there by the cairn.   And Laban said:

>   This cáirn which thou séest is wítness
>   Betwéen me and thée this dáy.

49a Therefore was the name of it called Galeed (Cairn of Witness;—an attempted etymology of "Gilead").

50
>   If thóu shalt afflíct my dáughters,
>   Or ádd other wíves to my dáughters,
>   No mán is présent wíth us;
>   See thése [stones] are wítness betwéen me and thée.

49b And [Jacob called the name of the place where he had pitched his tent] Mizpah (Watching-place), for he said:

>   Yáhweh wátch betwéen me and thée,
>   Whén we are hídden the óne from the óther.

The Story of Mahanaim and Jabboq. How Jacob wrestled with an angel and was called Israel.

32—3 And Jacob sent messengers before him to Esau his
4   brother unto the land of Seir.   And he commanded them, saying, Thus shall ye say unto my lord Esau; Thus saith thy servant Jacob, I have sojourned with Laban, and
5   stayed until now: and I have oxen, and asses, and flocks, and menservants and maidservants: and I have sent to
6   tell my lord, that I may find grace in thy sight.   And the messengers returned to Jacob, saying, We came to thy brother Esau, and moreover he cometh to meet thee,
7   and four hundred men with him.   Then Jacob was greatly afraid and was distressed: and he divided the people that was with him, and the flocks, and the herds, and the cam-
8   els, into two companies (*mahanaim*); and he said, If Esau come to the one company, and smite it, then the company which is left shall escape.   [Therefore was the name of
13b the place called Mahanaim.]   And he took of that which he had with him a present for Esau his brother; two
14   hundred she-goats and twenty he-goats, two hundred

ewes and twenty rams, thirty milch camels and their 15
colts, forty kine and ten bulls, twenty she-asses and ten
jacks. And he delivered them into the hand of his serv- 16
ants, every drove by itself: and said unto his servants,
Pass over before me, and put a space betwixt drove and
drove. And he commanded the foremost, saying, When 17
Esau my brother meeteth thee, and asketh thee, saying,
Whose art thou? and whither goest thou? and whose
are these before thee? then thou shalt say, [They be] 18
thy servant Jacob's; it is a present sent unto my lord
Esau: and, behold, he also is behind us. And he com- 19
manded also the second, and the third, and all that followed the droves, saying, On this manner shall ye speak
unto Esau, when ye find him; and ye shall say, More- 20
over, behold, thy servant Jacob is behind us. For he
said, I will appease him with the present that goeth
before me, and afterward I will see his face; peradventure he will accept me. So the present passed over 21
before him: and he himself lodged that night in the
company.

And he rose up that night, and took his two wives, and 22*a*
his two handmaids, and his eleven children, and sent 23
them over the stream, and sent over that he had. And 24
Jacob was left alone; and there wrestled (*jeabeq*, punning
etymology of Jabboq) a man with him until the breaking of
the day. And when he saw that he prevailed not against 25
him, he touched the hollow of his thigh; and the hollow of
Jacob's thigh was strained, as he wrestled with him. And 26
he said, Let me go, for the day breaketh. And he said, I
will not let thee go, except thou bless me. And he said 27
unto him, What is thy name? And he said, Jacob. And 28
he said, Thy name shall be called no more Jacob, but
Israel (God strives): for thou hast striven with God and
with men, and hast prevailed. And Jacob asked him, 29
and said, Tell me, I pray thee, thy name. And he said,
Wherefore is it that thou dost ask after my name? And
he blessed him there.

17

THE STORY OF PENUEL. HOW JACOB MET ESAU AND OBTAINED FORGIVENESS.

31 And the sun rose upon him as he passed over Penuel,
32 and he was limping upon his thigh. Therefore the children of Israel eat not the sinew of the hip which is upon the hollow of the thigh, unto this day: because he touched the hollow of Jacob's thigh in the sinew of the hip.

33 And Jacob lifted up his eyes, and looked, and, behold, Esau came, and with him four hundred men. And he divided the children unto Leah, and unto Rachel, and
2 unto the two handmaids. And he put the handmaids and their children foremost, and Leah and her children
3 after, and Rachel and Joseph hindermost. And he himself passed over before them, and bowed himself to the ground seven times, until he came near to his brother.
4–6 And Esau ran to meet him, and embraced him. Then the handmaids came near, they and their children, and
7 they bowed themselves. And Leah also and her children came near, and bowed themselves: and after came Joseph near and Rachel, and they bowed themselves.
8 And he said, What meanest thou by all this company which I met? And he said, To find favor in the sight of
9 my lord. And Esau said, I have enough; my brother,
10 let that thou hast be thine. And Israel said, Nay, I pray thee, if now I have found favor in thy sight, then receive my present at my hand: forasmuch as I have seen thy face, as one seeth the face of God
12 (*Peni-el*), and thou hast accepted me.* And he said, Let us take our journey, and let us go, and I will go
13 before thee. And he said unto him, My lord knoweth that the children are tender, and that the flocks and herds with me give suck: and if they overdrive them one day,
14 all the flocks will die. Let my lord, I pray thee, pass over

---

*I. e. Since I have propitiated thy wrath therewith, as one obtaineth acceptance at the sanctuary. Cf. xxxii. 20 and Ex. xxxiv. 20, last clause.

before his servant : and I will lead on in my quiet way,
according to the pace of the cattle that is before me and
according to the pace of the children, until I come unto
my lord unto Seir.   And Esau said, Let me now leave 15
with thee some of the folk that are with me.   And he
said, What needeth it? let me find favor in the sight of
my lord.   So Esau returned that day on his way unto 16
Seir.   And Israel journeyed to Succoth, and built him an 17
house, and made booths for his cattle : therefore the
name of the place is called Succoth (Booths).

THE STORY OF SHECHEM THE HIVITE.   HOW SIMEON AND
  LEVI CRUELLY AVENGED THEIR SISTER'S DISHONOUR.

And Shechem, the son of Hamor the Hivite, saw 34—2
Dinah, Jacob's daughter, and took her, and ravished her.
And his soul clave unto her, and he loved the damsel. 3
Now Israel heard of this thing while his sons were with 5
his cattle in the field : and Israel held his peace until they
came.   And the sons of Israel came in from the field when 7
they heard it : and the men were grieved, and they were
very wroth, because he had wrought folly in Israel in
lying with Israel's daughter ; which thing ought not to be
done. [. . .] And Shechem said unto her father and unto 11
her brethren, Let me find favor in your eyes, and what
ye shall say unto me, I will give.   Ask me never so much 12
bridal-money and gratuity, and I will give according as ye
shall say unto me : but give me the damsel to wife.   And 13
the sons of Israel answered Shechem with guile. [. . .]
And the young man deferred not to do the thing, because 19
he had delight in Israel's daughter : and he was honoured
above all the house of his father.   [. . .] And two of 25
the sons of Israel, Simeon and Levi, Dinah's brethren,
took each man his sword, [. . .] and slew Hamor and 26
Shechem his son with the edge of the sword, and took
Dinah out of Shechem's house, and went forth.   And 29*b*
they spoiled all that was in the house.   And Israel said to 30
Simeon and Levi, Ye have troubled me, to bring me into

bad odor with the inhabitants of the land, with the Canaanites and the Perizzites : and, I being few in number, they will gather themselves together against me and smite me ; and I shall be destroyed, I and my house.
31 And they said, Should he deal with our sister as with an harlot?

THE STORY OF THE "PILLAR" AT BETHEL. HOW ISRAEL CAME TO HEBRON (?).

[And Israel journeyed from Shechem, and came to the city of Luz.   And he lodged there that night.]
28—13   And, behold, Yahweh stood beside him and said,
> Í am Yahwéh,
> God of Ábram thy fáther, and of Ísaac.
> Thís very lánd whereupón thou líest,
> To thée and thy séed will I gíve it.

14
> And thy séed shall bé as the dúst of the éarth,
> Thou shalt spréad east and wést, north and sóuth ;
> And in thée all the tríbes of the lánd shall be bléssed.

16 And Israel awaked out of his sleep and said,
> Surely Yáhweh is ín this pláce,
> And Í was in ígnorance óf it.

35—14 And Israel set up a pillar in the place where he spake with him, a pillar of stone : and he poured out a libation thereon, and poured oil thereon.
28—19   And he called the name of that place Bethel (House
35—16 of God).   And they journeyed from Bethel ; and there was still some way to come to Ephrath : and Rachel
17 travailed, and she had hard labour.   And it came to pass, when she was in hard labour, that the midwife said unto her, Fear not : for this too is a son.
18 And it came to pass, as her soul was in departing (for she died), that she called his name Ben-oni (Son of my sorrow) : but his father called him Benjamin (Son of the
21 right hand).   And Israel journeyed, and spread his tent

beyond the tower of Eder. And it came to pass, while 22
Israel dwelt in that land, that Reuben went and lay with
Bilhah his father's concubine: and Israel heard of it
[. . .]

The Story of the Clans of Judah.

And it came to pass at that time, that Judah went 38
down from his brethren, and turned in to a certain
Adullamite, whose name was Hirah. And Judah saw 2
there a daughter of a certain Canaanite whose name was
Shua ; and he took her, and went in unto her. And she 3
conceived, and bare a son; and she called his name Er.
And she conceived again, and bare a son ; and she called 4
his name Onan. And she yet again bare a son, and called 5
his name Shelah : and she was at Chezib, when she bare
him. And Judah took a wife for Er his firstborn, and 6
her name was Tamar. And Er, Judah's firstborn, was 7
wicked in the sight of Yahweh ; and Yahweh slew him.
And Judah said unto Onan, Go in unto thy brother's 8
wife, and perform the duty of an husband's brother unto
her, and raise up seed to thy brother. And Onan knew 9
that the seed should not be his ; and it came to pass, whenever he went in unto his brother's wife, that he spilled
it on the ground, lest he should give seed to his brother.
And the thing which he did was evil in the sight of
Yahweh: and he slew him also. Then said Judah to 11
Tamar his daughter in law, Remain a widow in thy
father's house, till Shelah my son be grown up: for he
said, Lest he also die, like his brethren. And Tamar
went and dwelt in her father's house. And in process of 12
time Shua's daughter, the wife of Judah, died ; and Judah
was comforted, and went up unto his sheepshearers to
Timnah, he and his friend Hirah the Adullamite. And 13
it was told Tamar, saying, Behold, thy father in law
goeth up to Timnah to shear his sheep. And she put off 14
from her the garments of her widowhood, and covered
herself with her veil, and wrapped herself, and sat in the

gate of Enaim, which is by the way to Timnah ; for she
saw that Shelah was grown up, and she was not given
15 unto him to wife. When Judah saw her, he thought her
16 to be an harlot ; for she had covered her face. And he
turned unto her by the way, and said, Go to, I pray thee,
let me come in unto thee : for he knew not that she was
his daughter in law. And she said, What wilt thou give
17 me, that thou mayest come in unto me? And he said,
I will send thee a kid of the goats from the flock. And
she said, Wilt thou give me a pledge, till thou send it?
18 And he said, What pledge shall I give thee? And she
said, Thy signet and thy cord, and thy staff that is in
thine hand. And he gave them to her, and came in unto
19 her, and she conceived by him. And she arose, and went
away, and put off her veil from her, and put on the gar-
20 ments of her widowhood. And Judah sent the kid of the
goats by the hand of his friend the Adullamite, to receive
the pledge from the woman's hand : but he found her
21 not. Then he asked the men of her place, saying, Where
is the harlot (*kedeshah*) that was at Enaim by the way-
side? And they said, There hath been no harlot here.
22 And he returned to Judah, and said, I have not found
her ; and also the men of the place said, There hath been
23 no harlot here. And Judah said, Let her keep it, lest
we be put to shame : behold, I sent this kid, and thou
24 hast not found her. And it came to pass about three
months after, that it was told Judah, saying, Tamar thy
daughter in law hath played the harlot ; and moreover,
behold, she is with child by whoredom. And Judah said,
25 Bring her forth, and let her be burnt. When she was
brought forth, she sent to her father in law, saying, By
the man, whose these are, am I with child : and she said,
Discern, I pray thee, whose are these, the signet, and the
26 cords, and the staff. And Judah acknowledged them,
and said, She is more righteous than I ; forasmuch as I
gave her not to Shelah my son. And he knew her again
27 no more. And it came to pass in the time of her travail,

that, behold, twins were in her womb. And it came to 28
pass, when she travailed, that one put out a hand: and
the midwife took and bound upon his hand a scarlet
thread, saying, This came out first. And it came to pass, 29
as he drew back his hand, that, behold, his brother came
out: and she said, Wherefore hast thou made a breach
for thyself? therefore his name was called Perez (Breach).
And afterward came out his brother, that had the scarlet 30
thread upon his hand: and his name was called Zerah
(Putting forth).

*   *   *   *   *   *   *   *   *

THE STORY OF THE KINGS OF EDOM.

And these are the kings that reigned in the land of **36**—31
Edom, before there reigned any king over the children
of Israel. And Bela the son of Beor reigned in Edom ; 32
and the name of his city was Dinhabah. And Bela died, 33
and Jobab the son of Zerah of Bozrah reigned in his
stead. And Jobab died, and Husham of the land of the 34
Temanites reigned in his stead. And Husham died, and 35
Hadad the son of Bedad, who smote Midian in the field
of Moab, reigned in his stead: and the name of his city
was Avith. And Hadad died, and Samlah of Masrekah 36
reigned in his stead. And Samlah died, and Shaul of 37
Rehoboth by the River reigned in his stead. And Shaul 38
died, and Baal-hanan the son of Achbor reigned in his
stead. And Baal-hanan the son of Achbor died, and 39
Hadar reigned in his stead: and the name of his city was
Pau ; and his wife's name was Mehetabel, the daughter
of Matred, the daughter of Me-zahab.

THE STORY OF JOSEPH. HOW HIS BRETHREN SOLD HIM TO THE ISHMAELITES AND THESE BROUGHT HIM INTO EGYPT.

Now Israel loved Joseph more than all his children, **37**—3
because he was the son of his old age : and he made
him a sleeved tunic. And his brethren saw that their 4

father loved him more than all his brethren ; and they hated him, and could not speak peaceably unto him.
12 And his brethren went to feed their father's flock in
13 Shechem. And Israel said unto Joseph, Do not thy brethren feed the flock in Shechem? come, and I will send thee
14*b* unto them. So he sent him out of the vale of Hebron,
18 and he came to Shechem. And they saw him afar off, and before he came near unto them, they conspired against
21 him to slay him. And Judah heard it, and delivered him out of their hand ; and said, Let us not take his life.
23*b* [And they took off] the sleeved tunic that was on him,
25 and they lifted up their eyes and looked, and, behold, a travelling company of Ishmaelites came from Gilead, with their camels bearing tragacanth and balm and ladanum,
26 going to carry it down to Egypt. And Judah said unto his brethren, What profit is it if we slay our brother and
27 conceal his blood? Come, and let us sell him to the Ishmaelites, and let not our hand be upon him ; for he is our brother, our flesh. And his brethren hearkened unto
28*b* him, and sold Joseph to the Ishmaelites for twenty pieces
32 of silver. And they sent the sleeved tunic to their father ;
33*b* [and when Israel saw it he said,] Joseph is without doubt
35 torn in pieces. And all his sons and all his daughters rose up to comfort him ; but he refused to be comforted ; and he said, Nay, I will go down mourning to the lower regions to my son. So his father wept for him.

The Story of the Egyptian woman. How Joseph was tempted and unjustly imprisoned.

39 And Joseph was brought down to Egypt ; and an Egyptian bought him of the hand of the Ishmaelites,
2 which had brought him down thither. And Yahweh was with Joseph, and he was a prosperous man ; and he was
3 in the house of his master the Egyptian. And his master saw that Yahweh was with him, and that Yahweh made
4 all that he did to prosper in his hand. And Joseph found favor in his sight : and he made him overseer over his

house, and all that he had he put into his hand. And it 5
came to pass from the time that he made him overseer
in his house, and over all that he had, that Yahweh
blessed the Egyptian's house for Joseph's sake; and the
blessing of Yahweh was upon all that he had, in the
house and in the field. And he did not concern him- 6
self about anything in the house beside him, except
the bread which he himself ate. And Joseph was comely,
and well favoured. And it came to pass after these 7
things, that his master's wife cast her eyes upon Joseph;
and she said, Lie with me. But he refused, and said 8
unto his master's wife, Behold, my master doth not
concern himself about what is in the house beside
me, and he hath put all that he hath into my hand;
there is none greater in this house than I; neither hath 9
he kept back any thing from me but thee, because thou
art his wife: how then can I do this great wickedness,
and sin against God? And it came to pass, as she spake 10
to Joseph day by day, that he hearkened not unto her, to
lie by her. And it came to pass about this time, that he 11
went into the house to do his work; and there was none
of the men of the house there within. And she caught 12
him by his garment, saying, Lie with me: and he left his
garment in her hand, and fled, and got him out. And 13
it came to pass, when she saw that he had left his garment in her hand, and was fled forth, that she called 14
unto the men of her house, and spake unto them, saying,
See, he hath brought in an Hebrew unto us to mock us;
he came in unto me to lie with me, and I cried with a
loud voice: and it came to pass, when he heard that I 15
lifted up my voice and cried, that he left his garment by
me, and fled, and got him out. And she laid up his gar- 16
ment by her, until his master came home. And she spake 17
unto him according to these words, saying, The Hebrew
servant, which thou hast brought unto us, came in unto
me to mock me: and it came to pass, as I lifted up my 18
voice and cried, that he left his garment by me, and fled

19 out. And it came to pass, when his master heard the
words of his wife, which she spake unto him, saying,
After this manner did thy servant to me ; that his wrath

20 was kindled. And Joseph's master took him, and put
him into the prison : and he was there in the prison.

21 But Yahweh was with Joseph, and shewed kindness unto
him, and gave him favour in the sight of the keeper of

22 the prison. And the keeper of the prison committed to
Joseph's hand all the prisoners that were in the prison ;

23 and whatsoever they did there, he was the doer of it. The
keeper of the prison looked not to anything that was
under his hand, because Yahweh was with him ; and that
which he did, Yahweh made it to prosper.

.

The Story of the Butler's and Baker's dreams. How Joseph interpreted Pharaoh's dream and was made ruler of Egypt.

40—1 And the butler of the king of Egypt and his baker
offended their lord the king of Egypt, [and he cast them]

3 into the prison, the place where Joseph was bound.

5b [And each of them dreamed a dream,] the butler and the
baker of the king of Egypt, which were bound in the
prison. [And Joseph interpreted their dreams ; and as
he interpreted, so it came to pass. For unto the baker
he had said, Pharaoh will hang thee on a tree ; but unto
the butler he said, Pharaoh will restore thee to thine
office. But have me in remembrance, I pray thee, when
thou art delivered hence, for I was sold into bondage

15 unjustly,] and here also have I done nothing that they
should put me into the dungeon. [Yet the butler of the
king of Egypt forgat Joseph when he was restored.

41 And it came to pass thereafter that Pharaoh king of
Egypt dreamed a dream, and no man could interpret it.
Then did the king's butler remember Joseph, and told

14 Pharaoh. So Pharaoh sent for Joseph.] And they
brought him hastily out of the dungeon, [and he came

into Pharaoh's presence. And Pharaoh said unto Joseph, I have heard say of thee that thou canst interpret dreams. Behold, I saw in my dream, and lo, seven ears came up upon one stalk, full and good ; and, behold, seven ears, withered, thin and blasted with the east wind, came up after them ; and the thin ears swallowed up the good ears. And Joseph said, This is the interpretation of the dream. Behold there come seven years of great plenty throughout all the land of Egypt. And there shall arise after them seven years of famine,] and the plenty shall 31 not be noticed in the land by reason of that famine which followeth, for it shall be very grievous. Let Pharaoh 34*a* make [store-cities,] and let them lay up corn under the 35*b* hand of Pharaoh for food in the cities, and let them keep it. [. . .] And Pharaoh said unto Joseph, See, I have 41 set thee over all the land of Egypt. And Pharaoh took 42 off his signet ring from his hand, and put it upon Joseph's hand, and arrayed him in garments of byssus, and put a gold chain about his neck ; and he made him to ride in 43 the second chariot which he had ; and they cried before him, Abrech : and he set him over all the land of Egypt. And Pharaoh said unto Joseph, I am Pharaoh, and without 44 thee shall no man lift up his hand or his foot in all the land of Egypt. And Pharaoh called Joseph's name 45 Zaphenath-paneah ; and he gave him to wife Asenath the daughter of Poti-phera priest of On. And Joseph went 46*b* out from the presence of Pharaoh, and went throughout all the land of Egypt. And he gathered up all the food 48 of the seven years which were in the land of Egypt, and laid up food in the cities : the food of the field, which was round about every city, laid he up in the same. And the seven years of famine began to come, according 54*a* as Joseph had said. And when all the land of Egypt 55 was famished, the people cried to Pharaoh for bread : and Pharaoh said unto all the Egyptians, Go unto Joseph ; what he saith to you, do. And the famine was 56 over all the face of the earth : and Joseph opened all the storehouses, and sold unto the Egyptians; and the famine was sore in the land of Egypt.

How Joseph's brethren came to Egypt to buy corn.

42—5 And the sons of Israel came to buy among those that came: for the famine had reached the land of Canaan.

6 Now it was Joseph that sold to all the people of the land;

7 and Joseph saw his brethren, and he recognized them, but made himself strange unto them, and said unto them, Whence come ye? And they said, From the land of Canaan to buy food. [And* he asked them concerning their kindred, saying, Have ye a father or a brother? And they said unto him, My lord, we have a father, an old man, and a child of his old age, a little one; and his brother is dead, and he alone is left of his mother, and his father loveth him. And Joseph said unto them, Bring him down unto me, that I may set mine eyes upon him. And they said, My lord, the lad cannot leave his father: for if he should leave his father, his father would die. And he said unto them, Except your youngest brother come down with you, ye shall see my face no more. And Joseph commanded to fill their sacks with food, as much as they could carry, and to put every man's money in his sack's mouth. As soon as the morning was light, the men were sent away, they and their asses. And at evening they came to the lodging place.]

27 And as one of them opened his sack to give his ass provender in the lodging place, he espied his money; and,

28 behold, it was in the mouth of his sack. And he said unto his brethren, My money is returned; and, lo, it is even in my sack. [And† his brethren also opened their sacks, and, behold, every man's money was in the mouth of his sack, his money in full weight. And they came unto their father, and told him all that had befallen them.]

* Supplied from xliii. 7f and xliv. 18ff.
† Supplied from xliii. 21.

HOW JOSEPH'S BRETHREN CAME THE SECOND TIME, AND HE REVEALED HIMSELF TO THEM.

And the famine was sore in the land. And it came to **43** pass, when they had eaten up the corn which they had 2 brought out of Egypt, their father said unto them, Go again, buy us a little food. And Judah spake unto him, 3 saying, The man did solemnly protest unto us, saying, Ye shall not see my face, except your brother be with you. If thou wilt send our brother with us, we will go 4 down and buy thee food: but if thou wilt not send him, 5 we will not go down : for the man said unto us, Ye shall not see my face, except your brother be with you. And 6 Israel said, Wherefore dealt ye so ill with me, as to tell the man whether ye had yet a brother? And they said, 7 The man asked straitly concerning ourselves, and concerning our kindred, saying, Is your father yet alive? have ye [another] brother? and we told him according to the tenor of these words : could we in any wise know that he would say, Bring your brother down? And **42**—38 he said, My son shall not go down with you; for his brother is dead, and he only is left: if mischief befall him by the way in the which ye go, then shall ye bring down my gray hairs with sorrow to the grave. And **43**—8 Judah said unto Israel his father, Send the lad with me, and we will arise and go ; that we may live, and not die, both we, and thou, and also our little ones. I will be 9 surety for him ; of my hand shalt thou require him : if I bring him not unto thee, and set him before thee, then let me bear the blame for ever : for except we had lin- 10 gered, surely we had now returned a second time. And 11 their father Israel said unto them, If it be so now, do this ; take of the choice fruits of the land in your vessels, and carry down the man a present, a little balm, and a little honey, tragacanth and ladanum, pistachio-nuts and almonds : and take double money in your hand ; and the 12 money that was returned in the mouth of your sacks carry again in your hand ; peradventure it was an oversight :

13 take also your brother, and arise, go again unto the man.

15 And the men took that present, and they took double money in their hand, and Benjamin ; and rose up, and

16 went down to Egypt, and stood before Joseph. And when Joseph saw Benjamin with them, he said to the steward of his house, Bring the men into the house, and slay, and make ready ; for the men shall dine with me at noon.

17 And the man did as Joseph bade ; and the man brought

18 the men into Joseph's house. And the men were afraid, because they were brought into Joseph's house ; and they said, Because of the money that was returned in our sacks at the first time are we brought in ; that he may seek occasion against us, and fall upon us, and take us

19 for bondmen, and our asses. And they came near to the steward of Joseph's house, and they spake unto him at

20 the door of the house, and said, Oh my lord, we came

21 indeed down at the first time to buy food : and it came to pass, when we came to the lodging place, that we opened our sacks, and, behold, every man's money was in the mouth of his sack, our money in full weight : and we

22 have brought it again in our hand. And other money have we brought down in our hand to buy food : we

23 know not who put our money in our sacks. And he said, Peace be to you, fear not : your God, and the God of your father, hath given you treasure in your sacks : I had your

24 money. And the man brought the men into Joseph's house, and gave them water, and they washed their feet :

25 and he gave their asses provender. And they made ready the present against Joseph came at noon : for they

26 heard that they should eat bread there. And when Joseph came home, they brought him the present which was in their hand into the house, and bowed down them-

27 selves to him to the earth. And he asked them of their welfare, and said, Is your father well, the old man of

28 whom ye spake ? Is he yet alive ? And they said, Thy servant our father is well, he is yet alive. And they

bowed the head, and made obeisance. And he lifted up 29
his eyes, and saw Benjamin his brother, his mother's son,
and said, Is this your youngest brother, of whom ye
spake unto me? And he said, God be gracious unto thee,
my son. And Joseph made haste; for his heart did 30
yearn upon his brother: and he sought where to weep;
and he entered into his chamber, and wept there. And 31
he washed his face, and came out; and he refrained himself, and said, Set on bread. And they set on for him by 32
himself, and for them by themselves, and for the Egyptians, which did eat with him, by themselves: because
the Egyptians might not eat bread with the Hebrews;
for that is an abomination unto the Egyptians. And 33
they sat before him, the firstborn according to his birthright, and the youngest according to his youth: and the
men marvelled one with another. And he took [and 34
sent] messes unto them from before him: but Benjamin's
mess was five times so much as any of theirs. And they
drank, and were drunken with him.

And he commanded the steward of his house, saying, 44
Fill the men's sacks with food, as much as they can
carry, and put every man's money in his sack's mouth.
And put my cup, the silver cup, in the sack's mouth of 2
the youngest, and his corn money. And he did according to the word that Joseph had spoken. As soon as the 3
morning was light, the men were sent away, they and
their asses. Now when they were gone out of the city, 4
and were not yet far off, Joseph said unto his steward,
Up, follow after the men; and when thou dost overtake
them, say unto them, Wherefore have ye rewarded evil
for good? Why have ye stolen my silver cup? Is not 5
this it in which my lord drinketh, and whereby he indeed
divineth? ye have done evil in so doing. And he over- 6
took them, and he spake unto them these words. And 7
they said unto him, Wherefore speaketh my lord such
words as these? God forbid that thy servants should do
such a thing. Behold, the money, which we found in our 8

sacks' mouths, we brought again unto thee out of the
land of Canaan : how then should we steal out of thy
9 lord's house silver or gold? With whomsoever of thy
servants it be found, let him die, and we also will be my
10 lord's bondmen. And he said, Now also let it be according unto your words : he with whom it is found shall be
11 my bondman ; and ye shall be blameless. Then they
hasted, and took down every man his sack to the ground
12 and opened every man his sack. And he searched, beginning at the eldest, and leaving off at the youngest : and the
13 cup was found in Benjamin's sack. Then they rent their
clothes, and laded every man his ass, and returned to the
14 city. And Judah and his brethren came to Joseph's
house ; and he was yet there : and they fell before him
15 on the ground. And Joseph said unto them, What deed
is this that ye have done? know ye not that such a man
16 as I can indeed divine? And they said, What shall we
say unto my lord? what shall we speak? or how shall we
clear ourselves? God hath found out the iniquity of thy
servants : behold, we are my lord's bondmen, both we,
17 and he also in whose hand the cup is found. And he
said, God forbid that I should do so : the man in whose
hand the cup is found, he shall be my bondman ; but as
for you, get you up in peace unto your father.
18   Then Judah came near unto him, and said, Oh my
lord, let thy servant, I pray thee, speak a word in my
lord's ears, and let not thine anger burn against thy
19 servant : for thou art even as Pharaoh. My lord asked
his servants, saying, Have ye a father, or a brother?
20 And we said unto my lord, We have a father, an old man,
and a child of his old age, a little one ; and his brother is
dead, and he alone is left of his mother, and his father
21 loveth him. And thou saidst unto thy servants, Bring him
22 down unto me, that I may set mine eyes upon him. And
we said unto my lord, The lad cannot leave his father :
for if he should leave his father, his father would die.
23 And thou saidst unto thy servants, Except your youngest

brother come down with you, ye shall see my face no
more.   And it came to pass when we came up unto thy 24
servant my father, we told him the words of my lord.
And our father said, Go again, buy us a little food. 25
And we said, We cannot go down: if our youngest 26
brother be with us, then will we go down: for we may
not see the man's face, except our youngest brother be
with us.   And thy servant my father said unto us, Ye 27
know that my wife bare me two sons: and the one went 28
out from me, and I said, Surely he is torn in pieces; and
I have not seen him since: and if ye take this one also 29
from me, and mischief befall him, ye shall bring down
my gray hairs with sorrow to the grave.   Now therefore 30
when I come to thy servant my father, and the lad be not
with us; seeing that his life is bound up in the lad's life;
it shall come to pass, when he seeth that the lad is 31
missing, that he will die: and thy servant shall bring
down the gray hairs of thy servant our father with sorrow to the grave.   For thy servant became surety for 32
the lad unto my father, saying, If I bring him not unto
thee, then shall I bear the blame to my father for ever.
Now therefore, let thy servant, I pray thee, abide instead 33
of the lad a bondman to my lord; and let the lad go up
with his brethren.   For how shall I go up to my father, 34
and the lad be not with me? lest I see the evil that shall
come on my father.

Then Joseph could not refrain himself before all them 45
that stood by him; and he cried, Cause every man to go
out from me.   And he wept aloud, and the house of 2
Pharaoh heard.   And Joseph said unto his brethren, 4
Come near to me, I pray you.   And they came near.
And he said, I am Joseph your brother, whom ye sold
into Egypt.   And now be not grieved that ye sold me
thither.   [Go up now] and tell my father of all my glory 13
in Egypt, and of all that ye have seen, [and say to him,
Come down unto me], and thou shalt dwell in the land 10
of Goshen, and thou shalt be near unto me, thou, and thy
18

children, and thy children's children, and thy flocks, and
13*b* thy herds, and all that thou hast : and ye shall haste and
14 bring down my father hither. And he fell upon his
brother Benjamin's neck, and wept ; and Benjamin wept
upon his neck. [And the sons of Israel took their journey, and came unto their father, and told him all the
28 words of Joseph.] And Israel said, It is enough ; Joseph
my son is yet alive : I will go and see him before I die.

How Israel went down into Egypt.

46 And Israel took his journey with all that he had [to
28 go down into Egypt to Joseph]. And he sent Judah
before him unto Joseph, to Heroöpolis unto Goshen ;
29 and they came into the land of Goshen. And Joseph
made ready his chariot, and went up to meet his father,
to Goshen ; and he presented himself unto him, and fell
30 on his neck, and wept on his neck a good while. And
Israel said unto Joseph, Now let me die, since I have
31 seen thy face, that thou art yet alive. And Joseph said
unto his brethren, and unto his father's house, I will go
up, and tell Pharaoh, and will say unto him, My brethren,
and my father's house, which were in the land of Canaan,
32 are come unto me ; and the men are shepherds ; and they
have brought their flocks, and their herds, and all that
33 they have. And it shall come to pass, when Pharaoh
shall call you, and shall say, What is your occupa-
34 tion ? that ye shall say, Thy servants have been keepers
of cattle from our youth even until now, both we, and
our fathers : that ye may dwell in the land of Goshen ;
for every shepherd is an abomination unto the Egyptians.
47 Then Joseph went in and told Pharaoh, and said, My
father and brethren, and their flocks, and their herds,
and all that they have, are come out of the land of
Canaan ; and, behold, they are in the land of Goshen.
2 And from among his brethren he took five men, and pre-
3 sented them unto Pharaoh. And Pharaoh said unto his

brethren, What is your occupation?   And they said
unto Pharaoh, Thy servants are shepherds, both we,
and our fathers.   To sojourn in the land are we come; 4
for there is no pasture for thy servants' flocks; for
the famine is sore in the land of Canaan: now therefore, we pray thee, let thy servants dwell in the land
of Goshen.   [And Pharaoh said unto Joseph,] in the
land of Goshen let them dwell: and if thou knowest 6*b*
any able men among them, then make them rulers over
my cattle.   So Israel dwelt in the land of Goshen.   27

And there was no bread in all the land; for the famine 13
was very sore, so that the land of Egypt fainted by reason of the famine.   And Joseph gathered up all the 14
money that was found in the land of Egypt, for the corn
which they bought: and Joseph brought the money into
Pharaoh's house.   And when the money was all spent in 15
the land of Egypt, all the Egyptians came unto Joseph,
and said, Give us bread: for why should we die in thy
presence? for there is no more money.   And Joseph 16
said, Give your cattle; and I will give you for your
cattle, if there is no more money.   And they brought 17
their cattle unto Joseph: and Joseph gave them bread
in exchange for the horses, and for the flocks, and
for the herds, and for the asses: and he fed them with
bread in exchange for all their cattle for that year.
And when that year was ended, they came unto him 18
the second year, and said unto him, We will not hide
from my lord, how that our money is all spent; and the
herds of cattle are my lord's; there is nought left in the
sight of my lord, but our bodies, and our lands: where- 19
fore should we die before thine eyes, both we and our
land? buy us and our land for bread, and we and our
land will be servants unto Pharaoh: and give us seed,
that we may live, and not die, and that the land be not
desolate.   So Joseph bought all the land of Egypt for 20
Pharaoh; for the Egyptians sold every man his field,
because the famine was sore upon them: and the land

21 became Pharaoh's. And as for the people, he removed
   them to the cities from one end of the border of Egypt
22 even to the other end thereof. Only the land of the
   priests bought he not ; for the priests had a portion from
   Pharaoh, and did eat their portion which Pharaoh gave
23 them ; wherefore they sold not their land. Then Joseph
   said unto the people, Behold, I have bought you this
   day and your land for Pharaoh : lo, here is seed for you,
24 and ye shall sow the land. And it shall come to pass at
   the ingatherings, that ye shall give a fifth unto Pharaoh,
   and four parts shall be your own, for seed of the field,
   and for your food, and for them of your households, and
25 for food for your little ones. And they said, Thou hast
   saved our lives : let us find favor in the sight of my lord,
26 and we will be Pharaoh's servants. And Joseph made it
   a statute concerning the land of Egypt unto this day,
   that Pharaoh should have the fifth ; only the land of the
   priests alone became not Pharaoh's.

The Story of the Blessing of Israel. How Ephraim and Manasseh were received as tribes.

29   And the time drew near that Israel must die : and he
   called his son Joseph, and said unto him, If now I have
   found favor in thy sight, put, I pray thee, thy hand
   under my thigh, and deal kindly and truly with me ;
30 bury me not, I pray thee, in Egypt : but when I sleep
   with my fathers, thou shalt carry me out of Egypt, and
(50—5) bury me in [my grave which I have digged for me
   in the land of Canaan]. And he said, I will do as thou
31 hast said. And he said, Swear unto me : and he sware
   unto him. And Israel bowed himself upon the bed's
   head.
48—2*b* And Israel strengthened himself, and sat upon the
8*a*, 9*b* bed. And Israel beheld Joseph's sons. And he said,
   Bring them, I pray thee, unto me, and I will·bless them.
10 Now the eyes of Israel were dim for age, so that he
13 could not see. And Joseph took them both, Ephraim in

his right hand towards Israel's left hand, and Manasseh
in his left hand towards Israel's right hand, and brought
them near unto him.   And Israel stretched out his right 14
hand, and laid it upon Ephraim's head, who was the
younger, and his left hand upon Manasseh's head, crossing his hands; for Manasseh was the firstborn.   And 17
when Joseph saw that his father laid his right hand upon
the head of Ephraim, it displeased him : and he held up
his father's hand, to remove it from Ephraim's head unto
Manasseh's head.   And Joseph said unto his father, Not 18
so, my father: for this is the firstborn; put thy right
hand upon his head.   And his father refused, and said, 19
I know it, my son, I know it.

> He shall álso becóme a péople,
> And hé shall álso be gréat ;
> Nevertheléss his yóunger bróther
> Shall surpáss him in gréatness,
> And his séed be a fúlness of nátions.

[And Israel called his sons], and said: Gather your-**49**
selves together, that I may tell you that which shall befall you in the latter days.

> Assémble, and héar, sons of Jácob ;   2
> And héarken to Ísrael your fáther.

> Réuben, my fírstborn art thóu,   3
> My míght, and firstfrúits of my stréngth ;
> Pre-éminence of dígnity, pre-éminence of pówer.
> Wánton as wáter, thou shalt not háve the pre-émi-   4
>   nence,
> For thou moúntedst the béd of thy fáther,
> And defíledst his cóuch [. . .].*

> Símeon and Lévi are bréthren,   5
> Wéapons of víolence their (. . . ?)
> My sóul, come nót to their cóuncil,   6
> My glóry, join nót their assémbly.

* Vulgate, *Et maculasti stratum ejus.*

<blockquote>
For mén they sléw in their ánger,
And houghed óxen ín their self-wíll.
</blockquote>

7
<blockquote>
Cúrsed be their ráge, for its fiérceness,
And their wráth, for its crúelty :
I will divíde them in Jácob,
And scátter them in Israel.
</blockquote>

8
<blockquote>
Thée, Judah (Praise), thy bréthren shall práise ;
Thy hánd* be on the néck of thy fóes :
Thy fáther's sóns shall bow dówn to thee.
</blockquote>

9
<blockquote>
The whélp of a líon is Júdah,
From the préy art thou góne up, my són.
He coúches, he lies dówn like a líon,
Like a líoness; whó dares aróuse him ?
</blockquote>

10
<blockquote>
The scéptre shall nót pass from Júdah,
Nor the stáff from betwéen his féet,
Untíl he shall réach unto (. . . ?),
And tríbes not his ówn shall obéy him.
</blockquote>

11
<blockquote>
Bínding his áss to the víne,
And his cólt to the chóice of the vínes;
He shall wásh his gárments in wíne,
His róbe in the blóod of the grápe.
</blockquote>

12
<blockquote>
His éyes shall be réddened with wíne,
And his téeth shall be whíte with mílk.
</blockquote>

13
<blockquote>
Zébulun shall dwéll at the séa-beach,
And a béach for the shíps shall he bé ;
And his bórder shall bé upon Zídon.
</blockquote>

14
<blockquote>
A stróng-boned áss is Íssachar,
Knéeling betwéen the dúng-hills.
</blockquote>

15
<blockquote>
And he foúnd his résting-place góod,
And the lánd to be pléasant ;
So he bówed his shóulder to béar,
And becáme a sláve under táskwork.
</blockquote>

* Seemingly another play upon the name Judah, the Hebrew word for "hand" (*yad*) containing the same letters except the last. Cf. Dt. xxxiii. 7.

Dán (Judge) shall júdge his péople   16
As óne of the tríbes of Ísrael.
Let Dán be a snáke in the wáy,   17
An ádder in the páth,
Bíting the héels of the hórse,
So that báckward fálleth the ríder.

I awáit thy delíverance, O Yáhweh!   18

Gád, a crówd (*gedūd*) shall crówd (*gūd*) him,   19
But hé shall crówd on their réar.

Ásher, his bréad shall be fát,   20
And dáinties for kíngs he shall yíeld.

Náphtali ís a slim óak,   21
That séndeth forth góodly shóots.

A frúitful tree's (*phrath* for Ephrath?) óffshoot is 22
    Jóseph,
A frúitful trée by a foúntain ;
His bránches run óver the wáll.

The árchers have sórely besét him,   23
Shot át and harássed him.
But his bów abóde in stréngth,   24
And the árms of his hánds were made stróng
By the hánds of the Stróng One of Jácob,
By the árms (?) of the Róck of Ísrael.

By thy fáther's Gód who shall hélp thee,   25
By El-Sháddai, for hé shall bléss thee,
With bléssings of héaven from abóve,
Bléssings of th' abyss couched benéath,
Bléssings of bréasts and wómb.

Thy fáther's bléssings surpáss   26
The bléssings of th' áncient móuntains,
The wéalth of th' etérnal hílls :

> They shall bé on the héad of Jóseph,
> On the témples of the prínce 'mid his bréthren.

27   Bénjamin, a wólf that rávineth ;
> In the mórning devóuring the préy,
> And at éven divíding the spóil.

28 All these are the twelve tribes of Israel: and this is it
33 that their father spake unto them. And he gathered up
his feet into the bed [and gave up the ghost]

The Story of Israel's Death and Burial.

50   And Joseph fell upon his father's face, and wept upon
2 him, and kissed him. And Joseph commanded his servants the physicians to embalm his father: and the
3 physicians embalmed Israel. And forty days were fulfilled for him ; for so are fulfilled the days of embalming :
and the Egyptians wept for him threescore and ten days.
4 And when the days of weeping for him were past, Joseph
spake unto the house of Pharaoh, saying, If now I have
found favor in your eyes, speak, I pray you, in the ears
5 of Pharaoh, saying, My father made me swear, saying,
Lo, I die : in my grave which I have digged for me in
the land of Canaan, there shalt thou bury me. Now
therefore let me go up, I pray thee, and bury my father,
6 and I will come again. And Pharaoh said, Go up, and
7 bury thy father, according as he made thee swear. And
Joseph went up to bury his father : and with him went
up all the servants of Pharaoh, the elders of his house,
8 and all the elders of the land of Egypt, and all the house
of Joseph, and his brethren, and his father's house : only
their little ones, and their flocks, and their herds, they
9 left in the land of Goshen. And there went up with him
both chariots and horsemen : and it was a very great
10 company. And they came to the threshing-floor of Atad,
which is beyond Jordan, and there they lamented with a
very great and sore lamentation : and he made a mourn-

ing for his father seven days.   And when the inhabitants 11
of the land, the Canaanites, saw the mourning, they said,
This is a grievous mourning to the Egyptians : wherefore
the name of [the place] was called Abelmizraim (as if
Mourning (*ebel*) of the Egyptians), which is beyond Jordan.

And Joseph returned into Egypt, he, and his brethren, 14
and all that went up with him to bury his father, after he
had buried his father.

THE EPHRAIMITE PROPHETIC NARRATIVE E, CIRC. 750 B. C.

The Story of the Call of Abraham. How God brought the father of the Hebrews from beyond the River, and promised to make them a great nation.

. . . [Of old time the fathers dwelt beyond the River, even Terah the father of Abraham and the father of Nahor, and they served strange gods. And God took Abraham from beyond the River, and led him forth from his father's ·house unto Shechem in the land of Canaan.*] . . .

After these things God came unto Abraham in a **15**—1 vision, saying,

> Abraham, bé not afráid ;
> Í am a shiéld unto thée :
> Very gréat shall bé thy rewárd.

And Abraham said, Behold, to me thou hast given no 3*a* seed, and he that shall be possessor of my house is 2*b* Eliezer (?). And he brought him forth abroad, and said, 5 Look now toward heaven, and tell the stars, if thou be able to tell them : and he said unto him, So shall thy seed be.

The Story of Abraham and the Philistines. How Sarah was taken and restored.

And Abraham journeyed from thence toward the land 20 of the Negeb, and dwelt between Kadesh and Shur ; and he sojourned in Gerar. And Abraham said of Sarah his 2 wife, She is my sister : and Abimelech king of Gerar sent, and took Sarah. [But God suffered him not to touch her, for he smote Abimelech and his house with a great

* Supplied from Josh. xxiv. 2 ; Gen. xx. 13.

plague, and all the women of Abimelech's house were

3 barren.*] And God came to Abimelech in a dream of the night, and said to him, Behold, thou art but a dead man, because of the woman which thou hast taken ; for

4 · she is a man's wife. Now Abimelech had not come near her : and he said, Lord, wilt thou slay even a righteous

5 nation ? Said he not himself unto me, She is my sister ? and she, even she herself said, He is my brother : in the integrity of my heart and the innocency of my hands

6 have I done this. And God said unto him in the dream, Yea, I know that in the ·integrity of thy heart thou hast done this, and I also withheld thee from sinning against

7 me : therefore suffered I thee not to touch her. Now therefore restore the man's wife ; for he is a prophet, and he shall pray for thee, and thou shalt live : and if thou restore her not, know thou that thou shalt surely die,

8 thou, and all that are thine. And Abimelech rose early in the morning, and called all his servants, and told all these things in their ears : and the men were sore afraid.

9 Then Abimelech called Abraham, and said unto him, What hast thou done unto us? and wherein have I sinned against thee, that thou hast brought on me and on my kingdom a great sin ? thou hast done deeds unto me that

10 ought not to be done. And Abimelech said unto Abraham, What hadst thou in view, that thou hast done this thing ?

11 And Abraham said, Because I thought, Surely the fear of God is not in this place ; and they will slay me for my

12 wife's sake. (And moreover she is of a truth my sister, the daughter of my father, but not the daughter of my

13 mother ; and she became my wife :†) and it came to pass, when God caused me to wander from my father's house, that I said unto her, This is thy kindness which thou shalt shew unto me ; at every place whither we shall

14 come, say of me, He is my brother. And Abimelech

---

* Supplied according to vv. 6 and 17.

† Verse 12 is obviously parenthetic ; perhaps introduced by E into his material from apologetic motives.

took sheep and oxen, and gave them unto Abraham, and
restored him Sarah his wife. And Abimelech said, Be- 15
hold, my land is before thee: dwell where it pleaseth
thee. And unto Sarah he said, Behold, I have given thy 16
brother a thousand pieces of silver : behold, it is for thee
a covering of the eyes to all that are with thee ; and in
respect of all thou art righted (?). And Abraham prayed 17
unto God : and God healed Abimelech, and his wife,
and his maidservants ; and they bare children.

THE STORY OF ISAAC AND ISHMAEL. HOW HAGAR WAS DRIVEN OUT.

[And it came to pass after these things, that Sarah
conceived when she was old, and bare Abraham a
son.] And Sarah said, God hath prepared laughter 21—6
(from the same stem as Isaac) for me, [and she called his
name Isaac.] And the child grew, and was weaned : 8
and Abraham made a great feast on the day that Isaac
was weaned. And Sarah saw the son of Hagar the 9
Egyptian, which she had borne unto Abraham, playing
(from the same stem as Isaac). Wherefore she said unto 10
Abraham, Cast out this bondwoman and her son : for the
son of this bondwoman shall not be heir with my son,
even with Isaac. And the thing was very grievous in 11
Abraham's sight on account of his son. And God said 12
unto Abraham, Let it not be grievous in thy sight because of the lad, and because of thy bondwoman ; in all
that Sarah saith unto thee, hearken unto her voice ; for
in Isaac shall thy seed be called. And also of the son of 13
the bondwoman will I make a nation, because he is thy
seed. And Abraham rose up early in the morning, and 14
took bread and a skin of water, and gave it unto Hagar,
and put the child on her shoulder, and sent her away :
and she departed, and wandered in the wilderness of
Beer-sheba. And the water in the bottle was spent, and 15
she cast the child under one of the shrubs. And she 16
went, and sat her down over against him a good way off,

as it were a bow-shot: for she said, Let me not look upon the death of the child. Therefore did she sit down.

17 And the child lift up its voice, and wept. And God heard the voice of the lad: and the angel of God called to Hagar out of heaven, and said unto her, What aileth thee, Hagar? fear not; for God hath heard the voice of

18 the lad where he is. Arise, lift up the lad, and hold

19 him fast; for I will make him a great nation. And God opened her eyes, and she saw a well of water; and she went, and filled the bottle with water, and gave the

20 lad drink. And God was with the lad, and he grew; and he dwelt in the wilderness, and became an archer.

21 And he dwelt in the wilderness of Paran: and his mother took him a wife out of the land of Egypt.

The Story of the Wells of the Negeb. The Covenant at Beer-sheba.

[And Abraham departed from Gerar and dwelt in the valley of Gerar. And there Isaac's servants digged a well, and found running water. And the herdmen of Gerar strove with Abraham's herdmen, saying, The water is ours: and he called the name of the well Esek ("Contention"); because there they contended with him. And they digged another well, and they strove for that also; and he called the name of it Sitnah ("Enmity"). And he removed from thence, and digged another well; and for that they strove not. So he called the name of it Rehoboth ("Room"). And from thence he went up to Beer-sheba.*]

22 And it came to pass at that time, that Abimelech and Phicol the captain of his host spake unto Abraham, saying,

God is with thee in áll whatsoéver thou dóest;

23 Nów therefore swéar unto mé by Gód in this pláce, That thóu wilt not bréak faith with mé, nor my kíth and kín:

* Supplied in accordance with xxvi. 17–23 and xxi. 25.

Áfter my kíndness to thée thou shalt dó unto mé,
Ánd to the lánd wheréin thou hast dwélt.

And Abraham said, I will swear. And Abraham re- 24, 25
proved Abimelech because of the well of water, which
Abimelech's servants had violently taken away. And 26
Abimelech said, I know not who hath done this thing:
neither didst thou tell me, neither yet heard I of it, but
to-day. And Abraham took sheep and oxen, and gave 27
them unto Abimelech ; and they two made a covenant.
And Abraham set seven ewe lambs of the flock by them- 28
selves. And Abimelech said unto Abraham, What mean 29
these seven ewe lambs which thou hast set by themselves? And he said, These seven ewe lambs shalt thou 30
take of my hand, that it may be a witness unto me that
I have digged this well. And he called it Shibah 26—33
("Seven "): therefore the name of this city is Beer-sheba
unto this day.

And Abraham sojourned in the land of the Philis- 21—34
tines many days.

THE STORY OF THE MOUNT OF GOD(?). HOW GOD PROVED
ABRAHAM. THE SACRIFICE OF ISAAC.

And it came to pass after these things, that God did 22
prove Abraham, and said unto him, Abraham : and he
said, Here am I. And he said, Take now thy son, thine 2
only son, whom thou lovest, even Isaac, and get thee
into the land of (. . . . .), and offer him there for a
burnt offering upon one of the mountains which I will
tell thee of. And Abraham rose early in the morning, 3
and saddled his ass, and took his two young men with
him, and Isaac his son ; and he clave the wood for the
burnt offering, and rose up, and went unto the place of
which God had told him. On the third day Abraham 4
lifted up his eyes, and saw the place afar off. And 5
Abraham said unto his young men, Abide ye here with
the ass, and I and the lad will go yonder ; and we will

6 worship, and come again to you. And Abraham took the wood of the burnt offering, and laid it upon Isaac his son ; and he took in his hand the fire and the knife ; and
7 they went both of them together. And Isaac spake unto Abraham his father, and said, My father : and he said, Here am I, my son. And he said, Behold, the fire and the wood : but where is the lamb for a burnt offering?
8 And Abraham said, God will provide himself the lamb for a burnt offering, my son : so they went both of them
9 together. And they came to the place which God had told him of ; and Abraham built the altar there, and laid the wood in order, and bound Isaac his son, and laid him
10 on the altar, upon the wood. And Abraham stretched
11 forth his hand, and took the knife to slay his son. And the angel of God called unto him out of heaven, and said,
12 Abraham, Abraham : and he said, Here am I. And he said, Lay not thine hand upon the lad, neither do thou anything unto him: for now I know that thou fearest God, seeing thou hast not withheld thy son, thine only
13 son, from me. And Abraham lifted up his eyes, and looked, and behold, behind him a ram caught in the thicket by his horns : and Abraham went and took the ram, and offered him up for a burnt offering in the stead
14 of his son. And Abraham called the name of that place . . . ("God is provider?"), as it is said to this day, In
19 the Mount of God it shall be provided. So Abraham returned unto his young men, and they rose up and went together to Beer-sheba ; and Abraham dwelt at Beer-sheba.

The Story of Isaac.

20 And it came to pass after these things, that [Abraham sent and took a wife for Isaac his son from Aram Naharaim ; and her name was Rebekah, the daughter of Bethuel, the sister of Laban. And Bethuel was the son of Nahor, Abraham's brother.

And Abraham died, an old man, and full of years ; and Isaac his son buried him in Beer-sheba.   And Isaac dwelt in that land, and was fruitful.   And Rebekah bare Isaac two sons, at one birth.   And the firstborn was rough and hairy, and she called his name Esau, and the younger . . . and his name was called Jacob.]

THE STORY OF THE BLESSING OF ISAAC. HOW JACOB SUPPLANTED ESAU.

[And when Isaac was old,] he called Esau his elder 27—1 son, and said unto him, My son : and he said unto him, Here am I.   And he said, Behold now, I am old, I know 2 not the day of my death.   Now therefore make me sav- 4 oury meat, such as I love, and bring it to me, that I may eat ; that my soul may bless thee before I die.   And 5 Rebekah heard when Isaac spake to Esau his son.   [And she said to Jacob, Behold thy father hath called Esau to bless him ; for I heard him say,] make me savoury meat, 7 that I may eat, and bless thee before my death.   Now 8 therefore, my son, obey my voice according to that which I command thee.   Go now to the flock, and fetch 9 me from thence two good kids of the goats ; and I will make them savoury meat for thy father, such as he lov- eth : and thou shalt bring it to thy father, that he may 10 eat, so that he may bless thee before his death.   And 11 Jacob said to Rebekah his mother, Behold, Esau my brother is a hairy man, and I am a smooth man.   My 12 father peradventure will feel me, and I shall seem to him as a deceiver ; and I shall bring a curse upon me, and not a blessing.   And his mother said unto him, 13 Upon me be thy curse, my son : only obey my voice, and go fetch me them.   So he went, and fetched, and 14 brought them to his mother : and his mother made savoury meat, such as his father loved.   And she put the 16 skins of the kids of the goats upon his hands, and upon the smooth of his neck : and she gave the savoury meat 17

and the bread, which she had prepared, into the hand of
18 her son Jacob. And he came unto his father, and said,
21 My father : and he said, Here am I. And Isaac said unto
Jacob, Come near, I pray thee, that I may feel thee, my
22 son, whether thou be my very son Esau or not. And
Jacob went near unto Isaac his father ; and he felt him,
and said, The voice is Jacob's voice, but the hands are
23 the hands of Esau. And he discerned him not, because
his hands were hairy, as his brother. Esau's hands : so he
blessed him, [and said,]

28   Abúndance of déw, from the héavens thy Gód shall
            affórd thee,
       And the fátness of eárth [from benéath],
       With plénty of córn and wíne [. . . . .].
29   A lórd thou shalt bé to thy bréthren.
       To thée shall bow dówn all the sóns of thy móther.

30*b* And Jacob was yet scarce gone out from the presence
of Isaac his father, that Esau his brother came in from
31 his hunting. And he also made savoury meat, and
brought it unto his father. [And Isaac trembled very
exceedingly, and said, Who then is he that hath brought
me savoury meat, and I have eaten of all and blessed
him before thou camest? yea, he shall have the bless-
34 ing.] When Esau heard the words of his father, he
cried with an exceeding great and bitter cry, and said
unto his father, Bless me, even me also, O my father.
35 And he said, Thy brother came with guile, and hath
36*b* taken away thy blessing. And. he said, Hast thou not
37 reserved a blessing for me ? And Isaac answered and
said unto Esau, Behold, I have made him thy lord, and
all his brethren have I given to him for servants ; and
with corn and wine have I sustained him: and what then
38 shall I do for thee, my son ? And Esau said unto his
father, Is the blessing the only one thou hast, my father ?
bless me, even me also, O my father. And Esau lifted

up his voice, and wept.   And Isaac his father **answered** 39
and said unto him,

> Fár from the fátness of eárth hencefórth be thy
> dwélling,
> Fár from the déws of the héavens.
> Subsístence thou'llt gáin by thy swórd, subject stíll 40
> to thy bróther ;
> But, strúggling stíll to be frée,
> Shalt téar óff at léngth his yóke from thy shóulder.

And Esau said in his heart, The days of mourning for 41*b*
my father are at hand; then will I slay my brother
Jacob.   And the words of Esau her elder son were told 42
to Rebekah ; and she sent and called Jacob her younger
son, and said unto him, Behold, thy brother Esau, as
touching thee, doth comfort himself with the thought of
killing thee.   Now therefore, my son, obey my voice ; 43
and arise, flee thou to Laban my brother, to Haran ; 44
and tarry with him a few days, until thy brother's fury
turn away.

The Story of Bethel. How Jacob anointed the pillar there.

[So Jacob arose and fled.]   And he lighted upon 28—11
the [holy] place, and tarried there all night, because the
sun was set ; and he took one of the stones of the place,
and put it under his head, and lay down in that place to
sleep.   And he dreamed, and behold 'a ladder set up on 12
the earth, and the top of it reached to heaven : and behold
the angels of God ascending and descending on it.   And 17
he was afraid, and said,

> How dréadful a pláce is thís !
> Thís is naught élse than Gód's hóuse,
> And thís is the gáte of héaven.

And Jacob rose up early in the morning, and took the 18
stone that he had put under his head, and set it up for a

20 pillar, and poured oil upon the top of it. And Jacob
vowed a vow, saying, If God will be with me, and will
keep me in this way that I go, and will give me bread to
21 eat, and raiment to put on, so that I come again to my
22 father's house in peace, then shall this stone, which I
have set up for a pillar, be God's house (Beth-el): and of
all that thou shalt give me I will surely give the tenth
unto thee.

The Story of Jacob's Service with Laban. How Laban gave him Leah and Rachel to wife.

29   Then Jacob went on his journey, and came to the land
of the children of the east. [And he came to Laban his
14*b* mother's brother.] And he abode with him the space of
15 a month. And Laban said unto Jacob, Because thou art
my brother, shouldest thou therefore serve me for
16 nought? tell me, what shall thy wages be? And Laban
had two daughters: the name of the elder was Leah, and
17 the name of the younger was Rachel. And Leah's eyes
were weak; but Rachel was beautiful and well favoured.
18 And Jacob loved Rachel; and he said, I will serve thee
19 seven years for Rachel thy younger daughter. And
Laban said, It is better that I give her to thee, than that
20 I should give her to another man: abide with me. And
Jacob served seven years for Rachel; and they seemed
unto him but a few days, for the love he had to her.
21 And Jacob said unto Laban, Give me my wife, for my
22 days are fulfilled, that I may go in unto her. And
Laban gathered together all the men of the place, and
23 made a feast. And it came to pass in the evening, that
he took Leah his daughter, and brought her to him; and
25 he went in unto her. And it came to pass in the morning that, behold, it was Leah: and he said to Laban,
What is this thou hast done unto me? did not I serve
with thee for Rachel? wherefore then hast thou cheated
27 me? [And Laban said,] Fulfil the [festal] week of this

one, and we will give thee the other also for the service
which thou shalt serve with me yet seven other years.
And Jacob did so, and fulfilled her week: and he gave 28
him Rachel his daughter to wife. And he went in also 30
unto Rachel, and he loved Rachel more than Leah, and
served with him yet seven other years.

THE STORY OF THE RIVALRY OF LEAH AND RACHEL.
HOW THE PATRIARCHS WERE BORN AND NAMED.

[And Leah bare unto Jacob Reuben and Simeon, and
Levi and Judah.]

And when Rachel saw that she bare Jacob no children, **30**
Rachel envied her sister; and she said unto Jacob, Give
me children, or else I die. And Jacob's anger was kind- 2
led against Rachel: and he said, Am I in God's stead,
who hath withheld from thee the fruit of thy womb?
And she said, Behold my maid Bilhah, go in unto her; 3
that she may bear upon my knees: and Jacob went in 4*b*
unto her. And Bilhah conceived, and bare Jacob a son. 5
And Rachel said, God hath judged (*dan*) me, and hath 6
also heard my voice, and hath given me a son: therefore
called she his name Dan. And she conceived again, and 7
[bare a son]. And Rachel said, With wrestlings of God 8
have I wrestled (*niphtal*) with my sister, and have prevailed; and she called his name Naphtali. [And Leah
also gave her handmaid Zilpah to Jacob. And Zilpah
bare Gad and Asher. And Leah cried unto God.] And 17
God hearkened unto Leah, and she conceived, and bare
Jacob a fifth son. And Leah said, God hath given me my 18
hire (*sachar*), because I gave my handmaid to my husband:
so she called his name Issachar. And Leah conceived 19
again, and bare a sixth son to Jacob. And Leah said, 20
God hath endowed me with a good dowry (*zebed*); and
she called his name Zebulun. [And Rachel also cried
unto God.] And God hearkened to her. And she con- 22*b*
ceived, and bare a son: and said, God hath taken away 23
(*asaph*) my reproach: so she called his name Joseph.   24

The Story of Jacob's service with Laban. How God gave him the wealth of the Syrian.

26   [And Jacob said unto Laban,] Give me my wives and my children for whom I have served thee, and let me go: for thou knowest my service wherewith I have served
28   thee. And he said, Appoint me thy wages, and I will give it. [Whatsoever thou shalt ask me I will give, if thou wilt tarry] and keep [the flock. And Jacob said,]
32 I will pass through all thy flock to-day, removing from thence every speckled and spotted one, and every black one among the sheep, and the spotted and speckled
33 among the goats: and it shall be my hire. So shall my righteousness answer for me hereafter, when thou shalt come concerning my hire that is before thee: every one that is not speckled and spotted among the goats, and black among the sheep, that [if found] with me shall be counted stolen. [And Laban said, So let it be; the speckled shall be thy wages. So Jacob separated the flock, and he set the speckled and spotted by themselves for his own, and the white by themselves for Laban. But he set the faces of the white toward the speckled and
38*b* spotted in the flock of Laban,*] at the watering troughs where the flocks came to drink; for they rutted when they came to drink. [So all the flock bare speckled and spotted. And when Laban saw that all the flock bare speckled and spotted, he was very wroth, and said to Jacob, Thy wages are too much. Be content, and take the ringstraked and the black only. And Jacob said, I will serve thee for the ringstraked and the black. And again he separated the flock, and set the white and speckled by themselves for Laban, and the ringstraked
40*b* and the black by themselves for his own.] And he set the faces of the flocks toward the ringstraked and all the black in the flock of Laban. [So all the flock bare ringstraked and black.]

* Supplied from xxxi. 7-9.

The Story of Jacob's Return, and the Covenant at Gilead.

And Jacob beheld the countenance of Laban, and, 31—2
behold, it was not toward him as beforetime. And Jacob 4
sent and called Rachel and Leah to the field unto his
flock, and said unto them, I see your father's counten- 5
ance, that it is not toward me as beforetime; but the God
of my father hath been with me. And ye know that 6
with all my power I have served your father. And your 7
father hath deceived me, and changed my wages ten
times; but God suffered him not to hurt me. If he said thus, 8
The speckled shall be thy wages; then all the flock bare
speckled: and if he said thus, The ringstraked shall be
thy wages; then bare all the flock ringstraked. Thus 9
God hath taken away the cattle of your father, and given
them to me. And it came to pass at that time, that I 10
lifted up my eyes, and saw in a dream, ... and, 11
behold, the angel of God said unto me in the dream, Jacob:
and I said, Here am I. And he said, I am the God of Beth- 13
el, where thou anointedst a pillar, where thou vowedst a
vow unto me: now arise, get thee out from this land, and
return unto the land of thy nativity. And Rachel and 14
Leah answered and said unto him, Is there yet any portion or inheritance for us in our father's house? Are we 15
not counted of him strangers? for he hath sold us, and
hath also quite devoured the price paid for us. For all 16
the riches which God hath taken away from our father,
that is ours and our children's: now then, whatsoever
God hath said unto thee, do. Then Jacob rose up, and 17
set his sons and his wives upon the camels; and he car- 18
ried away all his cattle. Now Laban was gone to shear 19
his sheep: and Rachel stole the teraphim that were her
father's. And Jacob stole away unawares to Laban the 20
Syrian, in that he told him not that he fled. So he fled 21
with all that he had; and set his face toward the mountain of Gilead.

22 And it was told Laban on the third day that Jacob
23 was fled.   And he took his brethren with him, and pursued after him seven days' journey; and he overtook
24 him in the mountain of Gilead.   And God came to Laban
the Syrian in a dream of the night, and said unto him,
Take heed to thyself that thou speak not to Jacob either
26 good or bad.   And Laban said to Jacob:

> Whát hast thou dóne, that thou stólest awáy,
> And didst béar off my dáughters, as cáptives of the
> swórd?

28 Nor súfferedst me to kíss my sóns and my dáughters?
Nów hast thou ácted in fólly.

29 It is in the power of my hand to do you hurt: but the
God of your father spake unto me yesternight, saying,
Take heed to thyself that thou speak not to Jacob either
30 good or bad.   And now, if thou must by all means be
gone, because thou sore longedst after thy father's house,
32 yet wherefore hast thou stolen my gods?   And he said,
With whomsoever thou findest thy gods, he shall not
live: before our brethren discern thou what is thine
with me, and take it to thee.   For Jacob knew not that
33 Rachel had stolen them.   And Laban went into Jacob's
tent, and into Leah's tent; but he found them not.   And
he went out of Leah's tent, and entered into Rachel's
34 tent.   Now Rachel had taken the teraphim, and put
them in the camel's furniture, and sat upon them.   And
Laban felt about all the tent, but found them not.
35 And she said to her father, Let not my lord be angry
that I cannot rise up before thee; for the manner of
women is upon me.   And he searched, but found not the
36 teraphim.   And Jacob was wroth, and chode with Laban:
and Jacob answered, and said to Laban,

> Whát is my tréspass? whát is my sín?

37 That thóu hast pursúed me, and ránsacked my stúff?
Whát hast thou fóund of áll thy belóngings?

Sét it down hére before my kin and thy kin,
And théy shall be júdge betwéen us.

This twénty yéars I have béen with thée,   38
Thy éwes and thy shé-goats have nót cast their
  yóung ;
Nor éver a rám of thy flóck have I éaten.
The tórn of béasts I bróught not to thée: 39
Í bare its lóss ; of my hánd thou didst cláim it,
Whether stólen by dáy, or stólen by níght.

Thus wás I ; by dáy, consúmed of the héat,   40
By níght, of the fróst ; while my sléep fled mine éyes.
These twénty yéars have I béen in thy hóuse: 41
Foúrteen yéars I sérved for thy dáughters,
And síx years I sérved for thy flóck.
And thóu hast áltered my wáges ten tímes.

Bút for my fáther's Gód, God of Ábraham,   42
And hád not the Féar of Ísaac been wíth me,
Even now thou hadst sént me émpty awáy.
Mine afflíction, and tóil of my hánds God-hath séen,
And rebúked thee last níght.

And Jacob took a stone and set it up for a pillar. 45
And Laban [made a cairn and] called it Jegar-sahadutha 47
(In Aramaic, Cairn of Witness), but Jacob called it Gal-
eed (i. e. Gilead, as if = *gal éd*, Cairn of Witness in
Hebrew).   And Laban said to Jacob: 51

Behóld, and sée this cáirn,
Which Í have cast úp between mé and thée.
Wítness (*ed*) shall bé this cáirn (*gal*)   52
That Í pass not óver this cáirn unto thée,
And that thóu pass not óver to mé for hárm.
Abraham's Gód be júdge betwéen us.   53

And Jacob sware by the Fear of his father Isaac. And 54
Jacob offered a sacrifice in the mountain, and called his

brethren to eat bread: and they did eat bread, and
55 tarried all night in the mountain. And early in the morning Laban rose up, and kissed his sons and his daughters, and blessed them: and Laban departed, and returned unto his place.

The Story of Mahanaim and Peniel How Jacob met Esau again in peace.

32 And Jacob went on his way, and the angels of God
2 met him. And Jacob said when he saw them, This is God's host: and he called the name of that place Mahan-
13*a* aim (Two Hosts). And he lodged there that night. [And Jacob sent a gift unto Esau his brother from
3, 22 Mahanaim] unto the field of Edom. And he took [his household] and passed over the ford of Jabboq. [. . .]
30 And Jacob called the name of the place Peniel (Face of God): for, said he, I have seen God face to face, and my life is preserved. . . . . . .

[And, behold, Esau came to meet him, and when he
33—4*b* saw him,] he fell on his neck, and kissed him: and
5 they wept. And he lifted up his eyes, and saw the women and the children; and said, Who are these with thee? And he said, The children which God hath graciously given thy servant. [And Esau said, Wherefore hast thou sent me a gift. Keep that which is thine.
11 And Jacob said,] Take, I pray thee, my gift that is brought to thee; because God hath dealt graciously with me, and because I have abundance. And he urged him, and he took it.

The Story of the Pillar and Altar by Shechem.

18 So Jacob came in peace to Shechem, a city which is in the land of Canaan, and encamped before the city.
19 And he bought the parcel of ground, where he had spread his tent, at the hand of the children of Hamor,
20 Shechem's father, for an hundred *kesitas*. And he set up

a pillar there and called it El-elohe-Israel (God, the God
of Israel).

THE STORY OF THE CONQUEST OF SHECHEM. HOW JACOB AVENGED HIS DAUGHTER'S HONOR AND CONQUERED THE CITY.

And Dinah the daughter of Leah which she bare 34—1
unto Jacob, went out to see the daughters of the land.
[And Shechem the son of Hamor saw her,] and lay with 2
her.   And he spake comfortingly to the damsel.   And 3, 4
Shechem spake unto his father Hamor, saying, Get me
this damsel to wife.   And Hamor the father of Shechem 6
went out unto Jacob to commune with him.   And Hamor 8
communed with him, saying, The soul of my son Shechem longeth for your daughter : I pray you give her unto
him to wife.   And intermarry with us; give your 9
daughters unto us, and take our daughters unto you.
And ye shall dwell with us : and the land shall be before 10
you ; dwell and trade ye therein, and get you possessions
therein.   [And the sons of Jacob answered, and said,]
We cannot do this thing, to give our sister to one that is 14
uncircumcised ; for that were a reproach unto us : only 15
on this condition will we consent unto you : if ye will be
circumcised as we be; then will we give our daughters 16
unto you, and we will take your daughters to us, and we
will dwell with you, and we will become one people.
But if ye will not hearken unto us, to be circumcised ; 17
then will we take our daughter, and we will be gone.
And their words pleased Hamor.   And Hamor and 18, 20
Shechem his son came unto the gate of their city, and
communed with the men of their city, saying, These men 21
are peaceable with us; therefore let them dwell in the
land, and trade therein; for, behold, the land is large
enough for them ; let us take their daughters to us for
wives, and let us give them our daughters.   Only on this 22
condition will the men consent unto us to dwell with us,

to become one people, if we be circumcised, as they are

24 circumcised. And unto Hamor and unto Shechem his son hearkened all that went out of the gate of his city; all that went out of the gate of his city were circumcised.

25 And it came to pass on the third day, when they were sore, that [Jacob and his people] came upon the city all

27 unsuspecting, and slew them. The sons of Jacob came

28 upon the slain, and spoiled the city. They took their flocks and their herds and their asses, and that which was

29 in the city, and that which was in the field; and all their wealth, and all their little ones and their wives, took they captive.

The Story of the Altar at Bethel, and of the Oak of Deborah. How Jacob came to Bethel, and dwelt there.

35 And God said unto Jacob, Arise, go up to Bethel, and dwell there: and make there an altar unto God, who appeared unto thee when thou fleddest from the face of

2 Esau thy brother. Then Jacob said unto his household, and to all that were with him, Put away the strange gods that are among you, and purify yourselves, and change

3 your garments: and let us arise, and go up to Bethel; and I will make there an altar unto God, who answered me in the day of my distress, and was with me in the

4 way which I went. And they gave unto Jacob all the strange gods which were in their hand, and the rings which were in their ears; and Jacob hid them under the

5 oak which was by Shechem. And they journeyed: and a terror from God was upon the cities that were round about

6 them, and they did not pursue after Jacob. And Jacob came to Bethel, he and all the people that were with

7 him. And he built there an altar, and called the place El-beth-el (God of Bethel): because there God was revealed unto him, when he fled from the face of his

8 brother. And Deborah Rebekah's nurse died, and she

was buried below Bethel under the oak: and the name
of it was called Allon-bacuth (Oak of Weeping).

THE STORY OF THE PILLAR OF RACHEL'S TOMB.

And Rachel died, and was buried in the way to Eph- 19
rath. And Jacob set up a pillar upon her grave: the 20
same is the Pillar of Rachel's grave unto this day.

THE STORY OF JOSEPH. HOW HE DREAMED OF FUTURE THINGS, AND HOW, HIS BRETHREN PLOTTING AGAINST HIM, HE WAS STOLEN BY THE MIDIANITES.

Now Joseph was a lad, feeding the flock with his **37**—2
brethren: and Joseph brought the evil report of them
unto their father. And Joseph dreamed a dream, and 5
he told it to his brethren. And he said unto them, Hear, 6
I pray you, this dream which I have dreamed: for, be- 7
hold, we were binding sheaves in the field, and, lo, my
sheaf arose, and also stood upright; and, behold, your
sheaves came round about, and made obeisance to my
sheaf.

And his brethren said to him,   8

> Shalt thóu indeed réign over ús?
> Or shalt thóu have the rúle over ús?

And he dreamed yet another dream, and told it to his 9
brethren, and said, Behold I have dreamed yet a dream:
and, behold, the sun and the moon and eleven stars made
obeisance to me. And he told it to his father, and to his 10
brethren; and his father rebuked him, and said unto him,
What is this dream that thou hast dreamed? Shall I and
thy mother and thy brethren indeed come to bow down
ourselves to thee to the earth? And his brethren envied 11
him; but his father kept the saying in mind. [And it
came to pass after these things, that Jacob called Joseph,
and said unto him, Joseph.] And he said to him, Here 13*b*
am I. And he said to him, Go now, see whether it be 14
well with thy brethren, and well with the flock; and

bring me word again. [So Joseph went to find his

15 brethren.] And a certain man found him, and, behold, he was wandering in the field: and the man asked him,

16 saying, What seekest thou? And he said, I seek my brethren: tell me, I pray thee, where they are feeding

17 [the flock]. And the man said, They are departed hence: for I heard them say, Let us go to Dothan. And Joseph went after his brethren, and found them in Dothan.

19 And they said one to another, Behold, this dreamer

20 cometh. Come now therefore, and let us slay him, and cast him into one of the pits, and we will say, An evil beast hath devoured him: and we shall see what will

22 become of his dreams. And Reuben said unto them, Shed no blood; cast him into this pit that is in the wilderness, but lay no hand upon him: that he might deliver him out of their hand, to restore him to his father.

23 And it came to pass, when Joseph was come unto his brethren, that they stript Joseph of his coat, and they

24 took him, and cast him into the pit: and the pit was

25 empty, there was no water in it. And they sat down to

28 eat bread. And there passed by Midianites, merchantmen; and they drew and lifted up Joseph out of the pit,

29 and brought Joseph into Egypt. And Reuben returned unto the pit; and, behold, Joseph was not in the pit; and

30 he rent his clothes. And he returned unto his brethren, and said, The child is not; and I, whither shall I go?

31 And they took Joseph's coat, and killed a he-goat, and

32 dipped the coat in the blood; and they brought it to their father; and said, This have we found: know now

33 whether it be thy son's coat or not. And he knew it, and said, It is my son's coat; an evil beast hath devoured

34 him. And Jacob rent his garments, and put sackcloth upon his loins, and mourned for his son many days.

How Joseph was a slave in Egypt, and interpreted Pharaoh's dream.

36 And the Midianites sold him into Egypt unto Potiphar,

a eunuch of Pharaoh's, the chief executioner. And **39**—4*b* he ministered unto him. And he left all that he had in 6*a* Joseph's hand.

And it came to pass after these things, that Pharaoh **40**—2 was wroth against his two officers, against the chief of the butlers, and against the chief of the bakers. And he 3 put them in ward in the house of the chief executioner. And the chief executioner charged Joseph with them, 4 and he ministered unto them : and they continued a season in ward. And they dreamed a dream both of them, 5 each man his dream, in one night, each man according to the interpretation of his dream. And Joseph came in 6 unto them in the morning, and saw them, and, behold, they were sad. And he asked Pharaoh's officers that 7 were with him in ward in his master's house, saying, Wherefore look ye so sadly to-day ? And they said unto 8 him, We have dreamed a dream, and there is none that can interpret it. And Joseph said unto them, Do not interpretations belong to God? tell it me, I pray you. And the chief butler told his dream to Joseph, and said 9 to him,

> In my dréam, behóld, a víne was befóre me ;
> And ín the víne were three bránches :　　　　　　10
> And thís seemed to búd, its blóssoms shot fórth ;
> The clústers theréof ripened grápes.

And Pharaoh's cup was in my hand; and I took the 11 grapes, and pressed them into Pharaoh's cup, and I gave the cup into Pharaoh's hand. And Joseph said unto 12 him, This is the interpretation of it : the three branches 13 are three days ; within yet three days shall Pharaoh lift up thine head, and restore thee unto thine office : and thou shalt give Pharaoh's cup into his hand, after the former manner when thou wast his butler. But have 14 me in thy remembrance when it shall be well with thee, and shew kindness, I pray thee, unto me, and make mention of me unto Pharaoh, and bring me out of this house:

15 for indeed I was stolen away out of the land of the
16 Hebrews. When the chief baker saw that the interpretation was good, he said unto Joseph, I also was in
my dream, and, behold, three baskets of white bread
17 were on my head: and in the uppermost basket there
was of all manner of bakemeats for Pharaoh; and the
birds did eat them out of the basket upon my head.
18 And Joseph answered and said, This is the interpretation
19 thereof: the three baskets are three days; within yet
three days shall Pharaoh lift up thy head from off thee,
and shall hang thee on a tree; and the birds shall eat thy
20 flesh from off thee. And it came to pass the third day,
which was Pharaoh's birthday, that he made a feast unto
all his servants: and he lifted up the head of the chief
butler and the head of the chief baker among his serv-
21 ants. For he restored the chief butler unto his butlership
22 again; and he gave the cup into Pharaoh's hand: but he
hanged the chief baker: as Joseph had interpreted to
23 them. Yet did not the chief butler remember Joseph,
but forgat him.

41   And it came to pass at the end of two full years, that
Pharaoh dreamed: and, behold, he stood by the river.
2 And, behold, there came up out of the river seven kine,
well favoured and fat fleshed; and they fed in the reed-
3 grass. And, behold, seven other kine came up after them
out of the river, ill favoured and leanfleshed; and stood
4 by the other kine upon the brink of the river. And the
ill favoured and leanfleshed kine did eat up the seven
5 well favoured and fat kine. So Pharaoh awoke. And he
slept and dreamed a second time: and, behold, seven
ears of corn came up upon one stalk, rank and good.
6 And, behold, seven ears, thin and blasted with the east
7 wind, sprung up after them. And the thin ears swallowed up the seven rank and full ears. And Pharaoh
8 awoke, and, behold, it was a dream. And it came to pass
in the morning that his spirit was troubled; and he sent
and called for all the magicians of Egypt, and all the

wise men thereof : and Pharaoh told them his dream ;
but there was none that could interpret them unto Pharaoh. Then spake the chief butler unto Pharaoh, saying, 9
I do remember my faults this day : Pharaoh was wroth 10
with his servants, and put them in ward in the house of
the chief executioner, me and the chief baker : and we 11
dreamed a dream in one night, I and he ; we dreamed
each man according to the interpretation of his dream.
And there was with us there a young man, an Hebrew, 12
servant to the chief executioner ; and we told him,
and he interpreted to us our dreams ; to each man according to his dream he did interpret. And it came to 13
pass, as he interpreted to us, so it was ; I was restored
unto mine office, and he was hanged. Then Pharaoh sent 14
and called Joseph, and he shaved himself, and changed
his raiment, and came in unto Pharaoh. And Pharaoh 15
said unto Joseph, I have dreamed a dream, and there is
none that can interpret it : and I have heard say of thee,
that when thou hearest a dream thou canst interpret it.
And Joseph answered Pharaoh, saying, It is not in me : 16
God shall give Pharaoh an answer of peace. And Pha- 17
raoh spake unto Joseph, In my dream, behold, I stood
upon the brink of the river : and, behold, there came up 18
out of the river seven kine, fatfleshed and well favoured ;
and they fed in the reed-grass : and, behold, seven other 19
kine came up after them, poor and very ill favoured and
leanfleshed, such as I never saw in all the land of Egypt
for badness : and the lean and ill favoured kine did eat 20
up the first seven fat kine : and when they had eaten 21
them up, it could not be known that they had eaten
them ; but they were still ill favoured, as at the beginning. So I awoke. And I saw in my dream, and, behold, 22
seven ears came up upon one stalk, full and good : and, 23
behold, seven ears, withered, thin, [and] blasted with the
east wind, sprung up after them : and the thin ears swal- 24
lowed up the seven good ears : and I told it unto the
magicians ; but there was none that could declare it to

25 me. And Joseph said unto Pharaoh, The dream of Pharaoh is one : what God is about to do he hath declared
26 unto Pharaoh. The seven good kine are seven years ;
and the seven good ears are seven years : the dream is
27 one. And the seven lean and ill favoured kine that came
up after them are seven years, and also the seven empty
ears blasted with the east wind ; they shall be seven
28 years of famine. That is the thing which I spake unto
Pharaoh : what God is about to do he hath shewed unto
29 Pharaoh. Behold, there come seven years of great plenty
30 throughout all the land of Egypt : and there shall arise
after them seven years of famine ; and all the plenty
shall be forgotten in the land of Egypt ; and the famine
32 shall consume the land. And for that the dream was
doubled unto Pharaoh twice, it is because the thing is
established by God, and God will shortly bring it to pass.
33 Now therefore let Pharaoh look out a man discreet and
34 wise, and set him over the land of Egypt. And let him
appoint overseers over the land, and take up the fifth
part of the land of Egypt in the seven plenteous years.
35a And let them gather all the food of these good years that
36 come. And the food shall be for a store to the land
against the seven years of famine, which shall be in the
land of Egypt ; that the land perish not through the
37 famine. And the thing was good in the eyes of Pha-
38 raoh, and in the eyes of all his servants. And Pharaoh
said unto his servants, Can we find such a one as this, a
39 man in whom the spirit of God is ? And Pharaoh said
unto Joseph, Forasmuch as God hath shewed thee all
40 this, there is none so discreet and wise as thou : thou
shalt be over my house, and according unto thy word
shall all my people be ruled : only in the throne will I be
47 greater than thou. And in the seven plenteous years
49 the earth brought forth by handfuls. And Joseph laid
up corn as the sand of the sea, very much, until he left
50 numbering ; for it was without number. And unto
Joseph were born two sons before the year of famine

came. And Joseph called the name of the firstborn Man- 51
asseh (Making to forget): For, [said he,] God hath made
me forget all my toil, and all my father's house. And the 52
name of the second called he Ephraim (Fruitfulness):
For God hath made me fruitful in the land of my affliction. And the seven years of plenty, that was in the land 53
of Egypt, came to an end. And there was famine in all 54*b*
lands; but in all the land of Egypt there was bread. And 56*a*
the famine was over all the face of the earth. And all 57
countries came into Egypt to Joseph for to buy corn: because the famine was sore in all the earth.

How Joseph's dreams came to pass.

Now Jacob saw that there was corn in Egypt, and 42
Jacob said unto his sons, Why do ye look one upon another? And he said, Behold, I have heard that there is 2
corn in Egypt: get you down thither, and buy for us from
thence; that we may live, and not die. And Joseph's 3
ten brethren went down to buy corn from Egypt. But 4
Benjamin, Joseph's brother, Jacob sent not with his brethren. And Joseph was the governor over the land; and 6
Joseph's brethren came, and bowed down themselves to
him with their faces to the earth. And Joseph knew his 8
brethren, but they knew not him. And Joseph remem- 9*a*
bered the dreams which he dreamed of them; and he spake 7*b*
roughly with them; and said unto them, Ye are spies; to 9*b*
see the nakedness of the land ye are come. And they said 10
unto him, Nay, my lord, but to buy food are thy servants
come. We are all one man's sons; we are true men, thy 11
servants are no spies. And he said unto them, Nay, but 12
to see the nakedness of the land are ye come. And they 13
said, We thy servants are twelve brethren, the sons of one
man in the land of Canaan; and, behold, the youngest is
this day with our father, and one is not. And Joseph said 14
unto them, That is it that I spake unto you, saying, Ye
are spies: hereby ye shall be proved: by the life of Pha- 15
raoh ye shall not go forth hence, except your youngest

16 brother come hither. Send one of you, and let him fetch
your brother, and ye shall be bound, that your words may
be proved, whether there be truth in you : or else by the
17 life of Pharaoh surely ye are spies. And he put them
18 all together into ward three days. And Joseph said unto
19 them the third day, This do, and live ; for I fear God : if
ye be true men, let one of your brethren be bound in
your prison house ; but go ye, carry corn for the famine
20 of your houses : and bring your youngest brother unto
me ; so shall your words be verified, and ye shall not die.
21 And they did so. And they said one to another,

> We are vérily gúilty concérning our ·bróther,
> Ín that we sáw the distréss of his sóul,
> Whén he besóught us, and wé would not héar ;
> Thérefore is thís distréss come upón us.

22 And Reuben answered them, saying, Spake I not unto
you, saying, Do not sin against the child ; and ye would
not hear ? therefore also, behold, his blood is required.
23 And they knew not that Joseph understood them ; for
24 there was an interpreter between them. And he turned
himself about from them, and wept ; and he returned to
them, and spake to them, and took Simeon from among
25 them, and bound him before their eyes. Then Joseph
commanded to fill their vessels with corn, and to restore
every man's money into his sack, and to give them provision for the way : and thus was it done unto them.
26 And they laded their asses with their corn, and departed
29 thence. And they came unto Jacob their father unto the
land of Canaan, and told him all that had befallen them ;
30 saying, The man, the lord of the land, spake roughly
31 with us, and took us for spies of the country. And we
32 said unto him, We are true men ; we are no spies : we be
twelve brethren, sons of our father ; one is not, and the
youngest is this day with our father in the land of Ca-
33 naan. And the man, the lord of the land, said unto us,
Hereby shall I know that ye are true men ; leave one of

your brethren with me, and take [corn for] the famine of your houses, and go your way : and bring your young-est brother unto me : then shall I know that ye are no 34 spies, but that ye are true men : so will I deliver you your brother, and ye shall traffick in the land. And it 35 came to pass as they emptied their sacks, that, behold, every man's bundle of money was in his sack : and when they and their father saw their bundles of money, they were afraid ; and their heart failed them, and they turned 28*b* trembling one to another, saying, What is this that God hath done unto us? And Jacob their father said unto 36 them, Me have ye bereaved of my children : Joseph is not, and Simeon is not, and ye will take Benjamin away : all these things are against me.   And Reuben spake unto 37 his father, saying, Slay my two sons, if I bring him not to thee : deliver him into my hand, and I will bring him to thee again. [And Jacob said, If it be so, go, and Ben-jamin shall go with you,] and El-Shaddai give you 43—14 mercy before the man, that he may release unto you your other brother and Benjamin. And if I be bereaved of my children, I am bereaved.

[So the men departed, and came again to Joseph. And when Joseph saw Benjamin with them, his heart was moved toward his brethren, and he determined to make himself known to them.]

How Joseph revealed himself to his brethren.

And he brought Simeon out unto them [and sent away 23*b* all his servants]. And there stood no man with him, 45—1*b* while Joseph made himself known unto his brethren. And he wept aloud : and the Egyptians heard, and the 2 house of Pharaoh heard. And Joseph said unto his 3 brethren, I am Joseph ; doth my father yet live ? And his brethren could not answer him ; for they were troubled at his presence. [And Joseph saw that they remembered their fault, and were afraid, and he reassured them, and said, Be not troubled,] nor angry with yourselves, for 5*b*

6 God did send me before you to preserve life. For these
two years hath the famine been in the land : and there are
yet five years, in the which there shall be neither plowing

7 nor harvest. And God sent me before you to preserve
you a remnant in the earth, and to keep alive for you a

8 great survival. So now it was not you who sent me
hither, but God : and he hath made me a father to Pharaoh, and lord of all his house, and ruler over all the land

9 of Egypt. Haste ye, and go up to my father, and say
unto him, Thus saith thy son Joseph, God hath made me

11 lord of all Egypt : come down unto me, tarry not : and
there will I nourish thee ; for there are yet five years of
famine ; lest thou come to poverty, thou, and thy house-

12 hold, and all that thou hast. And, behold, your eyes see,
and the eyes of my brother Benjamin, that it is my

15 mouth that speaketh unto you. And he kissed all his
brethren, and wept upon them : and after that his brethren talked with him.

16   And the fame thereof was heard in Pharaoh's house,
saying, Joseph's brethren are come : and it pleased Pha-

17 raoh well, and his servants. And Pharaoh said unto
Joseph, Say unto thy brethren, This do ye ; lade your

18 beasts, and go, get you unto the land of Canaan ; and
take your father and your households, and come unto me :
and I will give you the good of the land of Egypt, and ye

21*b* shall eat the fat of the land. And Joseph gave them

22 wagons, and provision for the way. To all of them he
gave each man changes of raiment ; but to Benjamin he
gave three hundred pieces of silver, and five changes of

23 raiment. And to his father he sent after this manner ;
ten asses laden with the good things of Egypt, and ten
she-asses laden with corn and bread and victual for his

24 father by the way. So he sent his brethren away, and
they departed : and he said unto them, See that ye fall

25 not out by the way. And they went up out of Egypt,
and came into the land of Canaan unto Jacob their father.

26 And they told him, saying, Joseph is yet alive, and he is

ruler over all the land of Egypt. And his heart fainted, for he believed them not. And they told him all the 27 words of Joseph, which he had said unto them : and when he saw the wagons which Joseph had sent to carry him, the spirit of Jacob their father revived.

How Jacob came into Egypt.

And [Jacob] offered sacrifices unto the God of his 46—1b father Isaac. And God spake unto Jacob in the visions 2 of the night, and said, Jacob, Jacob. And he said, Here am I. And he said, 3

> Í am Gód, the Gód of thy fáther ;
> Féar thou nót to go dówn into Égypt,
> For Í will máke of thee thére a great nátion.

> Í will go dówn with thée into Égypt, 4
> And súrely I álso will bríng thee up thénce,
> And Jóseph shall clóse thine éyes in déath.

So Jacob rose up from Beer-sheba : [and went down 5 into Egypt to Joseph]. And Joseph nourished his father, and his brethren, and all his father's household with bread, according to the number of their little ones.

The Blessing of Jacob. How Ephraim and Manasseh
received a portion above their brethren.

And it came to pass after these things, that one said 48 to Joseph, Behold, thy father is sick : and he took with him his two sons, Manasseh and Ephraim. And one told 2 Jacob, and said, Behold, thy son Joseph cometh unto thee. [And Jacob saw Joseph and his sons,] and said, Who are these? And Joseph said unto his father, They are my 9 sons, whom God hath given me here. And he brought 10b them near unto him ; and he kissed them, and embraced them. And Jacob said unto Joseph, I had not thought 11 to see thy face : and, lo, God hath let me see thy seed also. And Joseph brought them out from between his 12

knees ; and he bowed himself with his face to the earth.
15 And he blessed Joseph, and said,

> The Gód before whóm my fáthers wálked, Ábraham
>   and Ísaac,
> The Gód who shépherded my from the fírst even
>   únto this dáy,
16 The Ángel who sáved me from évery évil, bléss the
>   láds ;
> And let my náme be námed on thém,
> And the náme of my fáthers, Ábraham and Ísaac ;
> A múltitude lét them becóme in the lánd.*

20 So he blessed them that day, saying, By thee shall
Israel bless, saying, God make thee as Ephraiin and as
21 Manasseh : and he set Ephraim before Manasseh. And
Jacob said unto Joseph, Behold, I die : but God shall be
with you, and bring you again unto the land of your
22 fathers. Moreover I have given unto thee one ridge
(Shechem) above thy brethren, which I took out of the
hand of the Amorite with my sword and with my bow.
50—15 And when Joseph's brethren saw that their father
was dead, they said, It may be that Joseph will hate us,
and will fully requite us all the evil which we did unto
16 him. And they sent a message unto Joseph, saying, Thy
17 father did command before he died, saying, So shall ye
say unto Joseph, Forgive, I pray thee now, the transgression of thy brethren, and their sin, for that they did unto
thee evil : and now, we pray thee, forgive the transgression of the servants of the God of thy father. And
18 Joseph wept when they spake unto him. And his brethren also went and fell down before his face ; and they
19 said, Behold, we be thy servants. And Joseph said unto
20 them, Fear not : for am I in the place of God ? And as
for you, ye meant evil against me ; but God meant it for
good, to bring to pass, as it is this day, to save much peo-

---

* Cf. the rendering of Prof. Briggs, *Biblical Study*, p. 269, and the remarks there
on the tristich, in illustration of which the above passage is cited.

ple alive. Now therefore fear ye not: I will nourish you 21 and your little ones.

And Joseph dwelt in Egypt, he, and his father's house: 22 And Joseph saw Ephraim's children of the third genera- 23 tion: the children also of Machir the son of Manasseh were born upon Joseph's knees. And Joseph said unto 24 his brethren, I die: but God will surely visit you, and bring you up out of this land unto the land which he sware to Abraham, to Isaac, and to Jacob. And Joseph 25 took an oath of the children of Israel, saying, God will surely visit you, and ye shall carry up my bones from hence. So Joseph died, being an hundred and ten years 26 old: and they embalmed him, and he was put in a coffin in Egypt.

2 4*a*. THIS IS THE GENEALOGY OF THE HEAVEN AND THE EARTH IN THE BEGINNING OF THEIR CREATION.

God created the heaven and the earth. And the earth 1–2 was waste and void; and darkness was upon the face of the abyss:* and the spirit of God was brooding upon the face of the waters. And God said, Let there be light: and 3 there was light. And God saw that the light was good: 4 and God divided the light from the darkness. And God 5 called the light Day, and the darkness he called Night. And there was evening and there was morning, one day.

And God said, Let there be a dome in the midst of the 6 waters, and let it be a partition between the different waters. And God made the dome, and divided the waters which 7 were under the dome from the waters which were above the dome: and it was so. And God called the dome 8 Heaven.† And there was evening and there was morning, a second day.

And God said, Let the waters under the heaven be 9 gathered together unto one place, and let the dry land appear: and it was so. And God called the dry land 10 Earth; and the gathering together of the waters called

---

*Heb. *tehom*, a technical term for the primeval ocean or *hulē* filling all space. Cf. Appendix I. Babylonian creation tablet. After the platform earth had been founded on its "pillars" (I Sam. ii. 8) and the dome of heaven erected upon it, this *tehom* is thereby divided into two parts (vs. 6f), "the waters which are above the dome," perhaps the same as "the River of God which is full of water" Ps. lxv. 9, whose floods stream down when "the windows of heaven are opened" Gen. vii. 11; and the waters which are "under the earth" (Ex. xx. 4) and which well up in fountains, streams and bodies of water (Gen. xlix. 25), or overwhelm the earth when the sluice-gates that control it are "broken up" (Gen. vii. 11; Job xxxviii. 8–11.)

†Were only the derivation from "heave" admissible! In the Egyptian cosmogony the deity Shu "heaves" up the vaulted roof over earth. "Dome" suggests a hemispherical idea not in the Hebrew word here used, but presents the conception better than "expanse" or "firmament." Cf. Job xxii. 14; xxvi. 8ff; xxxvii. 18.

315)

11 he Seas: and God saw that it was good. And God said,
Let the earth put forth verdure, herb yielding seed, and
fruit tree bearing fruit after its kind, wherein is the seed
12 thereof, upon the earth: and it was so. And the earth
brought forth verdure, herb yielding seed after its kind,
and tree bearing fruit, wherein is the seed thereof, after
13 its kind: and God saw that it was good. And there was
evening and there was morning, a third day.

14　And God said, Let there be lights in the dome of the
heaven to divide the day from the night; and let them be
for [calendar?] signs, and for [the reckoning of] sacred
15 seasons, and for days and years: and let them be for lights
in the dome of the heaven to give light upon the earth:
16 and it was so. And God made the two great lights: the
greater light to rule the day, and the lesser light to rule
17 the night: also the stars. And God set them in the dome
18 of the heaven to give light upon the earth, and to rule over
the day and over the night, and to divide the light from the
19 darkness: and God saw that it was good. And there was
evening and there was morning, a fourth day.

20　And God said, Let the waters swarm with swarms of
living creatures, and let fowl fly above the earth in the
21 open dome of heaven. And God created the great sea-
monsters, and every living creature that stirreth, which
the waters swarmed with, after their kinds, and every
winged fowl after its kind: and God saw that it was good.
22 And God blessed them, saying, Be fruitful, and multiply
and fill the waters in the seas, and let fowl multiply in
23 the earth. And there was evening and there was morning, a fifth day.

24　And God said, Let the earth bring forth the living creature after its kind, cattle and creeping thing and wild
25 beast of the earth after its kind: and it was so. And God
made the wild beast of the earth after its kind, and the
cattle after their kind, and every thing that creepeth upon
the ground after its kind: and God saw that it was good.
26 And God said, Let us make man in our image, after our

likeness: and let them have dominion over the fish of the sea, and over the fowl of the air, and over the cattle, and over every wild beast of the earth, and over every creeping thing that creepeth upon the earth. And God created 27 man in his own image, in the image of God created he him ; male and female created he them. And God blessed 28 them : and God said unto them, Be fruitful and multiply and replenish the earth and subdue it ; and have dominion over the fish of the sea and over the fowl of the air and over every living thing that creepeth upon the earth. And God said, Behold, I give you every herb yielding 29 seed, which is upon the face of all the earth, and every tree in which is the fruit of a tree yielding seed ; to you it shall be for meat : and to every beast of the earth and 30 to every fowl of the air and to every thing that creepeth upon the earth, wherein there is life, I give every green herb for meat : and it was so. And God saw every thing 31 that he had made, and behold, it was very good. And there was evening and there was morning, the sixth day.

So the heaven and the earth were finished, and all the 2 host of them. And on the seventh day God finished his 2 work which he had made ; and he rested on the seventh day from all his work which he had made. And God 3 blessed the seventh day, and hallowed it : because that in it he rested from all his work which God had made and [so] created.

5 1. THIS IS THE BOOK OF THE GENEALOGY OF ADAM.

In the day that God created man, in the likeness of God made he him ; male and female created he them ; and 2 blessed them, and called their name Adam, in the day when they were created.

And Adam lived   -   -   -   -   -   130 years
· and begat a son in his own likeness, after his
image ; and called his name Seth : and the days   4
of Adam after he begat Seth were   -   -   **800** years
and he begat sons and daughters.   And all the   5

days that Adam lived were -   -   -   -   **930** years
and he died.

6   And Seth lived   -   -   -   -   -   105 years
7 and begat Enosh : and Seth lived after he begat
Enosh -   -   -   -   -   -   -   **807** years
8 and begat sons and daughters : and all the days
of Seth were   -   -   -   -   -   -   **912** years
and he died.

9   And Enosh lived   -   -   -   -   -   90 years
10 and begat Kenan : and Enosh lived after he
begat Kenan   -   -   -   -   -   -   **815** years
11 and begat sons and daughters : and all the days
of Enosh were   -   -   -   -   -   -   **905** years
and he died.

12   And Kenan lived   -   -   -   -   -   70 years
13 and begat Mahalalel : and Kenan lived after he
begat Mahalalel   -   -   -   -   -   **840** years
14 and begat sons and daughters : and all the days
of Kenan were   -   -   -   -   -   -   **910** years
and he died.

15   And Mahalalel lived   -   -   -   -   65 years
16 and begat Jared : and Mahalalel lived after he
begat Jared   -   -   -   -   -   -   **830** years
17 and begat sons and daughters : and all the days
of Mahalalel were   -   -   -   -   -   **895** years
and he died.

18   And Jared lived   -   -   -   -   -   62 years*
19 and begat Enoch : and Jared lived after he
begat Enoch   -   -   -   -   -   -   **785** years
20 and begat sons and daughters : and all the days
of Jared were   -   -   -   -   -   -   **847** years
and he died.

21   And Enoch lived   -   -   -   -   -   65 years
22 and begat Methuselah : and Enoch walked with
God after he begat Methuselah   -   -   -   **300** years
23 and begat sons and daughters : and all the days

* In vv. 18ff the Sam. is followed. See p. 108, note.

of Enoch were   -   -   -   -   -   -   **365** years

and Enoch walked with God: and he was not;   24
for God took him.

And Methuselah lived   -   -   -   -   **67** years 25
and begat Lamech: and Methuselah lived after   26
he begat Lamech   -   -   -   -   -   **653** years
and begat sons and daughters: and all the days   27
of Methuselah were   -   -.   -   -   -   **720** years
and he died.

And Lamech lived   -   -   -   -   -   **53** years 28
and begat [Noah].   And Lamech lived after he   30
begat Noah -   -   -   -   -   -   -   **600** years
and begat sons and daughters: and all the days   31
of Lamech were   -   -   -   -   -   -   **653** years
and he died.

And Noah was -   -   -   -   -   -   **500** years 32
old: and Noah begat Shem, Ham, and Japheth.

6 9. THIS IS THE GENEALOGY OF NOAH.

Noah was a righteous man, blameless in his generation:
Noah walked with God.   And Noah begat three sons, 10
Shem, Ham and Japheth.

Now the earth grew corrupt before God, and the earth 11
became filled with violence.   And God saw the earth, and, 12
behold, it was corrupt; for all flesh had turned to corrupt
ways upon the earth.

And God said unto Noah, I have determined to make an 13
end of all flesh; for the earth is filled with their violence;
and behold, I will destroy them from off the earth.   Make 14
thee an ark of gopher wood; thou shalt make the ark of
compartments, and shalt pitch it within and without with
pitch.   And this is how thou shalt make it: the length of 15
the ark three hundred cubits, the breadth of it fifty cubits,
and the height of it thirty cubits.   Thou shalt make a light 16
for the ark at the top and shall finish it [accurately] to a
cubit; and the door of the ark shalt thou set in the side
thereof; with lower, second, and third stories shalt thou

17 make it. And I, behold, I do bring the flood upon the
earth, to destroy all flesh, wherein is the breath of life,
from under heaven ; every thing that is in the earth shall
18 expire. But I will establish my covenant with thee ; and
thou shalt come into the ark, thou, and thy sons, and thy
19 wife, and thy sons' wives with thee. And of every living
thing of all flesh, two of every sort shalt thou bring into
the ark, to keep them alive with thee ; they shall be male
20 and female. Of the fowl after their kind, and of the cattle after their kind, of every creeping thing of the ground
after its kind, two of every sort shall come unto thee, to
21 keep them alive. And take thou unto thee of all food that
is eaten, and gather it to thee ; and it shall be for food for
22 thee, and for them. Thus did Noah ; according to all that
God commanded him, so did he.
7—6   And Noah was six hundred years old when the flood
11 was upon the earth. In the six hundredth year of Noah's
life, in the second month, on the seventeenth day of the
month, on the same day all the sluicegates of the abyss
were broken up and the windows of the heaven were
13 opened. In the selfsame day entered Noah and Shem
and Ham and Japheth, the sons of Noah, and Noah's
wife, and the three wives of his sons with them, into the
14 ark ; they, and every wild beast after its kind, and all the
cattle after their kind, and every creeping thing that
creepeth upon the earth after its kind, and every fowl
15 after its kind, every bird of every sort. And they went
in unto Noah into the ark, two and two of all flesh
16 wherein is the breath of life. And they that went in,
went in male and female of all flesh, as God commanded
17-18 him : And the flood came upon the earth. And the
waters prevailed, and increased greatly upon the earth ;
19 and the ark went upon the face of the waters. And the
waters prevailed exceedingly upon the earth ; and all the
high mountains that were under the whole heaven were
20 covered. Fifteen cubits upward did the waters prevail ;
21 and the mountains were covered. And all flesh expired

that moved upon the earth, both fowl, and cattle, and beast, and every creeping thing that creepeth upon the earth, and every man : And the waters prevailed upon the earth 24 an hundred and fifty days.

And God remembered Noah and all the living crea- 8 tures, and all the cattle that were with him in the ark : and God made a wind to pass over the earth, and the waters assuaged : The sluicegates of the abyss and the openings 2 of the heaven were stopped : and after the end of the one 3 hundred and fifty days the waters began to decrease. And the ark rested in the seventh month, on the seven- 4 teenth day of the month, upon the mountains of Ararat. And the waters decreased continually until the tenth 5 month : in the tenth month, on the first day of the month, were the tops of the mountains seen. And it came to pass 13 in the six hundred and first year, in the first month, the first day of the month, the waters were dried up from off the earth ; And in the second month, on the seven and 14 twentieth day of the month, was the earth dry.

And God spake unto Noah, saying, Go forth of the 15-16 ark, thou, and thy wife, and thy sons, and thy sons' wives with thee. Bring forth with thee every living thing that is 17 with thee of all flesh, both fowl, and cattle, and every creeping thing that creepeth upon the earth ; that they may breed abundantly in the earth, and be fruitful, and multiply upon the earth. And Noah went forth, and his sons, and 18 his wife, and his sons' wives with him : every beast, every 19 creeping thing, and every fowl, whatsoever stirreth upon the earth, after their families, went forth out of the ark. And God blessed Noah and his sons, and said unto them, 9 Be fruitful, and multiply, and replenish the earth. And 2 the fear of you and the dread of you shall be upon every beast of the earth, and upon every fowl of the air : with all wherewith the ground teemeth, and all the fishes of the sea, into your hand are they delivered. Every moving 3 thing that liveth shall be food for you ; in like manner with the green herb have I given you all. But flesh with 4

the life thereof, which is the blood thereof, shall ye not eat.
5 And surely your blood, the blood of your lives, will I require ; at the hand of every beast will I require it : and at the hand of man, even at the hand of every man's
6 brother, will I require the life of man. Whoso sheddeth man's blood, by man shall his blood be shed : for in the
7 image of God made he man. And you, be ye fruitful, and multiply ; bring forth abundantly in the earth, and multiply therein.

8   And God spake unto Noah, and to his sons with him,
9 saying, And I, behold, I establish my covenant with you,
10 and with your seed after you ; and with every living creature that is with you, the fowl, the cattle, and every wild beast of the earth with you ; of all that go out of
11 the ark, even every wild beast of the earth. And I will establish my covenant with you, that all flesh shall not be cut off any more by the waters of the flood ; neither shall there any more be a flood to destroy the earth.
12 And God said, This is the token of the covenant which I make between me and you and every living creature
13 that is with you, for perpetual generations : I do set my bow in the cloud, and it shall be for a token of the
14 covenant between me and the earth. And it shall come to pass, when I bring a cloud over the earth, and the bow
15 shall be seen in the cloud, that I will remember my covenant, which is between me and you and every living creature of all flesh ; and the waters shall no more become a
16 flood to destroy all flesh. And the bow shall be in the cloud, so that when I look upon it I may remember the everlasting covenant between God and every living crea-
17 ture of all flesh that is upon the earth. And God said unto Noah, This is the token of the covenant which I have established between me and all flesh that is upon the earth.
28   And Noah lived after the flood   -   -   350 years.
29 And all the days of Noah were   -   -   **950** years and he died.

10—1 NOW THIS IS THE GENEALOGY OF THE SONS OF NOAH, SHEM, HAM AND JAPHETH.

The sons of Japheth :   2
    Gomer, and Magog, and Madai, and Javan, and Tubal, and Meshech, and Tiras.

And the sons of Gomer :   3
    Ashkenaz, and Riphath, and Togarmah.

And the sons of Javan :   4
    Elishah, and Tarshish, Kittim, and Rodanim.

Of these were the coast-lands of the Goiim divided in their lands.

[These are the sons of Japheth] every one after his tongue ; after their families, in their nations.

And the sons of Ham ;   6
    Cush, and Mizraim, and Put, and Canaan.

And the sons of Cush ;   7
    Seba, and Havilah, and Sabtah, and Raamah, and Sabteca.

And the sons of Raamah ;   8
    Sheba, and Dedan.

These are the sons of Ham, after their families, after 20 their tongues, in their lands, in their nations.

The sons of Shem ;   22
    Elam, and Asshur, and Arpachshad, and Lud, and Aram.

And the sons of Aram ;   23
    Uz, and Hul, and Gether, and Mash.

These are the sons of Shem, after their families, after 31 their tongues, in their lands, after their nations.

These are the families of the sons of Noah, after their 32 generations, in their nations : and from these the nations branched out in the earth after the flood.

11—10 THIS IS THE GENEALOGY OF SHEM.

Shem was   -   -   -   -   -   -   100 years old, and begat Arpachshad : and Shem lived   11

	after he begat Arpachshad	-	-	-	500 years
	and begat sons and daughters.				
12	And Arpachshad lived	-	-	-	35 years
13	and begat Shelah : and Arpachshad lived after				
	he begat Shelah	-	-	-	403 years
	and begat sons and daughters.				
14	And Shelah lived	-	-	-	30 years
15	and begat Eber : and Shelah lived after he begat				
	Eber	-	-	-	403 years
	and begat sons and daughters.				
16	And Eber lived	-	-	-	34 years
17	and begat Peleg and Eber lived after he begat				
	Peleg	-	-	-	430 years
	and begat sons and daughters.				
18	And Peleg lived	-	-	-	30 years
19	and begat Reu : and Peleg lived after he begat				
	Reu	-	-	-	209 years
	and begat sons and daughters.				
20	And Reu lived	-	-	-	32 years
21	and begat Serug : and Reu lived after he begat				
	Serug	-	-	-	207 years
	and begat sons and daughters.				
22	And Serug lived	-	-	-	30 years
23	and begat Nahor : and Serug lived after he be-				
	gat Nahor	-	-	-	200 years
	and begat sons and daughters.				
24	And Nahor lived	-	-	-	29 years
25	and begat Terah : and Nahor lived after he be-				
	gat Terah	-	-	-	119 years
	and begat sons and daughters.				
26	And Terah lived	-	-	-	70 years
	and begat Abram, Nahor, and Haran.				

27 Now this is the Genealogy of Terah.

Terah begat Abram, Nahor and Haran : and Haran be-
31 gat Lot.   And Terah took Abram his son, and Lot the
son of Haran, his son's son, and Sarai his daughter-in-law,

his son Abram's wife, and went forth with them from Ur of the Chaldees, to go into the land of Canaan : and they came unto Haran, and dwelt there.

And the days of Terah were -   -   -   205 years 32 and Terah died in Haran.

And Abram took Sarai his wife, and Lot his brother's 12—5a son, and all their substance that they had gathered, and the souls that they had gotten in Haran ; and they went forth to go into the land of Canaan ; and Abram was 4b seventy and five years old when he departed out of Haran.

And they came into the land of Canaan.   5b

And the land was not able to bear them, that they 13—6 might dwell together : for their substance was great. And 11b they separated themselves the one from the other ; Abram 12 dwelled in the land of Canaan, and Lot dwelled in the cities of the Plain.

And it came to pass, when God destroyed the 19—29 cities of the Plain, that God remembered Abram, and sent Lot out of the midst of the overthrow, when he overthrew the cities in the which Lot dwelt.

Now Sarai Abram's wife bare him no children, and 16—1, 3 Sarai Abram's wife took Hagar the Egyptian, her handmaid, after Abram had dwelt ten years in the land of Canaan, and gave her to Abram her husband to be his wife. And Hagar bare Abram a son : and Abram called 15 the name of his son, which Hagar bare, Ishmael. And 16 Abram was fourscore and six years old, when Hagar bare Ishmael to Abram.

And when Abram was ninety years old and nine God 17 appeared to Abram, and said unto him, I am El-Shaddai ; walk before me, and thou shalt be perfect. And I will 2 make my covenant between me and thee, and will multiply thee exceedingly. And Abram fell on his face : and 3 God talked with him, saying, As for my part, behold, my 4 covenant with thee is that thou shalt be the father of a multitude of nations. Neither shall thy name any more 5 be called Abram, but thy name shall be Abraham (as if—

"Father of a multitude ") ; for the father of a multitude of
6 nations do I make thee.   And I will make thee exceeding
fruitful, and I will make nations of thee, and kings shall
7 come out of thee.   And I will establish my covenant between me and thee and thy seed after thee throughout
their generations for an everlasting covenant, to be a God
8 unto thee and to thy seed after thee.   And I will give unto thee, and to thy seed after thee, the land of thy sojournings, all the land of Canaan, for an everlasting possession ;
and I will be their God.

9   And God said unto Abraham, And as for thy part, thou
shalt keep my covenant, thou, and thy seed after thee
10 throughout their generations.   This is my covenant, which
ye shall keep, between me and you and thy seed after thee ;
11 every male among you shall be circumcised.   And ye shall
be circumcised in the flesh of your foreskin ; and it shall
12 be a token of a covenant betwixt me and you.   And he
that is eight days old shall be circumcised among you,
every male throughout your generations, he that is born
in the house, or bought with money of any stranger, which
13 is not of thy seed.   He that is born in thy house, and he
that is bought with thy money, must needs be circumcised :
and my covenant shall be in your flesh for an everlasting
14 covenant.   And the uncircumcised male who is not circumcised in the flesh of his foreskin, that soul shall be cut
off from his people ; he hath broken my covenant.

15   And God said unto Abraham, As for Sarai thy wife, thou
shalt not call her name Sarai, but Sarah (i. e. "Princess")
16 shall her name be.   And I will bless her, and moreover I
will give thee a son of her : yea, I will bless her, and she
shall be a mother of nations ; kings of people shall be of
17 her.   Then Abraham fell upon his face, and laughed, and
said in his heart, Shall a child be born unto him that is an
hundred years old ? and shall Sarah, that is ninety years
18 old, bear ? And Abraham said unto God, Oh that Ishmael
19 might live before thee ! And God said, Nay, but Sarah
thy wife shall bear thee a son ; and thou shalt call his

name Isaac (from the stem meaning "to laugh"): and
I will establish my covenant with him for an everlasting
covenant for his seed after him.   And as for Ishmael (i. e. 20
"God heareth"), I have heard thee ; behold, I have blessed
him, and will make him fruitful, and will multiply him exceedingly ; twelve princes shall he beget, and I will make
him a great nation.   But my covenant will I establish with 21
Isaac, which Sarah shall bear unto thee at this set time in
the next year.   And he left off talking with him, and God 22
went up from Abraham.   And Abraham took Ishmael his 23
son, and all that were born in his house, and all that
were bought with his money, every male among the men
of Abraham's house, and circumcised the flesh of their foreskin in the selfsame day, as God had said unto him.   And 24
Abraham was ninety years old and nine, when he was circumcised in the flesh of his foreskin.   And Ishmael his 25
son was thirteen years old, when he was circumcised in the
flesh of his foreskin.   In the selfsame day was Abraham 26
circumcised, and Ishmael his son.   And all the men of his 27
house, those born in the house, and those bought with
money of the stranger, were circumcised with him.

And God did unto Sarah as he had promised, at **21**—1*b*–2*b*
the set time of which God had spoken to him.   And Abra- 3
ham called the name of his son that was born unto him,
whom Sarah bare to him, Isaac.   And Abraham circum- 4
cised his son Isaac when he was eight days old, as God had
commanded him.   And Abraham was an hundred years 5
old, when his son Isaac was born unto him.

And the life of Sarah was an hundred and seven and **23**
twenty years : these were the years of the life of Sarah.
And Sarah died in Kiriath-arba (the same is Hebron), in 2
the land of Canaan : and Abraham came to mourn for
Sarah, and to weep for her.   And Abraham rose up from 3
before his dead, and spake unto the children of Heth, saying, I am a stranger and a sojourner with you ; give me a 4
possession of a buryingplace with you, that I may bury
my dead out of my sight.   And the children of Heth an- 5

6 swered Abraham, saying Pray, hear us, my lord: thou
art a mighty prince among us: in the choice of our sepulchres bury thy dead; none of us shall withhold from thee
7 his sepulchre, but that thou mayest bury thy dead. And
Abraham rose up, and bowed himself to the people of the
8 land, even to the children of Heth. And he communed
with them, saying, If it be your mind that I should bury
my dead out of my sight, hear me, and entreat for me to
9 Ephron the son of Zohar, that he may give me the cave of
Machpelah, which he hath, which is in the end of his field;
for the full price let him give it to me in the midst of you
10 for a possession of a buryingplace. Now Ephron was sitting in the midst of the children of Heth: and Ephron
the Hittite answered Abraham in the audience of the children of Heth, even of all that went in at the gate of his
11 city, saying, Nay, my lord, hear me: the field I give thee,
and the cave that is therein, I give it thee; in the presence
of the sons of my people give I it thee: bury thy dead.
12 And Abraham bowed himself down before the people of
13 the land. And he spake unto Ephron in the audience of
the people of the land, saying, But if thou wilt, pray
hear me: I will give the price of the field; take it of me,
14 and I will bury my dead there. And Ephron answered
15 Abraham, saying unto him, My lord, hearken unto me: a
piece of land worth four hundred shekels of silver, what
. is that betwixt me and thee? bury therefore thy dead.
16 And Abraham hearkened unto Ephron; and Abraham
weighed to Ephron the silver, which he had named in the
audience of the children of Heth, four hundred shekels of
17 silver, current money with the merchant. So the field of
Ephron, which was in Machpelah, which was before Mamre,
the field, and the cave which was therein, and all the trees
that were in the field, that were in all the border thereof
18 round about, were made sure unto Abraham for a possession in the presence of the children of Heth, before all that
19 went in at the gate of his city. And after this, Abraham
buried Sarah his wife in the cave of the field of Machpelah

before Mamre (the same is Hebron) in the land of Canaan.
And the field, and the cave that is therein, were made sure 20
unto Abraham for a possession of a buryingplace by the
children of Heth.

And these are the days of the years of Abraham's life 25-7
which he lived, an hundred threescore and fifteen years.
And Abraham gave up the ghost, and died in a good old 8
age, an old man, and satisfied with life : and was gathered
to his people. And Isaac and Ishmael his sons buried him 9
in the cave of Machpelah, in the field of Ephron the son
of Zohar the Hittite, which is before Mamre ; the field 10
which Abraham purchased of the children of Heth : there
was Abraham buried, and Sarah his wife. And it came 11a
to pass after the death of Abraham, that God blessed Isaac
his son.

12 Now this is the Genealogy of Ishmael, Abraham's
son, whom Hagar the Egyptian, Sarah's
handmaid, bare unto Abraham.

These are the names of the sons of Ishmael, by their 13
names, according to their generations.
The firstborn of Ishmael,
Nebaioth ; and Kedar, and Adbeel,
and Mibsam, and Mishma, and Dumah,   14
and Massa ; Hadad, and Tema,   15
Jetur, Naphish, and Kedemah.
These are the sons of Ishmael, and these are their 16
names, by their villages, and by their encampments ;
twelve princes according to their nations. And these are 17
the years of the life of Ishmael, an hundred and thirty and
seven years, and he gave up the ghost and died ; and was
gathered unto his people.

19 And this is the Genealogy of Isaac, Abraham's son.

Abraham begat Isaac ; and Isaac was forty years old 20
when he took Rebekah, the daughter of Bethuel the Syrian
of Paddan-aram, the sister of Laban the Syrian, to be his
wife. [And Rebekah, Isaac's wife, bare him two sons, Esau

26*b* and Jacob]; and Isaac was threescore years old when she
bare them.

26–34   And when Esau was forty years old he took to wife
Judith the daughter of Beeri the Hittite, and Basemath
35 the daughter of Elon the Hittite : and they proved a grief
28 of mind unto Isaac and to Rebekah.   And Isaac called
Jacob, and blessed him, and charged him, and said unto
him, Thou shalt not take a wife of the daughters of Ca-
2 naan.   Arise, go to Paddan-aram, to the house of Bethuel
thy mother's father ; and take thee a wife from thence of
3 the daughters of Laban thy mother's brother.   And El
Shaddai bless thee, and make thee fruitful, and multiply
4 thee, that thou mayest be a company of peoples ; and give
thee the blessing of Abraham, to thee, and to thy seed
with thee ; that thou mayest inherit the land of thy so-
5 journings, which God gave unto Abraham.   And Isaac
sent away Jacob: and he went to Paddan-aram unto
Laban, son of Bethuel the Syrian, the brother of Re-
6 bekah, Jacob's and Esau's mother.   Now Esau saw that
Isaac had blessed Jacob and sent him away to Paddan-
aram, to take him a wife from thence ; and that as he
blessed him he gave him a charge, saying, Thou shalt not
7 take a wife of the daughters of Canaan ; and that Jacob
obeyed his father and his mother, and was gone to Pad-
8 dan-aram : and Esau saw that the daughters of Canaan
9 pleased not Isaac his father ; and Esau went unto Ishmael, and took unto the wives which he had Mahalath
the daughter of Ishmael Abraham's son, the sister of
Nebaioth, to be his wife.

[And Laban gave to Jacob his daughter Leah to wife].
29–24 And Laban gave Zilpah his handmaid to his daughter
Leah for an handmaid.   [And afterward he gave him also
29 Rachel his younger daughter to wife].   And Laban gave
to Rachel his daughter Bilhah his handmaid to be her
handmaid.   [And when Jacob had dwelt twenty(?) years
31–18 in Paddan-aram he took his wives and his children] and
all his substance which he had gathered, the cattle of his

getting, which he had gathered in Paddan-aram, for to go to
Isaac his father unto the land of Canaan.

And God appeared unto Jacob, when he came from 35–9
Paddan-aram, and blessed him.   And God said unto him, 10
Thy name is Jacob : thy name shall not be called any more
Jacob, but Israel shall be thy name : and he called his name
Israel.   And God said unto him, I am El Shaddai : be fruit- 11
ful and multiply ; a nation and a company of nations shall
be of thee, and kings shall come out of thy loins ; and 12
the land which I gave unto Abraham and Isaac, to thee I
will give it.   And God went up from him.   And Jacob 13, 15
called the name of the place where God spake with him,
Beth-el.

> Now the sons of Jacob were twelve :   22*b*
>> The sons of Leah ;   23
>>> Jacob's firstborn, Reuben, and Simeon, and Levi,
>>>> and Judah, and Issachar, and Zebulun :
>> The sons of Rachel ;   24
>>> Joseph and Benjamin :
>> And the sons of Bilhah, Rachel's handmaid ;   25
>>> Dan and Naphtali :
>> And the sons of Zilpah, Leah's handmaid ;   26
>>> Gad and Asher.

These are the sons of Jacob, which were born to him in
Paddan-aram.   And Jacob came unto Isaac his father to 27
Mamre, to Kiriath-arba (the same is Hebron), where Abraham and Isaac sojourned.   And the days of Isaac were an 28
hundred and fourscore years.   And Isaac gave up the 29
ghost, and died, and was gathered unto his people, old and
full of days ; and Esau and Jacob his sons buried him.

And Esau took his wives, and his sons, and his daugh- 36–6
ters, and all the souls of his house, and his cattle, and all
his beasts, and all his possessions, which he had gathered
in the land of Canaan ; and went into the land [of Seir]
away from his brother Jacob.   For their substance was 7
too great for them to dwell together ; and the land of their
sojournings could not bear them because of their cattle.

8—37—1 So Esau dwelt in mount Seir : and Jacob dwelt in the land of his father's sojournings, in the land of Canaan.

36—9 Now this is the Genealogy of Esau the father of the Edomites in Mount Seir.

40   These are the names of the sheikhs of Esau, according to their families, after their places, by their names.
Sheikh Timnah, Sheikh Alva, Sheikh Jetheth ;
41   Sheikh Oholibamah, Sheikh Elah, Sheikh Pinon ;
42   Sheikh Kenaz, Sheikh Teman, Sheikh Mibzar ;
43   Sheikh Magdiel, [Sheikh Zepho,] Sheikh Iram : these be the sheikhs of Edom, according to their habitations in the land of their possession.

37—2   This is the Genealogy of Jacob.

When Joseph was seventeen years old [he went forth unto his brethren into the field. And his brethren sold him into Egypt. And he was there in bondage twelve years. And Pharaoh king of Egypt heard of the wisdom of Joseph, and made him governor over the land.]
41—46   And Joseph was thirty years old when he stood before Pharaoh king of Egypt.

[And Joseph sent for his father and his brethren, saying, Come down unto me and dwell here, and I will give you
46—6 the best of the land]. And they took their cattle, and their goods, which they had gotten in the land of Canaan, and came into Egypt, Jacob, and all his seed with him :
7 his sons, and his sons' sons with him, his daughters, and his sons' daughters, and all his seed brought he with him into Egypt.
47—5b (LXX) So Jacob and his sons came to Joseph unto Egypt, and when Pharaoh the king of Egypt heard of it, Pharaoh spake unto Joseph, saying, Thy father and thy
6a brethren are come unto thee : the land of Egypt is before thee ; in the best of the land make thy father and thy breth-
7 ren to dwell ; And Joseph brought in Jacob his father, and
8 set him before Pharaoh : and Jacob blessed Pharaoh.   And

Pharaoh said unto Jacob, How many are the days of the years of thy life? And Jacob said unto Pharaoh, The 9 days of the years of my sojournings are an hundred and thirty years : few and evil have been the days of the years of my life, and they have not attained unto the days of the years of the life of my fathers in the days of their sojournings. And Jacob blessed Pharaoh, and went out from the 10 presence of Pharaoh. And Joseph placed his father and 11 his brethren, and gave them a possession in the land of Egypt, in the best of the land, in the land of Rameses, as Pharaoh had commanded. [So Israel dwelt] in the land 27 of Egypt, and they gat them possessions therein, and were fruitful, and multiplied exceedingly.

And Jacob lived in the land of Egypt seventeen years : 28 so the days of Jacob, the years of his life, were an hundred forty and seven years.

And Jacob called his sons and blessed them ; every 49—1, 28 one according to his blessing he blessed them. And 48— 3 Jacob said unto Joseph, El Shaddai appeared unto me at Luz in the land of Canaan, and blessed me, and said unto 4 me, Behold, I will make thee fruitful, and multiply thee, and I will make of thee a company of peoples ; and will give this land to thy seed after thee for an everlasting possession. And now thy two sons, which were born unto 5 thee in the land of Egypt before I came unto thee into Egypt, are mine ; Ephraim and Manasseh, even as Reuben and Simeon, shall be mine. And thy issue, which thou be- 6 gettest after them, shall be thine ; they shall be called after the name of their brethren in their inheritance.

And he charged them, and said unto them, I am 49—29 to be gathered unto my people : bury me with my fathers in the cave that is in the field of Ephron the Hittite, in the cave that is in the field of Machpelah, which is be- 30 fore Mamre, in the land of Canaan, which Abraham bought with the field from Ephron the Hittite for a possession of a buryingplace : there they buried Abraham and Sarah 31 his wife ; there they buried Isaac and Rebekah his wife ;

32 and there I buried Leah [and Rachel] : the field and the
cave that is therein, which was purchased from the chil-
33 dren of Heth. And when Jacob made an end of charging
his sons, he yielded up the ghost, and was gathered unto
his people.

50—12 And his sons did unto him according as he had com-
13 manded them : for his sons carried him into the land of
Canaan, and buried him in the cave of the field of Machpelah, which Abraham bought with the field, for a possession of a buryingplace, of Ephron the Hittite, before
Mamre.

APPENDIX I.

THE GREAT FLOOD-INTERPOLATION J',
CIRC. 700 B. C.

[When* God created the heaven and the earth, the earth was 1–2
waste and void; and darkness was upon the face of the abyss (Tehom), and the spirit of God was brooding upon the face of the
waters. And God said, Let there be light: and there was light. 3
And God saw that the light was good: and God divided the 4
light from the darkness. And God called the light Day, and the 5
darkness he called Night.

And God said, Let there be a dome in the midst of the waters, 6
and let it be a partition between the different waters. And God 7
made the dome, and divided the waters which were under the
dome from the waters which were above the dome: and it was so.
And God called the dome Heaven. 8

And God said, Let the waters under the heaven be gathered to- 9
gether unto one place, and let the dry land appear: and it was so.
And God called the dry land Earth; and the gathering together 10
of the waters called he Seas: and God saw that it was good. And 11
God said, Let the earth put forth verdure, herb yielding seed, and
fruit tree bearing fruit after its kind, wherein is the seed there-

FRAGMENTS OF TABLET I, ASSYRIAN COSMOGONIC EPOS.

When the heaven above was not yet set apart,
And the earth beneath was without a name—
For the Abyss was their generator,
The chaotic world-ocean (Tiamat) brought forth the whole—
Their waters mingled and flowed united.
The darkness was not yet removed, no plant had sprung up.
When none of the gods had yet been produced,
When they were still unnamed and no fate was [fixed],
Then were the [great] gods created.
(The gods) Lahmu and Lahamu were produced.
. . . . also grew up.
(The gods) Shar and Ki-shar (representing "the host of heaven and earth,"
    Gen. ii. 1) were created.
The days were prolonged . . . .
The god Anu . . . . . .
The god Shar . . . . . .

* Supplied from narrative of P. Gen. I.

(335)

12 of, upon the earth: and it was so. And the earth brought forth
verdure, herb yielding seed after its kind, and tree bearing fruit,
wherein is the seed thereof, after its kind: and God saw that it
was good.

14 And God said, Let there be lights in the dome of the heaven to
divide the day from the night; and let them be for signs, and for

15 seasons, and for days and years: and let them be for lights in the
dome of the heaven to give light upon the earth; and it was so.

16 And God made the two great lights; the greater light to rule the

17 day, and the lesser light to rule the night. And God set them in the

18 dome of the heaven to give light upon the earth, and to rule over
the day and over the night, and to divide the light from the darkness: and God saw that it was good.

FRAGMENTS OF THE FIFTH (?) TABLET.

Excellently he made the mansions twelve] in number for the great gods (zodi-
acal constellations).
He brought forth the stars like *lumasvi*.
He determined the year and appointed decades for it;
For each of the twelve months he appointed three stars
From the day when the year begins until its end.
He determined the mansions of the planets to define their orbits by a fixed time,
So that none of them may fall short, and none be turned aside.
He fixed the abodes of Bel and Ea near his own.
He opened also perfectly the great gates (of heaven),
Making their bolts solid to right and left;
And in his majesty he made himself steps there (the steps by which the sun
mounts from the morning "gate" at the eastern horizon to the meridian,
and descends to the evening "gate" at the western).
He made Nannar (the moon) to shine, he joined it to the night,
And fixed for it the seasons of its phases determining the days.
For the entire month without interruption he appointed the form of its disk.
In the beginning of the month when evening begins,
Thy horns shall be for a sign to determine the times of the heaven;
The seventh day thou shalt be filling out thy disk,
But the   . . . . will partly expose its dark side.
When the sun descends towards the horizon at the moment of thy rising,
The limits exactly defined [of thy fulness] form its circle,
[Afterwards] turn, draw near the path of the sun,
     . . . . . . turn, and let the sun transpose thy dark part,
. . . . walk in its path,
[Rise] and set, subject to the law of this destiny.

. . . .

. . . .

[Uncertain fragments, probably belonging to the third (?) and fourth (?)
tablets (cf. Geo. Smith, *Chaldean Account of Genesis,* Rev. Ed. p. 62ff.
Lenormant, *Beginnings of History*, p. 491f. Schrader, *Keilinschrif-
ten und altes Testament*, second edition, p. 15).]

And God said, Let the waters swarm with swarms of living 20 creatures, and let fowl fly above the earth in the open dome of heaven. And God created the great sea-monsters, and every living 21 creature that stirreth, which the waters swarmed with, after their kinds, and every winged fowl after its kind: and God saw that it was good. And God blessed them, saying, Be fruitful, and multi- 22 ply, and fill the waters in the seas, and let fowl multiply in the earth.

And God said, Let the earth bring forth the living creature after 24 its kind, cattle, and creeping thing, and wild beast of the earth after its kind: and it was so. And God made the wild beast of the 25 earth after its kind, and the cattle after their kind, and every thing that creepeth upon the ground after its kind: and God saw that it was good. And God said, Let us make man in our image, 26 after our likeness: and let them have dominion over the fish of the sea, and over the fowl of the air, and over the cattle, and over every beast of the earth, and over every creeping thing that creepeth upon the earth. So God created man in his own image, 27 in the image of God created he him; male and female created he them. And God blessed them: and God said unto them, Be fruit- 28 ful and multiply, and replenish the earth, and subdue it; and have dominion over the fish of the sea, and over the fowl of the air, and over every living thing that stirreth upon the earth. And 29 God said, Behold, I have given you every herb yielding seed, which is upon the face of all the earth, and every tree, in the which is the fruit of a tree yielding seed; to you it shall be for meat: and to every beast of the earth, and to every fowl of the air, and to every thing that creepeth upon the earth, wherein there is life, [I have given] every green herb for meat: and it was so. And God saw every thing that he had made, and, behold, it 31 was very good.

So the heaven and the earth were finished and all their host.] 2—1

FRAGMENTS FROM THE SEVENTH (?) CREATION TABLET.

When the gods collectively had created . . . . .
They made excellently the stout trunks of trees (?),
Brought forth living creatures . . . . .
The cattle of the field, the wild beasts of the field, and the creeping things of the [field].

. . . .

. . . .

. . . . . . [Uncertain fragments.] . . . .

22

2—9 . . . . . . The tree of life also . . . . . .
10 And a river went out of Eden to water the garden; and from
11 thence it was parted, and became four heads. The name of the
    first is Pishon: that is it which compasseth the whole land of
12 Havilah, where there is gold; and the gold of that land is good:
13 there is bdellium and the onyx stone. And the name of the second
    river is Gihon: the same is it that compasseth the whole land of
14 Cush. And the name of the third river is Hiddekel: that is it
    which goeth in front of Assyria. And the fourth river is Euphra-
15 tes. And Yahweh God took the man, and put him into the garden
    of Eden to dress it and to keep it.

The tree of life, or sacred plant of the Assyrian bas-reliefs, is guarded
by winged genii (*Kiroubim*—cherubim) with eagle's heads. In Indian
tradition (perhaps connected with the ancient Assyro-Babylonian) the
tree appears springing from over the sacred fountain, *Ardvi-çura*, in the
centre of the garden of the gods at the top of *Meru*, the holy mountain
of the north, and distilling the *soma* or drink of immortality. Cf. Ez.
xxviii. 13f. "Thou wast in Eden, the garden of God . . . . . thou
wast on the holy mountain of God." In Greek mythology the source of
celestial immortality is the food ambrosia. Among all Oriental peoples
traces remain of a primitive conception of a divine life resident in trees,
and the tree of life is therefore common property in Oriental folk-lore.
The tree of the knowledge of good and evil, on the contrary, is a meta-
physical conception or modification of the myth by J¹, the author of the
Eden story.

Eden—Assyrian *Idinu*. The geographical data may be compared
with Gen. x., as there the general story of xi. 1–9 is localized and made
specific, so here the garden, which originally, vs. 8, was only "eastward
in Eden," is localized; and the four "heads," which were perhaps
originally the same as the four divisions of the Indian holy fount,
Ardvi-çura, flowing to the four cardinal points, are localized and
identified.—**Pishon**—perhaps Accadian *Pisaanna*, Assyrian *Pisanu*,
"water-container."—**Gihon**—perhaps Accadian *Guhan-D I.*—**The whole
land of Cush** is obviously intended to include also south Arabia, besides
the country usually and properly designated Cush, i. e. Aethiopia and
Nubia. The author accordingly seems to find the source of the Nile in
Eden. The same remarkable conception of Cush extending to the
Persian Gulf reappears in Gen. x. 6–8 (P on the basis of J²), and appears
to rest upon a confusion of the Egyptian-Nubian *Kes* with the Babylonian *Kas*.—**Hiddekel**—Assyrian *Hidiglat*, Babylonian *Idiglat*; i. e. the
Tigris (Dan. x. 4).—**Euphrates**—Assyrian *Burat*; elsewhere simply
"the River" (cf. Gen. xxxi. 21).

And Yahweh said, Behold, the man is become as one of us, to 3—22
know good and evil; and now, lest he put forth his hand, and
take also of the tree of life, and eat, and live for ever: therefore
he drove out the man; and he placed at the east of the garden of 24
Eden the Cherubim, and the flame of a sword which whirled every
way, to keep the way of the tree of life.

And again she bare his brother Abel. And Abel was a keeper 4—2

Cherubim—Assyrian *Kiroubim*, the guardian genii represented by
human and eagle-headed, winged colossi, with bodies of bulls, at the
entrance of palaces and temples. Greek *Grups*—English "griffon:"
perhaps the same as *Cerberus*, the dragon guardian of the entrance to
the nether world. In Assyrian sculpture also they "keep the way of
the tree of life" (cf. Ez. i. 10; x. 14).—The flame (or "prodigy," "en-
chantment;" cf. Ex. vii. 11) **of a (sickle-shaped) sword whirling every
way**, is the peculiar attribute of the cherub (perhaps a weapon like the
Hindu *tchakra*). Cf. the "wheels," i. e. whirling disks, of the cherubs
in Ez. i. 15–21 ; x. 9–17, which are there said to contain the spirit of the
cherubim and accompany them everywhere. An Accadian lyric (*Cuneiform Inscriptions of West Asia*. Vol. II., pl. 19. No. 2) introduces
this whirling disc as the weapon of a god.

The Eden creation-story of J¹, as appears from a recent discovery by
Mr. Pinches (announced in *The Academy* of November 29, 1890), had
also a Babylonian parallel beginning with the statement that no plant
existed, placing the formation of man before that of plants and animals
and mentioning an abode of delights. Here also the Tigris and Euphrates are mentioned. The evidence is decisive that Gen. ii. and this
Babylonian story have at least a common stock. It is not impossible
that what appear to be additions to the primitive narrative of J¹ will
turn out to have been suggested by the Babylonian form of the story.

Abel perhaps—Assyr. *Abal* (*habal*) "son," Accadian *ibila*, suggesting
an Assyro-Babylonian origin for this section also, which in spite of its
obvious relation to J¹ (cf. vs. 7 with iii. 16; 11f. with iii. 17f. ; 14*b* with
16*b* ; 15*a* with 24) is not originally of a piece with this document. Jabal
here, vs. 20, is the father of shepherds, and Cain, after having become
"a fugitive and a wanderer," vs. 14f, reappears in 16*b*f as a settled
agriculturist and city-builder. The references to J¹ in vv. 7, 11, 14, 15,
also turn out on closer inspection to be evidence for diversity and not
identity of authorship. Verse 7, for example, misapplies the expression
of iii. 16. The double character of Cain as city-builder (J¹) and fratricide
(J²) may perhaps again be due to the double Assyro-Babylonian stock ;
for as Lenormant observes (*Beg. of Hist.*, pp. 146ff), in the duo-decimal
Babylonian calendar, the third month is called "the month of brick-
making," and also "the month of the twins," with the sign *Gemini*.

3 of sheep. And in process of time it came to pass, that Cain
   brought of the fruit of the ground an offering unto Yahweh.
4 And Abel, he also brought of the firstlings of his flock and of the
5 fat thereof. And Yahweh had respect unto Abel and to his offering:
   but unto Cain and to his offering he had not respect. And Cain
6 was very wroth, and his countenance fell. And Yahweh said unto
   Cain, Why art thou wroth? and why is thy countenance fallen?
7 If thou doest well, is it not lifted up? and if thou doest not well,
   sin coucheth at the door: and unto thee shall be his desire, and
8 thou shalt rule over him. And Cain said unto Abel his brother,
   . . . . . And it came to pass, when they were in the field, that
9 Cain rose up against Abel his brother, and slew him. And Yahweh said unto Cain, Where is Abel thy brother? And he said, I
10 know not: am I my brother's keeper? And he said, What hast
   thou done? the voice of thy brother's blood crieth unto me from
11 the ground. And now cursed art thou from the ground, which
   hath opened her mouth to receive thy brother's blood from thy
12 hand; when thou tillest the ground, it shall not henceforth yield
   unto thee her strength; a fugitive and a wanderer shalt thou
13 be in the earth. And Cain said unto Yahweh, My punishment
14 is greater than I can bear. Behold, thou hast driven me out
   this day from the face of the ground; and from thy face shall I
   be hid; and I shall be a fugitive and a wanderer (nad) in the
   earth; and it shall come to pass, that whosoever findeth me shall
15 slay me. And Yahweh said unto him, Therefore whosoever slay-

Each month had its peculiar myth and related zodiacal sign. Thus the
eleventh with the sign *Aquarius* was called "the month of the curse of
rain," and its myth was that of the Flood. (See next page.) That of the
first, called, "the month of the altar of the demiurge" was the creation
of the world ; of the second, "the month of the propitious bull" (i. e.
Ea, the god originator of humanity), was the creation of man. The
myth, or myths, belonging with the third month, and the sign *Gemini*,
have not yet been discovered, the only hint of their (its?) character
being in the two names, "month of brick-making" and "month of the
twins," with which Lenormant compares the Egyptian, Greek and
Roman myths connecting fratricide with the founding of a city, and
the Phœnician myth of Cain, twin brother of *Adam min-haadamah*.
"These are they," says Sanchoniathon, "who found out how to mix
chopped straw with clay to make bricks, how to dry them in the sun,
and to build houses with roofs."

Here we have perhaps a union of two ancient myths, one of fratricide
and the other of city-building, the former, neglected by J[1], having been
introduced by J[2].

eth Cain, vengeance shall be taken on him sevenfold. And Yahweh appointed a sign for Cain, lest any finding him should smite
him. So Cain went out from the presence of Yahweh.   16

And Adam knew his wife again; and she bare a son, and called 25
his name Seth: For, [said she,] God hath appointed (*shath*) me another seed instead of Abel; for Cain slew him. And to Seth, to 26
him also there was born a son; and he called his name Enosh:
then began men to call upon the name of Yahweh.

[And unto Enosh was born Kenan; and Kenan begat Enoch]
and Enoch walked before Yahweh, [and he was not, for Yahweh 5—22
took him].

> "Then Bel listened to reason and mounted to the interior of the vessel. He
> took my hand and made me to rise, lifted up my wife also, and laid her hand in
> mine; he turned himself to us, stood between us, and blessed us, [saying],
> 'Hitherto Shamash-napishti was human, but now shall Shamash-napishti and
> his wife be like unto the gods, they are lifted up to live like them, and Shamash-
> napishti shall dwell far off at the mouth of the rivers.' So they took me and
> gave me a dwelling far off at the mouth of the rivers."

IV. 25f. By the interpolation of these two verses the seven-linked
genealogy of J[1] is considered to have been expanded to nine links. The
substitution of Noah in place of Jabal, Jubal and Tubal, to be the
son (instead of grandson?) of Lamech, produced then a ten-linked genealogy, corresponding exactly with the Assyrian genealogy of ten primeval kings or patriarchs, of whom the tenth is Hasisadra, the flood-hero
and repopulator of the world. Very little inventive power was required,
since the names Seth and Enosh are respectively synonymous with Cain
and Adam. The expansion of the genealogy to correspond in number
with the Assyrian was apparently accompanied by a slight alteration of
the remaining names. As before, in the case of the Creation story, the
priestly writer naturally follows the amended version, so that what is
now missing from J[2]'s genealogy of the Sethites may be readily supplied
from P.

The singular notice which in P's genealogy of Adam is attached to
the name of Enoch, Budde (*Urgesch.* ch. v.) considers to be derived, like
v. 29, from his J source. But in J[1] the name of Enoch appears uncon-
nected with any tradition. Since in all of P's genealogies there is the
most rigid exclusion of every trace of material of this nature, we must
attribute to J[2] the interesting notice of the apotheosis of Enoch and very
possibly even the 365 years which apparently indicate his connection
with sun-myths. Budde further conjectures that this tradition also was
borrowed from the Assyro-Chaldæan epos. In Col. IV., lines 23–30,
Xisuthros-Hasisadra, whose name as usually written in the tablets is
Shamash-napishti—"sun of life," relates the story of his own apotheosis
as above.

[And Enoch begat Jared, and Jared begat Mahalalel, and Mahalalel begat Methuselah, and Methuselah begat Lamech. And
5—29 unto Lamech there was born] a son: and he called his name
Noah, saying, This same shall comfort (Heb. *nahem*) us for our
work and for the toil of our hands, from the ground which Yahweh hath cursed.
6—5   And Yahweh saw that the wickedness of man was great in

If this be the source of the tradition, J², in adopting the story, divided
the character of the Assyrian flood-hero in accordance with the significance of the name Hasis-adra ("prudent-reverent," nearly the equivalent of "righteous and perfect," Gen. vi. 9) as flood-hero, transmitting his
rôle to Noah, the tenth from Adam, and for Shamash-napishti, the "sun
of life," made immortal like the gods and taken to dwell with them, sub-
stituting Enoch the fifth from Adam.

The fragments of Berosus, which give the corresponding list of ten
ante-diluvian kings ending with the Flood-hero, can be corrected in a
few cases by the cuneiform tablets. The list is as follows, and we set
side by side with it the list of J¹ and the expanded list of J².

Chaldæo-Assyrian.	J¹	J²
Adoros (Adiuru)	Ha-adam	Adam
Alaparos		Seth
Almelon		Enosh
Ammenon (Hammanu)	Cain	[Kenan]
Amegalaros	Enoch	Enoch
Daonos	Irad	[Jared]
Edoranchos	Mehujael	[Mahalalel]
Amemphsinos	Methusael	[Methuselah]
Obartes (Ubaratutu)	Lamech	Lamech
	Jabal Jubal Tubal	
Xisuthros (Hasisadra	Noah	Noah
	Shem Japheth Canaan	Shem Ham Japheth

"Noah the husbandman" may have been suggested, not only by his
appropriate position in the original genealogy, and as the father of the
populations of West Asia, but also by the favorable etymology which the
writer of the original genealogy had attached to his name, as a suitable
character to be selected for the rôle of the Assyro-Babylonian flood-hero.

The cuneiform Flood-story is an episode of the so-called Izdubar
legends, which constitute the great Babylonian national epos, celebrating
the deeds of king Izdubar of Erech on twelve tablets containing a total
of some 3,000 lines. For an offense against the goddess Ishtar Izdubar
is smitten with disease, and betakes himself for healing to his ancestor

the earth, and that every imagination of the thoughts of his heart
was only evil continually. And it repented Yahweh that he had 6
made man on the earth, and it grieved him at his heart. And 7
Yahweh said, I will blot out man from the face of the ground;
for it repenteth me that I have made them. But Noah found 8
grace in the eyes of Yahweh.

(J² underlying P.) [And Yahweh said unto Noah, The end 6—13-16
of all flesh is come before me. Behold, 1 will blot out man from
the face of the ground because their wickedness is great, but thou
hast found grace in mine eyes: Therefore build thee an ark of
gopher wood; thou shalt make the ark of compartments and shalt
pitch it within and without with pitch. And this is how thou
shalt make it: the length of the ark three hundred cubits, the
breadth of it fifty cubits and the hight of it thirty cubits. Thou
shalt make a light for the ark at the top, and shalt finish it to a
cubit, and the door of the ark shalt thou set in the side thereof:
with lower, second and third stories shalt thou make it. And 22
Noah built the ark as Yahweh commanded him.]

Shamash-napishti, surnamed Hasisadra, " at the mouth of the rivers,"
whither he was removed by the gods.   Arrived there, Shamash-napishti
relates at his request the story of his escape from the Flood and subsequent apotheosis.   The narrative is as follows :—

> Shamash-napishti also said to Izdubar, Let me reveal to thee, O Izdubar, the
> narrative of my preservation, and let me tell thee the decree of the gods. The
> city Shurippak, the city which as thou knowest is situate on the Euphrates, this
> was already ancient when the gods in it were moved by their heart to institute
> a Deluge (Assyr. *Abubu*=Heb. *mabbul*, a *nomen proprium* of the Flood). The
> great gods were there : their father Anu, their counsellor, the warlike Bel, their
> throne-bearer Adar, their prince Ennugi. The lord of unsearchable wisdom
> also, the god Ea, sat [in counsel] among them and reported their conclusion to
> his worshipper (?). " Worshipper, worshipper, venerable, venerable (?) [said he]
> . . . . . worshipper, hear . . . . . and give heed, venerable Shurripa-
> kite, son of Ubara-tutu. Forsake thine house, build a ship, leave . . . . . of
> life, they are determined to destroy the seed of life. Preserve thou alive and
> bring up into the interior of the vessel the seed of life of every sort. The ship
> which thou shalt build . . . . . cubits shall be its measure in length [and]
> . . . . . cubits the equal measure of its breadth and hight ; and . . . . .
> sea it, provide it also with a deck." When I understood this, I said to Ea, my
> lord : "[The building of the ship] O lord, which thou hast commanded, [if] I carry
> it out, the people and the elders [will laugh at me].". [Ea opened his mouth
> and] spake, saying to me his servant : " [If they laugh at thee] thou shalt say to
> them, Whoever abuses me and . . . . . surely I . . . . . and I will
> . . . . . the vault of heaven . . . . . above and beneath I will judge.
> [But thou, shut not the door until be come] the time when I shall send th[ee]
> word. [Then] enter in through the door of the ship and bring [into] its interior
> thy store of grain, all thy possessions and wealth, thy [family], thy servants and
> thy handmaids and [thy] relatives."

7   And Yahweh said unto Noah, Come thou and all thy house into the ark; for thee have I seen righteous before me in this genera-
2   tion. Of every clean beast thou shalt take to thee seven and seven, the male and his female; and of the beasts that are not
3   clean two, the male and his female; of the fowl also of the air, seven and seven, to keep seed alive upon the face of all the earth.
4   For yet seven days, and I will cause it to rain upon the earth forty days and forty nights; and every living thing that I have
5   made will I blot out from off the face of the ground. And Noah did according unto all that Yahweh commanded him.

7   And Noah went in, and his sons, and his wife, and his sons wives with him, into the ark, because of the waters of the flood.
.8   Of clean beasts, and of beasts that are not clean, and of fowls, and
9   of every thing that creepeth upon the ground, there went in two and two unto Noah into the ark, as Yahweh commanded Noah.
16*b* And Yahweh shut him in.

The [cattle] of the field, the wild beasts of the field, everything that . . . . . [will I] send to thee, to the end that [thy] gate may preserve [them all].—[Adra]-hasis opened his mouth and spake and [s]aid to Ea [his] lord; O my lord, no [one] has ever built a vessel [in this fashion] 49 [upon the la]nd; . . . . . . 50 . . . . . . may I see and the ship . . . . . 51 . . . . . . upon the land . . . . . 52 . . . . . . as thou hast commanded . . . . .

25. I collected all that I had ; I collected all the silver I had ; 26. I collected all the gold I had ; 27. all that I had of seed of life of all kinds [I collected], and all this 28. I brought up into the ship ; all my company, male and female ; 29. the cattle of the field, the wild beasts of the field, and all my relatives, I made to go on board. 30. Now when the sun had brought the appointed time, 31. a voice (?) proclaimed: "In the evening the heavens shall rain destruction. 32. Enter in to the [int]erior of the ship and shut thy door ; 33. the appointed time is come. 34. In the evening, proclaimed the voice (?), the heavens shall rain destruction. 35. With terror I awaited the setting of the sun on that day (?). 36. I held in dread the day of embarkation. 37. But I entered in to the interior of the ship and shut my door behind me, 38. to close the vessel. To Buzurkurgal, the pilot, 39. I entrusted the great structure with its cargo.

Col. II. 1–24. [In these lines the building of the vessel was described in detail. The beginning of the description, which formed the conclu-sion of Col. I. is missing. According to line 6, it appears that the con-struction lasted exactly a week. As Noah divided the ark in three par-titions ("stories"), so Hasisadra also (line 7) divides the interior into different stories. The number unfortunately is missing. Lines 10–12 are also plain. "I saw fissures (leaks) and supplied that which was lacking. Three sar (a liquid measure) of bitumen I poured over the exterior. Three sar of pitch over the interior." At the close it may be gathered from the fragmentary lines that Hasisadra provisioned the ship with food and drink.] (See Schrader's *Keilinschr.*, pp. 7of.)

And it came to pass after the seven days, that the waters of 10 the flood were upon the earth. And the rain was upon the earth 12 forty days and forty nights. And the waters increased and bare 17*b* up the ark so that it was lift up above the earth. All in whose 22 nostrils was the breath of life, of all that was in the dry land, died. So he (Yahweh) blotted out every living thing which was 23 upon the face of the ground: and Noah only was left, and they that were with him in the ark.

[And it came to pass at the end of seven days that the storm 8—2*b*

40. Then arose Mu-sheri-ina-namari from the foundations of the sky, a black cloud, 42. in the midst of which Ramman thundered, 43. Nebo and Sherru march against one another, 44. the throne-bearers stride over mountain and plain. 45. The powerful god of pestilence looses the whirlwinds(?). 46. Adar makes the canals (?) to overflow incessantly, 47. the Anunaki bring floods, 48. they make the earth to tremble with their might. 49. Ramman's inundation mounts aloft to the sky, all light vanished before the [darkness].

Col. III. 1. . . . . . of the earth they destroy like . . . . . . 2. . . . . . . mountain (?) . . . . . . 3. the . . . . . . they bring nigh to fight against man. 4. The brother no longer looks after his brother, men no longer are concerned about one another. In heaven 5. the gods are afraid at the Deluge and 6. seek refuge, they mount aloft to the heaven of Anu. Like a dog in its kennel the gods cower together at the lattice of heaven. 8. Ishtar cries out like a woman in travail, 9. the great goddess cries with a loud voice [saying] 10. "mankind has returned to clay (slime); 11. the evil which I predicted before the gods. 12. Thus did I foretell the disaster before the gods. 13. I foretold the war of extermination which would be waged against them. 14. But I did not bring mankind to birth that 15. they like the spawn of fish should fill the sea!" 16. Then the gods wept with her for the (deed of the) Anunaki; 17. upon one spot the gods sat down with lamentation; 18. their lips they pressed together . . . . . destiny. 19. Six days and seven nights 20 wind, flood and storm prevailed, 21 but at the breaking of the seventh day the storm was quieted, the flood, which 22 had battled like a mighty army 23. was appeased; the sea diminished, and storm and flood ceased.

24. I sailed through the sea weeping, 25. that the dwellings of men were turned to slime; 26. like tree-trunks the corpses floated about. 27. I had opened a port-hole, and as the daylight fell upon my face, 28. I was overwhelmed with sorrow and sat down weeping; the tears flowed over my face. 30. I sailed through the territories, (now) a dreadful ocean; 31. then emerged a bit of land twelve measures high. 32. To the land of Nizir (the mountain region eastward from the Tigris, beyond the lower Zab, between the 35th and 36th parallels, which dominates the plain of Assyria. If Semitic, Nizir means "rescue") drifted the ship. 33. The mountain of the land of Nizir held the ship and would not let it pass. 34. The first and second day the mountain Nizir held the ship, etc. 35. The third and fourth day the mountain Nizir held, etc. 36. The fifth and sixth day the mountain Nizir held, etc. 37. At the breaking of the seventh day 38. I brought forth a dove and loosed it. The dove flew hither and thither; but when 39. no resting-place appeared, it returned again. 40. Then I brought forth a swallow and released it. The swallow flew hither and thither; but when 41. no resting-place appeared, it returned again. 42. Then I brought forth a raven and released it. 43. The raven flew away, and when it saw that the waters had diminished 44. it drew near again, cautiously wading, but did not return.

3   ceased], and the rain from heaven was restrained; and the waters
6   returned from off the earth continually. And it came to pass at
    the end of forty days, that Noah opened the window of the ark
7   which he had made: and he sent forth a raven, and it went forth
8   to and fro, until the waters were dried up from off the earth. And
    he [stayed seven days and] sent forth a dove from him, to see if
9   the waters were abated from off the face of the ground; but the
    dove found no rest for the sole of her foot, and she returned unto
    him to the ark, for the waters were on the face of the whole
    earth: and he put forth his hand, and took her, and brought her
10 in unto him into the ark. And he stayed yet other seven days;
11 and again he sent forth the dove out of the ark; and the dove
    came in to him at eventide; and, lo, in her mouth a fresh olive
    leaf: so Noah knew that the waters were abated from off the
12 earth. And he stayed yet other seven days; and sent forth the
13*b* dove; and she returned not again unto him any more. And
    Noah removed the cover of the ark, and looked, and, behold, the
    face of the ground was dried.
        [Then Noah and all that were with him in the ark went forth.]
20 And Noah builded an altar unto Yahweh, and took of every clean
    beast, and of every clean fowl, and offered burnt offerings on the
21 altar. And Yahweh smelled the sweet savour; and Yahweh said
    in his heart, I will not again curse the ground any more for
    man's sake; for the imagination of man's heart is evil from his
    youth; neither will I again smite any more every living thing,
22 as I have done. While the earth remaineth, seedtime and har-
    vest, and cold and heat, and summer and winter, and day and
    night shall not cease.

9—11-17 (J² underlying P.) [And Yahweh made a covenant with
    Noah, and said, Behold I do set my bow in the sky, and it shall
    be the token of this covenant between me and thee and all flesh,
    that the waters shall no more become a flood to destroy all flesh.]

45. Then I sent forth (all) toward the four winds; I offered a sacrifice. 46. I
built an altar on the peak of the mountain; 47. seven by seven I placed the
adagur-vases; 48. beneath them I spread out reeds, cedar and juniper. 49. The
gods inhaled the fragrance, the gods smelled the sweet savour, 50. like flies the
gods gathered above the head of the offerer.

51. When at length the goddess Ishtar drew near, 52. she raised aloft the great
bows which Anu had made according to . . . . . [and said] 53. "These gods be
the jewels of my neck! Col. IV. 1. I shall not forget these days, I will remember them and not forget them forever. 2. Let the gods come to the altar,
3. only Bel shall not come to the altar, 4. because he did heedlessly and made
the Deluge, 5. and delivered my men to destruction." 6. When at length Bel
drew near and saw the ship he was aghast, 7. he was filled with wrath (?)
against the gods and the Igigi (celestial spirits). 8. "What man is this that has

And the sons of Noah, that went forth of the ark, were Shem, 18
and Ham, and Japheth: and Ham is the father of Canaan.
These three were the sons of Noah, and unto them sons 19*a*—10—1*b*
were born after the flood, and of these was the whole earth 9—19*b*
overspread.

> escaped? No mortal is to remain alive in the destruction." 9. Then Adar
> opened his mouth and spake, saying to the warlike Bel, 10. "Who indeed but
> Ea can have contr[ived] this thing? 11. Ea knew of it and informed him of all."
> 12. Then Ea opened his mouth and spake to the warlike Bel, saying: 13. "Thou
> art the war[rior] prince of the gods; 14. but why, why hast thou wrought so
> recklessly and didst prep[are] the Deluge? 15. Let the sinner's iniquity fall
> upon him, let the presumption of the presumptuous fall upon him. 16. (But) be
> not relentless, that he be not blotted out; be merciful, so that he may not
> . . . . . 17. Instead of (thy) making a Deluge let lions come and decima[te]
> mankind; 18. instead of thy making a Deluge let hyænas come and deci[mate]
> mankind; 19. instead of thy making a Deluge let famine appear and [consume]
> the land; 20. instead of thy making a Deluge let the god of pestilence come and
> dec[imate] mankind! 21. I did not reveal to him the decision of the great gods.
> 22. I (only) sent a dream to Adrahasis and he understood the decision of the
> gods." (I. e. he possessed this power through his piety; an impious man would
> not have understood the revelation.) 23. Then Bel listened to reason,
> mounted to the interior of the ship, 24. took my hand and lifted me up, raised
> up my wife also and placed her hand in mine, 26. turned himself to us, stood
> between us and blessed us: "Hitherto Shamash-napishti was mortal, 28. but
> now shall Shamash-napishti and his wife be lifted up to be like unto the gods.
> 29. And Shamash-napishti shall dwell far off at the mouth of the rivers!" 30.
> Then they took me and gave me a dwelling-place far off at the mouth of the
> rivers.

"After the Flood." Hebrew *achar ham-mabbul*—Assyr. *arki a-bu-bi*, a phrase occurring in the title of an ancient Babylonian list of kings and in Berosus-Polyhistor : "These are the kings who reigned after the Flood." J², however, naturally does not confine himself to the idea of Noah as ancestor of a line of Babylonian kings, but returns to the Hebrew line through Shem. The Assyro-Chaldean conception which he has adopted of Noah as repopulator of the earth, compels him to alter the original triad of Noah's sons, from Shem,—the Hebrew stock, Japheth, —Philistine (or Phœnician?), and Canaan ; to a triad suggestive of the three world divisions, Asia, Africa and Europe. This is very simply done by introducing Ham (Egyptian *Chemi*) as father of Canaan. J² was of course not embarrassed by ethnological considerations, although the triad must have originally been of Semitic peoples. The table of nations, ch. x., then takes the place probably of a simple seven-linked genealogy in J¹. Here evidence might be found of Assyrian influence in the geographical knowledge displayed, for although no Assyrian table of nations like Gen. x. has been discovered, the isolated names are largely represented on Assyrian monuments. On the other hand, J² does not depend on J¹, for in iv. 22 we found Tubal as father of smiths.

10—2 (J² underlying P.) [Unto Japheth were born Gomer, and Ma·
gog, and Madai, and Javan, and Tubal, and Meschech, and Tiras.
3 And Gomer begat Ashkenaz, and Riphath, and Togarmah.
4 And Javan begat Elishah, and Tarshish, Kittim, and Rodanim.
6 (J² underlying P.) And unto Ham were born Cush, and Mizraim,
8 and Canaan.] And Cush begat Nimrod: he was the first *gibbor*
10 (tyrant?) in the earth. And the beginning of his kingdom was
Babel, and Erech, and Accad, and Calneh, in the land of Shinar.
11 Out of that land he went forth into Assyria, and builded

perhaps ancestor of the Armenian peoples, whereas in x. 2 (P on the
basis of J²) he is a son of Japheth. Sheba and Dedan are sons of Abraham in xxv. 3 (J¹); here descendants of Ham. Babylon, founded according to xi. 1–9 (J¹) by the primitive human community, is here, x. 10,
founded by Nimrod, who seems to be identified with the Assyrian Gilgames (Izdubar).

Gomer, Magog (?), Madai, Javan, Tubal, Meschech, Togarmah, are
all known to the Assyrian monuments by names nearly or quite identical. For the well-known Kittim (Cyprus, Kition) they use another name.

Cush and Mizraim—Assyr. *Kusu* and *Musur.* *Kash*, the land of the
Kashu, formed an important part of Babylonia, and occurs frequently.
Nimrod seems to be, like Noah, a Hebrew hero who is made to play the
part of the hero of Assyrian national epos, Gilgames (Izdubar). The
conjecture may perhaps be deemed not too hazardous that the Hebrew
Nimrod, the *gibbor-çayid* or hunter-hero, is the counterpart to Noah the
Ish-ha-adamah, or "husbandman," the two corresponding to Sanchoniathon's *Agros* and *Agrotes*, whom Lenormant (*Beg. of Hist.*, p. 160)
identifies with *Sadê* and *Çaid*, the husbandman and the hunter in the
cosmogonic narrative. **And the beginning of his kingdom was Babel,
and Erech, and Accad, and Calneh, in the land of Shinar.** A bit of
Assyrian history which records the northward progress of culture, religion, letters and political supremacy from Babylonia to Assyria.
The geographical names have as their Assyrian counterparts respectively *Bab-ilu, Uruk, Akkad, Kul-mu* (?), *Shumiru.*

Out of that land, etc. In agreement with Assyrian history. **Builded
Nineveh, etc.** Calah did not attain the eminence of a royal residence
until the ninth century B. C. Previously it had lain in ruins. Asur-
nazir-habal says :—

"The ancient city Kalhu, which Shalmanezer, the great, king of Assyria (1300
B. C.), who reigned before me, founded, this city lay waste and was ruined ; this
city I rebuilt."

The great city. An expression for the city-complex in which Nineveh,
Calah, and Resen (—Assyr. *Ninua, Kalhu,* and *Rishin* (?), are suburbs or

Nineveh, and Rehoboth-Ir, and Calah, and Resen between Nine- 12
veh and Calah (the same is the great city). And Mizraim begat 13
Ludim, and Anamim, and Lehabim, and Naphtuhim, and Pathru- 14
sim, and Casluhim (whence went forth the Philistines), and
Caphtorim.

And Canaan begat Zidon his firstborn, and Heth: and after- 15, 18*b*
ward were the families of the Canaanite spread abroad. And the 19
border of the Canaanite was from Zidon, as thou goest toward
Gerar, unto Gaza; as thou goest toward Sodom and Gomorrah,
and Admah and Zeboiim, unto Lasha.

quarters. It points to a time before Sennacherib, when the name Nineveh
had not yet become, as in Jonah and from 705 B. C. downward, the common
designation for the whole. **Rehoboth-Ir** is doubtless an expression for
the business and residence portion of the city as distinct from the three
palace mounds mentioned. It cannot be identified with the *dur Sharru-
kin*, or "city of Sargon," of the inscriptions, built 707 B. C. ; and the
omission furnishes important evidence for the date of this verse.
Equally significant, however, is the omission of all reference to the
founding of Asshur long before the elevation of Nineveh to its station as
capital of the empire. In spite of its former pre-eminent importance,
this former capital had already, in the 8th century B. C., long since
passed into oblivion.

Zidon and Heth. (Assyr. *Sidunu* and *Hatti*.) The latter properly
employed by Assyrian scribes from 1100–750 B. C. to designate the important people dwelling between the Euphrates and Mediterranean in
the extreme north of Syria. But with the gradual occupation of this
region by the Assyrians from the time of Tiglath-Pileser II. to Sargon
(745–727 and 722–705 B. C.), and the incorporation in 708 of the two Hittite
states, Carchemish and Commagene, the name was transferred to
Canaan, Philistia, Edom, Ammon, and Moab, a territory which previously cannot have had more than unimportant and isolated Hittite
colonies (Gen. xii. 6 ; xiii. 7), even if the so-called " Hittites " of Gen.
xxiii. and elsewhere, were not, as we should gather from a comparison of
the proper names, entirely unrelated to the true Hittites. Under Sennacherib and Esarhadon *mat Hatti*, " land of the Hittites," becomes the
uniform though incorrect designation of Palestine. " Canaan " is unknown. With this fact should be compared the division of the original
Canaanite stock by J², vs. 15, into Zidonians and Hittites, " *and afterward* the Canaanites," and more especially the practise of P, who,
perhaps with regard to this verse, makes it a point *always* to substitute
in his narrative " Hittite " for " Perizzite," " Jebusite," " Canaanite " or
" Hivite " of the prophetic narrative. (Cf. e. g. Gen. xxiii. with xxxiii.
18ff.)

21　　And unto Shem, the elder brother of Japheth, to him also were
25　children born. [Eber and . . . .] And unto Eber were born
　　　two sons: the name of the one was Peleg (Division); for in his
　　　days was the earth divided; and his brother's name was Joktan.
26　And Joktan begat Almodad, and Sheleph, and Hazarmaveth, and
27, 28 Jerah; and Hadoram, and Uzal, and Diklah; and Obal, and
29　Abimael, and Sheba; and Ophir, and Havilah, and Jobab; all
30　these were the sons of Joktan.　And their dwelling was from
　　　Mesha as thou goest toward Sephar, the mountain of the east.
　　　　(J² underlying 11 : 10–27.) [And Peleg begat Reu, and Reu be-
　　　gat Serug, and Serug begat Terah, and Terah begat Abram,
11—28 Nahor, and Haran.　And Terah dwelt] in Ur of the Chaldees.

From the critical standpoint it is impossible to accept **Ur of the Chaldees** (— *Ur Muqqayar* in southern Babylonia) as the "fatherland" of
Abram.　Not to speak of the fact that, as ancestor of Shem, Japheth, and
Canaan, Noah, in J¹, would be out of place in Babylonia, Gen. xxiv. 4, 7, 10,
makes it a positive certainity that in J¹ Abram's "fatherland" was Aram
Naharaim and the city of Nahor.　It is difficult to account for the
strange introduction here of the name of an extremely ancient town in
south Babylonia except as the necessity of the Flood-story compelled its
incorporator to adapt the story to its scene.　"Ur of the Chaldees"
may well be regarded as the last link by which the great Flood interpolation, based upon the Assyro-Chaldean national epos, was attached to the
primitive Hebrew saga.　Having taken Noah from Aram Naharaim, the
home of the vine, to the scene of the Babylonian Flood-story, he must
now bring back Noah's descendants from "Ur of the Chaldees" in order
to attach his interpolation to the primitive narrative of how Abram
went forth from Aram Naharaim and came into the land of Canaan.

APPENDIX II.

(1) Jud. 15:16. For

בלחי החמור חמור חמורתים
בלחי החמור הכיתי אלף איש

read

בלחי חמור חמורתים
בלחי הכיתי אלף איש

Since writing the foregoing, I have found the same emendation proposed by Schenckel in his *Bibellexikon*, s. v. Lehi. The emendation is so obvious that it may well have suggested itself to many students independently.

(2) Gen. 1:1 and 2:4a. Read אלה תולדות השמים והארץ בראשית הבראם : ויברא אלהים וגו'.

(3) 1:26. After כל insert חית.

(4) 4:22. For ויהי למך חרש, read קין לטש כל חרש נחשת נחשת.

(5) 6:1–4. Omit v. 3 and v. 4 to אשר and insert ו consecutive. The usual form of Hebrew sentence for a statement of the birth of children is

ויקחו להם נשים⋯ויבאו⋯ וילדו וגו'.

This form is interrupted and destroyed by 3,4a, the last named clause being in addition admittedly corrupt. The author prefers therefore to regard the first clause of v. 4 (to אשר) as a gloss intended to identify the נפלים of Num. 13:33 with the גברים of the original writer, whereas in the first place only the origin of the גברים was intended, rather than adopt any of the numerous conjectures which assume an identity in the mind of the original writer of נפלים and גברים.

(6) 9:26sq. Budde conjectures in v. 26 ברוך יהוה שם (cf. 24:31 and 27:29), and in v. 27 the alliterative reading יפת יהוה ליפת.

(351)

(7) 10:9 הוא היה can scarcely stand directly after וגו' הוא החל .
The גבר ציד Budde associates with the גברים of 6:4.

(8) 16:13sq. For הלם read אלהים and supply after it וחי . In
v. 14 the original sense of the name באר לחי ראי must have been
something like Well of Lookout Rock; but for ראי read רעי and we
may translate, Well of the antelope's jawbone. J, however, pronounced באר לחי ראי .

(9) 18:21 read כלם in place of כלה .

(10) 19:12 read חתניך for חתן ובניך .

(11) 21:20 קשת an ancient gloss explanatory of the unusual רבה
" archer."

·(12) 22:14. The author has suggested on page 141 the name הנגב
in place of המריה , and v. 8 shows that in v. 14 the etymology was
based upon the stem ראה . The very fact that the attempt to afford
an etymology for מריה is so far from satisfactory is evidence that no
new construction was undertaken, but a comparatively slight modification of the original. The author suggests the reading אל־ראי (cf.
16:13 and 35:7) for יהוה־יראה , and in 14b האלהים for יהוה .

(13) 24:61 sq. For ויקח העבד את־רבקה וילך: ויצחק בא read ויקח העבד את־רבקה וילך ליצחק: ויבא מבא באד וגו'
מבא באר וגו' .

(14) 33:18. For שלם read שכם .

(15) 49:24. For משם רעה read מזרעי .